Dedication:

To the memory of Bill Horwitz and
Dorothy Negrino, because they loved
learning.

Special Thanks to:

Big thanks to our editor Nancy Davis; her expert touch, warm compassion, and fierce dedication always make our work better.

Thanks to Tracey Croom for her excellent production work.

Our heartfelt thanks to Danielle Foster, the book's compositor, who laid out the book under incredible time pressure and pulled off the job with grace and aplomb.

We're grateful to Peachpit's Nancy Ruenzel for her support.

We'd like to express our special thanks to all of the high school, college, and university instructors who chose to use the previous editions of this book as a textbook for their classes.

Dori would like to thank the wonderful ladies in the W&S group for their loving kindness and virtual hugs. And thanks are also due to the Wise-Women's Web Design community (http://www.wise-women.org) for their patience, support, and inspiration as role models.

CONTENTS AT A GLANCE

TABLE OF CONTENTS

INTRODUCTION

Welcome to JavaScript! Using this easy-to-learn programming language, you'll be able to add pizzazz to your Web pages and make them more useful for you and for your site's visitors. We've written this book as a painless introduction to JavaScript, so you don't have to be a geek or a nerd to write a script. Pocket protectors will not be necessary at any time. As a friend of ours says, "We're geeky, so you don't have to be!"

We wrote this book for you

We figure that if you're interested in JavaScript, then you've already got some experience in creating HTML pages and Web sites, and you want to take the next step by adding some interactivity to your sites. We don't assume that you know anything about programming or scripting. We also don't assume that you are an HTML expert (though if you are, that's just fine). We do assume that you've got at least the basics of building Web pages down, and that you have some familiarity with common HTML, such as links, images, and forms.

We include some extra explanation of HTML in sidebars called "Just Enough HTML." You won't find these sidebars in every chapter, just the ones where we think you'll need a quick reference. Having this information handy means you won't need multiple books open just to remember the syntax of a particular HTML attribute.

If you already know something about programming, you should be aware that we don't take the same approach to JavaScript as you might have seen in other books. We don't delve deeply into JavaScript's syntax and structure, and we don't pretend that this book is a comprehensive language reference (though you'll find some valuable reference material in Appendix A, the color section in the back of the book). There are several other books on the market that do that job admirably, and we list them at the end of this book, in Appendix D. The difference between those books and this one is that instead of getting bogged down in formalism, we concentrate on showing you how to get useful tasks done with JavaScript without a lot of extraneous information.

In the previous edition, we added an introduction to Ajax, a technique that uses JavaScript and other common Web technologies to add extra interactivity to Web pages, and to improve the user experience of your Web sites. We covered the basics of Ajax and added some practical examples to allow you to Ajax-ify your sites without getting an advanced degree in Web programming. In this edition, we've added more Ajax examples and techniques, as we've found that interest in Ajax is continuing to grow.

How to use this book

Throughout the book, we've used some devices that should make it easier for you to work with both the book and with JavaScript itself.

In the step-by-step instructions that make up most of the book, we've used a special type style to denote either HTML or JavaScript code, like this:

```
<div align="center">
window.onload = initLinks;
```

You'll also notice that we show the HTML and the JavaScript in lowercase. We've done that because all of the scripts in this edition are compliant with the XHTML 1.0 Transitional standard from the W3C, the World Wide Web Consortium. Whenever you see a quote mark in a JavaScript, it is always a straight quote (like ' or "), never curly quotes (aka "smart" quotes, like ' or "). Curly quotes will prevent your JavaScript from working, so make sure that you avoid them when you write scripts.

In the illustrations accompanying the step-by-step instructions, we've highlighted the part of the scripts that we're discussing in red, so you can quickly find what we're talking about. We often also highlight parts of the screen shots of Web browser windows in red, to indicate the most important part of the picture.

Because book pages are narrower than computer screens, some of the lines of JavaScript code are too long to fit on the page. When this happens, we've broken the line of code up into one or more segments, inserted this gray arrow → to indicate that it's a continued line, and indented the rest of the line. Here's an example of how we show long lines in scripts.

```
dtString = "Hey, just what are you
→ doing up so late?";
```

You say browser, we say Kumbaya

In the previous edition, we made a big change: we ended our support for browsers that are very old or that don't do a good job of supporting Web standards. We'd found that virtually all Web users have upgraded and are enjoying the benefits of modern browsers, ones that do a good-to-excellent job of supporting commonly accepted Web standards like XHTML, CSS2, and the Document Object Model. That covers Internet Explorer 6 or later; Firefox 1.0 or later; Netscape 7 or later; all versions of Safari; and Opera 7 or later.

We've tested our scripts in a wide variety of browsers, on several different operating systems, including Windows (both XP and Vista), Mac OS X, and Ubuntu Linux.

We used the 600-pound gorilla of the browser world, Microsoft Internet Explorer for Windows, to test virtually everything in the book, including testing with beta of IE 8 (we went to press before the final version of IE 8 was released). We also tested the scripts with Firefox 2 and 3, and with Safari 3 for Mac. Working with the latter browser means that our scripts should also work in any browsers based on the WebKit engine (including Safari for Windows and Omni Group's OmniWeb), and on browsers (such as Konqueror for Linux) based on KHTML, the open-source rendering engine from which Safari got its start.

Don't type that code!

Some JavaScript books print the scripts, and expect you to type in the examples. We think that's way too retro for this day and age. It was tough enough for us to do all that typing, and there's no reason you should have to repeat that work. So we've prepared a companion Web site for this book, one that includes all of the scripts in the book, ready for you to just copy and paste into your own Web pages. The site also includes additional tips and scripts. If we discover any mistakes in the book that got through the editing process, we'll list the updates on the site, too. You can find our companion site at:

`http://www.javascriptworld.com/`

If for some reason you do plan to type in some script examples, you might find that the examples don't seem to work, because you don't have the supporting files that we used to create the examples. For example, in a task where an on-screen effect happens to an image, you'll need image files. No problem. We've put all of those files up on the book's Web site, nicely packaged for you to download. You'll find one downloadable file that contains all of the scripts, HTML files, CSS files, and any media files we used. If you have any questions, please check the FAQ (Frequently Asked Questions) page on the companion Web site. It's clearly marked.

If you've read the FAQ, and your question isn't answered there, you can contact us via email at: `js7@javascriptworld.com`. We regret that because of the large volume of email that we get, we cannot, and will not, answer email about the book sent to our personal email addresses. We can only guarantee that messages sent to the `js7@javascriptworld.com` address will be answered.

Time to get started

One of the best things about JavaScript is that it's easy to start with a simple script that makes cool things happen on your Web page then add more complicated stuff as you need it. You don't have to learn a whole book's worth of information before you can start improving your Web pages. But by the time you're done with the book, you'll be adding advanced interactivity to your sites with Ajax.

Of course, every journey begins with the first step, and if you've read this far, your journey into JavaScript and Ajax has already begun. Thanks for joining us; please keep your hands and feet inside the moving vehicle. And please, no flash photography.

GETTING ACQUAINTED WITH JAVASCRIPT

For Web site creators, the evolution of HTML has been a mixed blessing. In the early days of the World Wide Web, HTML was fairly simple, and it was easy to learn most everything you needed to learn about putting together Web pages. As the Web grew, page designers' aspirations grew as well, and their demand for greater control over the look of the page forced HTML to change and become more complex.

Because the Web is a dynamic medium, page designers also wanted their pages to interact with the user, and it soon became obvious that HTML was insufficient to handle the demand. Netscape invented JavaScript as a way to control the browser and add pizzazz and interactivity to Web pages.

Since its creation, JavaScript has evolved quite a bit (although occasionally in different directions, depending on the browser). Later, we'll discuss JavaScript's evolution in detail.

In this chapter, you'll learn what JavaScript is (and what it isn't); what it can do (and what it can't); some of the basics of the JavaScript language; and you'll get an introduction to Ajax, the exciting combination of JavaScript and other technologies that is enabling the next wave of interactivity and creativity for Web sites.

What JavaScript Is

JavaScript is a programming language that you can use to add interactivity to your Web pages. But if you're not a programmer, don't panic; there are lots of JavaScripts available on the Web that you can copy and modify for your own use with a minimum of effort. In fact, standing on the shoulders of other programmers in this way is a great technique for getting comfortable with JavaScript.

To make it easier for you to get up and running with JavaScript, we have set up a Web site that supplements this book. We've included all the scripts in the book (so you don't have to type them in yourself!), as well as additional notes, addenda, and updates. You can find our site at http://www.javascriptworld.com.

You'll often see JavaScript referred to as a "scripting language," with the implication that it is somehow easier to script than to program. It's a distinction without a difference, in this case. A JavaScript script is a program that either is contained internally in an HTML page (the original method of scripting) or resides in an external file (the now-preferred method). On HTML pages, because it is enclosed in the <script> tag, the text of the script doesn't appear on the user's screen, and the Web browser knows to run the JavaScript program. The <script> tag is most often found within the <head> section of the HTML page, though you can, if you wish, have scripts in the <body> section. Internal scripts that write text to the screen or that write HTML are best put in the <body> section, as in **Script 1.1**. If you're unfamiliar with these HTML concepts and you need more information about HTML, we suggest that you check out Elizabeth Castro's *HTML, XHTML, and CSS, Sixth Edition: Visual QuickStart Guide*, also available from Peachpit Press.

Script 1.1 This very simple script types "Hello, Cleveland!" into the browser window.

```
<!DOCTYPE html PUBLIC "-//W3C//DTD XHTML 1.0
→ Transitional//EN"
        "http://www.w3.org/TR/xhtml1/DTD/
          → xhtml1-transitional.dtd">
<html xmlns="http://www.w3.org/1999/xhtml">
<head>
    <title>Barely a script at all</title>
</head>
<body bgcolor="#FFFFFF">
<h1>
    <script type="text/javascript">
        document.write("Hello, Cleveland!");
    </script>
</h1>
</body>
</html>
```

JavaScript Isn't Java

Despite the name, JavaScript and Java have almost nothing to do with one another. Java is a full-featured programming language developed and marketed by Sun Microsystems. With Java, a descendant of the C and C++ programming languages, programmers can create entire applications and control consumer electronic devices. Unlike other languages, Java holds out the promise of cross-platform compatibility; that is, a programmer should be able to write one Java program that can then run on any kind of machine, whether that machine is running Windows, Mac OS X, or any of the different flavors of Unix. In practice, Java hasn't always realized that dream, due in no small part to bickering between Sun and Microsoft as to the direction of the language. Microsoft got involved because it first wanted to integrate Java into Windows in its own way (a way that Sun said would make Java work one way on Windows, and another way on other machines, thereby defeating Java's main purpose); then Microsoft dropped Sun's Java from Windows altogether, after creating its own Java-like language, C#. After a flurry of lawsuits between the two companies (and a big settlement in favor of Sun), Microsoft removed its Java from Windows, and you can now install the latest version of Sun's Java for Windows (or Linux) at http://www.java.com/getjava/. Mac OS X comes with Java installed as part of the operating system.

Besides standalone applications, Java's main use on the *client side*, that is, in the user's browser, is to create *applets*, small programs that download over the Internet and run inside Web browsers. Because of Java's cross-platform nature, these applets should run identically on any Java-enabled browser. In recent years, we've seen many Java applets for browsers replaced by Adobe Flash animations, which are generally easier to create than Java applets.

You embed Java applets in your Web pages using the <object> HTML tag, with additional information specifying the applet. When the browser sees the <object> tag, it downloads the Java applet from the server, and the applet then runs in the area of the screen specified in the tag (**Figure 1.1**).

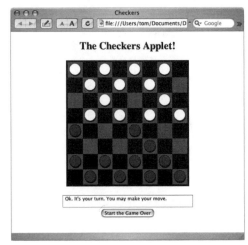

Figure 1.1 This Java applet plays a mean game of checkers.

Where JavaScript Came From

If JavaScript isn't related to Java, then why do they have such similar names? It's another example of one of the computer industry's most annoying traits: the triumph of marketing over substance.

Long ago, when Netscape added some basic scripting abilities to its Navigator Web browser, it originally called that scripting language LiveScript. Around the same time, Java was getting lots of press as the Next Big Thing In Computing. When Netscape revised Navigator to run Java applets in Navigator 2, it also renamed LiveScript to JavaScript, hoping that some of Java's glitter would rub off. The mere fact that JavaScript and Java were very different programming languages didn't stop Netscape's marketing geniuses, and ever since then, writers like us have made good money explaining that JavaScript and Java are very different things. Come to think of it, maybe we should be thanking those marketeers.

When Microsoft saw that JavaScript was becoming popular among Web developers, it realized that it would have to add some sort of scripting capabilities to Internet Explorer. It could have adopted JavaScript, but as is so often the case, Microsoft instead built its own language that works much like JavaScript but is not exactly the same. This Microsoft version of JavaScript is called JScript.

What JavaScript Can Do

There are many things that you can do with JavaScript to make your Web pages more interactive and provide your site's users with a better, more exciting experience. JavaScript lets you create an active user interface, giving the users feedback as they navigate your pages. For example, you've probably seen sites that have buttons that highlight as you move the mouse pointer over them. That's done with JavaScript, using a technique called a *rollover* (**Figure 1.2**).

You can use JavaScript to make sure that your users enter valid information in forms, which can save your business time and money. If your forms require calculations, you can do them in JavaScript on the user's machine without any server-side processing. That's a distinction you should know: programs that run on the user's machine are referred to as *client-side* programs; programs running on the server (including things called CGIs; more on them later) are called *server-side* programs.

With JavaScript, you have the ability to create customized Web pages, depending on actions that the user takes. Let's say that you are running a travel site, and the user clicks Hawaii as a destination. You can have the latest Hawaii travel deals appear in a new window. JavaScript controls the browser, so you can open up new windows, display alert boxes, and put custom messages in the status bar of the browser window. Because JavaScript has a set of date and time features, you can generate clocks, calendars, and time-stamp documents.

You can also use JavaScript to deal with forms, set cookies, build HTML pages on the fly, and create Web-based applications.

Figure 1.2 A rollover is an image that changes when you move the mouse pointer over it.

What JavaScript Can't Do

JavaScript is a *client-side* language; that is, it is designed to do its work on your machine, not on the server. Because of this, JavaScript has some limitations built-in, mostly for security reasons:

◆ JavaScript does not allow the reading or writing of files on client machines. That's a good thing, because you certainly don't want a Web page to be able to read files off of your hard disk, or be able to write viruses onto your disk, or be able to manipulate the files on your computer. The only exception is that JavaScript can write to the browser's cookie file, and even then there are limitations (for more information about cookies, see Chapter 10).

◆ JavaScript does not allow the writing of files on server machines. There are a number of ways in which this would be handy (such as storing page hit counts or filled-out form data), but JavaScript isn't allowed to do that. Instead, you'll need to have a program on your server to handle and store this data. This can be, for example, a CGI (a program that runs on the server) written in a language such as Perl or PHP, or a Java program.

◆ JavaScript cannot close a window that it hasn't opened. This is to avoid a situation where a site takes over your browser, closing windows from any other sites.

◆ JavaScript cannot read information from an opened Web page that came from another server. In other words, a Web page can't read any information from other open windows and find out what else a surfer visiting the site is up to.

What Is Ajax?

The short answer is that it's a way to create interactive Web applications. All right, now what does *that* mean? Let's think about things that you might want to do with a Web site. For example, you might want to go out to dinner with your spouse. (If you don't have a spouse, feel free to substitute "friend," "relative," or "pet" for "spouse" in the previous sentence. Though most people don't go to dinner with their pets. But we digress.) So you want to know how to get from your place to that fabulous new restaurant downtown that everyone's told you about. You decide to look up directions on a Web site that provides maps. You go to the site, type in the restaurant's address, and the site shows you a map with the restaurant marked. This particular site shows you the map, with a border that you can click if you want to change the map view (**Figure 1.3**). You click a border, wait five to ten seconds or so for the map to redraw, and, if you want to change the view again, repeat. It's a slow process and not very responsive to you. Wouldn't it be better to just click the map and drag it in the direction you want, and the map view moves as you drag?

That's the kind of dynamic responsiveness you can provide to your users with a Web application built with Ajax (**Figure 1.4**). There's almost no waiting; the user is in control; and it allows you to create Web-based applications with the kind of user experience found on a traditional desktop application. Plus, it makes it a lot faster and easier to find out how to get from home to that great dinner.

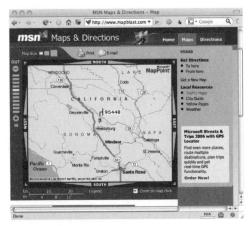

Figure 1.3 This MapQuest map takes a long time to respond to user clicks, because it needs a lot of refreshing from the server to make changes.

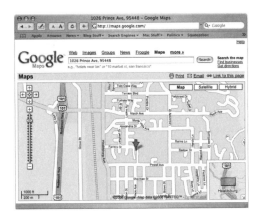

Figure 1.4 The Ajax-ified Google Maps allows a much more fluid and responsive user experience.

Ajax is shorthand for Asynchronous JavaScript and XML, and was first coined in early 2005 by Jesse James Garrett, a Web developer and author. Strictly speaking, Ajax is just a small (although particularly popular) part of JavaScript. As commonly used, though, the term no longer refers to a technology by itself (like, say, Java or JavaScript).

In the larger scheme of things, what's generally referred to as Ajax is the combination of these technologies:

◆ XHTML

◆ CSS (Cascading Style Sheets)

◆ The DOM (Document Object Model) accessed using JavaScript

◆ XML, the format of the data being transferred between the server and the client

◆ XMLHttpRequest to retrieve data from the server

Whew. That's quite a list, especially if you don't have much experience with JavaScript or other Web programming. But you shouldn't worry; throughout this book, we'll introduce each of these technologies. By the time you get to the Ajax chapters, the pieces that make it up should be old hat.

The benefit to Ajax is that most of the processing for the application is happening within the user's browser, and requests to the server for data are usually short. So with Ajax, you can give users the kind of rich applications that depend on Web-based data, without the performance penalty of older approaches, which required that the server send back entire pages of HTML in response to user actions.

WHAT IS AJAX?

Some companies have made huge investments in Ajax, notably Google, which has built several major Ajax applications, including Gmail (its Web-based email), Google Calendar, Google Docs, and Google Maps. Another big supporter of Ajax is Yahoo!, which uses Ajax to enhance its personalized My Yahoo! portal, the Yahoo! front page, Yahoo! Mail, and more. Both companies have made interfaces to their Web applications public, so that people can use them to make interesting new applications. For example, many people have created *mashups* for Google Maps, which take a map and overlay interesting, useful, or just wacky information on the map, such as the location of all Japanese restaurants or the filming locations for movies in the Los Angeles area.

✔ Tip

- For a nice listing of many Google Maps mashups, see Google Maps Mania (`googlemapsmania.blogspot.com`).

Figure 1.5 The cat object (this one's name is Pixel).

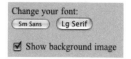

Figure 1.6 The buttons and check box are browser objects, which can be manipulated by JavaScript.

The Snap-Together Language

Here's another buzzword that we should get out of the way: JavaScript is an *object-oriented* language. So what does that mean?

Objects

First, let's think about objects. An *object* is some kind of a thing. A cat, a computer, and a bicycle are all objects (**Figure 1.5**) in the physical world. To JavaScript, there are objects it deals with in Web browsers, such as windows and forms, and the elements of the form, such as buttons and check boxes (**Figure 1.6**).

Because you can have more than one cat, or more than one window, it makes sense to give them names. While you could refer to your pets as Cat #1 and Cat #2, it's a bad idea for two reasons: first, it's easier to tell the cats apart if they have unique names, and second, it's just plain impolite. In the same way, all the examples in this book will give objects their own unique names.

✔ Tips

- Be aware that scripts you might see on the Internet will refer to objects like `window[0]` and `form[1]`. This is poor style for the reasons given above, and you'll find that it's much easier for you to keep track of the different objects in your scripts if you give them names instead of numbers.

- Some persnickety programmers will argue that JavaScript isn't really object-oriented, but rather, that it's actually *object-based*. For the purposes of this book, the two meanings are close enough that it makes no difference.

Properties

Objects have *properties*. A cat has fur, the computer has a keyboard, and the bicycle has wheels. In the JavaScript world, a window has a title, and a form can have a check box.

Changing a property of an object modifies that object, and the same property name can be a part of completely different objects. Let's say that you have a property called `empty`. It's okay to use `empty` wherever it applies, so you could say that both the cat's tummy is empty and the cat's bowl is empty.

Note that the computer's keyboard and the bicycle's wheels aren't only properties; they are also objects in their own right, which can have their own properties. So objects can have sub-objects.

Methods

The things that objects can do are called *methods*. Cats purr, computers crash, and bicycles roll. JavaScript objects also have methods: buttons `click()`, windows `open()`, and text can be `selected()`. The parentheses signal that we're referring to a method, rather than a property.

✔ Tip

■ It might help to think of objects and properties as nouns, and methods as verbs. The former are things, and the latter are actions that those things can do, or have done to them.

Putting the pieces together

You can put together objects, properties, and methods to get a better description of an object, or to describe a process. In JavaScript, these pieces are separated by periods (also known as dots, as in Internet addresses). This is called *dot syntax*. Here are some examples of objects and their properties written in this way:

THE SNAP-TOGETHER LANGUAGE

Figure 1.7 You can see a document's tree structure using the DOM Inspector, which is part of Firefox (shown here); there are similar features in Safari and Internet Explorer.

```
bicycle.wheels
```

```
cat.paws.front.left
```

```
computer.drive.dvd
```

```
document.images.name
```

```
window.status
```

And here are some examples of objects and methods written in dot syntax:

```
cat.purr()
```

```
document.write()
```

```
forms.elements.radio.click()
```

Introducing the Document Object Model

On a Web page, the objects that make up the page (or *document*) are represented in a tree structure. You've seen this sort of thing before when building HTML pages; the top level of the page is contained in the <html> tag, and inside that you'll find the <head> and <body> tags, with other tags within each of those, and so on. Some browsers can show you representations of this tree structure, as in **Figure 1.7**. JavaScript considers each of the items in the document tree to be objects, and you can use JavaScript to manipulate those objects. The representation of the objects within the document is called the *Document Object Model* (DOM).

Each of the objects on the tree is also called a *node* of the tree. We can use JavaScript to modify any aspect of the tree, including adding, accessing, changing, and deleting nodes on the tree. Each object on the tree is a node. If the node contains an HTML tag, it's referred to as an *element node*. Otherwise, it's referred to as a *text node*. Of course, element nodes can contain text nodes. That's all you need to know about the DOM and nodes for now; you'll learn more about them throughout the book, especially in Chapter 11.

Handling Events

Events are actions that the user performs while visiting your page. Submitting a form and moving a mouse over an image are two examples of events.

JavaScript deals with events using commands called *event handlers*. An action by the user on the page triggers an event handler in your script. The 12 most common JavaScript event handlers are listed in **Table 1.1**. We deal with other, more advanced event handlers in Chapter 9.

For example, let's say that our cat handles the event onpetting by performing the actions purr and stretch.

In JavaScript, if the user clicks a button, the onclick event handler takes note of the action and performs whatever duties it was assigned.

When you write a script, you don't have to anticipate every possible action that the user might take, just the ones where you want something special to occur. For instance, your page will load just fine without an onload event handler. But you need to use the onload command if you want to trigger a script as soon as the page loads.

Table 1.1

Event Handlers

EVENT	WHAT IT HANDLES
onabort	The user aborted loading the page
onblur	The user left the object
onchange	The user changed the object
onclick	The user clicked an object
onerror	The script encountered an error
onfocus	The user made an object active
onload	The object finished loading
onmouseover	The cursor moved over an object
onmouseout	The cursor moved off an object
onselect	The user selected the contents of an object
onsubmit	The user submitted a form
onunload	The user left the page

Table 1.2

Value Types		
TYPE	DESCRIPTION	EXAMPLE
Number	Any numeric value	3.141592654
String	Characters inside quote marks	"Hello, world!"
Boolean	True or False	true
Null	Empty and meaningless	
Object	Any value associated with the object	
Function	Value returned by a function	

Table 1.3

Operators	
OPERATOR	WHAT IT DOES
x + y (Numeric)	Adds x and y together
x + y (String)	Concatenates x and y together
x - y	Subtracts y from x
x * y	Multiplies x and y together
x / y	Divides x by y
x % y	Modulus of x and y (i.e., the remainder when x is divided by y)
x++, ++x	Adds one to x (same as x = x + 1)
x--, --x	Subtracts one from x (same as x = x - 1)
-x	Reverses the sign on x

Values and Variables

In JavaScript, a piece of information is a *value*. There are different kinds of values; the kind you're most familiar with are numbers. A *string* value is characters—such as a word or words—enclosed in quotes. Other kinds of JavaScript values are listed in **Table 1.2**.

Variables contain values. For example, the variable myName is assigned the string "Dori". Another way to write this is myName = "Dori". The equals sign can be read as "is set to." In other words, the variable myName now contains the value "Dori".

✔ Tips

- JavaScript is case sensitive. This means that myname is not the same as myName, and neither is the same as MyName.

- Variable names cannot contain spaces or other punctuation, or start with a digit. They also can't be one of the JavaScript reserved words. See Appendix B for a list of JavaScript reserved words.

Operators

Operators are the symbols used to work with variables. You're already familiar with operators from simple arithmetic; plus and minus are operators. See **Table 1.3** for the full list of operators.

✔ Tips

- While both x++ and ++x add one to x, they are not identical; the former increments x after the assignment is complete, and the latter before. For example, if x is 5, y=x++ results in y set to 5 and x set to 6, while y=++x results in both x and y set to 6. The operator -- (minus sign) works similarly.

- If you mix numeric and string values when adding two values together, the result is a string. For example, cat + 5 results in cat5.

Assignments and Comparisons

When you put a value into a variable, you are assigning that value to the variable, and you use an assignment operator to do the job. For example, you use the equals operator to make an assignment, such as hisName = "Tom". There are a whole set of assignment operators as listed in **Table 1.4**.

Other than the equals sign, the other assignment operators serve as shortcuts for modifying the value of variables. For example, a shorter way to say x=x+5 is to say x+=5. For the most part, we've used the longer version in this book for clarity's sake.

Comparisons

You'll often want to compare the value of one variable with another, or the value of a variable against a literal value (i.e., a value typed into the expression). For example, you might want to compare the value of the day of the week to "Tuesday", and you can do this by checking if todaysDate == "Tuesday" (note that double equal sign). A complete list of comparisons is in **Table 1.5**.

✔ Tip

- If you are comparing strings, be aware that "a" is greater than "A" and that "abracadabra" is less than "be".

Table 1.4

Assignments	
ASSIGNMENT	WHAT IT DOES
x = y	Sets x to the value of y
x += y	Same as x = x + y
x -= y	Same as x = x - y
x *= y	Same as x = x * y
x /= y	Same as x = x / y
x %= y	Same as x = x % y

Table 1.5

Comparisons	
COMPARISON	WHAT IT DOES
x == y	Returns true if x and y are equal
x != y	Returns true if x and y are not equal
x > y	Returns true if x is greater than y
x > = y	Returns true if x is greater than or equal to y
x < y	Returns true if x is less than y
x <= y	Returns true if x is less than or equal to y
x && y	Returns true if both x and y are true
x || y	Returns true if either x or y is true
!x	Returns true if x is false

Writing JavaScript-Friendly HTML

Because you'll be using JavaScript to manipulate the objects within a document, you want to write your HTML in a way that can be easily used by your scripts. That basically means writing modern, standards-compliant XHTML and using CSS to separate the document's structure from its presentation.

When we say modern XHTML, we don't just mean documents that pass W3C validation using the Web tool at `validator.w3.org`. We also recommend thinking ahead to what you are likely to do with a page and adding appropriate tags and attributes that will make it easy to access objects with JavaScript. What sort of markup, you wonder? Glad you asked.

Structure, presentation, and behavior

CSS (Cascading Style Sheets) is a standard layout language for the Web that controls typography, colors, and the size and placement of elements and images. Your XHTML documents should have external style sheets defining the styles used within the document. Your JavaScript should also be in an external document, one that contains only JavaScript code.

When split up this way, your sites will contain three types of text files:

◆ XHTML: contains the content and structure of the page

◆ CSS: controls the appearance and presentation of the page

◆ JavaScript: controls the behavior of the page

When you do this, it becomes straightforward to make changes to your site—even changes with site-wide effects.

Divs and spans

If you're used to the classic style of HTML, where you threw everything into tables and played with spacer GIFs until it all fell into more-or-less the layout you wanted, some of this will be new to you—so here's a quick overview to bring you up to date.

XHTML contains two tags that are finally getting the attention they deserve: `<div>` and `<span>`. They're used to break up your content into *semantic* chunks, that is, chunks that have a similar *meaning*. Things inside a single table cell or paragraph may or may not have anything in common, but the content within each `<div>` and `<span>` should.

Why use one over the other? A `<div>` is a block-level element, that is, there's a physical break between it and the elements above and below it. A `<span>` isn't block-level; instead, it's *inline*, so you can apply it to, for instance, a single phrase within a sentence.

We're not saying that you need to junk everything you've ever learned about HTML—far from it! But add these two tags to your toolkit of solutions, and you'll be surprised how often you use them.

Classes and ids

Inside your XHTML document, you'll mark up your content by breaking it down into those meaningful chunks. From there, you'll still need to identify those pieces of content where you want to change their presentation or behavior. For that, you'll primarily use two attributes: `class` and `id`. These attributes can be used by both CSS and JavaScript; a CSS style sheet uses those attributes as part of rules to define the appearance of a page, and the JavaScript file can use those attributes in code that affects the behavior of elements on the page.

◆ A *class* identifies an element that you may want to use more than once. For example, let's say that you're creating a page for a movie theater. You can define a class for the movie titles, specifying that the titles should be 14 pixel, bold, and dark blue.

```
.movieTitle {
    font: bold 14px;
    color: #000099;
}
```

You should then wrap each movie title on your page with a tag specifying the `class` of the title style, like so:

```
<p>We're currently showing
→ <span class="movieTitle">
→ The Aviator</span> and
→ <span class="movieTitle">
→ The Outlaw</span>.</p>
```

◆ An *id* identifies an element that is unique to that document. For example, if you only use the name of the movie theater once on your page, you can create a style rule using an `id` to define how the theater's name will look, like this:

```
#theaterName {
    font: bold 28px;
    color: #FF0000;
}
```

Then, when it's time to show the name of the theater, all you do is add that `id` attribute to the tag to get the effect:

```
<h1 id="theaterName">The Raven
→ Theater Presents:</h1>
```

What goes for CSS in the above examples also applies to JavaScript. Once we've assigned classes and ids to our divs and spans (and to any other elements as well), we can then modify those elements: not just their appearance with CSS, but also their behavior with JavaScript. And that's a topic that will take up the rest of this book.

✔ **Tip**

■ Having trouble remembering when to use # versus . in your CSS because you can't recall which one goes with `class` and which with `id`? Here's our method: an id can be on any given page one time, and *only* one time. One is a number, and the hash symbol (#) is also called a number sign—so it's the one that goes with id.

What Tools to Use?

Since JavaScript is just plain text, you could use almost any kind of text editor. You could even use a word processor like Microsoft Word, though you would always have to make sure that Word saved the file as Text Only, instead of in its native file format. HTML, JavaScript, and CSS files must always be in plain text format so Web servers can understand them.

You're better off using a program that has plain text as its standard format. On Windows, many people get away with using Notepad (**Figure 1.8**). On the Mac, you can use TextEdit, though a favorite of professionals is BBEdit, by Bare Bones Software (**Figure 1.9**). On Unix machines, Emacs is one of the best text editors available. No matter what program you use, don't forget to save your plain text files with the proper extension (`.html`, `.css`, or `.js`) so that things will go smoothly when you upload the file to a Web server.

You can also use some of the WYSIWYG (What You See Is What You Get) HTML editors available, such as Adobe Dreamweaver. Just switch to their HTML Source mode and script away.

✔ Tip

- If you're a Mac user, try TextWrangler, also from the Bare Bones folks (`www.barebones.com`). It's not as full-featured as BBEdit, but it has a big point in its favor: it's free.

```
<!DOCTYPE HTML PUBLIC "-//W3C//DTD HTML 4.01 Transitional//EN"
        "http://www.w3.org/TR/html4/loose.dtd">
<HTML>
<HEAD>
        <TITLE>Password Check</TITLE>
        <SCRIPT LANGUAGE="JAVASCRIPT" TYPE="TEXT/JAVASCRIPT">
                <!-- Hide script from older browsers

                function validForm(passForm) {
                        if (passForm.passwd1.value == "") {
                                alert("You must enter a password")
                                passForm.passwd1.focus()
                                return false
                        }
                        if (passForm.passwd1.value != passForm.passwd2.value) {
                                alert("Entered passwords did not match")
                                passForm.passwd1.focus()
                                passForm.passwd1.select()
                                return false
                        }
                        return true
                }

                // End hiding script -->
        </SCRIPT>
</HEAD>
<BODY BGCOLOR="WHITE">
<FORM onSubmit="return validForm(this)" ACTION="someAction.cgi">
        Your name: <INPUT TYPE="TEXT" SIZE="30">
        <P>Choose a password: <INPUT TYPE="PASSWORD" NAME="passwd1">
        <P>Verify password: <INPUT TYPE="PASSWORD" NAME="passwd2">
        <P><INPUT TYPE="SUBMIT" VALUE="Submit"> <INPUT TYPE="RESET">
</FORM>
</BODY>
</HTML>
```

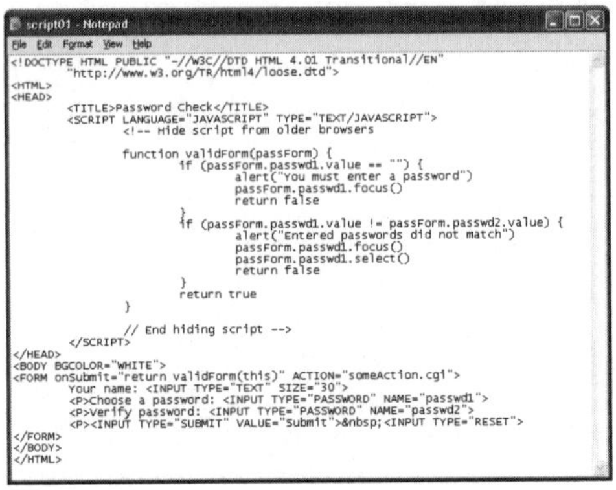

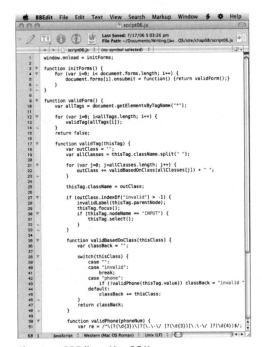

Figure 1.8 Notepad on Windows XP.

```
window.onload = initForms;

function initForms() {
    for (var i=0; i< document.forms.length; i++) {
        document.forms[i].onsubmit = function() {return validForm();}
    }
}

function validForm() {
    var allTags = document.getElementsByTagName("*");

    for (var i=0; i<allTags.length; i++) {
        validTag(allTags[i]);
    }
    return false;

    function validTag(thisTag) {
        var outClass = "";
        var allClasses = thisTag.className.split(" ");

        for (var j=0; j<allClasses.length; j++) {
            outClass += validBasedOnClass(allClasses[j]) + " ";
        }

        thisTag.className = outClass;

        if (outClass.indexOf("invalid") > -1) {
            invalidLabel(thisTag.parentNode);
            thisTag.focus();
            if (thisTag.nodeName == "INPUT") {
                thisTag.select();
            }
        }

        function validBasedOnClass(thisClass) {
            var classBack = "";

            switch(thisClass) {
                case "":
                case "invalid":
                    break;
                case "phone":
                    if (!validPhone(thisTag.value)) classBack = "invalid "
                default:
                    classBack += thisClass;
            }
            return classBack;
        }

        function validPhone(phoneNum) {
            var re = /^\(?(\d{3})\)?[\.\-\/ ]?(\d{3})[\.\-\/ ]?(\d{4})$/;
```

Figure 1.9 BBEdit on Mac OS X.

START ME UP!

Enough of the warm up; it's time to get scripting. In this chapter, you'll learn where to put your scripts in your HTML; how you can leave comments in your scripts so that you can more easily understand them at a later time; and how you can use scripts to communicate with the user. You'll also see how to make the page automatically change to another page (called *redirection*). Let's get to it!

Table 2.1

Just Enough HTML—The Basics		
TAG	**ATTRIBUTE**	**MEANING**
html		Contains the HTML part of the Web page
head		Contains the header part of the Web page
script		Contains the Web page's script or a reference to the external script file. Usually JavaScript, but not always.
	type	The programming language for the script. Required attribute.
	src	The location of an external script
title		Contains the title of the Web page
body		Contains the body part of the Web page
	bgcolor	Sets the background color of the page
h1…h6		Contents of this tag are emphasized as heading information; h1 is the largest heading size, down to h6 as the smallest heading
	align	Describes where the contents of this tag should be placed on the page in terms of horizontal or vertical alignment
a		Links to another Web page
	href	Specifies where the user should go when the link is clicked
	id	The id assigned to the link

Script 2.1 Scripts always need to be enclosed inside the <script> and </script> HTML tags.

```
script
<!DOCTYPE html PUBLIC "-//W3C//DTD XHTML 1.0
→ Transitional//EN"
        "http://www.w3.org/TR/xhtml1/DTD/
        → xhtml1-transitional.dtd">
<html xmlns="http://www.w3.org/1999/xhtml">
<head>
    <title>My first script</title>
</head>
<body bgcolor="#FFFFFF">
    <h1>
        <script type="text/javascript">

            document.write("Hello, world!");

        </script>
    </h1>
</body>
</html>
```

Figure 2.1 The "Hello, world" example is *de rigueur* in code books. We'd probably lose our union card if we left it out.

Where to Put Your Scripts

Scripts can be put in one of two places on an HTML page: between the <head> and </head> tags (called a *header script*), or between the <body> and </body> tags (a *body script*). **Script 2.1** is an example of a body script.

There is an HTML container tag that denotes scripts, which, as you would guess, begins with <script> and ends with </script>.

To write your first script:

1. `<script type="text/javascript">`

   Here's the opening script tag. This tells the browser to expect JavaScript instead of HTML. The type="text/javascript" attribute tells the browser that the script is plain text, organized as JavaScript.

2. `document.write("Hello, world!");`

   Here's the first line of JavaScript: It takes the document window and writes "Hello, world!" into it, as seen in **Figure 2.1**. Note the semicolon at the end of the line; this tells the browser's JavaScript interpreter that the line is ending. With rare exceptions, we'll be using semicolons at the end of each line of JavaScript in this book.

3. `</script>`

   This ends the JavaScript and tells the browser to start expecting HTML again.

✔ Tips

- There's no need to add attributes to the closing `script` tag.

- The `language` attribute of the `script` tag (which we're not using here) has been *deprecated* in XHTML, which means that the W3C, the standards body responsible for XHTML, has marked the attribute as one that will not necessarily be supported in future versions of the standard. There are plenty of older scripts that still use it, though.

- Using a semicolon at the end of a JavaScript line is optional, so long as you only have one statement per line. We've included them in this book for clarity, and we suggest that you get into the habit of including them in your code for the same reason.

- For most of the rest of this book, we've left out the `<script>` tags in our code explanations. As you'll see from the scripts themselves, they're still there and still needed, but we won't be cluttering our explanations with them.

- You can have as many `script` tags (and therefore, multiple scripts) on a page as you'd like.

About Functions

Before you get into the next example, you need to learn a bit about functions, which you'll use often when writing JavaScript. A *function* is a set of JavaScript statements that performs a task. Every function must be given a name (with one very rare exception, which we'll discuss much later in this book) and can be invoked, or *called*, by other parts of the script.

Functions can be called as many times as needed during the running of the script. For example, let's say that you've gotten some information that a user typed into a form, and you've saved it using JavaScript (there's more about this sort of thing in Chapter 7, "Form Handling"). If you need to use that information again and again, you could repeat the same code over and over in your script. But it's better to write that code once as a function and then call the function whenever you need it.

A function consists of the word `function` followed by the function name. There are always parentheses after the function name, followed by an opening brace. The statements that make up the function go on the following lines, and then the function is closed by another brace. Here's what a function looks like:

```
function saySomething() {
    alert("Four score and seven
    → years ago");
}
```

Notice that the line with `alert` is indented? That makes it easier to read your code. All of the statements between the first brace and the last one (and you probably noticed that those two lines are not indented) are part of the function. That's all you need to know for now about functions. You'll learn more about them in the next and subsequent chapters.

Using External Scripts

The problem with using scripts on the HTML page, as in the last example, is that the script is only available to that particular page. That's why those kinds of scripts are sometimes called *internal* scripts. But often, you'll want multiple HTML pages to share a script. You do this by including a reference to an *external* script, that is, a separate file that just contains JavaScript. This external file is called a .js file, because whatever it's called, the file name should end with the suffix .js. Individual pages call the .js file simply by adding a new attribute, src, to the script tag.

This saves a lot of code on every page and, more important, makes it easier to maintain your site. When you need to make changes to a script, you just change the .js file, and all HTML pages that reference that file automatically get the benefit of your changes.

In this first example of an external script, **Script 2.2** contains the HTML with the reference to the external file, and **Script 2.3** is the external JavaScript file.

To use an external script:

1. `<script type="text/javascript"`
   `→ src="script02.js">`

   This line is in Script 2.2. Adding the src attribute to the script tag causes browsers that support JavaScript 1.1 and later to look for that file. The resulting Web pages will look just as though the scripts were in their usual place inside the page's script tags, when really the script resides in the external .js file.

   By itself, this line is all we need to do to use an external script. Next, let's work through what is in that script.

Script 2.2 The simple HTML puts a reference to the external JavaScript file inside the script tag.

```
<!DOCTYPE html PUBLIC "-//W3C//DTD XHTML 1.0
→ Transitional//EN"
        "http://www.w3.org/TR/xhtml1/DTD/
            → xhtml1-transitional.dtd">
<html xmlns="http://www.w3.org/1999/xhtml">
<head>
    <title>My second script</title>
    <script type="text/javascript"
        → src="script02.js"></script>
</head>
<body bgcolor="#FFFFFF">
    <h1 id="helloMessage">
    </h1>
</body>
</html>
```

Script 2.3 Your first external JavaScript file.

```
window.onload = writeMessage;

function writeMessage() {
    document.getElementById("helloMessage").
        → innerHTML = "Hello, world!";
}
```

Figure 2.2 The result of moving your JavaScript to an external file looks eerily unchanged from the previous example. But it's still a better way of doing things.

2. `window.onload = writeMessage;`

Moving to Script 2.3, the first part of this line, `window.onload`, is an event handler, which we discussed in Chapter 1. After the equals sign there is the name of a function, `writeMessage`. In English, this line can be read as "When the window finishes loading, tell the `writeMessage` function to run."

3. `function writeMessage() {`

This line creates the `writeMessage()` function.

4. `document.getElementById`
   `→ ("helloMessage").innerHTML =`
   `→ "Hello, world!";`

Refer back to Script 2.2, and you'll see that there is an <h1> tag there with an id of `helloMessage`. You'll learn more about ids later, but for now, suffice it to say that an id is a unique identifier on a page for whatever it is attached to. In other words, on a given page, there can be only one element with a particular id. That makes it easy for JavaScript to retrieve and operate on the element by using its `getElementById()` method. The `innerHTML` property simply takes the string that is on the right-hand side of the equals sign and drops it directly into the page, just as if we'd written it into the HTML itself. So, reading the JavaScript line from right to left in English, we could say "Take the string "Hello, world!" and put it into the document, inside the element on the page that is named `helloMessage`." The result looks like **Figure 2.2**, which looks an awful lot like Figure 2.1.

✔ Tips

■ Browsers that support external JavaScript files include: Microsoft Internet Explorer 4 and later, Netscape 3 and later, and just about every other browser that's shipped since then, including modern browsers like Firefox and Safari.

■ Using external JavaScript files is sometimes used to try to hide JavaScript from users. It doesn't work if the user is technically savvy enough to check their browser cache files—everything that the browser has seen is stored there.

■ In Script 2.1 (and much earlier editions of this book), we used a technique for inserting information into the HTML page called `document.write()`. In this edition, we've mostly replaced that approach with setting `innerHTML`, because it is more versatile. Some people object to the use of the `innerHTML` property because it hasn't been blessed by the W3C. But even those people with issues agree that it's the simplest cross-browser way to work, so that's what we're primarily showing in this book. The "official" way to add or change an HTML page is covered in Chapter 11, "Objects and the DOM."

■ If you've seen functions before, you might be expecting the `writeMessage` reference in step 2 to instead be `writeMessage()`. It's not, because the two mean different things: a function shown with parentheses means that the function is being called, right then and there. When it's without parentheses, (as it is here) we're assigning it to the event handler, to be run later when that event happens.

Script 2.4 Here's how you can annotate your script with comments, which helps you and others understand your code.

```
●●●                 script
/*

    This is an example of a long JavaScript
    → comment. Note the characters at the
    → beginning and ending of the comment.


    This script adds the words "Hello, world!"
    → into the body area of the HTML page.
*/


window.onload = writeMessage; // Do this when
→ page finishes loading

function writeMessage() {
    // Here's where the actual work gets done

    document.getElementById("helloMessage").
    → innerHTML = "Hello, world!";
}
```

Putting Comments in Scripts

It's a good idea to get into the habit of adding comments to your scripts. You do this by inserting comments that JavaScript won't interpret as script commands. While your script may seem perfectly clear to you when you write it, if you come back to it a couple of months later it may seem as clear as mud. Comments help to explain why you solved the problem in a particular way. Another reason to comment your script is to help other people who may want to re-use and modify your script.

Script 2.4 shows examples of two kinds of script comments. The first kind is for longer, multi-line comments. The second example shows how to do single-line comments.

Note that we haven't included the HTML for this example, as it is (virtually) identical to Script 2.2. From now on in the book, when the HTML hasn't changed from a previous example, we won't be printing it again.

To comment your script:

1. ```
   /*
   This is an example of a long
   → JavaScript comment. Note the
   → characters at the beginning and
   → ending of the comment.
   This script adds the words "Hello,
   → world!" into the body area of the
   → HTML page.
   ```

   For multi-line comments, the /* at the beginning of the line tells JavaScript to ignore everything that follows until the end of the comment.

2. ```
   */
   ```

   This is the end of the comment.

   continues on next page

3.
```
window.onload = writeMessage;
    // Do this when page finishes
    → loading
function writeMessage() {
    // Here's where the actual work
    → gets done
    document.getElementById
    → ("helloMessage").innerHTML =
    → "Hello, world!";
}
```

And here's the script again, as in the previous example, with single-line comments. As you can see here, single-line comments can be on a line by themselves, or they can follow a line of code. You can't have any code on the same line after a single-line comment, nor can you have a multi-line comment on the same line as code.

Yes, we're as tired of seeing this one as you are, but it's traditional for all code books to start off with the "Hello, world!" example.

So much for tradition.

Script 2.5 The HTML for this example includes
<script> and <noscript> tags.

```
script
<!DOCTYPE html PUBLIC "-//W3C//DTD XHTML 1.0
→ Transitional//EN"
        "http://www.w3.org/TR/xhtml1/DTD/
        → xhtml1-transitional.dtd">
<html xmlns="http://www.w3.org/1999/xhtml">
<head>
    <title>My JavaScript page</title>
    <script type="text/javascript"
    → src="script04.js"></script>
</head>
<body bgcolor="#FFFFFF">
<noscript>
    <h2>This page requires JavaScript.</h2>
</noscript>
</body>
</html>
```

Script 2.6 Alert dialog boxes help you communicate
with the user.

```
script
alert("Welcome to my JavaScript page!");
```

Alerting the User

One of the main uses of JavaScript is to provide feedback to people browsing your site. You can create an alert window that pops up and gives users the vitally important information that they need to know about your page.

In user interface design, less is generally more. For example, you could get the user's attention with loud alarm sirens and big animated banners, but that would be just a bit over the top. Instead, **Scripts 2.5** (HTML, which just calls the external script) and **2.6** (JavaScript) show how to create a nice, tasteful alert window. Now you know why we're writers, not designers.

To alert a user:

◆ `alert("Welcome to my JavaScript`
`→ page!");`

Yes, that's all there is to it, as shown in **Figure 2.3**. Just put the text that you want to have appear within the `alert()` method in straight quotes.

✔ Tips

■ In most JavaScript alert boxes, you'll see some indication telling the user that the alert box was put up by a JavaScript command. This is a security feature to keep unscrupulous scripters from fooling hapless users. You can't code around this. On Safari for Mac OS X, for example, it shows the URL of the site that opened the alert, as shown in Figure 2.3. Firefox on both Windows and Mac does the same thing. In Internet Explorer 6, the window title is "Microsoft Internet Explorer." Internet Explorer 7 says "Windows Internet Explorer," an interesting bit of rebranding.

■ You'll also see the `<noscript>` tag used here. On non-JavaScript browsers (older browsers and browsers with JavaScript turned off), a message appears saying that this page requires JavaScript.

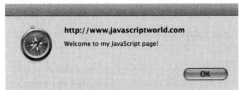

Figure 2.3 This script only puts up one dialog box; the four shown are examples of how the dialog box looks in, from top to bottom, Firefox 2 on Mac OS X; Microsoft Internet Explorer 6 on XP; Microsoft Internet Explorer 8 on Vista; and Safari 3 for Mac OS X.

Script 2.7 You can alter a reply, depending on how the user reacts to a prompt.

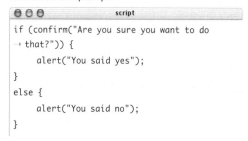

```
if (confirm("Are you sure you want to do
→ that?")) {
    alert("You said yes");
}
else {
    alert("You said no");
}
```

Figure 2.4 You can capture the result of a user's action and confirm the result in an alert box, as seen here. The top image asks the user a question, and the result of pressing the OK or Cancel button is shown below.

Confirming a User's Choice

While it's useful to give information to a user, sometimes you'll want to also get information back in return. **Script 2.7** shows how to find out if the user accepts or rejects your question. This script also introduces the idea of *conditionals*, which is where the script poses a test and performs different actions depending on the results of the test.

More about conditionals

Conditionals break down into three parts: the *if* section, where we do our test; the *then* section, where we put the part of the script we want to do if the result is true; and an optional *else* section, which contains the part of the script we want to have happen if the result of the test is not true. The contents of what we're testing in the *if* section are in parentheses, and the contents of the other two sections are each contained in braces.

To confirm a choice:

1. `if (confirm("Are you sure you want to` `→ do that?")) {`

   The `confirm()` method takes one parameter (the question we want to ask the user) and returns either true or false, depending on the user's response.

2. `alert("You said yes");`

   As shown in **Figure 2.4**, if the user clicked the OK button, `confirm()` returns true, and an alert displays, saying, "You said yes". As you can see, this is the *then* section of the code, even though there's no *then* operator in JavaScript. The braces serve as the delineation of the *then* area.

continues on next page

3. `}`

This brace ends the part that occurs when `confirm()` returned a value of true.

4. `else {`

Here, we begin the section that only happens when the user hits the Cancel button.

5. `alert("You said no");`

If the user clicked the Cancel button, `confirm()` returns false, and the message "You said no" is displayed.

6. `}`

This curly brace ends the entire `if/else` conditional statement.

✔ Tip

- You can put as many statements as you wish inside the *then* and *else* braces.

There's No One Right Way

There are, literally, a million ways to write any given script and still have it work correctly. For instance, braces are not required on conditionals if (and only if) there is only one statement in that code block.

In addition, there's an alternate method of writing a conditional that takes the form:

```
(condition) ? truePart : falsePart;
```

which is the rough equivalent of:

```
if (condition) {
        truePart;
}
else {
        falsePart;
}
```

That same shorthand method can also be used to set variables; for instance:

```
myNewVariable = (condition) ?
→ trueValue : falseValue;
```

is equivalent to:

```
if (condition) {
        myNewVariable = trueValue;
}
else {
        myNewVariable = falseValue;
}
```

There's also no requirement that the braces have to be at the end or beginning of lines, or that the true and false code blocks need to be indented. It's all a matter of style, and the correct style to use is the one you've found to work best for you.

In this book, for the most part and for clarity's sake, we've included the braces in the examples and chosen to use the longer form for conditionals.

Script 2.8 You can use a dialog box to query the user and work with the reply.

```
script
var ans = prompt("Are you sure you want to do
→ that?","");
if (ans) {
    alert("You said " + ans);
}
else {
    alert("You refused to answer");
}
```

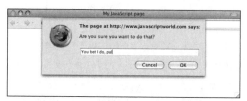

Figure 2.5 You can prompt a user for a text string, then act on that string.

Prompting the User

Sometimes, instead of just asking a Yes/No question, you'll want to get a more specific response. In that case, **Script 2.8** allows you to ask a question (with a default answer) and receive the reply in turn. **Figure 2.5** shows the results.

To prompt a user for a response:

1. `var ans = prompt("Are you sure you → want to do that?","");`

   Here, we're declaring a variable (as discussed in Chapter 1). We use the `var` keyword to declare variables. In this case, the variable is called `ans` and assigned the result of the `prompt()`, i.e., what the user types into the prompt dialog.

   The `prompt()` method is passed two bits of information (officially called *parameters*), separated by a comma: the question for the user and the default answer. It returns either the user's response or *null*; "null" occurs when the user hits Cancel, when there is no default and the user hits OK, or when the user clears the default answer and hits OK. For those browsers where a prompt shows a close box control, using that also returns a null result.

2. `if (ans) {`
   `    alert("You said " + ans);`
   `}`

   This conditional uses the variable that we just set. If `ans` exists (that is, if the user typed in a response), then the script puts up an alert window that says, "You said " (and note the extra space at the end of that text string above) and concatenates (appends to the end) the value of `ans`.

   continues on next page

3. else {
    alert("You refused to answer");
}

If ans is null, because the user didn't enter anything or clicked the Cancel button in the prompt dialog, then the else block of the condition is executed, and the alert pops up.

✔ Tips

- Using var does two things:
  - ▲ It tells JavaScript to create a variable (that is, to set aside some space in memory for this new object).
  - ▲ It defines the *scope* of the variable, that is, where JavaScript needs to know about this particular object (see the "What Is Scope?" sidebar). If a variable is created inside a function, other functions don't have access to it, as it's *local* to that function. If it's created outside any function, it's *global*, and everything has access to it. In this script, we're creating the ans global variable.

- In some browsers, if you leave off prompt's second parameter (the default response), everything works fine. However, in others, the prompt window will appear, displaying a default of "undefined." The answer is to always include *some* default, even if it's an empty string (as shown in Script 2.8).

What Is Scope?

In most of the world, when you talk about "Broadway," people know that you're referring to a street in New York City. While the street itself is in New York, people globally understand your reference. You can think of Broadway as a *global*.

However, if you're in San Diego, California, and you refer to "Broadway," people will think that you're referring to a major street in their downtown area. This is a *local* value. In San Diego, not being clear about whether you're referring to the locally known "Broadway" or the globally known "Broadway" can lead to confusion.

If you're in San Diego, the default is the local version, and you have to explicitly state "New York City's Broadway" in order to refer to the other. Outside of San Diego, people will think of New York's Broadway first, unless they have some other local version of Broadway.

The *scope* of each of these streets is where each is the default, that is, the one that will be automatically thought of if no other identifying information is given. The scope of San Diego's Broadway is local— inside the city and a few outlying suburbs. The scope of New York's Broadway is global; that is, people anywhere in the world will know to where you're referring.

With JavaScript code, the easiest way to avoid questions and confusion about a variable's scope is to avoid using two variables with the same name in two different places doing two different things. If you must go down this slippery slope, be clear about your variable's scope!

Script 2.9 This HTML allows you to redirect the user based on a link.

```
<!DOCTYPE html PUBLIC "-//W3C//DTD XHTML 1.0
→ Transitional//EN"
        "http://www.w3.org/TR/xhtml1/DTD/
        → xhtml1-transitional.dtd">
<html xmlns="http://www.w3.org/1999/xhtml">
<head>
    <title>Welcome to our site</title>
    <script type="text/javascript"
    → src="script07.js"></script>
</head>
<body bgcolor="#FFFFFF">
    <h2 align="center">
        <a href="script04.html" id="redirect">
        → Welcome to our site... c'mon in!</a>
    </h2>
</body>
</html>
```

Redirecting the User with a Link

You can check for the existence of JavaScript and then seamlessly *redirect*, or send users to another page, depending on if they have JavaScript turned on. This example shows you how to embed the redirection in a link. We'll use two HTML pages and one JavaScript file. The first HTML page, **Script 2.9**, gives the user the link to click. **Script 2.10** is the JavaScript file, and **Script 2.11** is the HTML page the user is redirected to if they have JavaScript enabled. **Figure 2.6** shows the starting point for users. When they click the link, they'll be taken to one of two pages, depending on whether or not they have JavaScript.

Script 2.10 By embedding the redirection inside the code, the user doesn't even know your script intervened in the link.

```
window.onload = initAll;

function initAll() {
    document.getElementById("redirect").
    → onclick = initRedirect;
}

function initRedirect() {
    window.location = "jswelcome.html";
    return false;
}
```

Script 2.11 This is the HTML for the page the JavaScript-enabled user ends up on.

```
<!DOCTYPE html PUBLIC "-//W3C//DTD XHTML 1.0
→ Transitional//EN"
        "http://www.w3.org/TR/xhtml1/DTD/
        → xhtml1-transitional.dtd">
<html xmlns="http://www.w3.org/1999/xhtml">
<head>
    <title>Our site</title>
</head>
<body bgcolor="#FFFFFF">
    <h1>Welcome to our web site, which features
    → lots of cutting-edge JavaScript</h1>
</body>
</html>
```

To redirect a user:

1. `<a href="script04.html"`
→ `id="redirect">Welcome to our`
→ `site... c'mon in!</a>`

In Script 2.9, this is the link the user clicks. If users don't have JavaScript and they click the link, they'll follow the usual `href` path and end up on a page that looks like **Figure 2.7**. If users have JavaScript and they click the link, the script (down in step 4) takes over and loads a new page.

2. `window.onload = initAll;`

Now we're in Script 2.10. When the page finishes loading, it triggers the `initAll()` function.

3. `function initAll() { document.`
→ `getElementById("redirect").onclick`
→ `= initRedirect;`
`}`

This function simply tells the element with the id `redirect` that it should call the `initRedirect()` function when a user clicks that link (that is, the link from step 1).

4. `function initRedirect() {`
    `window.location = "jswelcome.html";`
    `return false;`
`}`

If this function is called, then it sets `window.location` (the page loaded in the browser) to a new page. The `return false` says to stop processing the user's click, so the `href` page doesn't also get loaded.

What's so cool about this is that we've done a redirection without users having any idea that it happened. They're just on one of two different pages, depending on what they came in with. If they have JavaScript, they end up on a page shown in **Figure 2.8**.

Figure 2.6 This page has the link that contains the redirection code.

Figure 2.7 This message gives the user the heave-ho, if you've decided that JavaScript is essential to your site.

Figure 2.8 JavaScript-savvy browsers see this page instead.

✔ Tips

■ On first glance, we might think that we could just set the `onclick` handler globally—that is, as the page is loading—but we can't. There's a chance, particularly for a large and complex page, that the browser will not yet have come across that `redirect id`, and if that happens, JavaScript won't be able to assign the `onclick` handler. Instead, we have to wait until the page has completed loading, and that's done via `onload`.

■ Keep in mind that some users may object to being sent to a different page than the one they saw when they put their mouse over the link.

Script 2.12 The HTML, as usual, contains an `id` in the link tag that JavaScript can use.

```
                    script
<!DOCTYPE html PUBLIC "-//W3C//DTD XHTML 1.0
    Transitional//EN"
        "http://www.w3.org/TR/xhtml1/DTD/
    → xhtml1-transitional.dtd">
<html xmlns="http://www.w3.org/1999/xhtml">
<head>
    <title>Welcome to our site</title>
    <script type="text/javascript"
    → src="script08.js"></script>
</head>
<body bgcolor="#FFFFFF">
    <h2 align="center">
        Hey, check out <a href="http://www.
        → pixel.mu/" id="redirect">my cat's
        → Web site</a>.
    </h2>
</body>
</html>
```

Using JavaScript to Enhance Links

Sometimes, you may want to perform some sort of action after the user clicks a link, but before the browser loads the new page. A typical example would be when you want to put up an alert before the user goes to a particular page on your site, or to make it clear when the user leaves your site. In this example, we'll put up an alert dialog before continuing on to the ultimate destination. **Script 2.12** shows the HTML, and **Script 2.13** shows the small amount of changes we need to make to previous scripts.

Script 2.13 The link enhancement script.

```
                    script
window.onload = initAll;

function initAll() {
    document.getElementById("redirect").
    → onclick = initRedirect;
}

function initRedirect() {
    alert("We are not responsible for the
    → content of pages outside our site");
    window.location = this;
    return false;
}
```

USING JAVASCRIPT TO ENHANCE LINKS

To enhance links:

1. `Hey, check out <a href="http://www.`
`→ pixel.mu/" id="redirect">my cat's`
`→ Web site</a>.`

This line in Script 2.12 shows the link, with the `href` for the link's destination, and the `id` for the link, which will be used by Script 2.13. The page is shown in **Figure 2.9**.

2. `alert("We are not responsible for`
`→ the content of pages outside our`
`→ site");`

This alert appears after the link has been clicked, as shown in **Figure 2.10**.

3. `window.location = this;`

This line allows us to set the browser window to the location specified by the keyword `this`, which contains the link. For now, just think of `this` as a container— if you want to know more, see the "What is 'this'?" sidebar. When the user reaches their final destination, it looks like **Figure 2.11** (at least, using our cat's Web page as the destination).

Figure 2.9 Clicking the link will redirect the user to our cat's Web site.

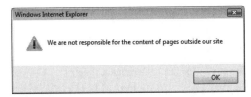

Figure 2.10 If the user has a JavaScript-capable browser, they'll see this warning message as they leave.

Figure 2.11 In this case, we'll admit that we actually are responsible for this cat's page (what, you think he does it himself?).

✔ Tips

- You may have noticed that nowhere in the code does it refer to a particular Web page—that's part of the power of `this`. One of the things the `this` keyword does for us is grab the URL from the HTML link (that is, the value of the `a` tag's `href` attribute). Because we're using this approach, we don't have to touch Script 2.13 if we someday change Script 2.12 to point to our kid instead of our cat. In fact, we could have links all over our Web site calling this same script, and that one line of code would automatically grab *their* `href` values as well.

- If that previous tip wasn't enough, think about it this way: with this approach, your HTML pages can be modified by WYSIWYG editors and people who know nothing about JavaScript—and so long as they only change the HTML pages, they can't screw up your script.

- That wasn't enough for you either? Here's another benefit: if the user's browser doesn't understand JavaScript, it loads in only the HTML page. When they click the link, it loads just as it normally would: no errors, no confusing "you must have some other browser," no problems.

- This kind of coding style—where the code is separated out from the HTML, so that both are more flexible—is referred to as *unobtrusive scripting*. If you want to know more about how this fits in with all the other buzzwords you hear about code on the Web, check out the "Just Enough Terminology" sidebar.

What is "this"?

In the example, you see the word `this` used, but it's not completely clear what `this` is.

The JavaScript keyword `this` allows the script to pass a value to a function, solely based on the context where the keyword is used. In this case, `this` is used inside a function triggered by an event attached to an `a` tag, so here, `this` is a link object. In later examples, you'll see `this` used elsewhere, and you should be able to tell what `this` is, simply based on the context where it's being used.

Just Enough Terminology

If you work with JavaScript for any length of time, you may start to feel overwhelmed by the amount of terminology that gets thrown around—and much of it, at its root, is about what JavaScript is and isn't. Here's a quick rundown of where we stand on these burning issues (and if you don't think they're burning issues, hang out with some scripters for a while!):

◆ **JavaScript**: While officially this term is owned by AOL (via Netscape), it's commonly used to cover all JavaScript-like scripting technologies such as Microsoft's JScript. We'll continue that trend in this book.

◆ **DHTML**: This stands for *Dynamic HTML*, but in real life, what *that* actually means depends on who's doing the talking. The DOM Scripting Task Force of the Web Standards Project defined DHTML (`webstandards.org/action/dstf/definitions/`) as "...an outdated scripting technique that is mainly characterized by the changes it makes to the style properties of certain elements, and by the use of the browser-specific DOMs `document.layers` and `document.all`." On the other hand, Myspace.com (in **Figure 2.12**) says that when you're editing your profile, "You may enter HTML/DHTML or CSS in any text field. JavaScript is not allowed," leading their huge user base to believe that DHTML has nothing to do with scripting (and is possibly interchangeable with XHTML).

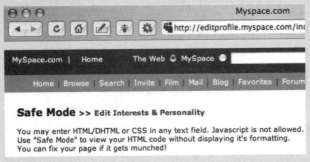

Our opinion is that DHTML is much too confusing and imprecise a term, so we no longer use it. If you come across anyone who does, make sure they define it.

continues on next page

Figure 2.12 Can (nearly) 100-million myspace.com users who've been told that DHTML isn't scripting all be wrong?

Just Enough Terminology *(continued)*

◆ **DOM scripting**: An approach to scripting Web pages using JavaScript, in which the code only modifies pages via manipulation of the W3C DOM (that is, no use of proprietary, non-standard, or deprecated properties). When Scripts 2.10 and 2.13 refer to `document. getElementById("redirect").onclick`, that's DOM scripting in action.

◆ **Unobtrusive scripting**: An approach to scripting Web pages using JavaScript in which the behavior of the Web page is kept separate from its content—that is, the HTML is in one file, and the JavaScript is in another. As a best-practices recommendation, it's comparable to the split between HTML and CSS, where the presentation (CSS) is in one file and the content (HTML) is in another. Additionally, the term "unobtrusive scripting" is used when code is written such that visitors without JavaScript (or with less-capable browsers) get all the functionality of a site, just with a less-rich user experience. Scripts 2.10 and 2.13 are also examples of unobtrusive scripting, in that you don't need JavaScript in order to click the links, but you'll have a richer experience when you do.

Throughout this book, we use a variety of scripting techniques. While we recommend the unobtrusive scripting approach wholeheartedly (and we try to demonstrate it whenever possible), we also know that you, as a budding scripter, will frequently need to be able to understand and support older, less-rigorously written code. And finally, this being the real world, we also know that sometimes the simplest way to hammer in a nail is to grab a rock and pound the nail into the wall. This, for instance, is why we used `innerHTML` back in Script 2.3, even though it's not part of the W3C DOM.

Using Multi-level Conditionals

There are times when you need more than two choices in a conditional test; `then` and `else` sometimes just aren't enough. While you can have nested levels of `if`, it's often simpler to just use a `switch/case` statement instead. The `switch/case` construct allows you to check a variable against multiple values. As you can see in **Figure 2.13**, this script returns one of three different Presidential quotes as alert dialogs, depending on which button the user clicks. **Script 2.14** shows the HTML, which is fairly simple. **Script 2.15**, the JavaScript, uses the `switch/case` construct to differentiate between presidents.

Script 2.14 The HTML sets up the page for multi-level conditionals.

```
<!DOCTYPE html PUBLIC "-//W3C//DTD XHTML 1.0
→ Transitional//EN"
        "http://www.w3.org/TR/xhtml1/DTD/
        → xhtml1-transitional.dtd">
<html xmlns="http://www.w3.org/1999/xhtml">
<head>
    <title>Switch/Case handling</title>
    <script type="text/javascript"
    → src="script09.js"></script>
</head>
<body bgcolor="#FFFFFF">
<h2>Famous Presidential Quotes</h2>
<form action="#">
    <input type="button" id="Lincoln"
    → value="Lincoln" />
    <input type="button" id="Kennedy"
    → value="Kennedy" />
    <input type="button" id="Nixon"
value="Nixon" />
</form>
</body>
</html>
```

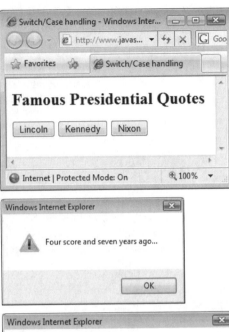

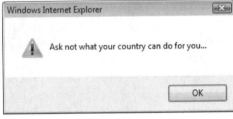

Figure 2.13 Calling the function with each of the three buttons in the top window results in three different responses, as shown in the three dialog boxes.

Script 2.15 This type of conditional allows you to check against multiple possibilities.

```
window.onload = initAll;

function initAll() {
    document.getElementById("Lincoln").onclick
    → = saySomething;
    document.getElementById("Kennedy").onclick
    → = saySomething;
    document.getElementById("Nixon").onclick =
    → saySomething;
}

function saySomething() {
    switch(this.id) {
        case "Lincoln":
            alert("Four score and seven years
            → ago...");
            break;
        case "Kennedy":
            alert("Ask not what your country can
            → do for you...");
            break;
        case "Nixon":
            alert("I am not a crook!");
            break;
        default:
    }
}
```

To use a switch/case statement:

1. `window.onload = initAll;`

   When the page loads, call the `initAll()` function.

2. ```
   function initAll() {
       document.getElementById
       → ("Lincoln").onclick =
       → saySomething;
       document.getElementById
       → ("Kennedy").onclick =
       → saySomething;
       document.getElementById("Nixon").
       → onclick = saySomething;
   ```

   In the function, we set the `onclick` handler for each of the buttons on the page. Because we set the `id` attribute along with the `value` attribute in the HTML, we're able to use `getElementById()` to set the event handler. If it existed, it would have been nice to be able to use a `getElement-ByValue()` call—then, we wouldn't have had to set the `id` attribute.

3. `function saySomething() {`

   This begins the `saySomething()` function.

4. `switch(this.id) {`

   The `id` of the `this` object is used as the parameter to `switch()`. Its value will decide which of the below `case` statements gets executed.

   continues on next page
   ```

5. `case "Lincoln":`
   `alert("Four score and seven years`
   `→ ago...");`
   `break;`

If the id of the `this` object is "Lincoln", this alert appears. Regarding `break`, if the user clicked Lincoln, we're in this section of code. However, we've done everything we want to do, and so we want to get out of the `switch`. In order to do that, we need to `break` out. Otherwise, we'll execute all of the code below, too. While that continued execution can be handy in certain circumstances, this isn't one of them.

6. `case "Kennedy":`
   `alert("Ask not what your country`
   `→ can do for you...");`
   `break;`

If the user clicked Kennedy, we end up in this `case` block.

7. `case "Nixon":`
   `alert("I am not a crook!");`
   `break;`

And finally, if the user clicked Nixon, we end up here, popping up another alert and then breaking out of the `switch`.

8. `default:`

If you were wondering what would happen if the user's entry didn't meet one of the above criteria, you're in the right place. The `default` section is where we end up if our `switch` value didn't match any of the `case` values. The `default` block is optional, but it's always good coding practice to include it, just in case (so to speak). In this script, there's no code here to execute, because we shouldn't ever get here.

9. `}`

This closing brace ends the `switch` statement.

✔ Tip

■ A `switch` statement can be passed other values besides strings. You can use it with a numeric value or even have it evaluate a mathematical result. If its result should be numeric, though, be sure that the `case` statements match—your `case` statements would then need to check for numbers, not strings (e.g., 5, not "5").

USING MULTI-LEVEL CONDITIONALS

Script 2.16 Use this script to have JavaScript gracefully handle errors.

```
script
window.onload = initAll;

function initAll() {
    var ans = prompt("Enter a number","");
    try {
        if (!ans || isNaN(ans) || ans<0) {
            throw new Error("Not a valid
            → number");
        }
        alert("The square root of " + ans + " is
        → " + Math.sqrt(ans));
    }
    catch (errMsg) {
        alert(errMsg.message);
    }
}
```

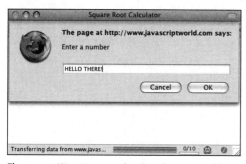

Figure 2.14 We want a number, but the user could enter anything, like this non-numeric entry.

Handling Errors

While you may have years of experience working with computers, it's a good bet that many of your site's visitors won't. Consequently, you'll want to give them meaningful error messages instead of the technobabble that most browsers return if they object to something the user does. **Script 2.16** shows how to use JavaScript's `try/throw/catch` commands to produce a friendly, useful error message. We've built this into a simple square root calculator.

To handle errors gracefully:

1. `var ans = prompt("Enter a number", "");`

   Here's an ordinary, everyday prompt, which stores its returned value in the `ans` variable for later use. In this case, we want the user to enter a number. If they do that successfully, JavaScript displays the square root of whatever they entered.

2. `try {`

   However, if they didn't enter a number, as in **Figure 2.14**, we want to be able to catch it gracefully and display something meaningful. Yes, we'll be polite about it, even though the user entered words when the alert asked for a number. We start off by using the `try` command. Inside its block of code, we'll check to see if the user's entry was valid.

continues on next page

3. `if (!ans || isNaN(ans) || ans<0) {`
    `throw new Error("Not a valid`
    `→ number");`
`}`

There are three things we care about: no entry at all, or if the user entered something but it was non-numeric, or if the entry was numeric but was a negative number (because the square root of a negative number is an imaginary number, and that's beyond this example). If `!ans` is true, that means that the user didn't enter anything. The built-in `isNaN()` method checks to see if the parameter it was passed is "Not a Number." If `isNaN()` returns true, we know that something invalid was entered. And if `ans` is less than 0, it's a negative number. In any of these cases, we want to `throw` an error; in this case, it says "Not a valid number". Once an error is thrown, JavaScript jumps out of the `try` block and looks for a corresponding `catch` statement. Everything between here and there is skipped over.

4. `alert("The square root of " + ans +`
    `→ " is " + Math.sqrt(ans));`

If something valid was entered, the square root is displayed, as shown in **Figure 2.15**.

5. `}`

This closing brace ends the `try` block.

6. `catch (errMsg) {`
    `alert(errMsg.message);`
`}`

Here's the promised and looked-for `catch` statement. The `error` is passed in as a parameter, and the `message` part of the error is displayed (**Figure 2.16**). If no error was thrown, the code inside the catch will never be executed.

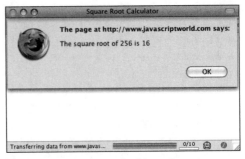

Figure 2.15 Here's the result of the script acting on a number.

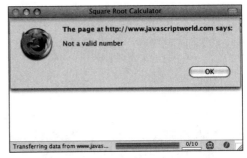

Figure 2.16 If bad data was entered, let the user know.

✔ Tip

■ There's another, optional part to this: the `finally {}` block. That would go after the `catch` and would contain code that should be executed whether the `try` threw an error or not.

HANDLING ERRORS

YOUR FIRST WEB APP

Now that you've gotten your feet wet, let's wade a bit deeper into the JavaScript language. In this chapter, we'll go into more detail about the basic elements of JavaScript and introduce you to other aspects of the JavaScript language, such as loops, arrays, and more about functions (don't let your eyes glaze over; we promise that it'll be easy).

You'll see how you can use JavaScript to write your Web pages for you, learn how JavaScript handles errors that the user makes, and much more.

Table 3.1

Just Enough HTML—The Basics	
TAG	MEANING
table	Presents tabular data on a Web page
tr	Begins a row inside the table
th	Heading cells for the columns in the table
td	Contains each cell in the table

Around and Around with Loops

It's common in programming to test for a particular condition and repeat the test as many times as needed. Let's use an example you probably know well: doing a search and replace in a word processor. You search for one bit of text, change it to a different text string, and then repeat the process for all of the instances of the first string in the document. Now imagine that you have a program that does it for you automatically. The program would execute a *loop*, which lets it repeat an action a specified number of times. In JavaScript, loops become a vital part of your scripting toolbox.

More about loops

The kind of loop that we mostly use in this book is the `for` loop, named after the command that begins the loop. This sort of loop uses a *counter*, which is a variable that begins with one value (usually 0) and ends when a conditional test inside the loop is satisfied.

The command that starts the loop structure is immediately followed by parentheses. Inside the parentheses you'll usually find the counter definition and the way the counter is incremented (i.e., the way the counter's value is increased).

Script 3.1 This HTML page creates the skeleton for the Bingo card.

```
<!DOCTYPE html PUBLIC "-//W3C//DTD XHTML 1.0
→ Transitional//EN"
        "http://www.w3.org/TR/xhtml1/DTD/
        → xhtml1-transitional.dtd">
<html xmlns="http://www.w3.org/1999/xhtml">
<head>
    <title>Make Your Own Bingo Card</title>
    <link type="text/css" rel="stylesheet"
    → href="script01.css" />
    <script type="text/javascript"
    → src="script01.js"></script>
</head>
<body>
<h1>Create A Bingo Card</h1>
<table>
    <tr>
        <th width="20%">B</th>
        <th width="20%">I</th>
        <th width="20%">N</th>
        <th width="20%">G</th>
        <th width="20%">O</th>
    </tr>
    <tr>
        <td id="square0"> </td>
        <td id="square5"> </td>
        <td id="square10"> </td>
        <td id="square14"> </td>
        <td id="square19"> </td>
    </tr>
    <tr>
        <td id="square1"> </td>
        <td id="square6"> </td>
        <td id="square11"> </td>
        <td id="square15"> </td>
        <td id="square20"> </td>
    </tr>
    <tr>
        <td id="square2"> </td>
        <td id="square7"> </td>
        <td id="free">Free</td>
        <td id="square16"> </td>
```

(script continues on next page)

Script 3.1 *continued*

```
            <td id="square21"> </td>
        </tr>
        <tr>
            <td id="square3"> </td>
            <td id="square8"> </td>
            <td id="square12"> </td>
            <td id="square17"> </td>
            <td id="square22"> </td>
        </tr>
        <tr>
            <td id="square4"> </td>
            <td id="square9"> </td>
            <td id="square13"> </td>
            <td id="square18"> </td>
            <td id="square23"> </td>
        </tr>
    </table>
    <p><a href="script01.html" id="reload">
    → Click here</a> to create a new card</p>
</body>
</html>
```

In the next several examples we're going to build a simple yet familiar application, a Bingo card. We'll use each example to show you a new aspect of JavaScript. We'll begin with an HTML page, **Script 3.1**. It contains the table that is the Bingo card's framework (**Figure 3.1**). Take a look at the script, and you'll see that the first row contains the letters at the top of the card, and each subsequent row contains five table cells. Most cells contain just a non-breaking space (using the HTML entity   ); however, the third row contains the Free space, so one table cell in that row contains the word "Free". Note that each cell has an id attribute, which the script uses to manipulate the cell contents. The id is in the form of square0, square1, square2, through square23, for reasons that we'll explain below. At the bottom of the page, there's a link that generates a new card.

Figure 3.1 This Bingo card has randomly generated numbers, but it isn't a valid Bingo card. Yet.

Script 3.2 is the CSS file that we're using to style the contents of the Bingo card. If you don't know CSS, don't worry about it, as it doesn't matter much here anyway. The HTML and CSS pages won't change for the rest of the Bingo card examples, so we're only going to print them once here.

This example shows you how to set up and use a loop to populate the contents of the Bingo card with randomly generated numbers. **Script 3.3** contains the JavaScript you need to make it happen. The card that is generated from this script is not a valid Bingo card, because there are constraints on which numbers can be in particular columns. Later examples add to the script until the resulting Bingo card is valid.

Script 3.2 This CSS file adds style to the Bingo card.

```
body {
    background-color: white;
    color: black;
    font-size: 20px;
    font-family: "Lucida Grande", Verdana,
    → Arial, Helvetica, sans-serif;
}

h1, th {
    font-family: Georgia, "Times New Roman",
    → Times, serif;
}

h1 {
    font-size: 28px;
}

table {
    border-collapse: collapse;
}

th, td {
    padding: 10px;
    border: 2px #666 solid;
    text-align: center;
}

#free, .pickedBG {
    background-color: #f66;
}

.winningBG {
    background-image: url(images/redFlash.gif);
}
```

Script 3.3 Welcome to your first JavaScript loop.

```
script
window.onload = initAll;

function initAll() {
    for (var i=0; i<24; i++) {
        var newNum = Math.floor(Math.random()
        → * 75) + 1;

        document.getElementById("square"
        → + i).innerHTML = newNum;
    }
}
```

What's in a Bingo Card?

Sure, you've seen them, but maybe you haven't looked carefully at a Bingo card lately. Bingo cards in the United States are 5 x 5 squares, with the columns labeled B-I-N-G-O and with spots containing numbers between 1 and 75. The center square typically is a free spot and often has the word "free" printed on it. Each column has a range of allowable numbers:

◆ Column B contains numbers 1–15

◆ Column I contains numbers 16–30

◆ Column N contains numbers 31–45

◆ Column G contains numbers 46–60

◆ Column O contains numbers 61–75

To use a loop to create the table's contents:

1. `window.onload = initAll;`

   This is in Script 3.3. This line calls the `initAll()` function when the window finishes loading. It's common to use an event handler to call a function.

2. `function initAll() {`

   This line begins the function.

3. `for (var i=0; i<24; i++) {`

   This line begins the loop. Programmers traditionally use the variable i to denote a variable used as a counter inside a loop. First i is set to 0. A semicolon signals the end of that statement and allows us to put another statement on the same line. The next part is read as "if i is less than 24, do the following code inside the braces." The final bit (after the second semicolon) adds 1 to the value of i. Because this is new, let's break that down a bit. The i++ part uses the ++ operator you saw in Chapter 1 to increment the value of i by 1. The loop will repeat 24 times, and the code inside the loop will execute 24 times. On the first go-through, i will be 0, and on the last go-through i will be 23.

   continues on next page

continues on next page

AROUND AND AROUND WITH LOOPS

4. `var newNum = Math.floor`
`→ (Math.random() * 75) + 1;`

Inside the loop, we create a new variable, `newNum`, and fill it with the result of the calculation on the right side of the equals sign. The built-in JavaScript command `Math.random()` gives us a number between 0 and 1, such as 0.123456789. Multiplying `Math.random()` by the maximum value (remember, values in Bingo cards can be from 1 to 75) gives us a result between 0 and one less than the max value. The `floor` of that result gives us the integer portion, i.e., an integer between 0 and (one less than the maximum value). Add one, and we have a number between 1 and our maximum value.

5. `document.getElementById("square"`
`→ + i).innerHTML = newNum;`

This is where we write into the table the value of the random number we just got. We get the element with the `id` named `square` with the current value of `i` concatenated onto it. For example, the first time through the loop, the value of `i` will be zero, so the line gets the element with the `id` of `square0`. Then the line sets the `innerHTML` property of the `square0` object to the current value of `newNum`. Then, because we're still inside the loop, steps 4 and 5 happen again, until the whole Bingo card is filled out.

Passing a Value to a Function

You'll often want to take some information and give it to a function to use. This is called *passing* the information to the function. For example, look at this function definition:

```
function playBall(batterup)
```

The variable `batterup` is a *parameter* of the function. When a function is called, a value can be passed into the function. Then, when you're inside the function, that data is in the `batterup` variable. Functions can be passed just about any data you want to use, including text strings, numbers, or even other JavaScript objects. For example, the `batterup` variable could be passed a player's name as a text string (`"Mantle"`), or his number in the lineup (7) (although mixing the two can be a very bad idea unless you really know what you're doing). Like all variables, you should give the ones you use as function parameters names that remind you what the variable is being used for.

You can have more than one parameter in a function. Just separate them inside the parentheses with commas like this:

```
function currentScore(hometeam,visitors)
```

We would like to underscore that parameters are variables, and so they can be passed a variety of different values when the function is called. So these code fragments are all equivalent:

```
currentScore(6,4);

var homeScore = 6;
var visitingScore = 4;
currentScore(homeScore,visitingScore);

currentScore(6,3+1);
```

Looping the Loop

A for loop has three parts, as shown in **Figure 3.2**:

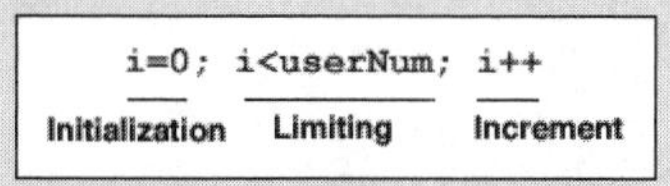

```
i=0;  i<userNum;  i++
────   ─────────   ───
Initialization  Limiting  Increment
```

Figure 3.2 The three parts of a loop.

1. **The initialization step**. The first time through the loop, this is what the loop variable (`i`, in this case) is set to.

2. **The limiting step**. This is where we say when to stop looping. While normal people count from one to ten, it's common in programming languages to count from zero to nine. In both cases, the code inside the loop is run ten times, but the latter method works better with languages (like JavaScript) where arrays start with a zero[th] position. That's why you'll see loops have a limitation of "less than `userNum`" instead of "less than or equal to `userNum`." Let's say that the variable `userNum` is 10, and you want the loop to run ten times. If you count from 0 to 9 (using the "less than" test), the loop runs ten times. If you count from 0 to 10 (using the "less than or equals to" test), the loop runs 11 times.

3. **The increment step**. This is where we say by how much to increase the loop counter on each pass through the loop. In this case, we add one each time through, using ++ to add one to `i`'s value.

For all three examples, once we're inside currentScore(), the value of hometeam is 6, and the value of visitors is 4 (which is great news for the home team).

In this example, we'll clean up some of the calculations from Script 3.3 by taking them out of the initAll() function, restating them a bit, and putting them into a function with passed values, in order to make it more obvious what's going on. It all happens in **Script 3.4**.

To pass a value to a function:

1. setSquare(i);

   This is inside the initAll() function. We're passing the value of i into the setSquare() function.

2. function setSquare(thisSquare) {

   This defines the setSquare() function, and it's being passed the current square number that we want to update. When we pass it in, it's the loop variable i. When the function receives it, it's the parameter thisSquare. What is a little tricky to understand is that this function is passed i, and does stuff with that value, but doesn't actually see i itself. Inside the function, all it knows about is the thisSquare variable.

3. var currSquare = "square" + thisSquare;

   In order to make the getElementById() call later in the script clearer, we're creating and setting a new variable: currSquare. This is the current square that we're working on. It takes the text string "square" and concatenates it with the thisSquare variable.

4. document.getElementById(currSquare).
   → innerHTML = newNum;

   This line gets the element with the name specified by currSquare and changes it to display newNum.

Script 3.4 By passing values to the setSquare() function, the script becomes easier to read and understand.

```
window.onload = initAll;

function initAll() {
    for (var i=0; i<24; i++) {
        setSquare(i);
    }
}

function setSquare(thisSquare) {
    var currSquare = "square" + thisSquare;
    var newNum = Math.floor(Math.random()
    → * 75) + 1;

    document.getElementById(currSquare).
    → innerHTML = newNum;
}
```

Script 3.5 Object detection is an important tool for scripters.

```
window.onload = initAll;

function initAll() {
    if (document.getElementById) {
        for (var i=0; i<24; i++) {
            setSquare(i);
        }
    }
    else {
        alert("Sorry, your browser doesn't
        → support this script");
    }
}

function setSquare(thisSquare) {
    var currSquare = "square" + thisSquare;
    var newNum = Math.floor(Math.random() * 75)
    → + 1;

    document.getElementById(currSquare).
    → innerHTML = newNum;
}
```

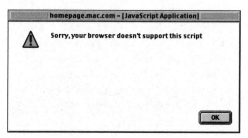

Figure 3.3 Object detection rejected this ancient browser (Netscape 4 for Mac) and displayed this error message.

Detecting Objects

When you're scripting, you may want to check to see if the browser is smart enough to understand the objects you want to use. There is a way to do this check, which is called *object detection*.

What you do is pose a question for the object you're looking for, like this:

```
if (document.getElementById) {
```

If the object exists, the `if` statement is `true`, and the script continues on its merry way. But if the browser doesn't understand the object, the test returns `false`, and the `else` portion of the conditional executes. **Script 3.5** gives you the JavaScript you need, and **Figure 3.3** shows you the result in an obsolete browser.

To detect an object:

1. `if (document.getElementById) {`

   This line begins the conditional. If the object inside the parentheses exists, the test returns true, and the rest of this block in the `initAll()` function runs.

2. `else {`
   `    alert("Sorry, your browser doesn't`
   `    → support this script");`
   `}`

   If the test in step 1 returns `false`, this line pops up an alert, and the script ends.

✔ Tips

- In a production environment, it's better to give users something else to do, or at least some version of the page that doesn't require this capability. Here, though, there's nothing to be done.

- It's important to understand that you won't always check for `document.getElementById`. What objects you check for depends on what objects your script uses. If your scripts use objects with less than 100% support, always check first if the browser can handle it—never assume that it can. We aren't showing object detection throughout this book to save space, but in the real world, it's vital.

Washed-Up Detectives

An alternate way to try to figure which objects a browser supports is to do a *browser detect*, which tries to identify the browser being used to view the page. It gets this by requesting the user agent string from the browser, which reports the browser name and version. The idea is that you would then write your scripts to work one way with particular browsers and another way for other browsers. This is an obsolete approach to scripting, because it doesn't work well.

Browser detection relies on you knowing that a particular browser supports the script you're writing, and another browser doesn't. But what about obscure browsers that you've never used? Or browsers that are released after your script is done?

Worse, many browsers try to get around browser detection by intentionally misrepresenting themselves. For example, Apple's Safari browser claims that it is a Mozilla browser, even though it is not. And some browsers, such as Safari and Opera, allow you to set which browser you want it to report itself as.

There's just no way that you can retrofit your script fast enough to keep up with all of the possible browser permutations. It's a losing game.

The same goes for attempting to detect which version of JavaScript a browser supports. We strongly suggest that you do not use these detection methods, and use object detection instead.

Script 3.6 This script limits the range of values that can go into each column.

```
window.onload = initAll;

function initAll() {
    if (document.getElementById) {
        for (var i=0; i<24; i++) {
            setSquare(i);
        }
    }
    else {
        alert("Sorry, your browser doesn't
→ support this script");
    }
}

function setSquare(thisSquare) {
    var currSquare = "square" + thisSquare;
    var colPlace = new Array(0,0,0,0,0,1,1,1,1,
→ 1,2,2,2,2,3,3,3,3,3,4,4,4,4,4);
    var colBasis = colPlace[thisSquare] * 15;
    var newNum = colBasis + Math.floor
→ (Math.random() * 15) + 1;

    document.getElementById(currSquare).
innerHTML = newNum;
}
```

Figure 3.4 This Bingo card is improved, but not quite right yet, because there are duplicate numbers in some of the columns.

Working with Arrays

In this example, we're introducing another useful JavaScript object, the *array*. An array is a kind of variable that can store a group of information. Like variables, arrays can contain any sort of data: text strings, numbers, other JavaScript objects, whatever. You declare an array with the elements of the array inside parentheses, separated by commas, like so:

```
var newCars = new Array("Toyota",
→ "Honda", "Nissan");
```

After this, the newCars array contains the three text strings with the car makes. To access the contents of the array, you use the variable name with the *index number* of the array member you want to use, in square brackets. So newCars[2] has the value "Nissan", because array numbering, like most other numbering in JavaScript, begins at zero.

In this example, shown in **Script 3.6**, we begin making sure the Bingo card is valid. On a real Bingo card, each column has a different range of numbers: B is 1–15, I is 16–30, N is 31–45, G is 46–60, and O is 61–75. If you look back at Figure 3.1, you'll see that it is not a valid card, because it was generated with a version of the script that simply put a random number between 1 and 75 in each square. This example fixes that, with only three lines of changed or new code. When we're done, the card will look something like **Figure 3.4**. It's still not a valid Bingo card (note how there are duplicate numbers in some of the columns), but we're getting there.

To use an array:

1. `var colPlace = new Array(0,0,0,0,0,`
`→ 1,1,1,1,1,2,2,2,2,3,3,3,3,3,4,4,`
`→ 4,4,4);`

We're concerned with limiting which random numbers go into which columns. The simplest way to keep track of this is to give each column a number (B: 0, I: 1, N: 2, G: 3, O: 4) and then calculate the numbers that can go into each column as (the column number × 15) + (a random number from 1–15).

The `colPlace` array keeps track of, for each square, which column it's in. It's the numbers 0–4 repeated five times (minus the free space; notice that the digit 2 is only used 4 times).

2. `var colBasis = colPlace[thisSquare]`
`→ * 15;`
`var newNum = colBasis + Math.`
`→ floor(Math.random() * 15) + 1;`

We start off by calculating the column basis: the number stored in `colPlace[thisSquare]` multiplied by 15. The `newNum` variable still generates the random numbers, but instead of coming up with a number from 1–75, it now calculates a random number from 1–15, and then adds that to the column basis. So, if our random number is 7, it would be 7 in the B column, 22 in the I column, 37 in the N column, 52 in the G column, and 67 in the O column.

Script 3.7 A function can return a value, which can then be checked.

```
window.onload = initAll;

function initAll() {
    if (document.getElementById) {
        for (var i=0; i<24; i++) {
            setSquare(i);
        }
    }
    else {
        alert("Sorry, your browser doesn't
        → support this script");
    }
}

function setSquare(thisSquare) {
    var currSquare = "square" + thisSquare;
    var colPlace = new Array(0,0,0,0,0,1,1,1,1,
    → 1,2,2,2,2,2,3,3,3,3,3,4,4,4,4,4);
    var colBasis = colPlace[thisSquare] * 15;
    var newNum = colBasis + getNewNum() + 1;

    document.getElementById(currSquare).
    → innerHTML = newNum;
}

function getNewNum() {
    return Math.floor(Math.random() * 15);
}
```

Working with Functions That Return Values

Up to this point, all the functions that you've seen simply do something and then return. Sometimes, though, you want to return a result of some kind. **Script 3.7** makes the overall script more understandable by breaking out some of the calculations in previous examples into a function which returns the random numbers for the cells on the Bingo card. Another function then uses this result.

To return a value from a function:

1. `var newNum = colBasis + getNewNum()`
`→ + 1;`

This line is again just setting the `newNum` variable to our desired number, but here we've moved that random number generator into a function, called `getNewNum()`. By breaking the calculation up, it makes it easier to understand what's going on in the script.

2. `function getNewNum() {`
`    return Math.floor(Math.random()`
`    → * 15);`
`}`

This code calculates a random number between 0 and 14 and returns it. This function can be used anywhere a variable or a number can be used.

✔ Tip

■ Any value can be returned. Strings, Booleans, and numbers work just fine.

Updating Arrays

As you saw in Figure 3.4, the Bingo card script doesn't yet have a way to make sure that duplicate numbers don't appears in a given column. This example fixes that problem, while simultaneously demonstrating that arrays don't have to be just initialized and then read—instead, they can be declared and then set on the fly. This gives you a great deal of flexibility, since you can use calculations or functions to change the values in the array while the script is running. **Script 3.8** shows you how, with only a few new lines of code.

To update an array on the fly:

1. `var usedNums = new Array(76);`

Here is a new way of declaring an array. We're creating `usedNums`, a new array with 76 objects. As mentioned before, those objects can be *anything*. In this case, they're going to be Booleans, that is, true/false values.

Script 3.8 Changing the contents of arrays to store the current situation is a very powerful technique.

```
window.onload = initAll;
var usedNums = new Array(76);

function initAll() {
    if (document.getElementById) {
        for (var i=0; i<24; i++) {
            setSquare(i);
        }
    }
    else {
        alert("Sorry, your browser doesn't
        → support this script");
    }
}

function setSquare(thisSquare) {
    var currSquare = "square" + thisSquare;
    var colPlace = new Array(0,0,0,0,0,1,1,1,1,
    → 1,2,2,2,2,3,3,3,3,3,4,4,4,4,4);
    var colBasis = colPlace[thisSquare] * 15;
    var newNum = colBasis + getNewNum() + 1;

    if (!usedNums[newNum]) {
        usedNums[newNum] = true;
        document.getElementById(currSquare).
        → innerHTML = newNum;
    }
}

function getNewNum() {
    return Math.floor(Math.random() * 15);
}
```

UPDATING ARRAYS

Figure 3.5 We've gotten rid of the duplicate numbers, but some of the spaces are now blank. Time to go back to the drawing board.

2. `if (!usedNums[newNum]) {`
    `usedNums[newNum] = true;`

If the `newNum` slot in the `usedNum` array is false (represented by the ! before the statement, meaning "not"), then we set it to true and write it out to the card. If it's true, we don't do anything at all, leaving us with no duplicates, but possibly blank spaces on our card (**Figure 3.5**). That's not good either, which leads us to the next task.

✔ Tips

■ Why is the array defined as containing 76 items? Because we want to use the values 1 to 75. If we initialized it to contain 75 items, the numbering would go from 0 to 74. 76 lets us use 1 through 75, and we'll just ignore item 0.

■ If you don't do anything to initialize Booleans, they'll automatically be false.

Using Do/While Loops

Sometimes you'll need to have a loop in your code that loops around a number of times, but there's no way of knowing in advance how many times you'll want to loop. That's when you'll want to use a do/while loop: you want to do something, while some value is true. **Script 3.9** writes out each row of numbers as always, but this time it checks first to see if a number has been used already before putting it in a cell. If it has, the script generates a new random number and repeats the process until it finds one that's unique. **Figure 3.6** shows the working, finally valid Bingo card.

To use a do/while loop:

1. `var newNum;`

   In the previous task, we initialized the `newNum` variable when we created it. Because we're going to be setting it multiple times, we're instead going to create it just the once, before we get into the loop.

2. `do {`

   This line starts the do block of code. One of the things you have to remember about this type of loop is that the code inside the do block will always be executed at least once.

3. `newNum = colBasis + getNewNum() + 1;`

   This line inside the loop sets the `newNum` variable to our desired number, as in previous examples.

Script 3.9 This script prevents numbers in a given column from being used more than once.

```
window.onload = initAll;
var usedNums = new Array(76);

function initAll() {
    if (document.getElementById) {
        for (var i=0; i<24; i++) {
            setSquare(i);
        }
    }
    else {
        alert("Sorry, your browser doesn't
        → support this script");
    }
}

function setSquare(thisSquare) {
    var currSquare = "square" + thisSquare;
    var colPlace = new Array(0,0,0,0,0,1,1,1,1,
    → 1,2,2,2,2,3,3,3,3,3,4,4,4,4,4);
    var colBasis = colPlace[thisSquare] * 15;
    var newNum;

    do {
        newNum = colBasis + getNewNum() + 1;
    }
    while (usedNums[newNum]);

    usedNums[newNum] = true;
    document.getElementById(currSquare).
    → innerHTML = newNum;
}

function getNewNum() {
    return Math.floor(Math.random() * 15);
}
```

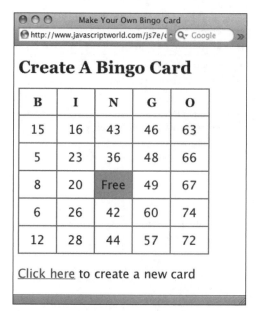

Figure 3.6 Finally, we've ended up with a valid Bingo card!

4. `}`

The closing brace signals the end of the do block.

5. `while (usedNums[newNum]);`

The `while` check causes the do block of code to repeat until the check evaluates to `false`. In this case, we're checking `newNum` against the `usedNums[]` array, to see if `newNum` has already been used. If it has, control is passed back to the top of the do block and the whole process starts again. Eventually, we'll find a number that hasn't been used. When we do, we drop out of the loop, set the `usedNums[]` item to true, and write it out to the card, as in the last task.

✔ Tip

■ A common use for a `do/while` loop would be to strip blanks or invalid characters off data entered by a user. But again, remember that the do block of code always gets executed at least once, whether the `while` check evaluates to true or false.

Calling Scripts Multiple Ways

Up to this point in the book, you've seen scripts that usually run automatically when the page loads. But in the real world, you'll often want to give the user more control over your scripts, even allowing them to run a script whenever they want. In this example (**Script 3.10**), the script still runs when the page loads. But we also allow the user to click the link at the bottom of the page to rerun the script that generates the Bingo card entirely in their browser, *without* needing to reload the page from the server. This gives the user fast response with zero server load.

To call a script multiple ways:

1. document.getElementById("reload").
   →onclick = anotherCard;
   newCard();
   The initAll() function we've seen before has one change and one addition. All it does that's new is set the link on the HTML page (the one with the id of reload; refer back to Script 3.1) to call anotherCard() when it's clicked. All the calculations that used to be in this function have now been moved to our new newCard() function—and that's all that's done there, so there's nothing new in that function for us to look at.

Script 3.10 Give your user the ability to run scripts themselves.

```
window.onload = initAll;
var usedNums = new Array(76);

function initAll() {
    if (document.getElementById) {
        document.getElementById("reload").
        →onclick = anotherCard;
        newCard();
    }
    else {
        alert("Sorry, your browser doesn't
        →support this script");
    }
}

function newCard() {
    for (var i=0; i<24; i++) {
        setSquare(i);
    }
}

function setSquare(thisSquare) {
    var currSquare = "square" + thisSquare;
    var colPlace = new Array(0,0,0,0,0,1,1,1,1,
    →1,2,2,2,2,3,3,3,3,3,4,4,4,4,4);
    var colBasis = colPlace[thisSquare] * 15;
    var newNum;

    do {
        newNum = colBasis + getNewNum() + 1;
    }
    while (usedNums[newNum]);

    usedNums[newNum] = true;
    document.getElementById(currSquare).
    →innerHTML = newNum;
}

function getNewNum() {
    return Math.floor(Math.random() * 15);
}
```

(script continues on next page)

Script 3.10 *continued*

```
                    script
function anotherCard() {
    for (var i=1; i<usedNums.length; i++) {
        usedNums[i] = false;
    }

    newCard();
    return false;
}
```

2.
```
function anotherCard() {
    for (var i=1; i<usedNums.length;
    → i++) {
        usedNums[i] = false;
    }

    newCard();
    return false;
}
```

Here's the anotherCard() function that's called when someone clicks the link. It does three things:

▲ Sets all the items in the usedNums[] array to false (so that we can reuse all the numbers again)

▲ Calls the newCard() function (generating another card)

▲ Returns a value of false so that the browser won't try to load the page in the href in the link (we covered this in Chapter 2).

✔ Tip

■ If you've gotten this far, you now know how to do something that many people consider to be a fundamental part of Ajax—using JavaScript to reload a part of a page instead of hitting the server and requesting an entirely new page. We'll be going into Ajax in much more detail in Chapters 13 and up.

Combining JavaScript and CSS

If you've been following along this far with the Bingo example, you may well be wondering, "Hey, they said that JavaScript was all about the interactivity—why haven't we seen any user interaction?" That's a reasonable question, and here, we show how to now let the user actually play that Bingo card you generated. To do that, **Script 3.11** uses some JavaScript to leverage the power of CSS.

To apply a style using JavaScript:

1. `document.getElementById(currSquare).`
   `→ className = "";`
   `document.getElementById(currSquare).`
   `→ onmousedown = toggleColor;`

   Because our Bingo card can be used and reused, we're going to make sure that we start off with a clean slate: for every square that's set in `setSquare()`, we're going to set the class attribute to `""` (the empty string), and the `onmousedown` event handler to call the new `toggleColor()` function.

Script 3.11 Adding a class via JavaScript allows our code to leverage the power of CSS.

```
window.onload = initAll;
var usedNums = new Array(76);

function initAll() {
    if (document.getElementById) {
        document.getElementById("reload").
        → onclick = anotherCard;
        newCard();
    }
    else {
        alert("Sorry, your browser doesn't
        → support this script");
    }
}

function newCard() {
    for (var i=0; i<24; i++) {
        setSquare(i);
    }
}

function setSquare(thisSquare) {
    var currSquare = "square" + thisSquare;
    var colPlace = new Array(0,0,0,0,0,1,1,1,1,
    → 1,2,2,2,2,2,3,3,3,3,3,4,4,4,4,4);
    var colBasis = colPlace[thisSquare] * 15;
    var newNum;

    do {
        newNum = colBasis + getNewNum() + 1;
    }
    while (usedNums[newNum]);

    usedNums[newNum] = true;
    document.getElementById(currSquare).
    → innerHTML = newNum;
    document.getElementById(currSquare).
    → className = "";
    document.getElementById(currSquare).
    → onmousedown = toggleColor;
}
```

(script continues on next page)

Script 3.11 *continued*

```
                    script
function getNewNum() {
    return Math.floor(Math.random() * 15);
}


function anotherCard() {
    for (var i=1; i<usedNums.length; i++) {
        usedNums[i] = false;
    }

    newCard();
    return false;
}


function toggleColor(evt) {
    if (evt) {
        var thisSquare = evt.target;
    }
    else {
        var thisSquare = window.event.
        → srcElement;
    }
    if (thisSquare.className == "") {
        thisSquare.className = "pickedBG";
    }
    else {
        thisSquare.className = "";
    }
}
```

2. `function toggleColor(evt) {`

   If you're a CSS wiz, you may have noticed back in Script 3.2 that we declared styles that we've never used. Now, inside the new `toggleColor()` function we're going to change that. The user can now click any of the squares on the card, and that square's background will change color to show that that number was called.

3. ```
   if (evt) {
       var thisSquare = evt.target;
   }
   else {
       var thisSquare = window.event.
       → srcElement;
   }
   ```

   First off, we need to figure out which square was clicked. Unfortunately, there are two ways to do this: the IE way, and the way every other browser handles events.

   If a value called `evt` was passed into this function, we know we're in a non-IE browser, and we can look at its target. If we're in IE, we instead need to look at the `event` property of the `window` object, and then at its `srcElement` property. Either way, we end up with the `thisSquare` object, which we can then examine and modify.

4. ```
   if (thisSquare.className == "") {
       thisSquare.className = "pickedBG";
   }
   else {
       thisSquare.className = "";
   }
   ```

   Here, we check to see if the class attribute of the clicked square has a value. If it doesn't, we want to give it one: `pickedBG`, named because the background of the square shows that the number has been picked.

   continues on next page

COMBINING JAVASCRIPT AND CSS

Now, normally, just changing a class attribute wouldn't actually change anything visually on the page—but remember the CSS back in Script 3.2? Any tag with a class of pickedBG gets the same background color as the free square. Changing the class here automatically makes that style apply to this square, causing it to also have a pink background (**Figure 3.7**).

Of course, squares can be picked accidentally, and we need to make sure there's a way to reset the value. Click the square again, and this time around, className has a value, so we toggle it to once again be the empty string.

✔ Tip

■ Instead of changing the class attribute on the square, we could instead change its style attribute, and then we wouldn't have to worry about the CSS file. That's the wrong approach, though—because we're leveraging the CSS file, it's simple to change the page's visual appearance without having to touch its behavior.

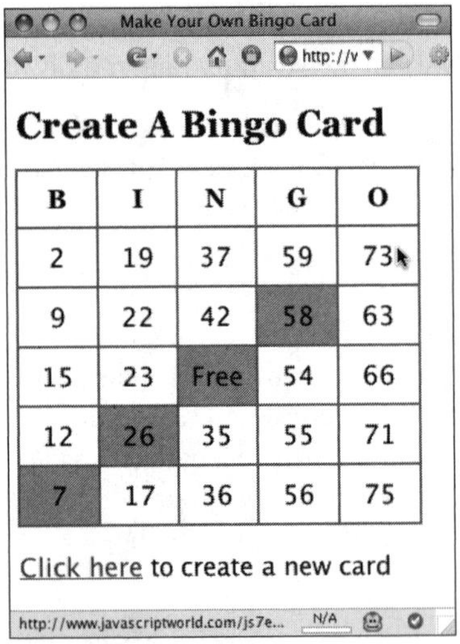

Figure 3.7 Being able to mark squares when numbers are called lets the user interact with the card.

A Bit About Bits

Whenever you use a Boolean, you're dealing with a value that's either true or false. Another way to think about these variables is as containing either zero or one, which is how computers handle everything internally (true being 1 and false being 0).

Those values—0 and 1—are called *bits*. They're single *bits* of information that the computer keeps track of. If it helps, you can instead think of each bit as a light switch that's either on or off.

Because everything on a computer is just a whole bunch of bits, you need to be able to do things with those bits. And in particular, you need to be able to compare them to each other. Here's some of what's going on inside:

◆ and (&)

When we *and* two bits together, if they're both true (that is, both 1), the result is true. Otherwise, the result is false.

◆ or (|)

When we *or* two bits together, if either is true (that is, either is 1), then the result is true. If they're both false, the result is false.

When you use *and* and *or* on numbers greater than one, it's referred to as *bitwise arithmetic*. Internally, your computer converts each number to its binary value and then compares the bits against each other. Because it's done internally, you don't have to do the conversion yourself (whew!).

Script 3.12 Complex math makes this script simple: a winning combination.

```
window.onload = initAll;
var usedNums = new Array(76);

function initAll() {
    if (document.getElementById) {
        document.getElementById("reload").
        → onclick = anotherCard;
        newCard();
    }
    else {
        alert("Sorry, your browser doesn't
        → support this script");
    }
}

function newCard() {
    for (var i=0; i<24; i++) {
        setSquare(i);
    }
}

function setSquare(thisSquare) {
    var currSquare = "square" + thisSquare;
    var colPlace = new Array(0,0,0,0,0,1,1,1,1,
    → 1,2,2,2,2,3,3,3,3,3,4,4,4,4,4);
    var colBasis = colPlace[thisSquare] * 15;
    var newNum;

    do {
        newNum = colBasis + getNewNum() + 1;
    }
    while (usedNums[newNum]);

    usedNums[newNum] = true;
    document.getElementById(currSquare).
    → innerHTML = newNum;
    document.getElementById(currSquare).
    → className = "";
    document.getElementById(currSquare).
    → onmousedown = toggleColor;
}
```

(script continues on next page)

Checking State

Along with interaction to let the user set a square, we can also check to see if the squares form a winning pattern. In this penultimate example, the user checks off which numbers have been called, and then **Script 3.12** lets the user know when they've won.

There's some powerful math going on in this example; if you've never had to deal with binary before, you'll want to read the sidebar, "A Bit About Bits." And if you want to get into the details, check out the sidebar, "Getting Wise About Bits" (but you can skip that one if you feel your eyes glazing over!).

To check for the winning state:

1. `checkWin();`

   Any time the user toggles a square, it's possible that the winning status has changed, so here's a call to `checkWin()` at the end of `toggleColor()`.

2. `var winningOption = -1;`
   `var setSquares = 0;`
   `var winners = new Array(31, 992,`
   `→ 15360, 507904, 541729, 557328,`
   `→ 1083458, 2162820, 4329736,`
   `→ 8519745, 8659472, 16252928);`

   Three new variables are created at the beginning of `checkWin()`:

   ▲ `winningOption`, which stores which of the possible winning options the user has hit (if any),

   ▲ `setSquares`, which stores which squares have been clicked, and

   ▲ `winners`, an array of numbers, each of which is the encoded value of a possible winning line.

continues on next page

3.
```
for (var i=0; i<24; i++) {
    var currSquare = "square" + i;
    if (document.getElementById
→ (currSquare).className != "") {
```

For each square on the card, we need to check to see whether or not its number has already been called. We'll use the square's class attribute as a flag—if it's empty, then it hasn't been clicked. If there is a class attribute, do the following lines.

4.
```
document.getElementById(currSquare).
→ className = "pickedBG";
setSquares = setSquares |
→ Math.pow(2,i);
```

The first line here is straightforward, and in fact, should be redundant—the class attribute should already be set to pickedBG. However, there's a chance it might not be, such as when someone clicks a square they didn't mean to click, gets a win (resetting the attribute to winningBG instead of pickedBG), and then clicks it again to turn it off. If it actually is a winner, that'll be reset later.

The second line uses *bitwise* arithmetic to set setSquares to a number based on each possible state of the card. The single bar (|) does a bitwise or of two values: setSquares itself and the number 2^i, which is the result of Math.pow(2,i). That is, 2^0 is 1, 2^1 is 2, 2^2 is 4, and so on. Or'ing each of these numbers together results in a unique variable storing which of the 16-some million possible states we're in.

Script 3.12 *continued*

```
                    script
function getNewNum() {
    return Math.floor(Math.random() * 15);
}


function anotherCard() {
    for (var i=1; i<usedNums.length; i++) {
        usedNums[i] = false;
    }


    newCard();
    return false;
}


function toggleColor(evt) {
    if (evt) {
        var thisSquare = evt.target;
    }
    else {
        var thisSquare = window.event.
        → srcElement;
    }
    if (thisSquare.className == "") {
        thisSquare.className = "pickedBG";
    }
    else {
        thisSquare.className = "";
    }
    checkWin();
}


function checkWin() {
    var winningOption = -1;
    var setSquares = 0;
    var winners = new Array(31,992,15360,
    → 507904,541729,557328,1083458,2162820,
    → 4329736,8519745,8659472,16252928);


    for (var i=0; i<24; i++) {
        var currSquare = "square" + i;
        if (document.getElementById(currSquare).
        → className != "") {
```

(script continues on next page)

Script 3.12 *continued*

```
document.getElementById(currSquare).
→ className = "pickedBG";
setSquares = setSquares | Math.
→ pow(2,i);
      }
    }

    for (var i=0; i<winners.length; i++) {
      if ((winners[i] & setSquares) ==
      → winners[i]) {
        winningOption = i;
      }
    }

    if (winningOption > -1) {
      for (var i=0; i<24; i++) {
        if (winners[winningOption] & Math.
        → pow(2,i)) {
          currSquare = "square" + i;
          document.getElementById
          → (currSquare).className =
          → "winningBG";
        }
      }
    }
  }
}
```

5.
```
for (var i=0; i<winners.length; i++) {
  if ((winners[i] & setSquares) ==
  → winners[i]) {
    winningOption = i;
  }
}
```

Here's the second complex section: now that we know just what state the card is currently in, we want to know if it's a winning state. In a common Bingo game, there are 12 winning states, and this section compares our card's current state to each. We do a bitwise *and* between each winning state and the current state, which results in a new state that only has true values for each square that is in both of the two. Comparing that back to the same winning state allows us to see if we've fully hit this pattern—that is, the result will have no hits outside the winning state (as they aren't found in the winning state) and so long as everything found in the winning pattern is also in the current pattern, we've got ourselves a winner. In that case, set `winningOption` to i, the pattern we matched.

continues on next page

6.
```
if (winningOption > -1) {
    for (var i=0; i<24; i++) {
        if (winners[winningOption] &
        → Math.pow(2,i)) {
            currSquare = "square" + i;
            document.getElementById
            → (currSquare).className =
            → "winningBG";
        }
    }
}
```

Finally, if winningOption is a number greater than -1, we know we've got a winner. In that case, we want to loop through each square and check to see if it's found in the winning pattern. If it is, we set the class attribute to winningBG, and we're done, as seen in **Figure 3.8**.

✔ **Tips**

■ Again, just setting the class attribute of the winning squares to match a particular CSS style is enough to change the card's appearance. Because this is paper, though, you can't see how it truly looks: the winningBG rule sets the background to an animated gif which slowly flashes between red and white. A friend of mine described it as "delightfully obnoxious."

■ There are a number of different Bingo games, each with different winning patterns. By modifying the single line of code that initializes the winners array, your script can fit any result someone might want.

■ If you've ever wondered why conditionals use && and || (for and and or, respectively), now you know: the single version of those operators tells JavaScript that you're doing binary math, not decimal math.

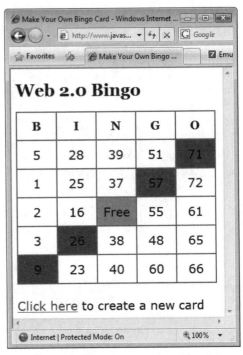

Figure 3.8 Looks like we've got a winner! (In print, you can't see the pulsing colors.)

CHECKING STATE

Getting Wise About Bits

(As we said above, this is the sidebar for geeks, so please be advised to put on your propeller beanie *and* pocket protector before continuing. If you don't already own these accoutrements, feel free to just skip this section.)

Given that there are (at least in this version of Bingo) only 12 possible winning patterns, we could easily write code that would check for each of those. Because of the many variations of Bingo, though, that would mean that any time you wanted to play a different version you'd have to change the entire way the script checks for wins.

Instead, we're using what's called bitwise arithmetic (see the sidebar, "A Bit About Bits") to store the winning patterns. That means that we're taking advantage of the way computers internally keep track of everything as 1s and 0s. So, we create the programming equivalent of making a list:

0	✔	1		13		8192
1		2		14	✔	16384
2		4		15		32768
3		8		16		65536
4		16		17		131072
5	✔	32		18		262144
6		64		19	✔	524288
7		128		20		1048576
8		256		21		2097152
9		512		22		4194304
10	✔	1024		23		8388608
11		2048				
12		4096				

If you compare the numbers in the left-hand column next to the checked boxes, you'll see that we've picked the top row of the card: `square0`, `square5`, `square10`, `square14`, and `square19`. The right-hand column is 2 to the power of the left-hand number.

To figure out the numeric equivalent of a winning pattern, we just add up the right-hand numbers that are part of the pattern. In this case, that's 1+32+1024+16384+524288, or 541729—which you'll see is included in the list of winners.

To calculate what you get with a vertical line in the B column, you add up 1+2+4+8+16, for a result of 31. That's another winner. And so on, for each possible winning pattern.

continues on next page

Getting Wise About Bits (continued)

Here's the secret: if you flip that chart above on its side so that it goes from 23 to 0, replace the check marks with 1s and the blanks with 0s, you'll have a 24-digit binary number. So, you could (if you wanted to) think of our first winning pattern as `000010000100010000100001` and our second as `000000000000000000011111`—although why you'd want to, we have no idea. But take our word for it: the first is the binary representation of 541729, and the latter for 31.

When we go through each square and check to see if it's set, we store the result in `setSquares`. That value is the sum of all the squares the player has selected, which, again, you could think of as a line of 24 ones and zeros if you prefer.

We get `setSquares` by or'ing all those values together. When a zero and a zero are or'ed together (using a single bar |), the result is a zero. Any other combination, and the result is a one.

Let's say that our end result in `setSquares` is 557840—that means that the player set squares 4, 8, 12, 15, and 19, for a binary value of `000010001001000100010000`. Now, 557840 isn't on our list of winners. But when we and the number above with 557328 (which is a winner), we get:

`000010001001000100010000` and
`000010001000000100010000`
`000010001000000100010000`

When a one and a one are and'ed together (using a single ampersand &), the result is a one. Any other combination, and the result is a zero.

Looking at the code, we then compare the resulting value back to the winning value, and if they're the same (as they are in this case), we've got a winner; here, it's the diagonal going from the bottom left to the top right.

If you're now wondering if this is really easier than calculating everything out manually, think about it this way: in order to play a round where getting all four corners also counts as a win, all you have to do is add the number 1362912 to the array of winners—and everything else just works (that's squares 0, 4, 19, and 23, by the way).

Script 3.13 A private game of Buzzword Bingo will liven up that next deadly dull staff meeting—just add your own text strings

```
script
var buzzwords = new Array ("Aggregate",
    "Ajax",
    "API",
    "Bandwidth",
    "Beta",
    "Bleeding edge",
    "Convergence",
    "Design pattern",
    "Disruptive",
    "DRM",
    "Enterprise",
    "Facilitate",
    "Folksonomy",
    "Framework",
    "Impact",
    "Innovate",
    "Long tail",
    "Mashup",
    "Microformats",
    "Mobile",
    "Monetize",
    "Open social",
    "Paradigm",
    "Podcast",
    "Proactive",
    "Rails",
    "Scalable",
    "Social bookmarks",
    "Social graph",
    "Social software",
    "Spam",
    "Synergy",
    "Tagging",
    "Tipping point",
    "Truthiness",
    "User-generated",
    "Vlog",
    "Webinar",
    "Wiki",
    "Workflow"
);
```

(script continues on next page)

Working with String Arrays

Up to this point, all the arrays we've dealt with have consisted of Booleans or numbers. As our final Bingo-related example, **Script 3.13** combines everything we've done previously with a string array to create the popular "Buzzword Bingo" game.

To use string arrays:

1. ```
   var buzzwords = new Array("Aggregate",
   →"Ajax", "API", "Bandwidth", "Beta",
   → "Bleeding edge", "Convergence",
   → "Design pattern", "Disruptive",
   → "DRM", "Enterprise", "Facilitate",
   → "Folksonomy", "Framework",
   → "Impact", "Innovate", "Long tail",
   → "Mashup", "Microformats", "Mobile",
   → "Monetize", "Open social",
   → "Paradigm", "Podcast", "Proactive",
   → "Rails", "Scalable",
   → "Social bookmarks",
   → "Social graph", "Social software",
   → "Spam", "Synergy", "Tagging",
   → "Tipping point", "Truthiness",
   → "User-generated", "Vlog", "Webinar",
   → "Wiki", "Workflow");
   ```

   ```
   var usedWords = new Array(buzzwords.
   → length);
   ```

   This game of Buzzword Bingo has a "Web 2.0" theme, but you can put strings based around any topic inside the buzzwords array. You'll need to have at least 24 entries (more is better), and you won't want them to be too lengthy (or they won't fit in the squares) but other than those restrictions, the only limit is your imagination.

   Along with initializing the string array, we also need to initialize the new usedWords array of Booleans. Giving it a size of buzzwords.length means that nothing needs to change when we add new entries—it will automatically be the right length.

   continues on next page
   ```

2.
```
do {
    var randomWord = Math.floor((Math.
    →random() * buzzwords.length));
}
while (usedWords[randomWord]);

usedWords[randomWord] = true;
var currSquare = "square" +
→ thisSquare;
document.getElementById(currSquare).
→ innerHTML = buzzwords[randomWord];
```

Figuring out what strings to put in what squares is actually simpler, as any string can go in any square (unlike the number restrictions in standard Bingo). All we're doing here is making sure that we're getting an as-yet-unused word, marking it as used, and then writing it into the square.

3.
```
for (var i=0; i<buzzwords.length;
→ i++) {
    usedWords[i] = false;
}
```

When a new card is generated, just like with the standard Bingo card, we have to set all the flags in usedWords back to false so they're once again available.

Script 3.13 *continued*

```
var usedWords = new Array(buzzwords.length);
window.onload = initAll;

function initAll() {
    if (document.getElementById) {
        document.getElementById("reload").
        →onclick = anotherCard;
        newCard();
    }
    else {
        alert("Sorry, your browser doesn't
        →support this script");
    }
}

function newCard() {
    for (var i=0; i<24; i++) {
        setSquare(i);
    }
}

function setSquare(thisSquare) {
    do {
        var randomWord = Math.floor((Math.
        → random() * buzzwords.length));
    }
    while (usedWords[randomWord]);

    usedWords[randomWord] = true;
    var currSquare = "square" + thisSquare;
    document.getElementById(currSquare).
    → innerHTML = buzzwords[randomWord];
    document.getElementById(currSquare).
    →className = "";
    document.getElementById(currSquare).
    →onmousedown = toggleColor;
}

function anotherCard() {
    for (var i=0; i<buzzwords.length; i++) {
        usedWords[i] = false;
    }
}
```

(script continues on next page)

Script 3.13 *continued*

```
                                    script
    newCard();
    return false;
}

function toggleColor(evt) {
    if (evt) {
        var thisSquare = evt.target;
    }
    else {
        var thisSquare = window.event.srcElement;
    }
    if (thisSquare.className == "") {
        thisSquare.className = "pickedBG";
    }
    else {
        thisSquare.className = "";
    }
    checkWin();
}

function checkWin() {
    var winningOption = -1;
    var setSquares = 0;
    var winners = new Array(31,992,15360,507904,541729,557328,1083458,2162820,4329736,8519745,8659472,
    → 16252928);

    for (var i=0; i<24; i++) {
        var currSquare = "square" + i;
        if (document.getElementById(currSquare).className != "") {
            document.getElementById(currSquare).className = "pickedBG";
            setSquares = setSquares | Math.pow(2,i);
        }
    }

    for (var i=0; i<winners.length; i++) {
        if ((winners[i] & setSquares) == winners[i]) {
            winningOption = i;
        }
    }

    if (winningOption > -1) {
        for (var i=0; i<24; i++) {
            if (winners[winningOption] & Math.pow(2,i)) {
                currSquare = "square" + i;
                document.getElementById(currSquare).className = "winningBG";
            }
        }
    }
}
```

WORKING WITH STRING ARRAYS

✔ Tip

■ At the annual Macworld Expo in San Francisco, it's traditional for the opening keynote to be given by Steve Jobs—which is, therefore, referred to as the "SteveNote." Also somewhat traditional are audience members playing "SteveNote Bingo," seeing which of Steve's pet phrases (such as "Boom!" and "One more thing…") are said and which of the rumored products actually appear.

Because the iPhone comes with the standard Safari browser, I was able to easily come up with an interactive version of this game (see **Figure 3.9**) for the Macworld following the iPhone's introduction. It was very well received, although no one actually yelled out "Bingo!" during the keynote

Figure 3.9 With a mobile browser and a little imagination, you can write a bingo game of your own for almost any occasion.

WORKING WITH IMAGES

One of the best (and most common) uses of JavaScript is to add visual interest to Web pages by animating graphics, and that's what this chapter is all about. Making an image on a Web page change when the user moves the mouse over the image, thereby making the page react to the user, is one of the most common—and effective—tricks you can learn in JavaScript. This *rollover*, as it is called, is easy to implement, yet has many applications, as you'll see.

Rollovers are a great tool, but you can do much more than rollovers with JavaScript, such as automatically change images, create ad banners, build slideshows, and display random images on a page.

In this chapter, you'll learn how to make JavaScript do all of these image tricks. Let's get started.

Table 4.1

Just Enough HTML—Images		

TAG	ATTRIBUTE	MEANING
img		Contains the attributes that describe the image to be displayed by the browser
	src	Contains the URL of the image, relative to the URL of the Web page
	width	Contains the width (in pixels) at which the browser will display the image
	height	Contains the height (in pixels) at which the browser will display the image
	border	The width of the border to be displayed
	name	The name that JavaScript uses to refer to this image; as with other JavaScript objects, no spaces or other punctuation is allowed, and it cannot start with a number
	alt	Used for non-visual browsers in place of the image
	hspace	A horizontal buffer area around the image
	vspace	A vertical buffer area around the image
	align	Describes where this image should be placed on the page in terms of horizontal or vertical alignment
	id	A unique identifier, which JavaScript will use to manipulate the image

Script 4.1 Here's the simplest way to do a rollover, within a link tag.

```
script
<!DOCTYPE html PUBLIC "-//W3C//DTD XHTML 1.0
→ Transitional//EN"
        "http://www.w3.org/TR/xhtml1/DTD/
          → xhtml1-transitional.dtd">
<html xmlns="http://www.w3.org/1999/xhtml">
<head>
        <title>A Simple Rollover</title>
</head>
<body bgcolor="#FFFFFF">
        <a href="next.html" onmouseover="document.
        → arrow.src='images/arrow_on.gif'"
        → onmouseout="document.arrow.src='images/
        → arrow_off.gif'"><img src="images/
        → arrow_off.gif" width="147" height="82"
        → border="0" name="arrow" alt="arrow" /></a>
</body>
</html>
```

Creating Rollovers

The idea behind rollovers is simple. You have two images. The first, or *original* image, is loaded and displayed along with the rest of the Web page by the user. When the user moves the mouse over the first image, the browser quickly swaps out the first image for the second, or *replacement* image, giving the illusion of movement or animation.

Script 4.1 gives you the bare-bones rollover; the whole thing is done within a standard image link. First a blue arrow is loaded (**Figure 4.1**), and then it is overwritten by a red arrow when the user moves the mouse over the image (**Figure 4.2**). The blue arrow is redrawn when the user moves the mouse away.

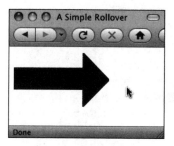

Figure 4.1
The first image, before the user moves the mouse over it.

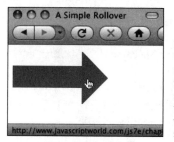

Figure 4.2
When the mouse is over the image, the script replaces the first image with the second image.

To create a rollover:

1. `<a href="next.html"`

The link begins by specifying where the browser will go when the user clicks the image, in this case to the page `next.html`.

2. `onmouseover="document.arrow.src=`
→ `'images/arrow_on.gif'"`

When the user moves the mouse over the image, the replacement image `arrow_on.gif`, which is inside the `images` directory, is written to the document window.

3. `onmouseout="document.arrow.src=`
→ `'images/arrow_off.gif'">`

Then, when the mouse moves away, the image `arrow_off.gif` is swapped back in.

4. `<img src="images/arrow_off.gif"`
→ `width="147" height="82" border="0"`
→ `name="arrow" alt="arrow" />`

The image link defines the source of the original image for the page. We have included the `alt` attribute inside the image tag because `alt` attributes (which give non-graphical browsers a name or description of an image) are required if you want your HTML to be compliant with the W3C standards, and because using `alt` attributes helps make your page accessible to disabled users, such as visually impaired users who browse using screen readers.

Disadvantages to This Kind of Rollover

This method of doing rollovers is very simple, but you should be aware that there are several problems and drawbacks with it.

◆ Because the second image is downloaded from the server at the time the user rolls over the first image, there can be a perceptible delay before the second image replaces the first one, especially for people browsing your site with a slower connection.

◆ Using this method causes an error message in ancient browsers, such as Netscape 2.0 or earlier, Internet Explorer 3.0 or earlier, or the America Online 2.7 browser. Since there are so few of these vintage browsers still in use, it's not much of a problem these days.

Instead of using this method, we suggest that you use the following way to create rollovers, in the "Creating More Effective Rollovers" section, which solves all these problems and more.

Creating More Effective Rollovers

To make the illusion of animation work, you need to make sure that the replacement image appears immediately, with no delay while it is fetched from the server. To do that, you use JavaScript to place the images into variables used by your script, which preloads all the images into the browser's cache (so that they are already on the user's hard disk when they are needed). Then, when the user moves the mouse over an image, the script swaps out one variable containing an image for a second variable containing the replacement image. **Script 4.2** shows how it is done. The visible result is the same as in Figures 4.1 and 4.2, but the apparent animation is smoother.

To keep your JavaScript more manageable, we'll extract the JavaScript code from the HTML page and put it in an external `.js` file, as in **Script 4.3** (see Chapter 2 for more about `.js` files).

To create a better rollover:

1. ```
<script type="text/javascript"
→ src="script02.js"></script>
```

   This tag is in Script 4.2, the HTML page. It uses the `src` attribute to tell the browser where to find the external `.js` file, which is where the JavaScript resides.

2. ```
<a href="next1.html"><img
→ src="images/button1_off.gif"
→ width="113" height="33"
→ border="0" alt="button1"
→ id="button1" /></a>  
→ <a href="next2.html"><img
→ src="images/button2_off.gif"
→ width="113" height="33" border="0"
→ alt="button2" id="button2" /></a>
```

   Still in Script 4.2, these are two typical link tags for the buttons, with image tags embedded in them. The `href` attribute describes the destination of the link when the user clicks it. In the `img` tag, the `src` attribute provides the path to the image before the user rolls over it. The rest of the attributes are descriptive and familiar: the image's `width`, `height`, `border`, and `alt` text. Note that each of the two buttons also has an `id` attribute; as described in Chapter 1, the `id` must be unique for each object. The script uses the image's `id` to make the rollover work.

Script 4.2 The only JavaScript on this HTML page is the pointer to the external `.js` file.

```
script
<!DOCTYPE html PUBLIC "-//W3C//DTD XHTML 1.0
→ Transitional//EN"
        "http://www.w3.org/TR/xhtml1/DTD/
        → xhtml1-transitional.dtd">
<html xmlns="http://www.w3.org/1999/xhtml">
<head>
    <title>A More Effective Rollover</title>
    <script type="text/javascript"
    → src="script02.js"></script>
</head>
<body bgcolor="#FFFFFF">
    <a href="next1.html"><img src="images/
    → button1_off.gif" width="113" height="33"
    → border="0" alt="button1" id="button1"
    → /></a>  
    <a href="next2.html"><img src="images/
    → button2_off.gif" width="113" height="33"
    → border="0" alt="button2" id="button2"
    → /></a>
</body>
</html>
```

Script 4.3 This is a better way to do rollovers than in Script 4.1, because it is much more flexible.

```
window.onload = rolloverInit;

function rolloverInit() {
    for (var i=0; i<document.images.length;
    → i++) {
        if (document.images[i].parentNode.
        → tagName == "A") {
            setupRollover(document.images[i]);
        }
    }
}

function setupRollover(thisImage) {
    thisImage.outImage = new Image();
    thisImage.outImage.src = thisImage.src;
    thisImage.onmouseout = function() {
        this.src = this.outImage.src;
    }

    thisImage.overImage = new Image();
    thisImage.overImage.src = "images/" +
    → thisImage.id + "_on.gif";
    thisImage.onmouseover = function() {
        this.src = this.overImage.src;
    }
}
```

3. `window.onload = rolloverInit;`

   Moving to Script 4.3, the `window.onload` event handler is triggered when the page has finished loading. The handler calls the `rolloverInit()` function.

   This handler is used here to make sure that the script doesn't execute before the page is done loading. That's because referring to items on the page before the page has finished loading can cause errors if some of the page's elements haven't yet been loaded.

4. `function rolloverInit() {`
   `    for (var i=0; i<document.images.`
   `    → length; i++) {`

   The `rolloverInit()` function scans each image on the page, looking to see if the tag around the image is an <a> tag, indicating that it is a link. The first of these two lines begins the function. The second begins a for…next loop that goes through all of the images. The loop begins by setting the counter variable i to 0. Then, each time the loop goes around, if the value of i is less than the number of images in the document, increment i by 1.

5. `if (document.images[i].parentNode.`
   `→ tagName == "A") {`

   This is where we test to see if the tag surrounding the image is an anchor tag. We do it by looking at an object and seeing if the object's value is A (the anchor tag). Let's break that object apart a bit. The first part of the object, `document.images[i]`, is the current image. Its `parentNode` property is the container tag that surrounds it, and `tagName` then provides the name of that container tag. So in English, you can read the part of the line in the parentheses as "For this particular image, is the tag around it an 'A'?"

   continues on next page

6. `setupRollover(document.images[i]);`

If the result of the test in step 5 is true, then the `setupRollover` function is called and passed the current image.

7. `function setupRollover(thisImage) {`

Take a minute to look at the whole function before we go through it line by line. Here's the overview: this function adds two new properties to the image object that's passed in. The new properties are `outImage` (the version of the image when you're not on it) and `overImage` (the version of the image when you are on it), both of which are image objects themselves. Because they're image objects, once they're created, we can add their `src` property. The `src` for `outImage` is the current (off) image `src`. The `src` value for `overImage` is calculated based on the `id` attribute of the original image.

This line starts off the function with the image that was passed to it by the `rolloverInit()` function.

8. `thisImage.outImage = new Image();`

This line takes the image object that was passed in and adds the new `outImage` property to it. Because you can add a property of any kind to an object, and because properties are just objects themselves, what's happening here is that we're adding an image object to an image. The parentheses for the new image object are optional, but it's good coding practice to include them; if needed, you can set properties of the new image object by passing certain parameters.

9. `thisImage.outImage.src = thisImage.src;`

Now we set the source for the new `outImage` to be the same as the source of `thisImage`. The default image on the page is always the version you see when the cursor is off the image.

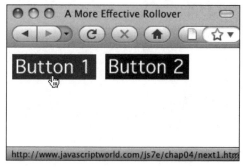

Figure 4.3 You can also put multiple rollovers on the same page.

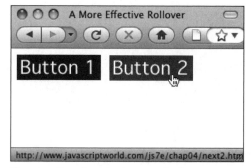

Figure 4.4 Hovering over the second rollover.

10. `thisImage.onmouseout = function() {`
   `    this.src = this.outImage.src;`
`}`

The first line here starts off what's called an *anonymous* function—that is, it's a function without a name. We could name it (say, `rollOut()`), but as it's only one line it's not so necessary.

In this section, we're telling the browser to trigger what should happen when the user moves the mouse away from the image. Whenever that happens, we want to set the image source back to the initial source value, that is, the `outImage` version of the image.

11. `thisImage.overImage = new Image();`
   `thisImage.overImage.src = "images/"`
   `→ + thisImage.id + "_on.gif";`

In the first line, we create a new image object that will contain the `overImage` version of the image. The second line sets the source for `overImage`. It builds the name of the source file on the fly, concatenating `"images/"` with the `id` of the image (remember, in Script 4.2, we saw that those `id`s were `button1` and `button2`) and adding `"_on.gif"`.

12. `thisImage.onmouseover = function() {`
   `    this.src = this.overImage.src;`
`}`

Here we have another anonymous function. This one tells the browser that when the user moves the cursor over the image, it should reset the current image's source to that of the `overImage` version, as seen in **Figures 4.3** and **4.4**.

✔ Tips

- When you prepare your graphics for roll-overs, make sure that all your GIF images are *not* transparent. If they are, you will see the image you are trying to replace beneath the transparent image—and that's not what you want.

- Both the original and the replacement images need to have identical dimensions. Otherwise, some browsers resize the images for you, and you probably won't like the distorted result.

- In the previous example, the rollover happened when you moved the cursor over the link; here, the rollover happens when you move the cursor over the image— that is, the onmouseover and onmouseout are now attached to the image, not the link. While these methods usually give the same effect, there's one big difference: some older browsers (Netscape 4 and earlier, IE 3 and earlier) don't support onmouseover and onmouseout on the img tag.

- While you might think that because all of the tags on the HTML page are lowercase (as required by XHTML), tagName should be compared to a lowercase "a". That's not the way it works. tagName always returns an uppercase value.

This Looks Very Different...

If you're thinking about now that hey, this isn't the way I remember JavaScript code looking before—don't panic! Things have changed a little on the face of it, which you'll particularly notice if you're familiar with the code in some older editions of this book.

Styles change over the years, and (as mentioned in Chapter 1) the recommended way to write JavaScript has changed. If you're more familiar with the older approach, it won't be that hard to switch, and you'll soon wonder how on earth you ever made do with all that JavaScript and HTML jumbled together.

For example, the scripts on the next page show what the same functionality from "Creating More Effective Rollovers" looked like in a previous edition compared to this edition. In previous editions, the script was called "Putting Multiple Rollovers On a Page," a task we've since eliminated because the "Creating More Effective Rollovers" script is more flexible now.

What you're likely to notice first is that the two are just about the same length—but that's a little misleading, because the page (in both cases) has only two buttons. Once you add a third button, while you have to add one line of HTML to both, you also have to add *seven* lines of JavaScript to the old-style code to handle that button. The new version? Zero new lines of code.

Additionally, you have to remember to add the onmouseover and onmouseout event handler attributes to your link when you're using the old method. If not, you'll find that no matter how much JavaScript you add, your rollovers won't roll. With the newer method, your HTML page requires no JavaScript mixed in. This is especially handy if you work in a larger group, where some people do JavaScript and some just do HTML.

And finally, the new style is preferable because you don't have to have all that JavaScript in every single page! If you've got rollovers, you almost definitely have a site with multiple pages. If every page has to load that same JavaScript, your site will load and feel slow. If all your pages reference a single external JavaScript file, however, it only has to load once, and as long as your pages refer to it, it never needs to be downloaded again. That means less bandwidth hits for your site and faster browsing for your visitors. And best of all: if you need to make a change to your JavaScript, you only need to change the one file, and the change is immediately propagated to the entire site.

Previous edition

```
○○○                script
<!DOCTYPE html PUBLIC "-//W3C//DTD XHTML 1.0
→ Transitional//EN">
<html xmlns="http://www.w3.org/1999/xhtml">
<head>
      <title>A Simple Rollover</title>
      <script language="Javascript"
      → type="text/javascript">
      <!-- Hide script from old browsers

      if (document.images) {
         button1Red = new Image
         button1Blue = new Image
         button2Red = new Image
         button2Blue = new Image

         button1Red.src = "images/redButton1.gif"
         button1Blue.src = "images/blueButton1.gif"
         button2Red.src = "images/redButton2.gif"
         button2Blue.src = "images/blueButton2.gif"
      }
      else {
         button1Red = ""
         button1Blue = ""
         button2Red = ""
         button2Blue = ""

         document.button1 = ""
         document.button2 = ""
      }

      // End hiding script from old browsers -->
      </script>
</head>
<body bgcolor="#FFFFFF">
      <a href="next1.html" onmouseover=
      → "document.button1.src=button1Red.src"
      → onmouseout="document.button1.
      → src=button1Blue.src"><img src="images/
      → blueButton1.gif" width="113" height="33"
      → border="0" name="button1" alt="button1"
      → /></a>  
      <a href="next2.html" onmouseover=
      → "document.button2.src=button2Red.src"
      → onmouseout="document.button2.
      → src=button2Blue.src"><img src="images/
      → blueButton2.gif" width="113" height="33"
      → border="0" name="button2" alt="button2"
      → /></a>
</body>
</html>
```

This edition

```
○○○                script
<!DOCTYPE html PUBLIC "-//W3C//DTD XHTML 1.0
Transitional//EN"
"http://www.w3.org/TR/xhtml1/DTD/xhtml1-
transitional.dtd">
<html xmlns="http://www.w3.org/1999/xhtml">
<head>
      <title>A More Effective Rollover</title>
      <script type="text/javascript"
      → src="script02.js"></script>
</head>
<body bgcolor="#FFFFFF">
      <a href="next1.html"><img src="images/
      → button1_off.gif" width="113" height="33"
      → border="0" alt="button1" id="button1"
      → /></a>  
      <a href="next2.html"><img src="images/
      → button2_off.gif" width="113" height="33"
      → border="0" alt="button2" id="button2"
      → /></a>
</body>
</html>
- - - - - - - - - - - - - - - -
window.onload = rolloverInit;

function rolloverInit() {
      for (var i=0; i<document.images.length;
      → i++) {
         if (document.images[i].parentNode.
         → tagName == "A") {
            setupRollover(document.images[i]);
         }
      }
}

function setupRollover(thisImage) {
      thisImage.outImage = new Image();
      thisImage.outImage.src = thisImage.src;
      thisImage.onmouseout = function() {
         this.src = this.outImage.src;
      }

      thisImage.overImage = new Image();
      thisImage.overImage.src = "images/" +
      → thisImage.id + "_on.gif";
      thisImage.onmouseover = function() {
         this.src = this.overImage.src;
      }
}
```

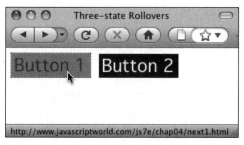

Figure 4.5 When the button is clicked, you get a third image (hard to see in this grayscale image; check our companion Web site for the full effect).

Script 4.4 By putting your JavaScript in an external file, the HTML for a three-state rollover is virtually identical to a two-state rollover.

```
script
<!DOCTYPE html PUBLIC "-//W3C//DTD XHTML 1.0
Transitional//EN"
        "http://www.w3.org/TR/xhtml1/DTD/
        → xhtml1-transitional.dtd">
<html xmlns="http://www.w3.org/1999/xhtml">
<head>
    <title>Three-state Rollovers</title>
    <script type="text/javascript"
    → src="script03.js"></script>
</head>
<body bgcolor="#FFFFFF">
    <a href="next1.html"><img src="images/
    → button1_off.gif" width="113" height="33"
    → border="0" alt="button1" id="button1"
    → /></a>  
    <a href="next2.html"><img src="images/
    → button2_off.gif" width="113" height="33"
    → border="0" alt="button2" id="button2"
    → /></a>
</body>
</html>
```

Building Three-State Rollovers

A three-state rollover is one where the rollover has three versions. Besides the original image and the version that appears when the user places the cursor over the image, there is a third version of the image when the button itself is clicked, as shown in **Figure 4.5**.

Script 4.4, the HTML file, looks almost exactly the same as Script 4.2 from the previous task. In fact, the only differences are the document's title and the name of the external JavaScript file that is being called. That's it. This is an example of why putting all your JavaScript into an external file is so powerful; you can add functionality to your pages without having to rework your HTML pages.

In **Script 4.5**, the external JavaScript file, there are only a few changes from Script 4.3. Rather than go through the whole script again, we'll just focus on the changes. Remember, the parts of the script that we're covering are shown in red in the code.

To build a three-state rollover:

1. `thisImage.clickImage = new Image();`
   `thisImage.clickImage.src = "images/"`
   `→ + thisImage.id + "_click.gif";`

   In the `setupRollover()` function, we now need to add a third image property for the click state. In the first line, we create a new image object that will contain the `clickImage` version of the image. The second line sets the source for `clickImage`. It builds the name of the source file on the fly, concatenating `"images/"` with the `id` of the image, and adding `"_click.gif"`.

2. `thisImage.onclick = function() {`
   `    this.src = this.clickImage.src;`
   `}`

   This tells the browser what to do when the user clicks the mouse on the image: in this case, we want to set the image source to its `clickImage` version.

Script 4.5 This script powers the three-state rollover.

```
window.onload = rolloverInit;

function rolloverInit() {
    for (var i=0; i<document.images.length;
    → i++) {
        if (document.images[i].parentNode.
        → tagName == "A") {
            setupRollover(document.images[i]);
        }
    }
}

function setupRollover(thisImage) {
    thisImage.outImage = new Image();
    thisImage.outImage.src = thisImage.src;
    thisImage.onmouseout = function() {
        this.src = this.outImage.src;
    }

    thisImage.clickImage = new Image();
    thisImage.clickImage.src = "images/" +
    → thisImage.id + "_click.gif";
    thisImage.onclick = function() {
        this.src = this.clickImage.src;
    }

    thisImage.overImage = new Image();
    thisImage.overImage.src = "images/" +
    → thisImage.id + "_on.gif";
    thisImage.onmouseover = function() {
        this.src = this.overImage.src;
    }
}
```

Figure 4.6 The text link is the triggering device for this rollover.

Figure 4.7 When the user points at the link, the graphic below changes.

Script 4.6 This script shows the HTML for a rollover from a text link.

```
script
<!DOCTYPE html PUBLIC "-//W3C//DTD XHTML 1.0
→ Transitional//EN"
        "http://www.w3.org/TR/xhtml1/DTD/
        → xhtml1-transitional.dtd">
<html xmlns="http://www.w3.org/1999/xhtml">
<head>
    <title>Link Rollover</title>
    <script type="text/javascript"
    → src="script04.js"></script>
</head>
<body bgcolor="#FFFFFF">
    <h1><a href="next.html" id="arrow">Next
    → page</a></h1>
    <img src="images/arrow_off.gif" width="147"
    → height="82" id="arrowImg" alt="arrow" />
</body>
</html>
```

Triggering Rollovers from a Link

In earlier examples, the user triggered the rollover by moving the mouse over an image. But you can also make a rollover occur when the user hovers over a text link, as in **Figures 4.6** and **4.7**. The HTML is an unexciting page with one link and one image, shown in **Script 4.6**. We'll do the rollover by modifying the script used in previous examples, as in **Script 4.7**.

To trigger a rollover from a link:

1. `function rolloverInit() {`
    `for (var i=0; i<document.links.`
    → `length; i++) {`

After beginning the `rolloverInit()` function, we start a loop, much like previous examples in this chapter. But there we were looking for images (`document.images.length`), and here we're looking for links (`document.links.length`). The loop begins by setting the counter variable i to zero. Every time around, if the value of i is less than the number of links in the document, increment i by 1.

2. `var linkObj = document.links[i];`

We create the `linkObj` variable and set it to the current link.

3. `if (linkObj.id) {`
    `var imgObj = document.`
    → `getElementById(linkObj.id +`
    → `"Img");`

If `linkObj` has an `id`, then we check to see if there's another element on the page that has an `id` that's the same plus `Img`. If so, put that element into the new variable `imgObj`.

4. `if (imgObj) {`
    `setupRollover(linkObj,imgObj);`

If `imgObj` exists, then call the `setupRollover()` function, passing it the link object and the image object.

Script 4.7 Here is the JavaScript for a rollover from a text link.

```
window.onload = rolloverInit;

function rolloverInit() {
    for (var i=0; i<document.links.length; i++) {
        var linkObj = document.links[i];
        if (linkObj.id) {
            var imgObj = document.getElementById
            → (linkObj.id + "Img");
            if (imgObj) {
                setupRollover(linkObj,imgObj);
            }
        }
    }
}

function setupRollover(thisLink,thisImage) {
    thisLink.imgToChange = thisImage;
    thisLink.onmouseout = function() {
        this.imgToChange.src = this.outImage.src;
    }
    thisLink.onmouseover = function() {
        this.imgToChange.src = this.overImage.src;
    }

    thisLink.outImage = new Image();
    thisLink.outImage.src = thisImage.src;

    thisLink.overImage = new Image();
    thisLink.overImage.src = "images/" +
    → thisLink.id + "_on.gif";
}
```

5. `function setupRollover(thisLink,`
`→ thisImage) {`
    `thisLink.imgToChange = thisImage;`

The `setupRollover()` function begins with the link and image parameters that were passed to it in step 4. Then we add a new property, `imgToChange`, to the link object. JavaScript needs some way of knowing what image is to be changed when the link is moused over, and this is where it's stored.

6. `thisLink.onmouseout = function() {`
    `this.imgToChange.src = this.`
    `→ outImage.src;`
`}`
`thisLink.onmouseover = function() {`
    `this.imgToChange.src = this.`
    `→ overImage.src;`
`}`

When the `mouseover` and `mouseout` are triggered, they're slightly different from the previous examples in this chapter: now, `this.imgToChange.src` is being reset instead of `this.src` itself.

✔ Tip

- This technique is useful when you want to provide the user with a preview of what they will see if they click the link at which they are pointing. For example, say you have a travel site describing trips to Scotland, Tahiti, and Cleveland. On the left of the page could be a column of text links for each destination, while on the right could be a preview area where an image appears. As the user points at the name of a destination, a picture of that place appears in the preview area. Clicking the link takes the user to a page detailing their fabulous vacation spot.

Making Multiple Links Change a Single Rollover

Up to now, you've seen how mousing over a single image (or actually, the link associated with that image) can trigger a rollover effect. But you can also have several different images that trigger a rollover. This can be very useful when you have several images that you want to annotate. Rolling over each of the images makes the description of that image appear. In this example, we've done just this with images of three of Leonardo da Vinci's inventions. As you roll over each image, the description of that image appears in a text box. The description itself is another image. Actually, it's three images, one for each of the three inventions. **Figure 4.8** shows **Script 4.8** (HTML) and **Script 4.9** (JavaScript) in action. As with most of the scripts in this book, it builds on previous examples, so we'll just explain the new concepts. There are just a few lines that are different between Script 4.7 and Script 4.9.

Figure 4.8 This page has three interactive images, a flying machine, a tank, and a helicopter. When you roll over an image, its description appears under Leonardo's face.

Script 4.8 Note that the links and images on this page all have unique ids.

```
●●●                 script
<!DOCTYPE html PUBLIC "-//W3C//DTD XHTML 1.0
→ Transitional//EN"
        "http://www.w3.org/TR/xhtml1/DTD/
          → xhtml1-transitional.dtd">
<html xmlns="http://www.w3.org/1999/xhtml">
<head>
    <title>Multiple Links, Single
      → Rollover</title>
    <script type="text/javascript"
      → src="script05.js"></script>
</head>
<body bgcolor="#EECC99">
    <img src="images/DaVinci.jpg" width="144"
      → height="219" alt="DaVinci" align="right"
      → hspace="50" />
    <img src="images/leoText.gif" width="375"
      → height="26" alt="Leonardo's Inventions" />
    <a href="flyPage.html" class="textField"
      → id="flyer"><img src="images/flyer.gif"
      → width="293" height="165" border="0"
      → alt="Flying Machine" vspace="10"
      → id="flyerImg" /></a><br clear="right" />
    <img src="images/bg.gif" width="208"
      → height="27" id="textField" alt="Text
      → Field" align="right" vspace="20" />
    <a href="tankPage.html" class="textField"
      → id="tank"><img src="images/tank.gif"
      → width="325" height="92" border="0"
      → alt="Tank" id="tankImg" /></a><br />
    <a href="heliPage.html" class="textField"
      → id="helicopter"><img src="images/
      → helicopter.gif" width="224" height="160"
      → border="0" alt="Helicopter"
      → id="helicopterImg" /></a>
</body>
</html>
```

Script 4.9 This script shows you how to use multiple links to trigger a single rollover.

```
window.onload = rolloverInit;

function rolloverInit() {
    for (var i=0; i<document.links.length;
    → i++) {
        var linkObj = document.links[i];
        if (linkObj.className) {
            var imgObj = document.getElementById
            → (linkObj.className);
            if (imgObj) {
                setupRollover(linkObj,imgObj);
            }
        }
    }
}

function setupRollover(thisLink,textImage) {
    thisLink.imgToChange = textImage;
    thisLink.onmouseout = function() {
        this.imgToChange.src = this.outImage.src;
    }
    thisLink.onmouseover = function() {
        this.imgToChange.src = this.overImage.src;
    }

    thisLink.outImage = new Image();
    thisLink.outImage.src = textImage.src;

    thisLink.overImage = new Image();
    thisLink.overImage.src = "images/" +
    → thisLink.id + "Text.gif";
}
```

To make multiple links change a single rollover:

1. ```
   if (linkObj.className) {
       var imgObj = document.
       → getElementById(linkObj.
       → className);
   ```

   We can't use the id of the rolled-over images to calculate the id of the changed image—that's because an id has to be unique, and all of the rolled-over images have to come up with the same value for the changed image destination. Instead, we're using the class attribute (because you can have multiple page elements sharing the same class). In this line, we're looking for the className of the link object.

2. ```
   function setupRollover(thisLink,
   → textImage) {
       thisLink.imgToChange = textImage;
   ```

   The setupRollover() function is passed the current link object (thisLink) and the image object, which we're calling textImage. Note that when we passed these objects (which can also be referred to as variables) in, we called them linkObj and imgObj, respectively.

   The rest of the script works the same way as the previous examples in this chapter.

Working with Multiple Rollovers

What if you want the image that triggers the rollover to also be a rollover itself? **Figure 4.9** builds on the last example and shows how we've added this feature. When you roll over one of the invention images, it makes the description image appear, as before, but this time also swaps out the invention image for another image with a drop shadow. This gives the user visual feedback about what they're pointing at (as if the mouse pointer isn't enough!). **Script 4.10** is the HTML page (no changes except for the title and the name of the external JavaScript file being called), and **Script 4.11** shows the additions to the JavaScript from the previous example.

Figure 4.9 When you roll over one of the images, a description appears and a drop shadow appears around the image itself.

Script 4.10 This HTML is identical to Script 4.8, except for the title and reference to the external script.

```
●○○                    script

<!DOCTYPE html PUBLIC "-//W3C//DTD XHTML 1.0
→ Transitional//EN"
        "http://www.w3.org/TR/xhtml1/DTD/
        → xhtml1-transitional.dtd">
<html xmlns="http://www.w3.org/1999/xhtml">
<head>
      <title>Multiple Links, Multiple Rollovers
      → </title>
      <script type="text/javascript"
      → src="script06.js"></script>
</head>
<body bgcolor="#EECC99">
      <img src="images/DaVinci.jpg" width="144"
      → height="219" alt="DaVinci" align="right"
      → hspace="50" />
      <img src="images/leoText.gif" width="375"
      → height="26" alt="Leonardo's Inventions" />
      <a href="flyPage.html" class="textField"
      → id="flyer"><img src="images/flyer.gif"
      → width="293" height="165" border="0"
      → alt="Flying Machine" vspace="10"
      → id="flyerImg" /></a><br clear="right" />
      <img src="images/bg.gif" width="208"
      → height="27" id="textField" alt="Text
      → Field" align="right" vspace="20" />
      <a href="tankPage.html" class="textField"
      → id="tank"><img src="images/tank.gif"
      → width="325" height="92" border="0"
      → alt="Tank" id="tankImg" /></a><br />
      <a href="heliPage.html" class="textField"
      → id="helicopter"><img src="images/
      → helicopter.gif" width="224" height="160"
      → border="0" alt="Helicopter"
      → id="helicopterImg" /></a>
</body>
</html>
```

To work with multiple rollovers:

1. `thisLink.imgToChange = new Array;`
   `thisLink.outImage = new Array;`
   `thisLink.overImage = new Array;`

   These lines were added because the script has more images to work with (two for each rollover). In each line, we're creating a new property of `thisLink`, each of which is an array.

2. `thisLink.imgToChange[0] = textImage;`

   In the previous task, `imgToChange` was an image, but in this task, it's an array that will contain images. Here, `textImage` is stored in the first element of `imgToChange`.

3. `thisLink.outImage[0] = new Image();`
   `thisLink.outImage[0].src =`
   `→ textImage.src;`

   As previously, we need to store the out (off) version of the image, but this time it's stored in the first element of the `outImage` array.

4. `thisLink.overImage[0] = new Image();`
   `thisLink.overImage[0].src =`
   `→ "images/" + thisLink.id +`
   `→ "Text.gif";`

   Similarly, the over (on) version of the image is calculated and stored in the first element of `overImage`.

   continues on next page

5. `var rolloverObj = document.`
`→ getElementById(thisLink.id +`
`→ "Img");`
`if (rolloverObj) {`

Now we need to figure out if this rollover will trigger multiple images, not just an individual image. If that's the case, there will be an element on the HTML page whose id is the same as this one, but with Img appended. That is, if we're working on flyer, we'll be checking to see if there's a flyerImg element on the page. If there is, it's saved in rolloverObj, and we should do the next three steps.

6. `thisLink.imgToChange[1] =`
`→ rolloverObj;`

In the same way that we set imgToChange[0] above, we now set imgToChange[1] (the second element in the array) to the new rolloverObj. When the onmouseout and onmouseover event handlers are triggered, both images swap to their alternate versions, as we'll see later.

7. `thisLink.outImage[1] = new Image();`
`thisLink.outImage[1].src =`
`→ rolloverObj.src;`

This sets the second array element of outImage to the out (off) version of the image.

8. `thisLink.overImage[1] = new Image();`
`thisLink.overImage[1].src =`
`→ "images/" + thisLink.id +`
`→ "_on.gif";`

And here, the over (on) version of the image is calculated and stored in the second element of overImage.

If, for some reason, we wanted a third image to also change during this same rollover, we'd repeat steps 6–8 with the third image object.

Script 4.11 This script handles the multiple rollovers.

```
window.onload = rolloverInit;

function rolloverInit() {
    for (var i=0; i<document.links.length; i++) {
        var linkObj = document.links[i];
        if (linkObj.className) {
            var imgObj = document.getElementById
            → (linkObj.className);
            if (imgObj) {
                setupRollover(linkObj,imgObj);
            }
        }
    }
}

function setupRollover(thisLink,textImage) {
    thisLink.imgToChange = new Array;
    thisLink.outImage = new Array;
    thisLink.overImage = new Array;

    thisLink.imgToChange[0] = textImage;
    thisLink.onmouseout = rollOut;
    thisLink.onmouseover = rollOver;

    thisLink.outImage[0] = new Image();
    thisLink.outImage[0].src = textImage.src;

    thisLink.overImage[0] = new Image();
    thisLink.overImage[0].src = "images/" +
    → thisLink.id + "Text.gif";

    var rolloverObj = document.getElementById
    → (thisLink.id + "Img");
    if (rolloverObj) {
        thisLink.imgToChange[1] = rolloverObj;

        thisLink.outImage[1] = new Image();
        thisLink.outImage[1].src = rolloverObj.
        → src;

        thisLink.overImage[1] = new Image();
```

(script continues on next page)

Script 4.11 *continued*

```
                    script
      thisLink.overImage[1].src = "images/" +
      → thisLink.id + "_on.gif";
   }
}

function rollOver() {
   for (var i=0;i<this.imgToChange.length;
   → i++) {
      this.imgToChange[i].src = this.
      → overImage[i].src;
   }
}

function rollOut() {
   for (var i=0;i<this.imgToChange.length;
   → i++) {
      this.imgToChange[i].src = this.
      → outImage[i].src;
   }
}
```

9. `for (var i=0; i<this.imgToChange.`
   `→ length; i++) {`
      `this.imgToChange[i].src =`
      `→ this.overImage[i].src;`
   `}`

Here inside the rollOver() function is where the images get swapped. Because one or more images can be changed, we need to start by asking how many images we have stored— that's the value of this.imgToChange. length. Here, the value is 2, because we want two images to change. We then loop through two times, setting the source of imgToChange[0] and then imgToChange[1] to their respective over values.

10. `for (var i=0; i<this.imgToChange.`
   `→ length; i++) {`
      `this.imgToChange[i].src =`
      `→ this.outImage[i].src;`
   `}`

This code in the rollOut() function is virtually the same as that in the previous step; the only difference is that we're now resetting those images to their out source values.

✔ Tips

- It's important to remember that every image that ever gets rolled over must have a unique id.

- What if you want some of the links on your page to trigger multiple rollovers, but others to be individual rollovers? No problem — you don't even need to change a line of JavaScript. So long as the check in step 5 doesn't find the alternate id on the page, no second element is stored, and the rollOver() and rollOut() loops only animate the initial image.

Creating Cycling Banners

When you surf the Web, it's common to see advertising banners that periodically switch between images. Some of these are animated GIF files, which are GIF files that contain a number of frames that play in succession; others are Flash animations. If you want to have a page that cycles through a number of GIFs (either animated or not), you can use JavaScript to do the job, as in **Script 4.13**. This example uses three GIFs and cycles repeatedly through them, as shown in **Figures 4.10**, **4.11**, and **4.12**. The simple HTML page is shown in **Script 4.12**.

To create cycling banners:

1. `var thisAd = 0;`

Our script starts by creating `thisAd`, which is given its beginning value in this code.

2. `function rotate() {`
  `var adImages = new Array("images/`
  `→ reading1.gif","images/reading2.`
  `→ gif","images/reading3.gif");`

We start off with a new function called `rotate()`. The next line creates a new array called `adImages`. In this case, the array contains the names of the three GIF files that make up the cycling banner.

3. `thisAd++;`

Take the value of `thisAd`, and add one to it.

4. `if (thisAd == adImages.length) {`
  `thisAd = 0;`

This code checks to see if the value of `thisAd` is equal to the number of items in the `adImages` array; if it is, then set the value of `thisAd` back to zero.

Script 4.12 The HTML loads the first image in the cycling banner; the JavaScript handles the rest.

```
<!DOCTYPE html PUBLIC "-//W3C//DTD XHTML 1.0
→ Transitional//EN"
       "http://www.w3.org/TR/xhtml1/DTD/
       → xhtml1-transitional.dtd">
<html xmlns="http://www.w3.org/1999/xhtml">
<head>
    <title>Rotating Banner</title>
    <script type="text/javascript"
    → src="script07.js"></script>
</head>
<body bgcolor="#FFFFFF">
    <div align="center">
        <img src="images/reading1.gif"
        → width="400" height="75" id="adBanner"
        → alt="Ad Banner" />
    </div>
</body>
</html>
```

Script 4.13 You can use JavaScript to cycle between images in a banner.

```
window.onload = rotate;

var thisAd = 0;

function rotate() {
    var adImages = new Array("images/reading1.
    → gif","images/reading2.gif","images/
    → reading3.gif");

    thisAd++;
    if (thisAd == adImages.length) {
        thisAd = 0;
    }
    document.getElementById("adBanner").src =
    → adImages[thisAd];

    setTimeout(rotate, 3 * 1000);
}
```

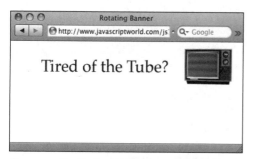

Figure 4.10 The first image, which starts the cycling banner...

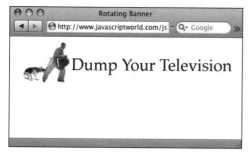

Figure 4.11 ...the second image...

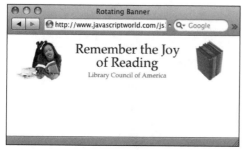

Figure 4.12 ...the final image. Once the page loads and the banner begins cycling, the animation continues with no user intervention required.

5. `document.getElementById("adBanner").`
`→ src = adImages[thisAd];`

The image on the Web that is being cycled has the `id` adBanner; you define the name as part of the `img` tag, as shown in Script 4.12. This line of code says that the new sources for `adBanner` are in the array `adImages`, and the value of the variable `thisAd` defines which of the three GIFs the browser should use at this moment.

6. `setTimeout(rotate, 3 * 1000);`

This line tells the script how often to change GIFs in the banner. The built-in JavaScript command `setTimeout` lets you specify that an action should occur on a particular schedule, always measured in milliseconds. In this case, the function `rotate()` is called every 3,000 milliseconds, or every 3 seconds, so the GIFs will cycle in the banner every three seconds.

✔ Tips

- You might be wondering why you would want to use JavaScript for a cycling banner, rather than just create an animated GIF. One good reason is that it lets you use JPEGs or PNGs in the banner, which gives you higher quality images. With these higher-quality images, you can use photographs in your banners.

- Unlike in some of the previous examples in this chapter, the images in this task are not pre-cached. Each downloads from the server the first time that it's displayed. This is because you might have any number of images in your ad array, and it's not polite to force users to download, for example, 100 images if they're only going to see 2 or 3 of them.

Adding Links to Cycling Banners

Banners are often used in advertising, and you'll want to know how to make a banner into a link that will take a visitor somewhere when the visitor clicks the banner. **Script 4.14** shows the HTML page, which differs from the last example only in that it adds a link around the img tag. **Script 4.15** shows a variation of the previous script. In this script, we'll add a new array. This new array contains destinations that users will be sent to when they click the banner. In this case, the "Eat at Joe's" banner takes you to negrino.com, "Drink more Java" goes to sun.com, and "Heartburn" goes to microsoft.com, as shown in **Figure 4.13**. No editorial comments implied, of course.

To add links to cycling banners:

1. `window.onload = initBannerLink;`

   When the window finishes loading, trigger the `initBannerLink()` function.

Script 4.14 The HTML needed for an ad banner.

```
<!DOCTYPE html PUBLIC "-//W3C//DTD XHTML 1.0
→ Transitional//EN"
        "http://www.w3.org/TR/xhtml1/DTD/
          → xhtml1-transitional.dtd">
<html xmlns="http://www.w3.org/1999/xhtml">
<head>
    <title>Rotating Banner with Links</title>
    <script type="text/javascript"
    → src="script08.js"></script>
</head>
<body bgcolor="#FFFFFF">
    <div align="center">
      <a href="linkPage.html">
      → <img src="images/banner1.gif"
      → width="400" height="75" id="adBanner"
      → border="0" alt="ad banner" /></a>
    </div>
</body>
</html>
```

Script 4.15 This script shows how you can turn cycling banners into real, clickable ad banners.

```
window.onload = initBannerLink;

var thisAd = 0;

function initBannerLink() {
    if (document.getElementById("adBanner").
    → parentNode.tagName == "A") {
        document.getElementById("adBanner").
        → parentNode.onclick = newLocation;
    }

    rotate();
}

function newLocation() {
    var adURL = new Array("negrino.com",
    → "sun.com","microsoft.com");
    document.location.href = "http://www." +
    → adURL[thisAd];
    return false;
}

function rotate() {
    var adImages = new Array("images/banner1.
    → gif","images/banner2.gif","images/
    → banner3.gif");

    thisAd++;
    if (thisAd == adImages.length) {
        thisAd = 0;
    }
    document.getElementById("adBanner").src =
    → adImages[thisAd];

    setTimeout(rotate, 3 * 1000);
}
```

Figure 4.13 Each of these three images is a link, and clicking each image takes you to one of three different Web sites.

2.
```
if (document.getElementById
  → ("adBanner").parentNode.tagName ==
  → "A") {
    document.getElementById
      → ("adBanner").parentNode.onclick
      → = newLocation;
}

rotate();
```
This code, inside the `initBannerLink()` function, first checks to see if the `adBanner` object is surrounded by a link tag. If so, when the link is clicked, the `newLocation()` function will be called. Finally, the `rotate()` function is called.

3.
```
function newLocation() {
    var adURL = new Array("negrino.
      → com","sun.com","microsoft.com");
```
In the new function `newLocation()`, the `adURL` variable gets assigned the three constituents of a new array. Just the domain names need to go in here, because we'll complete the URLs next.

4.
```
document.location.href =
  → "http://www." + adURL[thisAd];
return false;
```
Still inside `newLocation()`, we set the `document.location.href` object (in other words, the current document window) to the value of the text string `http://www.` (notice the period), plus the value of one item from `adURL`. Since `adURL` is an array, you need to specify a member of the array. That's stored in `thisAd`, and the resulting string can be any of the three links, depending on when the user clicks. Last, it returns false, which tells the browser that it should *not* also load in the `href`. Otherwise, the browser would do both. We've handled everything within JavaScript, so the `href` doesn't need to be loaded.

✔ Tip

■ The `adURL` array needs to have the same number of array items as the `adImages` array for this script to work correctly.

Building Wraparound Slideshows

Slideshows on Web sites present the user with an image and let the user control the progression (either forward or backward) of the images. JavaScript gives the user the interactive control needed. **Script 4.16** shows the HTML needed, and the JavaScript in **Script 4.17** has what you need to add slideshows to your pages.

This script builds a slideshow that wraps around—that is, if you go past the end of the list you go back to the beginning and vice versa. **Figure 4.14** shows the new slideshow.

Script 4.16 This HTML page creates a slideshow.

```
<!DOCTYPE html PUBLIC "-//W3C//DTD XHTML 1.0
→ Transitional//EN"
        "http://www.w3.org/TR/xhtml1/DTD/
        → xhtml1-transitional.dtd">
<html xmlns="http://www.w3.org/1999/xhtml">
<head>
    <title>Image Slideshow</title>
    <script type="text/javascript"
    → src="script09.js"></script>
</head>
<body bgcolor="#FFFFFF">
    <div align="center">
        <h1>Welcome, Robot Overlords!</h1>
        <img src="images/robot1.jpg"
        → id="myPicture" width="200"
        → height="400" alt="Slideshow" />
        <h2><a href="previous.html"
        → id="prevLink">&lt;&lt;
        → Previous</a>  <a
        → href="next.html" id="nextLink">Next
        → &gt;&gt;</a></h2>
    </div>
</body>
</html>
```

Script 4.17 This script builds a slideshow that the user can click through using links to control movement forward and back.

```
window.onload = initLinks;

var myPix = new Array("images/robot1.jpg",
→ "images/robot2.jpg","images/robot3.jpg");
var thisPic = 0;

function initLinks() {
    document.getElementById("prevLink").
    → onclick = processPrevious;
    document.getElementById("nextLink").
    → onclick = processNext;
}

function processPrevious() {
    if (thisPic == 0) {
        thisPic = myPix.length;
    }
    thisPic--;
    document.getElementById("myPicture").src =
    → myPix[thisPic];
    return false;
}

function processNext() {
    thisPic++;
    if (thisPic == myPix.length) {
        thisPic = 0;
    }
    document.getElementById("myPicture").src =
    → myPix[thisPic];
    return false;
}
```

To build a wraparound slideshow:

1. `window.onload = initLinks;`

   When the window finishes loading, trigger the `initLinks()` function.

2. ```
   function initLinks() {
       document.getElementById
       → ("prevLink").onclick =
       → processPrevious;
       document.getElementById
       → ("nextLink").onclick =
       → processNext;
   }
   ```

   This function sets up the `onclick` event handlers for the Previous and Next links.

   continues on next page

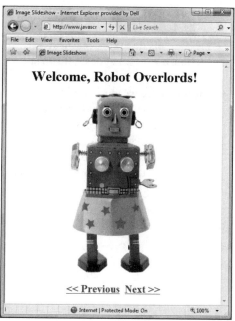

Figure 4.14 Clicking the Previous or Next link calls the `processPrevious()` or `processNext()` function, respectively.

109
   ```

3.
```
function processPrevious() {
    if (thisPic == 0) {
        thisPic = myPix.length;
```
This function makes the slideshow run in the Previous direction. This first part checks to see if thisPic is equal to 0. If it is, the function gets the number of pictures in the myPix array.

4.
```
thisPic--;
document.getElementById
→ ("myPicture").src = myPix[thisPic];
```
The first line reduces the value of thisPic by 1. The next line sets the src of myPicture to the element of the myPix array represented by the current value of thisPic.

5.
```
thisPic++;
if (thisPic == myPix.length) {
    thisPic = 0;
}
document.getElementById
→ ("myPicture").src = myPix[thisPic];
```
This code, inside the processNext() function, makes the slideshow run in the Next direction and is much like the processPrevious() function. The first thing it does is increment the value of thisPic by 1. Then it checks to see if the value of thisPic is the same as the number of items in the myPix array. If so, it sets thisPic back to 0. The next line sets the src of myPicture.

Script 4.18 This simple HTML creates the page for a random image.

```
<!DOCTYPE html PUBLIC "-//W3C//DTD XHTML 1.0
→ Transitional//EN"
        "http://www.w3.org/TR/xhtml1/DTD/
        → xhtml1-transitional.dtd">
<html xmlns="http://www.w3.org/1999/xhtml">
<head>
    <title>Random Image</title>
    <script type="text/javascript"
    → src="script10.js"></script>
</head>
<body bgcolor="#FFFFFF">
    <img src="images/spacer.gif" width="305"
    → height="312" id="myPicture"
    → alt="some image" />
</body>
</html>
```

Script 4.19 You can display random images on your page with this script, which uses JavaScript's Math. random method to generate a random number.

```
window.onload = choosePic;

function choosePic() {
    var myPix = new Array("images/lion.jpg",
    → "images/tiger.jpg","images/bear.jpg");
    var randomNum = Math.floor((Math.random() *
    → myPix.length));
    document.getElementById("myPicture").src =
    → myPix[randomNum];
}
```

Displaying a Random Image

If your site is rich with graphics, or if you are displaying digital artwork, then you may want to have a random image from your collection appear when the user enters your site. Once again, JavaScript to the rescue! The extremely simple **Script 4.18** shows the required HTML, and **Script 4.19** provides the JavaScript. **Figure 4.15** shows the result of the script, in this case images of a stuffed lion, tiger, and bear (oh, my!).

To display a random image:

1. `var myPix = new Array("images/lion.` `→ jpg", "images/tiger.jpg",` `→ "images/bear.jpg");`

   Inside the function `choosePic()`, as is now familiar, build an array of three images, and stuff it into the variable `myPix`.

2. `randomNum = Math.floor((Math.` `→ random() * myPix.length));`

   The variable called `randomNum` gets the value of a math expression that's best read from the inside outwards. `Math.random` generates a random number between 0 and 1, which is then multiplied by `myPix.length`, which is the number of items in the array (in this case, it's 3). `Math.floor` rounds the result down to an integer, which means that the number must be between 0 and 2.

   continues on next page

3. `document.getElementById`
    `→ ("myPicture").src =`
    `→ myPix[randomNum];`

This says that the source of the image myPicture is set based on the array myPix, and the value at this moment is dependent on the value of randomNum.

Figure 4.15 Depending on the value of the random number generated by the script, the user is presented with the lion, the tiger, or the bear.

Script 4.20 There's a spacer GIF in the HTML file, which is a placeholder until the ad banner appears.

```
script
<!DOCTYPE html PUBLIC "-//W3C//DTD XHTML 1.0
→ Transitional//EN"
         "http://www.w3.org/TR/xhtml1/DTD/
         → xhtml1-transitional.dtd">
<html xmlns="http://www.w3.org/1999/xhtml">
<head>
    <title>Rotating Random Banner</title>
    <script type="text/javascript"
    → src="script11.js"></script>
</head>
<body bgcolor="#FFFFFF">
    <div align="center">
        <img src="images/spacer.gif"
        → width="400" height="75" id="adBanner"
        → alt="Ad Banner" />
    </div>
</body>
</html>
```

Cycling Images with a Random Start

If you have a number of images that you want to display, you may not want to display them beginning with the same image each time the page is loaded. **Script 4.20** has the HTML, and **Script 4.21** combines the code used earlier for the cycling ad banners with the random image code.

Script 4.21 This script allows you to start your cycling image show with a random image.

```
script
window.onload = choosePic;

var adImages = new Array("images/reading1.gif","images/reading2.gif","images/reading3.gif");
var thisAd = 0;

function choosePic() {
    thisAd = Math.floor((Math.random() * adImages.length));
    document.getElementById("adBanner").src = adImages[thisAd];

    rotate();
}

function rotate() {
    thisAd++;
    if (thisAd == adImages.length) {
        thisAd = 0;
    }
    document.getElementById("adBanner").src = adImages[thisAd];

    setTimeout(rotate, 3 * 1000);
}
```

To start images cycling from a random start:

1. `var adImages = new Array("images/`
   `→ reading1.gif","images/reading2.`
   `→ gif","images/reading3.gif");`

   As in previous examples, set up the array and the variable that contains the number of items in the array.

2. `function choosePic() {`

   This function is similar to the `choosePic()` function in Script 4.19. See that explanation for the details of how it works.

3. `function rotate() {`

   This function is similar to the `rotate()` function in Script 4.13. See that explanation for the details of how it works.

FRAMES, FRAMES, AND MORE FRAMES

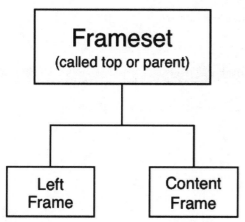

Figure 5.1 Layout of a frameset that contains two frames, "left" and "content".

Frames are a useful feature of HTML, though they have fallen somewhat out of favor over the past few years. In this chapter, we'll demonstrate how to harness the power of JavaScript to make frames even more useful.

A frame consists of at least three pages of HTML. The first, called the *frameset*, sets up the dimensions of each of the child frames. The frameset is referred to in JavaScript as *top* or *parent*. The remainder of the pages fit into the panes that the frameset has created and are the *child* pages. These can be named anything you choose. **Figure 5.1** shows a frameset that creates two child frames, "left" and "content".

Table 5.1

Just Enough HTML—Frames		

TAG	ATTRIBUTE	MEANING
frameset		Specifies that the page consists of two or more framed pages; contains the frame tags that specify the particular pages.
	cols	The column dimensions (proportional or fixed), in pixels, of each frame.
frame		The location and attributes of each framed page.
	id	Used by JavaScript to refer to one of the pages in the frameset.
	name	An alternate method by which JavaScript can refer to one of the pages in the frameset.
	src	The physical location (i.e., the URL) of the page loaded into the frame.
iframe		An internal frame, displayed inside the calling HTML page.
	id	JavaScript uses this to refer to the iframe.
	name	JavaScript can alternately use this to refer to the iframe.
	src	The URL of the iframe page.
	width	The width (in pixels or percent) of the iframe.
	height	The height (in pixels or percent) of the iframe.
	align	Aligns the iframe right or left.
	frameborder	Displays a border around the iframe.

FRAMES, FRAMES, AND MORE FRAMES

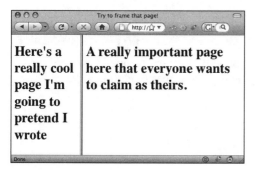

Figure 5.2 Our page, buried in someone else's frameset.

Script 5.1 Here is an HTML page that people want to hijack.

```
● ● ●                    script
<!DOCTYPE html PUBLIC "-//W3C//DTD XHTML 1.0
→ Transitional//EN"
        "http://www.w3.org/TR/xhtml1/DTD/
          → xhtml1-transitional.dtd">
<html xmlns="http://www.w3.org/1999/xhtml">
<head>
    <title>Can't be in a frame</title>
    <script type="text/javascript"
    → src="script01.js"></script>
</head>
<body bgcolor="#FFFFFF">
    <h1>A really important page here that
    → everyone wants to claim as theirs.</h1>
</body>
</html>
```

Keeping a Page out of a Frame

Other people can put one of your pages inside a frame on their site, making it appear that your page is part of their content. In JavaScript, windows appear in a hierarchy, with the parent window at the top of the heap. When someone hijacks your page, they are forcing it to be a child frame to their parent window. **Figure 5.2** shows how the page would appear as part of someone else's site. With these scripts, you can prevent this page hijacking and force your page to always be in a browser window by itself. There are two scripts; **Script 5.1** is the HTML page that should always stand alone and has the <script> tag that calls the JavaScript; **Script 5.2** is the JavaScript document, which we'll describe next.

Script 5.2 JavaScript provides a way to force our page to always appear on a separate page.

```
● ● ●                    script
if (top.location != self.location) {
    top.location.replace(self.location);
}
```

To isolate a page:

1. `if (top.location != self.location) {`

   First, check to see if the location of the current page (`self`) is the top-most in the browser window hierarchy. If it is, there's no need to do anything.

2. `top.location.replace(self.location);`

   If the current page isn't at the top, replace the top page with the location of the current page. This forces the current window to be our page and our page only. **Figure 5.3** shows our page as we designed it.

✔ Tip

- We could just set `top.location` to `self.location`, but this has one nasty side effect: users can no longer use the browser's back button. If they try to, going back to the previous page automatically jumps them back to the current page. Using the `replace()` method shown above replaces the current page in the history, which allows the back button to display the previous page.

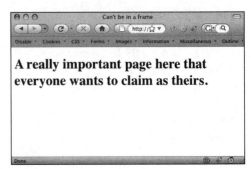

Figure 5.3 Our page, after escaping from the evil hijacking frameset.

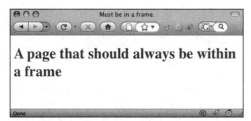

Figure 5.4 A lonely page, stranded by itself.

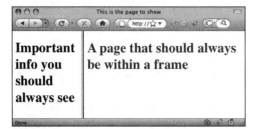

Figure 5.5 Our page, happily reunited with its parent and sibling.

Script 5.3 The frameset page.

```
<!DOCTYPE html PUBLIC "-//W3C//DTD XHTML 1.0
→ Frameset//EN"
        "http://www.w3.org/TR/xhtml1/DTD/
        → xhtml1-frameset.dtd">
<html xmlns="http://www.w3.org/1999/xhtml">
<head>
    <title>This is the page to show</title>
</head>
<frameset cols="30%,70%">
    <frame src="left2.html" name="left"
    → id="left" />
    <frame src="frame2.html" name="content"
    → id="content" />
</frameset>
</html>
```

Script 5.4 Use JavaScript to force your page into the frameset.

```
if (top.location == self.location) {
    self.location.replace("frameset2.html");
}
```

Forcing a Page into a Frame

When a search engine catalogs one of your pages, it doesn't know that the page is part of a frame. When a user finds your page via the search engine, clicking the link shows just the single page, not the full frameset as you designed it. **Script 5.3** shows the frameset. The page the user landed on (not shown) contains a call (just like the one in Script 5.1) to the JavaScript. **Script 5.4** shows you how to force the full frameset to display even though Google or another search engine doesn't know about the frameset. **Figure 5.4** shows the page looking out-of-place, and **Figure 5.5** shows it at home, snug in its frame.

To force a page into a frame:

1. `if (top.location == self.location) {`

   Check to see if the current page (`self`) is at the top-most level. If it isn't, we're in a frameset.

2. `self.location.replace`
   `→ ("frameset2. html");`

   If the location of the current page is at the top, then replace the current page with the URL of the frameset. This then displays our framed site as we designed it.

✔ Tip

■ This method works fine if you only have a few pages that might be called from outside their frames, because it requires a separate frameset page for every page that you might want loaded (in this example) into the content frame. The next example shows a way to handle a large site.

Forcing a Site into a Frame

If you have a large site, with numerous pages that you want inside a frame, the method described on the preceding page can easily become unwieldy. Here's a method that works better for larger sites. **Script 5.5** shows the frameset, which also calls the JavaScript, shown in **Script 5.6** (detailed below). **Figure 5.6** shows our page by itself, and **Figure 5.7** shows how we intended our site to look. Not shown is the simple HTML page that makes up the left-hand navigation bar in Figure 5.7, or the equally simple HTML pages that make up the content frames. The latter call the JavaScript (just in case they are loaded directly), in the same way as Script 5.5.

To force a site into a frame:

1. `var framesetPage = "frameset3.html";`
   `var currPage = justTheFilename`
   `→ (self.location.pathname);`

   We start off by creating and setting two variables: `framesetPage` and `currPage`. The former is the frameset page that we always want to load overall, so that's hard-coded to `frameset3.html`. The latter is the name of the HTML page that called this external JavaScript file. It needs to be calculated, as JavaScript doesn't have a built-in function that does this (although it should!). We'll use the `justTheFilename()` function to do that, as explained in step 10.

Script 5.5 The frameset page calls the external JavaScript file.

```
<!DOCTYPE html PUBLIC "-//W3C//DTD XHTML 1.0
→ Frameset//EN"
        "http://www.w3.org/TR/xhtml1/DTD/
            → xhtml1-frameset.dtd">
<html xmlns="http://www.w3.org/1999/xhtml">
<head>
    <title>Site Frameset</title>
    <script type="text/javascript"
        → src="script03.js"></script>
</head>
<frameset cols="30%,70%">
    <frame src="left3.html" name="left"
        → id="left" />
    <frame src="frame3a.html" name="content"
        → id="content" />
</frameset>
</html>
```

Figure 5.6 Here's our page outside the frame.

Figure 5.7 But here's how we really want it to look.

Script 5.6 This JavaScript forces the site we want into the frame we want.

```
                    script
var framesetPage = "frameset3.html";
var currPage = justTheFilename
→ (self.location.pathname);

if (top.location == self.location &&
→ framesetPage != currPage) {
    self.location.replace(framesetPage + "?" +
    → currPage);
}

window.onload = chgFrame;

function chgFrame() {
    if (top.location == self.location &&
    → document.location.search) {
        var linkURL = justTheFilename
        → (document.location.search);
        var contentWin = document.getElementById
        → ("content").contentWindow;
        var currURL = justTheFilename
        → (contentWin.location.pathname);

        if (currURL != linkURL) {
            contentWin.location.replace
            → (linkURL);
        }
    }
}

function justTheFilename(thisFile) {
    if (thisFile.indexOf("/") > -1) {
        thisFile = thisFile.substring
        → (thisFile.lastIndexOf("/")+1);
    }

    if (thisFile.indexOf("?") == 0) {
        thisFile = thisFile.substring(1);
    }

    return thisFile;
}
```

In this step, that function gets passed `self.location.pathname` (a variable that holds that part of a URL that comes *after* the domain name). For example, if you are viewing `http://www.peachpit.com/index.html`, `self.location.pathname` is `/index.html`. If you are at `http://www.peachpit.com/books/index.html`, `self.location.pathname` is `/books/index.html`. In either case, all we want is `index.html`, so that's what `justTheFilename()` will calculate and return, and that's what will be stored in `currPage`.

2. ```
   if (top.location == self.location &&
   → framesetPage != currPage) {
       self.location.replace
       → (framesetPage + "?" + currPage);
   }
   ```
   Now we do the usual check to see if `top.location` is the same as `self.location` that we've done previously, with one thing added: a check to see if we're currently on the frameset page. If we are, that's great; we don't need to reload anything. But if `currPage` isn't the frameset, something's wrong—so we need to reload this page, going to the frameset page, and passing `currPage` in the bargain so that it ends up in the content frameset.

3. ```
   window.onload = chgFrame;
   ```
   The `onload` handler is here because we want every page that uses this external JavaScript file to call the `chgFrame()` function.

4. ```
   function chgFrame() {
   ```
   This function checks to see if (a) it's the frameset page and (b) there was a question mark in the URL followed by a file name. If that's the case, that file needs to be loaded into the content frame.

continues on next page
   ```

5. `if (top.location == self.location &&`
`→ document.location.search) {`

Once again, we're doing the usual check to see if `top.location` is the same as `self.location`—in this case, if the two are equal, we know we're in the frameset. After that, we look at `document.location.search`, another built-in field that will contain everything in a URL from a question mark (if one exists) to the end. If there's no question mark, `document.location.search` has no value, and we get kicked out of this function.

6. `var linkURL = justTheFilename`
`→ (document.location.search);`

This is the first of three variables we'll need to set before we load in a new content frame. The first, `linkURL`, is the file to load in the content frame. The `linkURL` field is set by calling `justTheFilename()` and passing in `document.location.search`.

7. `var contentWin = document.`
`→ getElementById("content").`
`→ contentWindow;`

The `contentWin` variable needs to contain what JavaScript knows about the content frame. Set it by looking for the id `content`, taking its result (which will be a frame), and then getting `contentWindow` of that frame—which is the page loaded into that frame.

8. `var currURL = justTheFilename`
`→ (contentWin.location.pathname);`

The `currURL` variable is set here to the current content frame page, that is, the current HTML page loaded in the content frame. That is done by calling `justTheFilename()`, this time passing it `contentWin.location.pathname`, and storing the result.

9.
```
if (currURL != linkURL) {
   contentWin.location.replace
   ⇢(linkURL);
}
```

At this point, we could reload the content page, as we've got everything we need—but we can make things smarter by adding one more step. Why bother reloading the content page, if what we're going to load is already there? Here's where we check to see if `currURL` is equal to `linkURL`. If it is, we're on the right page already, so don't do anything. If it isn't, call that same old `replace()`, and we're done.

10.
```
if (thisFile.indexOf("/") > -1) {
   thisFile = thisFile.substring
   ⇢(thisFile.lastIndexOf("/")+1);
}

if (thisFile.indexOf("?") == 0) {
   thisFile = thisFile.substring(1);
}

return thisFile;
```

All that's left now is the `justTheFilename()` function. This function takes in a string and tries to clean it up and turn it into a filename. First, we check to see if it contains a /. If it does, then we look for the *last* / in the filename (note that `lastIndexOf`), and then reset the filename to be everything after it. Then, we look for a question mark. If it's the first character in the filename (i.e., at position zero), then we reset the filename to be everything from position one to the end. The filename is returned to wherever the function was called.

FORCING A SITE INTO A FRAME

✔ Tips

■ Search engines aren't the only reason why someone might be trying to load a single page of your framed site. If you've bookmarked a page inside a frame, your browser may or may not understand that you're on a particular framed content page, which isn't necessarily the default view of the frameset. If someone has bookmarked a particular single page of your site (so that they can come back to this particular content), this script will set everything up just the way it should be.

■ If you find yourself getting a little confused by the numbering in step 10, take a look at the sidebar, "JavaScript Strings."

JavaScript Strings

When does a word like "cat" have a "t" in the second position? When it's a JavaScript string.

In JavaScript, the first character is at position 0. So, using the example of "cat", "c" would be at position 0, "a" would be at position 1, and "t" would be at position 2.

Only when checking the length of cat do we actually see a value of 3. All other string methods are zero-based; that is, they start with 0.

Script 5.7 When you're using XHTML Strict in your frameset, you need JavaScript to set frame targets.

```
script
<!DOCTYPE html PUBLIC "-//W3C//DTD XHTML 1.0
→ Strict//EN"
        "http://www.w3.org/TR/xhtml1/DTD/
        → xhtml1-strict.dtd">
<html xmlns="http://www.w3.org/1999/xhtml">
<head>
    <title>Nav Bar</title>
    <script type="text/javascript"
    → src="script04.js"></script>
</head>
<body>
    <h1>Navigation Bar</h1>
    <h2>
    <a href="frame4a.html">Page 1</a><br />
    <a href="frame4b.html">Page 2</a><br />
    <a href="frame4c.html">Page 3</a>
    </h2>
</body>
</html>
```

Script 5.8 And here is the JavaScript you need to do the job.

```
script
window.onload = initLinks;

function initLinks() {
    for (var i=0; i<document.links.length; i++) {
        document.links[i].target = "content";
    }
}
```

Figure 5.8 Here's a frame acting as a navigation bar with the content page appearing in a content frame.

Setting a Target

If your site uses frames, it's common to have a framed navigation bar that loads the different pages into the main frame. The main frame is the target for the links in the navigation bar, and to load that main frame using HTML, you use the `target` attribute of the `<a>` tag. But if you want to use both frames and XHTML Strict, JavaScript is the only way to set the target. That's because the `target` attribute isn't allowed in XHTML Strict, and you have to set the target in order to use frames.

The XHTML Strict frameset in **Script 5.7** allows you to load your choice of page into the main content frame, just by clicking a link in the left frame (**Script 5.8**, detailed below). The result is shown in **Figure 5.8**.

To set the target for a frame:

1. `window.onload = initLinks;`

   When the page loads, call the `initLinks()` function.

2. `for (var i=0; i<document.links.` `→ length; i++) {` `document.links[i].target =` `→ "content";` `}`

   The `initLinks()` function loops through all of the links on the page. When the loop finds a link, it sets the `target` property to the string `"content"`. And that's all it takes.

✔ Tip

- If JavaScript is turned off, visitors will find that the first link that gets clicked loads into the navigation frame, not the content frame. Sorry, but that's the way frames and XHTML Strict work.

Creating and Loading a Dynamic Frame

Because JavaScript can create page content on-the-fly, it's useful for loading dynamic data into frames based on a user's choice in another frame. **Script 5.9** is a frameset that loads a dummy content page (frame5.html, referred to here as **Script 5.10**) and a left navbar page, left5.html (not shown). The latter calls **Script 5.11**, detailed next, that can create a page and load it into the main content frame. It creates a page that looks like **Figure 5.9**.

To load a dynamic frame from another frame:

1. for (var i=0; i<document.links.
→ length; i++) {
    document.links[i].onclick =
    → writeContent;
    document.links[i].thisPage = i+1;
}

The initLinks() function begins in the same way as in Script 5.8, by looping through the links on the page. Then, for each link, two things are set: the onclick handler for that link, and a new property is added: thisPage. The latter contains the page number to be displayed when that link is clicked, i.e., link 0 is "page 1", link 1 is "page 2", and so on. The onclick handler in the loop sets every link to call the writeContent() function when they're clicked.

Script 5.9 This frameset loads a dummy page, ready to be replaced by JavaScript.

```
<!DOCTYPE html PUBLIC "-//W3C//DTD XHTML 1.0
→ Frameset//EN"
        "http://www.w3.org/TR/xhtml1/DTD/
        → xhtml1-frameset.dtd">
<html xmlns="http://www.w3.org/1999/xhtml">
<head>
    <title>Setting one frame from another</title>
</head>
<frameset cols="30%,70%">
    <frame src="left5.html" name="left"
    → id="left" />
    <frame src="frame5.html" name="content"
id="content" />
</frameset>
</html>
```

Script 5.10 Speaking of which, here is the dummy page.

```
<!DOCTYPE html PUBLIC "-//W3C//DTD XHTML 1.0
→ Transitional//EN"
        "http://www.w3.org/TR/xhtml1/DTD/
        → xhtml1-transitional.dtd">
<html xmlns="http://www.w3.org/1999/xhtml">
<head>
    <title>Content frame</title>
</head>
<body bgcolor="#FFFFFF">
</body>
</html>
```

Script 5.11 This script creates a page and loads it into the main content frame.

```
                    script
window.onload = initLinks;

function initLinks() {
    for (var i=0; i<document.links.length; i++) {
        document.links[i].onclick =
        → writeContent;
        document.links[i].thisPage = i+1;
    }
}

function writeContent() {
    var newText = "<h1>You are now looking at
    → page " + this.thisPage + ".<\/h1>";

    var contentWin = parent.document.
    → getElementById("content").contentWindow;
    contentWin.document.body.innerHTML =
    newText;
    return false;
}
```

Figure 5.9 Here's the result of Script 5.11, a Web page written by a JavaScript. The content of the frame on the right was generated under script control.

2. `var newText = "<h1>You are now`
   `→ looking at page " + this.thisPage +`
   `→ ".<\/h1>";`

   `var contentWin = parent.document.`
   `→ getElementById("content").`
   `→ contentWindow;`
   `contentWin.document.body.innerHTML =`
   `→ newText;`

   Here is the meat of the `writeContent()` function, which first declares and sets a variable, `newText`, and assigns it some text. Next, the `contentWin` variable is set based on the `content` element, and then we reset `contentWin.document.body.innerHTML` to `newText`. To explain this a bit further, we find an element with a given `id` (in this case, `content`), and then store that element's `contentWindow` in the variable `contentWin`. Given `contentWin`, we want the `document` it contains; then we get the `body` of that `document`, and then we reset `innerHTML`, which is the HTML contained *within* that `body` tag.

3. `return false;`

   Lastly, `writeContent()` returns false, which tells the browser that it should *not* also load in the `hrefs` in the navigation bar's frame. Otherwise, the browser would do both. We've handled everything within JavaScript, so the `href` doesn't need to be loaded.

✔ Tips

- Why is there a backslash ("\") before the slash ("/") in step 2? According to the HTML standards, the browser may interpret the beginning of a closing tag ("</") as the end of the line. The backslash "escapes" the slash, allowing us to write out HTML without the chance of causing an error.

- We're using `parent.document.getElement...` here versus `document.getElement...` that we used back in Script 5.6. That's because that JavaScript was going to be called by the *frameset* page, whereas here, it's being called by one of the *framed* pages. In the latter case, JavaScript has to go back up to its parent (i.e., the frameset) in order to look at the content page (another child of the parent).

Figure 5.10 The information in the right, or content, frame is created by code called from the frameset.

Sharing Functions between Frames

One common frame layout uses a permanent navigation frame and a content frame that might display a variety of different pages. Once again, it makes sense to put the call to the external JavaScript file into the page that's always present (the frameset page) instead of duplicating it for every possible content page. In **Figure 5.10**, we use this capability to have many pages share an identical function that returns a random banner image. **Script 5.12** loads the pages into the frameset.

Script 5.12 This script allows you to share functions between multiple frames.

```
var bannerArray = new Array("images/redBanner.gif", "images/greenBanner.gif", "images/blueBanner.gif");

window.onload = initFrames;

function initFrames() {
    var leftWin = document.getElementById("left").contentWindow.document;

    for (var i=0; i<leftWin.links.length; i++) {
        leftWin.links[i].target = "content";
        leftWin.links[i].onclick = resetBanner;
    }

    setBanner();
}

function setBanner() {
    var contentWin = document.getElementById("content").contentWindow.document;
    var randomNum = Math.floor(Math.random() * bannerArray.length);

    contentWin.getElementById("adBanner").src = bannerArray[randomNum];
}

function resetBanner() {
    setTimeout(setBanner,1000);
}
```

To use a function on another page:

1. `var bannerArray = new Array`
`→ ("images/redBanner.gif",`
`→ "images/greenBanner.gif",`
`→ "images/blueBanner.gif");`

Start by creating a new array that contains all the possible banner image names, and assign the array to the `bannerArray` variable.

2. `window.onload = initFrames;`

When the frameset loads, call `initFrames()`.

3. `var leftWin = document.`
`→ getElementById("left").`
`→ contentWindow.document;`

Now we start the code inside the `initFrames()` function. We begin by creating the `leftWin` variable and setting it the same way we've previously stored framed pages: given the frame name (`left`), get that element (`document.getElementById("left")`); given that element, get the `contentWindow` property (`document.getElementById("left").contentWindow`); and given the `contentWindow` property, get its `document` property.

4. `for (var i=0; i<leftWin.links.`
`→ length; i++) {`
`  leftWin.links[i].target =`
`  → "content";`
`  leftWin.links[i].onclick =`
`  → resetBanner;`

Because this function is being called from the frameset's context, setting the left navigation bar's links is slightly different than in previous examples. This time, we reset both the `target` property and the `onclick` handler for each link. The `target` is set to `"content"` and the `onclick` handler is set to the `resetBanner` function.

5. `setBanner();`

As the last initialization step, the `setBanner()` function is called.

6. `var contentWin = document.`
`→ etElementById("content").`
`→ contentWindow.document;`

The `setBanner()` function loads up the content window and calculates a random number. Then, the ad banner in the content window is set to a random ad from the array. We begin by creating the `contentWin` variable and setting it the same way we've previously stored framed pages: given the frame name (content), get that element (`document.getElementById("content")`); given that element, get the `contentWindow` property (`document.getElementById("content").contentWindow`); and given the `contentWindow` property, get its `document` property.

7. `var randomNum = Math.floor`
`→ (Math.random() * bannerArray.`
`→ length);`

This line uses the `Math.random()` function multiplied by the number of elements in the `bannerArray` array to calculate a random number between 0 and the number of elements in the array. Then it places the result into the `randomNum` variable.

8. `contentWin.getElementById`
`→ ("adBanner").src =`
`→ bannerArray[randomNum];`

Here, we set the `src` for `adBanner` to the current item in the array. That's the new image name, which will then be displayed on the page.

continues on next page

SHARING FUNCTIONS BETWEEN FRAMES

9.
```
function resetBanner() {
    setTimeout(setBanner,1000);
}
```

The resetBanner() function is a little tricky, although it only has a single line of code. What it's doing is waiting for the content frame to load with its new page (one second should be sufficient), after which it can then call setBanner() to reset the banner.

If we instead called setBanner() immediately, the new content page might not have loaded yet. In that case, we would have a problem, as we would then either get an error (because adBanner wasn't found), or we would reset the old adBanner—the one from the page that's being unloaded.

✔ Tip

■ Note that resetBanner does *not* return false—this means that the browser will both do what's here *and* load the page from the href. This script depends on that, which is why both the onclick handler and target were set.

Script 5.13 JavaScript lets you load multiple frames with a single user click.

```
window.onload = initFrames;

function initFrames() {
    var leftWin = document.getElementById
    → ("left").contentWindow.document;

    for (var i=0; i<leftWin.links.length; i++) {
        leftWin.links[i].onclick = setFrames;
    }
}

function setFrames() {
    document.getElementById("left").
    → contentWindow.document.location.href =
    → this.id + ".html";
    document.getElementById("content").
    → contentWindow.document.location.href =
    → this.href;
    setTimeout(initFrames,1000);
    return false;
}
```

Figure 5.11 The page looks like this initially.

Figure 5.12 But when a link is clicked, both frames change.

Loading Multiple Frames at Once

It just takes a single link with a `target` attribute to change the content of a frame; that's simple HTML. To change the content of multiple frames with one click, you need JavaScript. The HTML files are trivial; all the action takes pace in **Script 5.13**. Two of the possible states the window can take are shown in **Figures 5.11** and **5.12**.

To load multiple frames at once:

1. ```
   var leftWin = document.
   → getElementById("left").
   → contentWindow.document;

   for (var i=0; i<leftWin.links.
   → length; i++) {
     leftWin.links[i].onclick =
     → setFrames;
   }
   ```

   The `initFrames()` function is pretty similar to what it's been previously in this chapter. It's called `onload`, as always. The function loops through the navigation bar (left) links. This time, it sets the `onclick` handlers to the `setFrames()` function.

   continues on next page
   ```

2. `document.getElementById("left").`
`↪ contentWindow.document.location.`
`↪ href = this.id + ".html";`
`document.getElementById("content").`
`↪ contentWindow.document.location.`
`↪ href = this.href;`
`setTimeout(initFrames,1000);`

The `setFrames()` function first resets the left frame based on the `id` of the link that called it. The function then resets the content frame based on the `href` of the link that called it—yes, we have access to that via JavaScript, so why not use it?

The function waits a second (by using `setTimeout`) and then calls the `initFrames()` function. This has to happen again because it's what sets the `onclick` handlers in the navigation bar, and as soon as we loaded a new navigation page into the bar, all those `onclick` handlers went away. In order to keep things working, they've all got to be reset for the new page, and this is how it's done.

3. `return false;`

And finally, we return false, so the browser won't load the new page in.

✔ Tip

■ If you click links in the navigation bar quickly, you'll get an unexpected result; a content page replaces the navigation bar. That's because the navigation page must finish loading before it is ready to accept the next click.

Script 5.14 This page creates the iframe and calls the external JavaScript.

```
<!DOCTYPE html PUBLIC "-//W3C//DTD XHTML 1.0
→ Transitional//EN"
        "http://www.w3.org/TR/xhtml1/DTD/
        → xhtml1-transitional.dtd">
<html xmlns="http://www.w3.org/1999/xhtml">
<head>
    <title>iframes</title>
    <script type="text/javascript"
    → src="script08.js"></script>
</head>
<body bgcolor="#FFFFFF">
    <iframe src="frame8b.html" width="550"
    → height="300" name="content" id="content"
    → align="right" frameborder="1">Your
    → browser does not support iframes</iframe>
    <h1>Navigation Bar</h1>
    <h2>
    <a href="page1.html">Page 1</a><br />
    <a href="page2.html">Page 2</a><br />
    <a href="page3.html">Page 3</a>
    </h2>
</body>
</html>
```

Script 5.15 The initial page that goes in the iframe.

```
<!DOCTYPE html PUBLIC "-//W3C//DTD XHTML 1.0
→ Transitional//EN"
        "http://www.w3.org/TR/xhtml1/DTD/
        → xhtml1-transitional.dtd">
<html xmlns="http://www.w3.org/1999/xhtml">
<head>
    <title>Content frame</title>
</head>
<body bgcolor="#FFFFFF">
    Please load a page
</body>
</html>
```

Working with Iframes

An *iframe* is an inline frame, that is, a frame that can be embedded within a regular HTML page instead of needing to be inside a frameset. Like a regular frame, an iframe is a separate HTML document. You can use an iframe as the target of a script, so you can create content on the fly under script control and display it in the page without having to use a frameset.

In this task, we have a regular HTML page with a content area that is an iframe. The content of the iframe is created using JavaScript. **Script 5.14** creates the regular page. **Script 5.15** is the placeholder HTML document that shows the user the initial content in the iframe, namely the "Please load a page" instruction, as shown in **Figure 5.13**. That content will be replaced by the product of **Script 5.16**; when the user clicks one of the links, JavaScript writes out new code to the iframe. In this case, it's displaying the name of the page and how many times the user has gone to that page in this session. As you will see, most of this script is built of pieces you've seen earlier in this chapter.

To create the content for an iframe:

1. ```
   <iframe src="frame8b.html"
   → width="550" height="300"
   → name="content" id="content"
   → align="right" frameborder="1">Your
   → browser does not support
   → iframes</iframe>
   ```

   In Script 5.14, the iframe tag tells the browser that the initial source for the iframe's content will be found in frame8b.html. Inside the tag, there's a message that will be displayed by browsers that don't understand iframes.

2. ```
   function writeContent() {
   ```
   Script 5.16 has a function called writeContent, which is used to build the content inside the iframe.

3. ```
   pageCount[this.thisPage]++;
   ```
   This line increments the pageCount array, so that we can keep track of how many times we've visited this particular page.

4. ```
   var newText = "<h1>You are now
   → looking at page " + this.thisPage;
   newText += ".<br \/>You have been to
   → this page ";
   newText += pageCount[this.thisPage]
   → + " times.<\/h1>";
   ```
   These lines create what will be the content of the iframe on the fly.

Figure 5.13 The iframe, on the right, initially contains an instruction to click a link.

Script 5.16 This script calculates the content of the iframe and writes it into the window.

```
var pageCount = new Array(0,0,0,0);

window.onload = initFrames;

function initFrames() {
    for (var i=0; i<document.links.length; i++) {
        document.links[i].onclick =
        → writeContent;
        document.links[i].thisPage = i+1;
    }
}

function writeContent() {
    pageCount[this.thisPage]++;

    var newText = "<h1>You are now looking at
    → page " + this.thisPage;
    newText += ".<br \/>You have been to this
    → page ";
    newText += pageCount[this.thisPage] +
    → " times.<\/h1>";

    var contentWin = document.getElementById
    → ("content").contentWindow.document;
    contentWin.body.innerHTML = newText;
    return false;
}
```

WORKING WITH IFRAMES

Figure 5.14 Each time you click a link in the navigation bar, the content in the iframe updates.

5. var contentWin = document.
→ getElementById("content").
→ contentWindow.document;
contentWin.body.innerHTML = newText;
return false;

As with previous examples, we get contentWin and reset the innerHTML property of its body. Resetting innerHTML writes the two lines of text in the iframe, and the result is shown in **Figure 5.14**. And because that's everything, we end with a return false so that the browser doesn't do things it shouldn't.

✔ Tip

■ Note that unlike previous times we've written out to a content frame from a non-frameset page, we're using document. getElementById("content") instead of parent.document.getElementById ("content"). That's because the iframe is a child of the main page, not a frameset, and consequently, we can address it directly instead of only via the parent.

Loading Iframes with JavaScript

Of course, you don't have to write into the contents of an iframe with JavaScript; chances are you'll want to load other HTML pages. This example shows you how. Once again, we'll have a main page that sets up the iframe and will be virtually identical to Script 5.14. Similarly, there is a page with the initial content of the iframe, like Script 5.15. There are also three other simple HTML pages (not shown) that we load into the iframe with **Script 5.17**.

To load an iframe with JavaScript:

◆
```
function setiFrame() {
    document.getElementById
    → ("content").contentWindow.
    → document.location.href =
    → this.href;
    return false;
}
```

In much the same way that Script 5.12 set both the `target` and the `onclick` handler for the links, Script 5.17 does the same for an iframe. In this example, clicking any of the links triggers the `setiFrame()` function, which then loads the new page into the iframe, as shown in **Figure 5.15**.

Script 5.17 This script loads HTML pages into the content iframe.

```
window.onload = initiFrame;

function initiFrame() {
    for (var i=0; i<document.links.length; i++) {
        document.links[i].target = "content";
        document.links[i].onclick = setiFrame;
    }
}

function setiFrame() {
    document.getElementById("content").
    → contentWindow.document.location.href =
    → this.href;
    return false;
}
```

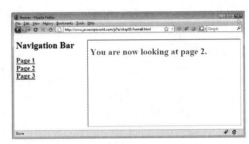

Figure 5.15 The content iframe gets loaded when you click a link in the navigation bar.

Working with Windows

The window is the most important interface element in a Web browser, and as you might expect, JavaScript provides you with many tools to manipulate windows

JavaScript deals with windows in ways similar to that of frames. This makes perfect sense, since frames are just other document windows within the overall browser window.

In this chapter, you'll learn how to use JavaScript to open and close, update, and position windows. You'll see how you can use JavaScript to write information into windows, so you can build a Web page on the fly.

Don't Kill Those Pop-Ups!

This chapter is about creating and working with windows using JavaScript. There's a name for these windows; they're called pop-up windows, and they've become a bane to many a Web surfer. We're going to be showing you some benign uses of pop-up windows, but if you're having trouble getting these examples to work, it may be because you've turned off pop-up windows in your browser, or because you have other software running that kills pop-up windows. While most browsers should open any pop-up that you've explicitly chosen to open, some don't. So while you're working on this chapter, make sure your pop-up killers are turned off.

However, some browsers, allegedly for security reasons (we're looking at *you*, Internet Explorer), will decide they know better than you and will not open pop-up windows from scripts no matter if you've asked them to or not.

Opening a New Window

You'll often want to create new windows to show users additional information without losing the information that they are reading. For example, you could open up an annotation window for a technical paper or for a news story. Although it is possible to open a new browser window with HTML, using JavaScript gives you more control over the new window's content and features. **Figure 6.1** shows you a standard browser window with all the parts labeled. You can create windows that have any or all of these parts. **Script 6.1** shows the HTML, and **Script 6.2** shows the JavaScript that creates a window from a page (**Figure 6.2**) where clicking a link brings up a new window (that contains an image of our cat, in this example).

Script 6.1 The HTML page that calls the external JavaScript that opens a new window.

```
script
<!DOCTYPE html PUBLIC "-//W3C//DTD XHTML 1.0
→ Transitional//EN"
        "http://www.w3.org/TR/xhtml1/DTD/
        → xhtml1-transitional.dtd">
<html xmlns="http://www.w3.org/1999/xhtml">
<head>
    <title>Opening a Window</title>
    <script type="text/javascript"
    → src="script01.js"></script>
</head>
<body bgcolor="#FFFFFF">
    <h1>The Master of the House</h1>
    <h2>Click on His name to behold He Who Must
    → Be Adored</h2>
    <h2><a href="#" class="newWin">Pixel</a>
    → </h2>
</body>
</html>
```

Figure 6.1 The elements of a browser window. The names in this figure correspond to the parameters you can apply in the open() command.

Script 6.2 Use this script to open a new window.

```
window.onload = newWinLinks;

function newWinLinks() {
    for (var i=0; i<document.links.length; i++) {
        if (document.links[i].className ==
        → "newWin") {
            document.links[i].onclick =
            → newWindow;
        }
    }
}

function newWindow() {
    var catWindow = window.open
    → ("images/pixel1.jpg", "catWin",
    → "resizable=no,width=350,height=260");
    return false;
}
```

Figure 6.2 Opening a new window.

You'll note that there is no JavaScript in Script 6.1, just a call to the external JavaScript file, and we also include an attribute to the link tag on the page: a class called newWin. As with the frames examples in Chapter 5, Script 6.2 includes an onload event handler that calls a function, in this case called newWinLinks. The newWinLinks function cycles through the links on the page and looks to see if any of the links include a class of newWin. If so, when the link is clicked, the function calls the newWindow function. Because very similar functions were used throughout Chapter 5, we've not detailed them in the steps below.

To open a new window:

1. function newWindow() {
   First, define a function called newWindow().

2. var catWindow = window.open
   → ("images/pixel1.jpg", "catWin",
   → "resizable=no,width=350,
   → height=260");
   The variable catWindow contains a new window object, referencing the image file pixel1.jpg. The name of this new window is catWin. Names are required, because we might want to reference this window later in a link or in another script. The new window has a width of 350 pixels and a height of 260 pixels; these parameters are optional.

✔ Tips

- In step 2, you can't have any spaces between the commas in the width and height parameters. If you do, your script may not work in some browsers. In general, when you get script errors and you need to debug your scripts, look for little problems like this. Syntax errors are a major cause of frustration to the beginning coder.

- Internet Explorer 6 and later does some funky and inconsistent window stuff for security reasons (scripting windows will work, or not; that sort of thing). If security is turned off, everything in this chapter works fine, but we don't recommend turning off security or requiring your site visitors to turn off security. Additionally, some new windows in IE7 and later may open in new tabs instead, based on your tabbed browsing settings.

Adding Parameters to Windows

To add one or more of the parameters listed in Figure 6.1 to your windows, state them in the `open()` command enclosed in quotes, with `=yes` after the name of a feature you want and `=no` after one you don't want (though `=no` is usually the default, so you can often skip even mentioning those features). For example, if you want a window of a specified size with a toolbar, location box, and scrollbars, you would type

```
"toolbar=yes,location=yes,scrollbars=yes,width=300,height=300"
```

as part of the `open()` command. Note that the window created would not have a menu bar or a status bar, and would not be resizable.

Given that leaving a parameter off entirely is (usually, see below for some exceptions) the same as setting it to `=no`; you can also just use the name of the parameter itself (without the `=yes`) to turn it on. Because there are some exceptions, we've preferred to make it a little more obvious in these scripts as to what we're turning on and off—consequently, we've combined them, followed by a yes or no; i.e., we've used `"location,scrollbars=yes"` to mean the same thing as `"location=yes,scrollbars=yes"`. We could also just say `"location,scrollbars"`, but it wouldn't be as clear what was going on.

Figure 6.3 shows the results of Script 6.2 in Firefox 3 for Mac, Firefox 2 for Windows, IE8, and Safari for Mac. As you can see, no two browsers produce identical results. In fact, the only browsers that did just what we wanted were Firefox 2 for Mac (as seen in Figure 6.2) and Internet Explorer. You may get results that differ from ours; for example, Firefox gives the user ultimate control—if they have their options set to require the status bar to show, it always will, no matter what your script says to do.

Figure 6.3 Different browsers use different window defaults, so items like the location appear in Firefox even though you've told it not to.

Ultimately, you'll still need to test your scripts in all the browsers that you think your site's users are most likely to be using, which may mean keeping both Windows and Mac (and maybe Linux) machines around for testing. Testing (and if necessary, script revision) will help make sure that your intentions for the script will work with whatever the browser hands you.

Loading Different Contents into a Window

In the previous task, clicking a link created a new window, filled with an image. But what if you have several links on a page, and you want them all to target a single new window? **Script 6.3** demonstrates this technique. The main window in **Figure 6.4** has three links. Clicking any of the links opens a new window, filled with the corresponding image of our cat. If you switch back to the main window and click another link, the image in the smaller window is replaced.

To load different contents into a window:

1. `document.links[i].onclick =`
   `→ newWindow;`

   In the newWinLinks() function, we've added the newWindow() function call as the onclick handler via JavaScript. When newWindow() is called, it uses this.href—that is, the href attribute value from HTML.

2. `function newWindow() {`

   Here, we're defining a new function called newWindow().

Script 6.3 With this script, you can open a new window and fill it with a variety of content, triggered by clicking different links.

```
script
window.onload = newWinLinks;

function newWinLinks() {
    for (var i=0; i<document.links.length; i++) {
        if (document.links[i].className ==
        → "newWin") {
            document.links[i].onclick =
            → newWindow;
        }
    }
}

function newWindow() {
    var catWindow = window.open
    → (this.href,"catWin","width=350,
    → height=260");
    catWindow.focus();
    return false;
}
```

Figure 6.4 Clicking any of the three links opens the smaller window and fills it with the appropriate image of our cat.

3. `var catWindow = window.open`
   `→ (this.href,"catWin","width=350,`
   `→ height=260");`

   Here in the variable `catWindow`, we're opening a new window object, followed by the window's parameters. First, we pass it the value of `this.href`. The name of the new window is `catWin`, and the width and height parameters set the size of the window.

4. `catWindow.focus();`

   This line uses the `focus()` method to tell the window we just opened to come to the front. You can use `focus()` whenever you need to make a window visible; if there are several windows open, using `focus()` brings the window to the top.

5. `return false;`

   The function needs to end with `return false` so that the HTML knows to not also load the `href` in.

✔ Tip

- The opposite of the `focus()` method used in step 4 is `blur()`. Using `blur()` pushes a window behind any other windows that are open. The `focus()` and `blur()` methods of the `window` object have associated `onfocus` and `onblur` event handlers, which let you take action when a window gains or loses focus.

Opening Multiple Windows

Sometimes you'll want to open multiple windows using a script; for example, you might want to create a script that opens a different window every time the user clicks an on-screen control. Or possibly you want to open several windows, all at the same time. As usual, JavaScript is up to the task. In this example, we have a page with a link; clicking it opens up several separate windows, each containing an image. **Script 6.4** shows you how it's done, and **Figure 6.5** shows the result.

To open multiple windows:

1. `document.links[i].onclick =`
   → `newWindows;`

   In the newWinLinks() function, we've changed this line to call the `newWindows()` function, since we're opening more than one window.

2. `for (var i=1; i<5;i++) {`

   The loop will execute four times—note that we're starting to i set to one instead of the usual zero. That's because we know that our four images are numbered 1, 2, 3, and 4, so why not use those same values for i?

3. `var imgName = "images/pixel" + i +`
   → `".jpg";`
   `var winName = "window" + i;`

   The imgName variable contains the constructed path of the images. The winName variable gets the current value of i and appends it to window.

Script 6.4 This script opens multiple windows with a single click on a link.

```
window.onload = newWinLinks;

function newWinLinks() {
    for (var i=0; i<document.links.length; i++) {
        if (document.links[i].className ==
        → "newWin") {
            document.links[i].onclick =
            → newWindows;
        }
    }
}

function newWindows() {
    for (var i=1; i<5;i++) {
        var imgName = "images/pixel" + i +
        → ".jpg";
        var winName = "window" + i;
        var catWindow = window.open
        → (imgName,winName,"width=350,
        → height=260");
    }
    return false;
}
```

Figure 6.5 Clicking the link opened all four child windows; the placement was determined by the browser. In this case, Safari opened all the windows on top of one another, and we moved them for clarity's sake.

4. `var catWindow = window.open`
   `→ (imgName,winName,"width=350,`
   `→ height=260");`

The `catWindow` variable opens the window with the image, adds the window's name, and specifies the window size. The key to this script is that `winName` (the second parameter to `window.open`) is unique. So long as each window name is different, new windows will open. The result of all this looping is shown in Figure 6.5.

✔ Tips

■ The placement of the windows is up to wherever the browser decides to put the windows. If you want to control those locations, Script 6.11 shows how to place a window in a specific location on the screen. See "Putting Windows in Their Place" later in this chapter.

■ If you want a new window to open up every time a user clicks a link (versus refreshing an existing window), add a random number to the window name.

■ There's some code in Script 6.3 that's missing from this script, namely `catWindow.focus()`. In Script 6.3, it makes the opened window the focus, i.e., the front-most window. But from a user interface standpoint, when multiple windows are opened at once it's not clear where the focus should be.

Updating One Window from Another

If you deal with forms and data entered by your users, you'll want to know how to send information entered in one window to another window for display. You might use this in a situation where you are selling a product to replicate the user's information in a summary window. In this example, we'll use two windows: the main window is the parent window, which will receive and display information entered in a child window. **Script 6.5** and **Script 6.6** show the parent and child HTML pages, respectively. **Script 6.7** shows the script, which is called from both the parent and child windows.

Script 6.5 The HTML for the parent window.

```
<!DOCTYPE html PUBLIC "-//W3C//DTD XHTML 1.0
→ Transitional//EN"
        "http://www.w3.org/TR/xhtml1/DTD/
        → xhtml1-transitional.dtd">
<html xmlns="http://www.w3.org/1999/xhtml">
<head>
    <title>Big Window</title>
    <script type="text/javascript"
    → src="script04.js"></script>
</head>
<body bgcolor="#FFFFFF">
<div align="center">
    <h1>Welcome to this page!</h1>
    <form action="#">
        <input type="text" size="20"
        → id="msgLine" readonly="readonly" />
    </form>
</div>
</body>
</html>
```

Script 6.6 The HTML for the child window.

```
<!DOCTYPE html PUBLIC "-//W3C//DTD XHTML 1.0
→ Transitional//EN"
        "http://www.w3.org/TR/xhtml1/DTD/
        → xhtml1-transitional.dtd">
<html xmlns="http://www.w3.org/1999/xhtml">
<head>
    <title>Little Window</title>
    <script type="text/javascript"
    → src="script04.js"></script>
</head>
<body bgcolor="#FFFFFF">
    <h1>What's your name?</h1>
    <form action="#">
        <input type="text" id="childField"
        → size="20" />
    </form>
</body>
</html>
```

Script 6.7 This script is called from both the parent and child windows.

```
window.onload = initWindows;

function initWindows() {
    if (document.getElementById("childField")) {
        document.getElementById("childField").
        → onchange = updateParent;
    }
    else {
        newWindow = window.open("child.html",
        → "newWin","status=yes,width=300,
        → height=300");
    }
}

function updateParent() {
    opener.document.getElementById("msgLine").
    → value = "Hello " + this.value + "!";
}
```

Figure 6.6 The child window is where the user enters data.

To update one window from another:

1. `window.onload = initWindows;`

When the window loads, call the `initWindows()` function.

2. `if (document.getElementById`
`→ ("childField")) {`
`document.getElementById`
`→ ("childField").onchange =`
`→ updateParent;`
`}`

The script is called by both HTML pages (the parent and the child pages), but it needs to do different things for each file. The way it tells which one it's on is to check for the existence of the `childField` object, which only exists in the child window. If we're there, and the user changes the object, then we call the `updateParent()` function.

3. `else {`
`newWindow = window.open`
`→ ("child.html","newWin",`
`→ "status=yes,width=300,`
`→ height=300");`

If the `childField` object doesn't exist, it's time to open the child window, using the `child.html` file. The rest of the line specifies the child window's parameters. (**Figure 6.6**).

4. `function updateParent() {`

Here we create the `updateParent` function.

continues on next page

5. opener.document.getElementById
→ ("msgLine").value = "Hello " +
→ this.value + "!";

This line introduces the opener property, which is how JavaScript references back to the parent document that opened the child window. This line tells the opener document (that is, the parent) window to find the element named msgLine and set its value to the word "Hello" and the contents of this.value, ending with an exclamation point (**Figure 6.7**).

Figure 6.7 The updated parent window after calling information from the child window.

✔ Tips

- Forms, fields, and how to script them are covered in depth in Chapter 7, "Form Handling."

- In Script 6.5, we've added the readonly="readonly" attribute to the parent window's msgLine field. It just makes it clear that visitors to your site can't edit that themselves; it can only be set elsewhere.

Script 6.8 Note the id tags for the two links in this HTML page.

```
● ● ●                    script
<!DOCTYPE html PUBLIC "-//W3C//DTD XHTML 1.0
→ Transitional//EN"
        "http://www.w3.org/TR/xhtml1/DTD/
        → xhtml1-transitional.dtd">
<html xmlns="http://www.w3.org/1999/xhtml">
<head>
    <title>Window Test</title>
    <script type="text/javascript"
    → src="script05.js"></script>
</head>
<body bgcolor="#FFFFFF">
    <div align="center">
        <h1>Let's play with windows!</h1>
        <h3>
            <a href="#" id="openWin">Open a new
            → window</a>  
            <a href="#" id="closeWin">Close the
            → window</a>
        </h3>
    </div>
</body>
</html>
```

Closing a Window

Just as you can create windows, you should know how to get rid of windows by closing them. In **Script 6.8**, the parent window has "open" and "close" links that create and close the child window, and each link has a unique id that we use in the script. The external JavaScript is in **Script 6.9**.

To close a window:

1. `var newWindow = null;`

This line initializes the value for the `newWindow` object that we're going to use later. While most browsers do this automatically, some don't, so it needs to be set here to avoid errors later.

2. `document.links[i].onclick =`
`→ chgWindowState;`

In the `newWinLinks()` function, we're stepping through the links in the document as usual. The only difference here is that we'll call `chgWindowState()` if we detect a click on one of the links.

3. `function windowOpen() {`
`    if (newWindow && !newWindow.`
`    → closed) {`
`        return true;`
`    }`
`    return false;`
`}`

The `if` statement poses a logical test using the `&&` operator, which returns a true result only if all the values being checked are true. So in this case, `newWindow` must exist and `newWindow` must not have been closed (the `!` is the logical "not" operator). This function returns `true` if a window is open and `false` if it isn't.

continues on next page

4. `function chgWindowState() {`
  `if (this.id == "closeWin") {`

Here, we're checking to see if the `id` of the clicked link is `closeWin`. If it's `closeWin`, the user clicked the close link. If it's `openWin`, they clicked the open link.

5. `if (windowOpen()) {`
  `newWindow.close();`
`}`

If the user clicked close and the window is open, these lines close it.

6. `else {`
  `alert("The window isn't open");`
`}`

If the user clicked close and the window is already closed, an alert pops up saying so.

Script 6.9 This script opens and closes a child window.

```
var newWindow = null;
window.onload = newWinLinks;

function newWinLinks() {
    for (var i=0; i<document.links.length; i++) {
        document.links[i].onclick =
        → chgWindowState;
    }
}

function windowOpen() {
    if (newWindow && !newWindow.closed) {
        return true;
    }
    return false;
}

function chgWindowState() {
    if (this.id == "closeWin") {
        if (windowOpen()) {
            newWindow.close();
        }
        else {
            alert("The window isn't open");
        }
    }
    if (this.id == "openWin") {
        if (windowOpen()) {
            alert("The window is already open!");
        }
        else {
            newWindow = window.open("","newWin",
            → "toolbar,location=yes,width=300,
            → height=200");
        }
    }
    return false;
}
```

Figure 6.8 The links in this window create and close a child window.

7. ```
if (this.id == "openWin") {
    if (windowOpen()) {
        alert("The window is already
        ⇢ open!");
    }
```

Similarly, if the user clicked open and the window is already open, an alert pops up saying so.

8. ```
else {
    newWindow = window.open("",
    ⇢ "newWin","toolbar,location=yes,
    ⇢ width=300,height=200");
}
```

If the user clicked open and there's no current window, the window opens up, showing the parameters set in the line (**Figure 6.8**). In this case, the toolbar and location are visible.

9. ```
return false;
```

We end with a `return false` so that the `href` from the link doesn't get triggered.
```

Putting Windows in Their Place

Sometimes you want to open a window in a particular spot on the screen. In this example, you'll have your choice of opening a small window in any of the four corners of your screen. Like the previous example, we also provide a link to close the child window. The HTML is similar to previous examples, as shown in **Script 6.10**. As you would expect, each of the links is tagged with its own unique id. The JavaScript, in **Script 6.11**, builds on Script 6.9.

Script 6.10 Clicking on these links tells JavaScript where you want your window located.

```
<!DOCTYPE html PUBLIC "-//W3C//DTD XHTML 1.0 Transitional//EN"
        "http://www.w3.org/TR/xhtml1/DTD/xhtml1-transitional.dtd">
<html xmlns="http://www.w3.org/1999/xhtml">
<head>
    <title>Window Test</title>
    <script type="text/javascript" src="script06.js"></script>
</head>
<body bgcolor="#FFFFFF">
    <div align="center">
        <h1>Let's play with windows!</h1>
        <h3>
            <a href="#" id="topLeftWin">Move/open window in the top left</a>  
            <a href="#" id="topRightWin">Move/open window in the top right</a><br />
            <a href="#" id="bottomLeftWin">Move/open window in the bottom left</a>  
            <a href="#" id="bottomRightWin">Move/open window in the bottom right</a><br />
            <a href="#" id="closeWin">Close the window</a>
        </h3>
    </div>
</body>
</html>
```

Script 6.11 If you need to move windows to specified spots, this script does the job.

```
● ● ●                    script
var newWindow = null;
window.onload = newWinLinks;

function newWinLinks() {
    for (var i=0; i<document.links.length; i++) {
        document.links[i].onclick =
        → chgWindowState;
    }
}

function windowOpen() {
    if (newWindow && !newWindow.closed) {
        return true;
    }
    return false;
}

function chgWindowState() {
    if (this.id == "closeWin") {
        if (windowOpen()) {
            newWindow.close();
        }
        else {
            alert("The window isn't open");
        }
        return false;
    }

    var topPos = 0;
    var leftPos = 0;

    if (this.id.indexOf("bottom") > -1) {
        topPos = screen.availHeight-200;
    }
    if (this.id.indexOf("Right") > -1) {
        leftPos = screen.availWidth-300;
    }
```

(script continues on next page)

To place a window in a particular location:

1.
```
var topPos = 0;
var leftPos = 0;

if (this.id.indexOf("bottom") > -1) {
    topPos = screen.availHeight-200;
}
if (this.id.indexOf("Right") > -1) {
    leftPos = screen.availWidth-300;
}
```

We're creating two new variables, topPos and leftPos, based on screen.availHeight and screen.availWidth. Here's the way it works: if the word "bottom" is in the id (that is, id as specified in Script 6.10 is either bottomLeftWin or bottomRightWin), we know that the newly opened window needs to be pegged to the bottom of the screen. So, topPos will be set to whatever the available height is of the screen minus 200 (the height of the window being opened). If "bottom" isn't in the id (causing the indexOf() check to return -1, meaning not found), then topPos is left at its initialized value of zero, because it should be pegged to the top of the screen. And ditto for leftPos and "Right".

2.
```
if (windowOpen()) {
    newWindow.moveTo(leftPos,topPos);
}
```

If the window is already open, we do a newWindow.moveTo() and pass in leftPos and topPos, which we just defined. That's all there is to it.

continues on next page

3. `else {`
```
    newWindow = window.open("",
  → "newWin","toolbar,location=yes,
  → width=300,height=200,
  → left="+leftPos+",top="+topPos);
```

If the window wasn't open, we open it in the specified location by setting the `left` and `top` values in `window.open`, as seen in **Figure 6.9**.

✔ Tips

- The `availHeight` and `availWidth` properties look at only one monitor at a time, so if you have a multi-monitor setup, you can't suddenly make a window fly somewhere else; the windows will open on the same monitor that the parent window is on.

- If you want to change a window's dimensions instead of its location, use `resizeTo()` instead of `moveTo()`.

- Both the `resizeTo()` and `moveTo()` commands can be used on the current window—not just newly opened windows. However, it's been found that visitors to sites hate having their main window moved even more than they hate pop-up windows, so don't do it.

Script 6.11 *continued*

```
if (windowOpen()) {
    newWindow.moveTo(leftPos,topPos);
}
else {
    newWindow = window.open("","newWin",
  → "toolbar,location=yes,width=300,
  → height=200,left="+leftPos+",
  → top="+topPos);
}
    return false;
}
```

Figure 6.9 The links in the parent window open a child window in the specified spot on your screen. If a window is already open but not where we now want it, clicking the new placement link moves it to the specified location.

PUTTING WINDOWS IN THEIR PLACE

FORM HANDLING

Any time you need to gather information from the users of your Web sites, you'll need to use a form.

Forms can contain most of the usual graphical interface elements, including entry fields, radio buttons, check boxes, pop-up menus, and entry lists. In addition, HTML forms can contain password fields, shielding the user's input from prying eyes.

Once the form is filled out, a click on the form's Submit button sends the form's information to your Web server, where a CGI (that stands for Common Gateway Interface, and it's a script that runs on the Web server) interprets the data and acts on it. Often, the data is then stored in a database for later use. It's useful to make sure that the data the user enters is "clean," that is, accurate and in the correct format, before it gets stored on the server side. JavaScript is the perfect way to check the data; this is called *form validation*. Though the CGI can do the validation (and should as a backup measure, since some people will have JavaScript turned off in their browsers), it's much faster and more efficient for your users to also do it on the client's machine with JavaScript.

continues on next page

In this chapter, you'll learn how to use
JavaScript to make sure that your forms
contain valid information, check data in one
field against the data in another field, and
highlight incorrect information to let the user
know what needs to be changed.

Table 7.1

Just Enough HTML—Forms		
TAG	**ATTRIBUTE**	**MEANING**
form		A tag that contains any of the following tags, making them into a valid HTML form
	action	The name of the server-side CGI that is run when control is passed back to the Web server
input		A form field of varying types, depending on the value of the type attribute
	class	The class assigned to the element
	id	The unique id assigned to the element
	name	Primarily used to group sets of radio buttons; also is a name that JavaScript can use to refer to this field; as with other JavaScript objects, no spaces or other punctuation is allowed, and it cannot start with a number
	maxlength	The maximum length entry that the user may enter in this field
	size	The number of characters that are displayed on the page
	type	The type of input required; possible values are button, checkbox, image, password, radio, reset, submit, and text
	value	The preset value of this form field
label		Used to specify labels for controls that do not have built-in labels, such as text fields, check boxes, radio buttons, and menus
	for	Associates the label with a specific element's id
option		The possible options available inside a select tag
	selected	Indicates whether this option is selected as the default
	value	The preset value of each option
select		A form field that is either a pop-up menu or scrolling list, based on the size attribute
	class	The class assigned to the element
	id	The unique id assigned to the element
	size	The number of options that are displayed on the page; if the attribute is set to 1, or this attribute is not present, the result is a pop-up menu

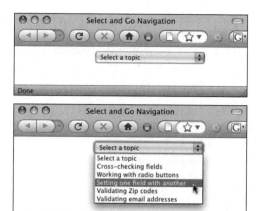

Figure 7.1 Picking any of the choices in this menu jumps you directly to the page containing that topic, without requiring a separate Go button.

Select-and-Go Navigation

You've probably seen lots of examples of the standard navigation menu on the Web; you pick a choice from a menu and click a Go button, which takes you to your destination. For example, many online stores use such menus to move you to different departments. But with a bit of JavaScript, you can launch users on their way with just the menu choice, eliminating the Go button (**Figure 7.1**). This makes your site feel snappier and more responsive, which is always a good idea. We call these JavaScript-enhanced menus select-and-go menus, and they're easy to create. The HTML is in **Script 7.1**, and the JavaScript is shown in **Script 7.2**. You'll never want to use a Go button again!

Script 7.1 The HTML for a select-and-go menu is fairly simple.

```
<!DOCTYPE html PUBLIC "-//W3C//DTD XHTML 1.0 Transitional//EN"
        "http://www.w3.org/TR/xhtml1/DTD/xhtml1-transitional.dtd">
<html xmlns="http://www.w3.org/1999/xhtml">
<head>
    <title>Select and Go Navigation</title>
    <script type="text/javascript" src="script01.js"></script>
</head>
<body bgcolor="#FFFFFF">
<div align="center">
    <form action="gotoLocation.cgi">
        <select id="newLocation">
            <option selected="selected">Select a topic</option>
            <option value="script06.html">Cross-checking fields</option>
            <option value="script07.html">Working with radio buttons</option>
            <option value="script08.html">Setting one field with another</option>
            <option value="script09.html">Validating Zip codes</option>
            <option value="script10.html">Validating email addresses</option>
        </select>
        <noscript>
            <input type="submit" value="Go There!" />
        </noscript>
    </form>
</div>
</body>
</html>
```

To create a select-and-go menu:

1. `window.onload = initForm;`
   `window.onunload = function() {};`

   When the window loads, call the initForm() function. The next line needs some explanation, because it is a workaround for the odd behavior of some browsers.

   When the window unloads (i.e., when it is closed or the browser goes to another location), we call an *anonymous function*, that is, a function that doesn't have a name. In this case, it not only doesn't have a name, it doesn't have anything at all. It's here because we have to set onunload to *something*—otherwise, the onload event isn't triggered when the browser's back button is clicked, because the page is cached in some browsers, such as Firefox and Safari. Having onunload do anything at all causes the page to be uncached, and therefore, when we come back, the onload happens.

   The *anonymous* part of the term refers to the fact that there's no name between function and (). This is the simplest way to trigger onunload but not have it do anything. The braces are just like any function; they would hold the contents of the function. They're empty here because this particular function does nothing.

Script 7.2 You can use JavaScript and forms for active site navigation.

```
window.onload = initForm;
window.onunload = function() {};

function initForm() {
    document.getElementById("newLocation").
    → selectedIndex = 0;
    document.getElementById("newLocation").
    → onchange = jumpPage;
}


function jumpPage() {
    var newLoc = document.getElementById
    → ("newLocation");
    var newPage = newLoc.options
    → [newLoc.selectedIndex].value;

    if (newPage != "") {
        window.location = newPage;
    }
}
```

SELECT-AND-GO NAVIGATION

2. `document.getElementById`
`→("newLocation").selectedIndex = 0;`
`document.getElementById`
`→("newLocation").onchange = jumpPage;`

In the `initForm()` function, the first line gets the menu on the HTML page, which has the `id` of `newLocation`, and sets its `selectedIndex` property to zero, which forces it to say "Select a topic".

The second line tells the script to call the `jumpPage()` function when the menu selection changes.

3. `var newLoc = document.getElementById`
`→("newLocation");`

Inside the `jumpPage()` function, the `newLoc` variable looks up the value chosen in the menu by the visitor.

4. `var newPage = newLoc.options`
`→[newLoc.selectedIndex].value;`

Start from the code inside the brackets and work outward. The object `newLoc.selectedIndex` will be a number from 0 to 5 (because there are six possible menu choices; remember that JavaScript arrays are zero-based). Given that number, we next get the value for the corresponding menu option, which is the name of the Web page we want to jump to. Then we assign the result to the variable `newPage`.

5. `if (newPage != "") {`
`    window.location = newPage;`

This conditional first checks to see that `newPage` is not equal to nothing (that is, it's not empty). In other words, if `newPage` has a value, then tell the window to go to the URL specified by the menu option chosen.

SELECT-AND-GO NAVIGATION

✔ Tips

- One of the nicest things about this script is that once the JavaScript function has been added, there's no need to modify the function when pull-down options are added, modified, or changed. Only the values of the options (i.e., the URLs that the menu options jump to) need to be set. For this reason, this script works well with WYSIWYG page editors.

- As mentioned above, Firefox caches pages, causing `onload` events to not be triggered when the back button is clicked. One way to work around this is covered above; another way we can do this is to add the line:

```
window.onpageshow = initForm;
```

  We didn't use this because it doesn't work in Safari (the other caching trouble-maker). But if you are specifically targeting Firefox, it's worth knowing that there are two new non-standard window event handlers, `onpageshow` and `onpagehide`, which can be used to handle events that we only want triggered in Firefox.

- We call these "select-and-go" menus, which isn't especially elegant but clearly tells you what's going on. You may see other names for the same functionality; for example, Dreamweaver calls them "jump menus." By the way, if you're a Dreamweaver user and need a great book on getting the most out of Dreamweaver, let us suggest *Dreamweaver for Windows and Macintosh: Visual QuickStart Guide* (Peachpit Press), by, uh, us.

Accommodating the JavaScript-impaired User

The point of this task is to use JavaScript to eliminate the need for a Go button when using a form to jump from one page to another. But what if the user has an old, non-JavaScript-capable browser, or just has JavaScript turned off? No problem; Script 7.1 handles those users just fine, by putting in a Go button that's only visible in the absence of JavaScript.

The only way to get from one page to another with a form but without JavaScript is to use a CGI, a program running on the Web server. Script 7.1 sets that up in this line:

```
<form action="gotoLocation.cgi">
```

Figure 7.2 If the user doesn't have JavaScript, they'll still be able to get around on your site, because the Go There! button automagically appears.

The form tag has the action attribute, which calls the CGI. But a form action requires the user to click a submit button, and there's no such button in Figure 7.1. Ah, but there is in **Figure 7.2**, which shows what happens when you turn JavaScript off. These lines contain the button, wrapped in the noscript tags, which are only executed if JavaScript is missing.

```
<noscript> <input type="submit"
 value="Go There!"> </noscript>
```

The really cool thing about all this is that the CGI only ever gets called if JavaScript is missing; if the user has a JavaScript-enabled browser, then the submit button doesn't appear, and the CGI is unnecessary.

Changing Menus Dynamically

It's often useful to offer the user a choice of inputs via pop-up menus, and to be able to change the contents of one or more pop-up menus depending on the choice the user makes in another pop-up menu. You've probably seen this on Web sites that ask you to choose the country you live in from a pop-up menu and then fill a second menu with state or province names, based on the choice you made. In **Scripts 7.3** (HTML) and **7.4** (JavaScript), we're using two pop-up menus (**Figure 7.3**). The first menu is for months. When the user picks a month, the script populates the second pop-up menu with the correct number of days for the selected month (**Figure 7.4**).

Script 7.3 The HTML for the pop-up menus lists the months but not the days.

```
<!DOCTYPE html PUBLIC "-//W3C//DTD XHTML 1.0
Transitional//EN"
        "http://www.w3.org/TR/xhtml1/DTD/
        → xhtml1-transitional.dtd">
<html xmlns="http://www.w3.org/1999/xhtml">
<head>
    <title>Dynamic Menus</title>
    <script type="text/javascript"
        → src="script02.js"></script>
</head>
<body bgcolor="#FFFFFF">
<form action="#">
    <select id="months">
        <option value="">Month</option>
        <option value="0">January</option>
        <option value="1">February</option>
        <option value="2">March</option>
        <option value="3">April</option>
        <option value="4">May</option>
        <option value="5">June</option>
        <option value="6">July</option>
        <option value="7">August</option>
        <option value="8">September</option>
        <option value="9">October</option>
        <option value="10">November</option>
        <option value="11">December</option>
    </select>
     

    <select id="days">
        <option>Day</option>
    </select>
</form>

</body>
</html>
```

To change menus dynamically:

1. `var monthDays = new Array(31,28,31,` `→ 30,31,30,31,31,30,31,30,31);`

This new array contains 12 values for the 12 months, with the correct number of days in each month. The array is stored in the variable `monthDays`.

2. `var monthStr = this.options` `→ [this.selectedIndex].value;`

We're using `this` (the month the user picked from the first menu) to get the value from the menu, and storing it in `monthStr`.

continues on next page

Script 7.4 By selecting a value from one pop-up menu, you can create the contents of a second pop-up menu.

```
window.onload = initForm;

function initForm() {
    document.getElementById("months").selectedIndex = 0;
    document.getElementById("months").onchange = populateDays;
}

function populateDays() {
    var monthDays = new Array(31,28,31,30,31,30,31,31,30,31,30,31);
    var monthStr = this.options[this.selectedIndex].value;

    if (monthStr != "") {
        var theMonth = parseInt(monthStr);

        document.getElementById("days").options.length = 0;
        for(var i=0; i<monthDays[theMonth]; i++) {
            document.getElementById("days").options[i] = new Option(i+1);
        }
    }
}
```

CHANGING MENUS DYNAMICALLY

3. `if (monthStr != "") {`
`    var theMonth = parseInt(monthStr);`

If the value of `monthStr` is `""`, then the user chose the word "Month" in the menu, rather than a month name. What these lines do is check to see that the value of `monthStr` is not `""`; if that condition is true, then `monthStr` is turned into a number with the `parseInt` method, and the variable `theMonth` is set to the result.

4. `document.getElementById("days").`
`  → options.length = 0;`
`for (var i=0; i<monthDays[theMonth];`
`  → i++) {`
`    document.getElementById("days").`
`    → options[i] = new Option(i+1);`

Start changing the day menu by setting its options length to zero. That clears out whatever happened to be there before, so we're starting fresh. The loop simply goes through the number of days in whatever the chosen month is, adding a new option to the menu for each day. Option is passed `i+1`, so that it shows 1 to 31 instead of 0 to 30.

✔ Tip

■ The `monthDays` array contains the number of days in each month, which works fine except in the case of leap years. To get your script to work in a leap year, you'll need to change the February value in `monthDays`.

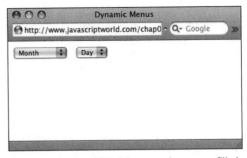

Figure 7.3 The contents of the second menu are filled in automatically when the user makes a selection from the first menu.

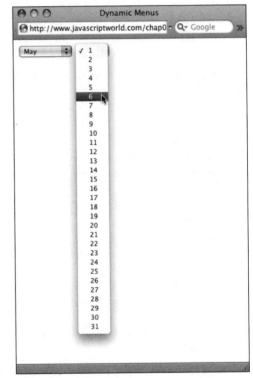

Figure 7.4 The result of choosing a month: the correct number of days of that month appear in the Day menu.

Figure 7.5 Make sure that passwords are entered correctly by highlighting the background to let the user know there's a problem with a particular field.

Making Fields Required

When filling out a form, you may want to specify particular fields that are required to be filled out by the user before the form can be submitted. You can use JavaScript to check that some or all fields are filled out. In this example, we use HTML, CSS, and JavaScript (**Scripts 7.5**, **7.6**, and **7.7**, respectively) to highlight fields that are not filled out with a red border and a yellow interior. The check occurs when the user clicks the form's Submit button.

Here's the big picture: the `class` attributes in the HTML store which checks we want the JavaScript to do. If a check is failed, we add `invalid` to the list of `class` attributes. Doing that causes (1) the form submission to fail, and (2) the CSS in Script 7.6 to change the appearance of the field on the page (**Figure 7.5**).

Script 7.5 The HTML for the password check example.

```
<!DOCTYPE html PUBLIC "-//W3C//DTD XHTML 1.0 Transitional//EN"
        "http://www.w3.org/TR/xhtml1/DTD/xhtml1-transitional.dtd">
<html xmlns="http://www.w3.org/1999/xhtml">
<head>
    <title>Password Check</title>
    <link type="text/css" rel="stylesheet" href="script03.css" />
    <script type="text/javascript" src="script03.js"></script>
</head>
<body>
<form action="#">
    <p><label for="userName">Your name: <input type="text" size="30" id="userName" class="reqd"
    → /></label></p>
    <p><label for="passwd1">Choose a password: <input type="password" id="passwd1" class="reqd"
    → /></label></p>
    <p><label for="passwd2">Verify password: <input type="password" id="passwd2" class="reqd passwd1"
    → /></label></p>
    <p><input type="submit" value="Submit" /> <input type="reset" /></p>
</form>
</body>
</html>
```

To make fields required:

1.
```
function initForms() {
   for (var i=0; i< document.forms.
   → length; i++) {
      document.forms[i].onsubmit =
      → function()
      → {return validForm();}
```

When the page first loads, the `initForms()` function is called. This function loops through every form on the page. For each one, it adds an event handler to that form's onsubmit: a call to `function() {return validForm();}`. This is another anonymous function, but this time it does something: it returns true or false to tell the browser whether or not to continue with the action attribute. When an `onsubmit` handler returns a value of false, the form doesn't get passed back to the server. The server only gets the form (running whatever CGI is stored in the action attribute) when we return a value of true.

2.
```
var allTags = document.
→ getElementsByTagName("*");
```

The `document.getElementsByTagName("*")` object is very useful—that asterisk tells JavaScript to return an array containing *every* tag on the page. Once we have that, we can then just loop through the `allTags` array looking for things of interest.

3.
```
for (var i=0; i<allTags.length; i++) {
   if (!validTag(allTags[i])) {
      allGood = false;
```

This loop searches through `allTags`, and the `if` conditional calls the `validTag()` function, which checks each tag to see if there's anything there that should keep the form from submitting this page. It's passed `allTags[i]`, which is the object that we're currently processing. If any tag causes `validTag()` to return false, we set `allGood` to false. However, even if one is false, we still keep going through all the tags.

Script 7.6 The CSS sets the style for invalid form elements.

```
body {
    color: #000;
    background-color: #FFF;
}

input.invalid {
    background-color: #FF9;
    border: 2px red inset;
}

label.invalid {
    color: #F00;
    font-weight: bold;
}
```

Script 7.7 This script serves as the basis for all the rest of the examples in this chapter; it's a framework that you can use to add additional validation checks.

```
window.onload = initForms;

function initForms() {
    for (var i=0; i< document.forms.length;
    → i++) {
        document.forms[i].onsubmit = function()
        → {return validForm();}
    }
}

function validForm() {
    var allGood = true;
    var allTags = document.getElementsByTagName
    → ("*");

    for (var i=0; i<allTags.length; i++) {
        if (!validTag(allTags[i])) {
            allGood = false;
        }
    }
    return allGood;

    function validTag(thisTag) {
        var outClass = "";
        var allClasses = thisTag.className.
        → split(" ");

        for (var j=0; j<allClasses.length;
        → j++) {
            outClass += validBasedOnClass
            → (allClasses[j]) + " ";
        }

        thisTag.className = outClass;

        if (outClass.indexOf("invalid") > -1) {
            thisTag.focus();
            if (thisTag.nodeName == "INPUT") {
                thisTag.select();
            }
```

(script continues on next page)

4. `return allGood;`

We return `allGood`, to signify whether or not we're good to go.

5. `function validTag(thisTag) {`

Create the `validTag()` function, and set it to receive the parameter `thisTag`.

6. `var allClasses = thisTag.className.`
`→ split(" ");`

For each tag, we want to look at every `class` attribute (remember, `class` can be set to have multiple attributes "like so and so and so"). The `allClasses` array is created and set based on `thisTag.className.split(" ");` which splits a string up into an array, broken up by the string that's passed in. Here, the string is a space, which would, for example, cause the string "this that and the other" to turn into an array of five elements: this, that, and, the, other.

We want to look at each `class` attribute, because `class` is where we're storing what we want each form field to have to provide. In this task, the one we care about is `reqd`—required. If any form field has a `class` that includes `reqd`, it's got to contain something.

7. `for (var j=0; j<allClasses.length;`
`→ j++) {`
`outClass += validBasedOnClass`
`→ (allClasses[j]) + " ";`
`}`

This loop uses j as its loop variable because we're inside a loop that's using i. We loop around once for each `class` attribute in `allClasses`.

For each class, we perform: `outClass += validBasedOnClass(allClasses[j]) + " ";` This calls the `validBasedOnClass()` function (explained below), passing in the current class we're looking at. That function returns something, and that something, plus a space, is appended onto the `outClass` variable.

continues on next page

8. `thisTag.className = outClass;`

When we've finished with the `allClasses` loop, we take the contents of `outClass` and put it into `thisTag.className`, overwriting the current `class` attribute for this form field. That's because it can change during this process, as we'll see very shortly.

9. `if (outClass.indexOf("invalid") > -1) {`

Something that can be returned in the new `class` attribute is the word "invalid", so we check for it. If that's found anywhere in the new class, do the following, as there's a problem.

10. `thisTag.focus();`

If this form field can take focus (remember, we discussed focus in Chapter 5), we want to put the focus into the field, and that's what this line does. This is a way of forcing the user to know which field is the problem.

11. `if (thisTag.nodeName == "INPUT") {`
`    thisTag.select();`
`}`

Basically, these lines say, "This tag I'm looking at: is it an `<input>` tag? If so, select its value so that the user has an easier time modifying it."

12. `return false;`

We're still inside the "invalid was returned" block, so we return false back to where we were called.

13. `return true;`

If all is good and valid, we return true.

14. `function validBasedOnClass(thisClass) {`

Begin the new `validBasedOnClass()` function, and set it to receive the value `thisClass`.

Script 7.7 *continued*

```
        return false;
    }
    return true;

function validBasedOnClass(thisClass) {
    var classBack = "";

    switch(thisClass) {
        case "":
        case "invalid":
            break;
        case "reqd":
            if (allGood && thisTag.
            → value == "") {
                classBack = "invalid ";
            }
            classBack += thisClass;
            break;
        default:
            classBack += thisClass;
    }
    return classBack;
    }
}
```

15. `var classBack = "";`

Create the `classBack` variable, and fill it with nothing for now. This is going to contain the class to be returned, that is, the value we want to send back.

16. `switch(thisClass) {`

The `switch` statement looks at the single `class` attribute that was passed in (in `thisClass`) and does something based on it.

17. `case "":`
`case "invalid":`
    `break;`

If `thisClass` is empty or `invalid`, then break out of the conditional; otherwise, continue.

18. `case "reqd":`
    `if (allGood && thisTag.value ==`
  `→ "") {`
      `classBack = "invalid ";`
    `}`
    `classBack += thisClass;`
    `break;`

If the attribute being processed is reqd *and* `allGood` is true *and* the current value of the current tag is "" (i.e., nothing), then we set `classBack` to be `invalid`, because there's a problem, and we want to notify the user. After that, whether there was a problem or not, we append the current class to `classBack` so that it doesn't get lost.

19. `default:`
    `classBack += thisClass;`

The `default` block is executed whenever something happens that isn't caught by one of the above cases. When that happens, it's a class we don't care about, so we just stick it onto `classBack` and don't fret.

20. `return classBack;`

Finally, we return `classBack`.

Checking Fields against Each Other

It's common to want to check one field against another, especially when you're asking the user to type in a password. You want to make them type it in twice for accuracy, and you want to make sure that they typed the same thing both times.

This example reuses Scripts 7.5 (HTML) and 7.6 (CSS); and only a few lines of JavaScript need to be added to Script 7.7 (**Script 7.8**) to give the script the extra crosschecking functionality. The result is shown in **Figure 7.6**; once again, when the check fails, the offending field gets a red border.

Figure 7.6 The two password fields cross-check to make sure their contents are identical. In this case, not so much.

Script 7.8 Use this script to compare the value of one field to another. Do they match?

```
window.onload = initForms;

function initForms() {
    for (var i=0; i< document.forms.length; i++) {
        document.forms[i].onsubmit = function() {return validForm();}
    }
}

function validForm() {
    var allGood = true;
    var allTags = document.getElementsByTagName("*");

    for (var i=0; i<allTags.length; i++) {
        if (!validTag(allTags[i])) {
            allGood = false;
        }
    }
    return allGood;

    function validTag(thisTag) {
        var outClass = "";
        var allClasses = thisTag.className.split(" ");

        for (var j=0; j<allClasses.length; j++) {
```

(script continues on next page)

Script 7.8 *continued*

```
                outClass += validBasedOnClass
                → (allClasses[j]) + " ";
            }

        thisTag.className = outClass;

        if (outClass.indexOf("invalid") > -1) {
            thisTag.focus();
            if (thisTag.nodeName == "INPUT") {
                thisTag.select();
            }
            return false;
        }
        return true;

    function validBasedOnClass(thisClass) {
        var classBack = "";

        switch(thisClass) {
            case "":
            case "invalid":
                break;
            case "reqd":
                if (allGood && thisTag.value
                → == "") {
                    classBack = "invalid ";
                }
                classBack += thisClass;
                break;
            default:
                if (allGood && !crossCheck
                → (thisTag,thisClass)) {
                    classBack = "invalid ";
                }
                classBack += thisClass;
        }
        return classBack;
    }

    function crossCheck(inTag,otherFieldID) {
        if (!document.getElementById
        → (otherFieldID)) {
            return false;
        }
        return (inTag.value == document.
        →getElementById(otherFieldID).value);
    }
  }
 }
}
```

To check one field against another:

1. `if (allGood &&`
`!crossCheck(thisTag,thisClass)) {`
`    classBack = "invalid ";`
`}`

We're now checking to make sure that the two password fields are the same. Because (see Script 7.5) the second password field has a class containing passwd1, this JavaScript knows that it has to crosscheck the second field against the first. Here in the default block of the conditional is where that's handled. If allGood is true *and* the crossCheck() function (see below) spotted a problem (and returned false), then we want to set classBack to invalid.

2. `function`
`crossCheck(inTag,otherFieldID) {`
`    if (!document.getElementById`
`    →(otherFieldID)) {`
`        return false;`
`    }`
`    return (inTag.value == document.`
`    →getElementById(otherFieldID).`
`    →value);`
`}`

Here's the crossCheck() function. It takes in the current tag and the id of the other field to check against. In this case, the current tag is the passwd2 <input> and the id of the other field is passwd1. If the other field doesn't exist, no check can be done; that's a problem, so the function returns false. Otherwise, the fields both exist, so we compare their values: if they're equivalent, true is returned; if they aren't, false is returned.

✔ Tip

■ This script does not check against a master password database to see if the password the user entered is valid; that requires a CGI on the server. It just makes sure that when a password is entered twice, it is the same value both times.

CHECKING FIELDS AGAINST EACH OTHER

Identifying Problem Fields

Changing the border of the input field to red is nice and all, but it would be better if we could make it a little clearer which field was the problem. In this example, you'll learn how to set the label around the field to be red and bold, making it clear where the problem lies (**Figure 7.7**). Once again, the HTML and CSS files have not changed (they're still Scripts 7.5 and 7.6). In **Script 7.9**, we've added a few lines of JavaScript to the previous Script 7.8 to help point out entry errors.

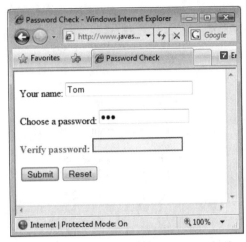

Figure 7.7 When there's a problem, you can make the field's label red and bold, as well as the field itself.

Script 7.9 This script highlights the incorrect field's label when it finds an error.

```
window.onload = initForms;

function initForms() {
    for (var i=0; i< document.forms.length; i++) {
        document.forms[i].onsubmit = function() {return validForm();}
    }
}

function validForm() {
    var allGood = true;
    var allTags = document.getElementsByTagName("*");

    for (var i=0; i<allTags.length; i++) {
        if (!validTag(allTags[i])) {
            allGood = false;
        }
    }
    return allGood;

    function validTag(thisTag) {
        var outClass = "";
        var allClasses = thisTag.className.split(" ");

        for (var j=0; j<allClasses.length; j++) {
            outClass += validBasedOnClass(allClasses[j]) + " ";
        }
```

(script continues on next page)

Script 7.9 *continued*

```
     thisTag.className = outClass;

     if (outClass.indexOf("invalid") > -1) {
         invalidLabel(thisTag.parentNode);
         thisTag.focus();
         if (thisTag.nodeName == "INPUT") {
             thisTag.select();
         }
         return false;
     }
     return true;

     function validBasedOnClass(thisClass) {
         var classBack = "";

         switch(thisClass) {
             case "":
             case "invalid":
                 break;
             case "reqd":
                 if (allGood && thisTag.value == "") {
                     classBack = "invalid ";
                 }
                 classBack += thisClass;
                 break;
             default:
                 if (allGood && !crossCheck(thisTag,thisClass)) {
                     classBack = "invalid ";
                 }
                 classBack += thisClass;
         }
         return classBack;
     }

     function crossCheck(inTag,otherFieldID) {
         if (!document.getElementById(otherFieldID)) {
             return false;
         }
         return (inTag.value == document.getElementById(otherFieldID).value);
     }

     function invalidLabel(parentTag) {
         if (parentTag.nodeName == "LABEL") {
             parentTag.className += " invalid";
         }
     }
    }
}
```

To identify a problem form field:

1. `invalidLabel(thisTag.parentNode);`

This line of code has been added to the invalid check inside `validTag()`. When the current field fails validation, we want to check to see if we can also invalidate the label surrounding the problem child. To do this, call the new `invalidLabel()` function (explained below) and pass it the *parent* of our current tag. That is, if there's a problem with the `passwd1` input field, we want both that tag *and* the `label` tag around it to be assigned a `class` of `invalid`. So, once we know that the `passwd1` input field has a problem, we pass its parent (the `label` tag) over to `invalidLabel()` to see if it's an appropriate element to mark invalid.

2.
```
function invalidLabel(parentTag) {
    if (parentTag.nodeName == "LABEL") {
        parentTag.className += " invalid";
    }
}
```

This function takes in a tag and checks to see if that tag is a label. If it is, it adds the attribute `invalid` to its class.

If we now try to submit the form and there's an error, we'll notice that the field labels for the problem fields turn bold and red when there's a problem. Fix the error, submit the form, and they'll turn black again.

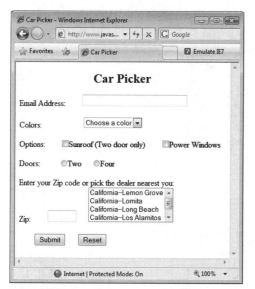

Figure 7.8 The Car Picker form uses text fields, a pop-up menu, check boxes, and radio buttons—all common form elements.

Putting Form Validation into Action

One interesting thing about the script that we built up in the last few examples is that it is largely independent of the HTML page that we used with it. In other words, you can substitute an entirely different page, with a completely different form, and you need to only make minor changes to the script to have it do all the validation tasks you want.

For example, take a look at **Figure 7.8**, which is a simplistic version of a form that could be used to customize a car that you want to purchase. The form includes a variety of options and interface elements, including radio buttons, menus, check boxes, and text fields that need validation for correct data entry. You'll find the HTML for this form in **Script 7.10**; we'll be using this HTML for the rest of the examples in this chapter.

The JavaScript file, **Script 7.11**, builds on the script that we've used earlier in this chapter. We've added a few lines to the script to handle the new interface elements, but otherwise the form is the same. In this example, you'll see what needed to be added to prepare the script for more validation, and subsequent examples will go deeper into specific types of form elements.

Script 7.10 Here's the entire HTML page for the Car Picker example.

```
                                          script
<!DOCTYPE html PUBLIC "-//W3C//DTD XHTML 1.0 Transitional//EN"
       "http://www.w3.org/TR/xhtml1/DTD/xhtml1-transitional.dtd">
<html xmlns="http://www.w3.org/1999/xhtml">
<head>
    <title>Car Picker</title>
    <link type="text/css" rel="stylesheet" href="script06.css" />
    <script type="text/javascript" src="script06.js"></script>
</head>
<body>
<h2 align="center">Car Picker</h2>
<form action="someAction.cgi">
    <p><label for="emailAddr">Email Address:
        <input id="emailAddr" type="text" size="30" class="reqd email" />
    </label></p>
    <p><label for="color">Colors:
        <select id="color" class="reqd">
            <option value="" selected="selected">Choose a color</option>
            <option value="Red">Red</option>
            <option value="Green">Green</option>
            <option value="Blue">Blue</option>
        </select>
    </label></p>
    <p>Options:
        <label for="sunroof"><input type="checkbox" id="sunroof" value="Yes" />Sunroof (Two door only)</
        → label>
        <label for="pWindows"><input type="checkbox" id="pWindows" value="Yes" />Power Windows</label>
    </p>
    <p><label for="DoorCt">Doors:  
        <input type="radio" id="twoDoor" name="DoorCt" value="twoDoor" class="radio" />Two
        <input type="radio" id="fourDoor" name="DoorCt" value="fourDoor" class="radio" />Four
    </label></p>
    <p><label for="zip">Enter your Zip code or pick the dealer nearest you:<br />
        Zip: <input id="zip" type="text" size="5" maxlength="5" class="isZip dealerList" />
        <select id="dealerList" size="4" class="zip">
            <option value="California--Lemon Grove">California--Lemon Grove</option>
            <option value="California--Lomita">California--Lomita</option>
            <option value="California--Long Beach">California--Long Beach</option>
            <option value="California--Los Alamitos">California--Los Alamitos</option>
            <option value="California--Los Angeles">California--Los Angeles</option>
        </select>
    </label></p>
    <p><input type="submit" value="Submit" /> <input type="reset" /></p>
</form>
</body>
</html>
```

Script 7.11 This script adds several blocks to the switch/case conditional, setting it up for later examples.

```
window.onload = initForms;

function initForms() {
    for (var i=0; i< document.forms.length; i++) {
        document.forms[i].onsubmit = function() {return validForm();}
    }
}

function validForm() {
    var allGood = true;
    var allTags = document.getElementsByTagName("*");

    for (var i=0; i<allTags.length; i++) {
        if (!validTag(allTags[i])) {
            allGood = false;
        }
    }
    return allGood;

    function validTag(thisTag) {
        var outClass = "";
        var allClasses = thisTag.className.split(" ");

        for (var j=0; j<allClasses.length; j++) {
            outClass += validBasedOnClass(allClasses[j]) + " ";
        }

        thisTag.className = outClass;

        if (outClass.indexOf("invalid") > -1) {
            invalidLabel(thisTag.parentNode);
            thisTag.focus();
            if (thisTag.nodeName == "INPUT") {
                thisTag.select();
            }
            return false;
        }
        return true;

        function validBasedOnClass(thisClass) {
            var classBack = "";

            switch(thisClass) {
                case "":
```

(script continues on next page)

To validate a form with many elements:

1. ```
   case "radio":
   case "isNum":
   case "isZip":
   case "email":
       classBack += thisClass;
       break;
   ```

   By adding additional blocks to the switch/case conditional inside the validBasedOnClass() function, we allow the script to check more fields and more situations. We've added radio, isNum, isZip, and email to the list. Although we're not validating them in this task, we want to prevent a problem when we do, so we add each to the list of attributes handled by the switch/case. Because there are no instructions in the first three blocks, all of them fall through to email, which just adds the attribute currently being checked onto classBack.

2. ```
   return (inTag.value != "" ||
   → document.getElementById
   → (otherFieldID).value != "");
   ```

   This line in crossCheck() has changed a bit. Instead of comparing the two fields to make sure they're the same, we're comparing two fields to make sure that at least one of them is set (this is in preparation for dealing with the Zip code and list elements at the end of the form). If either field contains a value, we return true. If not, we return false.

Script 7.11 *continued*

```
case "invalid":
    break;
case "reqd":
    if (allGood && thisTag.value
    → == "") {
        classBack = "invalid ";
    }
    classBack += thisClass;
    break;
case "radio":
case "isNum":
case "isZip":
case "email":
    classBack += thisClass;
    break;
default:
    if (allGood && !crossCheck
    → (thisTag,thisClass)) {
        classBack = "invalid ";
    }
    classBack += thisClass;
}
    return classBack;
}

function crossCheck(inTag,otherFieldID) {
    if (!document.getElementById
    → (otherFieldID)) {
        return false;
    }
    return (inTag.value != "" || document.
    → getElementById(otherFieldID).
    → value != "");
}

function invalidLabel(parentTag) {
    if (parentTag.nodeName == "LABEL") {
        parentTag.className += " invalid";
    }
}
}
}
}
```

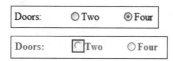

Figure 7.9 Radio buttons are the best way to let the user pick only one choice from a group of options.

Script 7.12 Only one radio button may be checked, and this JavaScript is there to enforce the interface law.

```
window.onload = initForms;

function initForms() {
    for (var i=0; i< document.forms.length;
    → i++) {
        document.forms[i].onsubmit = function()
        → {return validForm();}
    }
}

function validForm() {
    var allGood = true;
    var allTags = document.getElementsByTagName
    → ("*");

    for (var i=0; i<allTags.length; i++) {
        if (!validTag(allTags[i])) {
            allGood = false;
        }
    }
    return allGood;

    function validTag(thisTag) {
        var outClass = "";
        var allClasses = thisTag.className.split
        → (" ");

        for (var j=0; j<allClasses.length; j++) {
            outClass += validBasedOnClass
            → (allClasses[j]) + " ";
        }

        thisTag.className = outClass;
```

(script continues on next page)

Working with Radio Buttons

Radio buttons are an either/or interface element that let the user pick one (and only one) choice within a group of options. Radio buttons should be used when one of those options is required. As shown in **Figure 7.9**, the form uses radio buttons to let the hypothetical car buyer choose between a two-door or four-door automobile. In this case, you can only pick one of these choices, and you must make a choice.

As seen in **Script 7.12**, it doesn't take much scripting to check that one button is selected. We use a technique where we loop through each button and check its status and then turn the radio buttons' label and buttons red and bold if no button is picked.

To make sure that the user picks a radio button:

1. `if (allGood && !radioPicked`
`→ (thisTag.name)) {`
`    classBack = "invalid ";`

This goes into the `radio` block of the `switch/case` conditional. We want to check to make sure at least one of the radio buttons was picked, and the new `radioPicked()` function handles that. If it returns false, then we set `classBack` to `invalid`.

2. `function radioPicked(radioName) {`
`    var radioSet = "";`

Start the new `radioPicked()` function, and initialize the `radioSet` variable.

This function takes in the name of the *set* of radio buttons—in this case, `DoorCt`, as found in Script 7.10. Note that that's not the `id` of the current tag or a `class` or anything that we usually see, but its *name*. The `name` attribute of `<input>` tags is how HTML knows which radio buttons are grouped together; that is, all `<input>` tags with the same name attribute are part of one radio button set.

Script 7.12 *continued*

```
if (outClass.indexOf("invalid") > -1) {
    invalidLabel(thisTag.parentNode);
    thisTag.focus();
    if (thisTag.nodeName == "INPUT") {
        thisTag.select();
    }
    return false;
}
return true;

function validBasedOnClass(thisClass) {
    var classBack = "";

    switch(thisClass) {
        case "":
        case "invalid":
            break;
        case "reqd":
            if (allGood && thisTag.value
→ == "") {
                classBack = "invalid ";
            }
            classBack += thisClass;
            break;
        case "radio":
            if (allGood && !radioPicked
→ (thisTag.name)) {
                classBack = "invalid ";
            }
            classBack += thisClass;
            break;
        case "isNum":
        case "isZip":
        case "email":
            classBack += thisClass;
            break;
        default:
            if (allGood && !crossCheck
→ (thisTag,thisClass)) {
                classBack = "invalid ";
            }
```

(script continues on next page)

Script 7.12 *continued*

```
                classBack += thisClass;
        }
        return classBack;
    }

    function crossCheck(inTag,otherFieldID) {
        if (!document.getElementById
        → (otherFieldID)) {
            return false;
        }
        return (inTag.value != "" ||
        → document.getElementById
        → (otherFieldID).value != "");
    }

    function radioPicked(radioName) {
        var radioSet = "";

        for (var k=0; k<document.forms.length;
        k++) {
            if (!radioSet) {
                radioSet = document.forms[k]
                → [radioName];
            }
        }
        if (!radioSet) {
            return false;
        }
        for (k=0; k<radioSet.length; k++) {
            if (radioSet[k].checked) {
                return true;
            }
        }
        return false;
    }

    function invalidLabel(parentTag) {
        if (parentTag.nodeName == "LABEL") {
            parentTag.className += " invalid";
        }
    }
}
```

3. `for (var k=0; k<document.forms.`
`→ length; k++) {`
`    if (!radioSet) {`
`        radioSet = document.forms[k]`
`        → [radioName];`
`    }`
`}`

We next loop through all the forms on the current page. We know the name of the radio button set, but we don't know what form it's a part of, and any given page can have several forms. Because this function is inside another function looping on j, we use k for our loop here.

We then try to set `radioSet` to the name of this set of radio buttons inside the form we're looking at. If it's found, `radioSet` will then have a value.

4. `if (!radioSet) {`
`    return false;`

When the loop is done, we look at `radioSet`—if it hasn't been set, we return false, because we couldn't find it, and so, couldn't check it.

5. `for (k=0; k<radioSet.length; k++) {`
`    if (radioSet[k].checked) {`
`        return true;`
`    }`
`}`

Okay, we've got the radio button set we want to inspect. Now, we start another loop to look through each button. When we find one that's checked, we return true, because we're done.

6. `return false;`

If we make it to the end of the loop, we've looked at the entire set and nothing was clicked. In that case, return false and change the radio buttons' label and make the buttons red and bold.

Setting One Field with Another

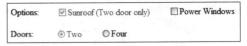

Options:	☑ Sunroof (Two door only)	☐ Power Windows
Doors:	◉ Two	○ Four

Figure 7.10 When the user checks the sunroof option, the script automatically sets the two-door radio button.

With your forms, you'll often find that if the user makes one choice, that choice dictates the value of other fields on the form. For example, let's say that the sunroof option is only available on a two-door model. You could deal with this in two ways. First, you could check the entry and put up an alert dialog if the user makes the wrong choice. But it's a slicker design to simply make the entry for the user. So if they pick the sunroof, the script automatically clicks the two-door button, as in **Figure 7.10. Script 7.13** shows you how.

To set a field value automatically:

1. `document.getElementById("sunroof").` → `onclick = doorSet;`

   This line of code has been added to `initForms()`. When the user clicks the sunroof check box, the `doorSet()` function will be called.

2. ```
   function doorSet() {
       if (this.checked) {
           document.getElementById
           → ("twoDoor").checked = true;
       }
   }
   ```

   This new function checks to see if the sunroof field was checked; if so, it sets the `twoDoor` radio button to true. If we've clicked the sunroof check box to turn it off, nothing happens.

✔ Tip

■ You may have noticed that there's no check to see if the user clicked the sunroof and then reset the `fourDoor` radio button. We'll leave that as an exercise for you, the reader.

Script 7.13 A sophisticated way to handle user choices lets you control and set field entries based on other choices made by the user.

```
window.onload = initForms;

function initForms() {
    for (var i=0; i< document.forms.length;
    → i++) {
        document.forms[i].onsubmit = function()
        → {return validForm();}
    }
    document.getElementById("sunroof").onclick
    → = doorSet;
}

function validForm() {
    var allGood = true;
    var allTags = document.getElementsByTagName
    → ("*");

    for (var i=0; i<allTags.length; i++) {
        if (!validTag(allTags[i])) {
            allGood = false;
        }
    }
    return allGood;

    function validTag(thisTag) {
        var outClass = "";
        var allClasses = thisTag.className.split
        → (" ");

        for (var j=0; j<allClasses.length; j++) {
            outClass += validBasedOnClass
            → (allClasses[j]) + " ";
        }
```

(script continues on next page)
```

Script 7.13 *continued*

```
                                                  script
      thisTag.className = outClass;

      if (outClass.indexOf("invalid") > -1) {
         invalidLabel(thisTag.parentNode);
         thisTag.focus();
         if (thisTag.nodeName == "INPUT") {
            thisTag.select();
         }
         return false;
      }
      return true;

      function validBasedOnClass(thisClass) {
         var classBack = "";

         switch(thisClass) {
            case "":
            case "invalid":
               break;
            case "reqd":
               if (allGood && thisTag.value == "") {
                  classBack = "invalid ";
               }
               classBack += thisClass;
               break;
            case "radio":
               if (allGood && !radioPicked(thisTag.name)) {
                  classBack = "invalid ";
               }
               classBack += thisClass;
               break;
            case "isNum":
            case "isZip":
            case "email":
               classBack += thisClass;
               break;
            default:
               if (allGood && !crossCheck(thisTag,thisClass)) {
                  classBack = "invalid ";
               }
               classBack += thisClass;
```

(script continues on next page)

SETTING ONE FIELD WITH ANOTHER

Script 7.13 *continued*

```
        }
        return classBack;
    }

    function crossCheck(inTag,otherFieldID) {
        if (!document.getElementById(otherFieldID)) {
            return false;
        }
        return (inTag.value != "" || document.getElementById(otherFieldID).value != "");
    }

    function radioPicked(radioName) {
        var radioSet = "";

        for (var k=0; k<document.forms.length; k++) {
            if (!radioSet) {
                radioSet = document.forms[k][radioName];
            }
        }
        if (!radioSet) {
            return false;
        }
        for (k=0; k<radioSet.length; k++) {
            if (radioSet[k].checked) {
                return true;
            }
        }
        return false;
    }

    function invalidLabel(parentTag) {
        if (parentTag.nodeName == "LABEL") {
            parentTag.className += " invalid";
        }
    }
}

function doorSet() {
    if (this.checked) {
        document.getElementById("twoDoor").checked = true;
    }
}
```

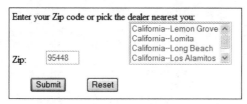

Figure 7.11 You can make sure that the user either enters a Zip code or makes a selection from the scrolling list.

Script 7.14 Banish incorrect letters from your Zip codes with just a few lines of JavaScript.

```
window.onload = initForms;

function initForms() {
    for (var i=0; i< document.forms.length;
    → i++) {
        document.forms[i].onsubmit = function()
        → {return validForm();}
    }
    document.getElementById("sunroof").onclick
    → = doorSet;
}

function validForm() {
    var allGood = true;
    var allTags = document.getElementsByTagName
    → ("*");

    for (var i=0; i<allTags.length; i++) {
        if (!validTag(allTags[i])) {
            allGood = false;
        }
    }
    return allGood;

    function validTag(thisTag) {
        var outClass = "";
        var allClasses = thisTag.className.split
        → (" ");
```

(script continues on next page)

Validating Zip Codes

Those wacky users can type almost anything into a form, so you'll want to make sure that if they entered anything into the Zip code field (**Figure 7.11**) that it contains only numbers. **Script 7.14** shows you how.

To make sure Zip codes are valid:

1. `if (allGood && !isNum(thisTag.`
   `→ value)) {`
      `classBack = "invalid ";`
   `}`
   `classBack += thisClass;`

   This goes into the isNum block of the switch/case conditional. If the entry is non-numeric, isNum() returns false.

2. `if (allGood && !isZip(thisTag.`
   `→ value)) {`
      `classBack = "invalid ";`

   This line has been added to the isZip switch/case block. If the field is not blank and it's not a Zip code, isZip() returns false.

3. `if (passedVal == "") {`
      `return false;`
   `}`

   Inside the isNum() function, if passedVal is empty, then the field we're looking at isn't a number. When that happens, return false, signaling an error.

4. `for (var k=0; k<passedVal.length;`
   `→ k++) {`

   Now scan through the length of passedVal, incrementing the k counter each time it goes through the loop. We're using k because we're already inside two other loops (i and j).

continues on next page

5. `if (passedVal.charAt(k) < "0") {`
   `return false;`
`}`
`if (passedVal.charAt(k) > "9") {`
   `return false;`
`}`

The charAt() operator checks the character at the position k. If the character is less than "0" or greater than "9," it isn't a digit, so bail out and declare the input to be non-numeric, or false.

6. `return true;`

If we make it here, we've got a number, so we return true.

7. `function isZip(inZip) {`
   `if (inZip == "") {`
     `return true;`
   `}`
   `return (isNum(inZip));`
`}`

In the context of this form, it's valid for the Zip code field to be empty. Because of that, we first check the field to see if the user entered anything, and if they didn't, we return true—it's a valid entry. If they did enter anything, though, it needs to be numeric, so that's the next check.

✔ Tips

- If at some later point we wanted to add a new field to the HTML form that had to be numeric, no new JavaScript code would need to be written. Instead, we'd just use the now-existing isNum check.

- Remember, it's the World Wide Web, not the American Web. If your site is likely to draw attention from outside the United States, don't require that the user enter a Zip code. Addresses outside the United States may or may not have postal codes, and those postal codes may not be numeric.

Script 7.14 *continued*

```
for (var j=0; j<allClasses.length; j++) {
    outClass += validBasedOnClass
    → (allClasses[j]) + " ";
}

thisTag.className = outClass;

if (outClass.indexOf("invalid") > -1) {
    invalidLabel(thisTag.parentNode);
    thisTag.focus();
    if (thisTag.nodeName == "INPUT") {
        thisTag.select();
    }
    return false;
}
return true;
}

function validBasedOnClass(thisClass) {
    var classBack = "";

    switch(thisClass) {
        case "":
        case "invalid":
            break;
        case "reqd":
            if (allGood && thisTag.value
            → == "") {
                classBack = "invalid ";
            }
            classBack += thisClass;
            break;
        case "radio":
            if (allGood && !radioPicked
            → (thisTag.name)) {
                classBack = "invalid ";
            }
            classBack += thisClass;
            break;
        case "isNum":
            if (allGood && !isNum(thisTag.
            → value)) {
```

(script continues on next page)

Script 7.14 *continued*

```
                    classBack = "invalid ";
                }
                classBack += thisClass;
                break;
            case "isZip":
                if (allGood && !isZip(thisTag.value)) {
                    classBack = "invalid ";
                }
                classBack += thisClass;
                break;
            case "email":
                classBack += thisClass;
                break;
            default:
                if (allGood && !crossCheck(thisTag,thisClass)) {
                    classBack = "invalid ";
                }
                classBack += thisClass;
        }
        return classBack;
    }

    function crossCheck(inTag,otherFieldID) {
        if (!document.getElementById(otherFieldID)) {
            return false;
        }
        return (inTag.value != "" || document.getElementById(otherFieldID).value != "");
    }

    function radioPicked(radioName) {
        var radioSet = "";

        for (var k=0; k<document.forms.length; k++) {
            if (!radioSet) {
                radioSet = document.forms[k][radioName];
            }
        }
        if (!radioSet) {
            return false;
        }
        for (k=0; k<radioSet.length; k++) {
```

(script continues on next page)

Script 7.14 *continued*

```
                  if (radioSet[k].checked) {
                      return true;
                  }
              }
              return false;
          }

          function isNum(passedVal) {
              if (passedVal == "") {
                  return false;
              }
              for (var k=0; k<passedVal.length; k++) {
                  if (passedVal.charAt(k) < "0") {
                      return false;
                  }
                  if (passedVal.charAt(k) > "9") {
                      return false;
                  }
              }
              return true;
          }

          function isZip(inZip) {
              if (inZip == "") {
                  return true;
              }
              return (isNum(inZip));
          }

          function invalidLabel(parentTag) {
              if (parentTag.nodeName == "LABEL") {
                  parentTag.className += " invalid";
              }
          }
      }
  }

  function doorSet() {
      if (this.checked) {
          document.getElementById("twoDoor").checked = true;
      }
  }
```

Email Address: badaddress@chalcedony/.com

Figure 7.12 Here's an example of the kind of entry error that the email validation script will catch.

Script 7.15 By scanning through the text within an email field on your form, you can ensure that you get proper email addresses.

```
window.onload = initForms;

function initForms() {
    for (var i=0; i< document.forms.length;
    → i++) {
        document.forms[i].onsubmit = function()
        → {return validForm();}
    }
    document.getElementById("sunroof").onclick
    → = doorSet;
}

function validForm() {
    var allGood = true;
    var allTags = document.getElementsByTagName
    → ("*");

    for (var i=0; i<allTags.length; i++) {
        if (!validTag(allTags[i])) {
            allGood = false;
        }
    }
    return allGood;

    function validTag(thisTag) {
        var outClass = "";
        var allClasses = thisTag.className.split
        → (" ");

        for (var j=0; j<allClasses.length; j++) {
            outClass += validBasedOnClass
            → (allClasses[j]) + " ";
        }
```

(script continues on next page)

Validating Email Addresses

Internet addresses can be tricky things for users—especially new users—to type. You can help them out by scanning the email address they enter and checking it for proper form. For example, you can check that there's only one @ sign, and that there are no invalid characters, as there are in **Figure 7.12**. The limit, of course, is that your script can't catch misspellings, so if the user meant to type in joe@myprovider.com and instead entered joe@yprovider.com, the mistake will go through. **Script 7.15** shows you how to snoop through an address for errors.

To validate an email address:

1. `if (allGood && !validEmail(thisTag.`
   `→ value)) {`
       `classBack = "invalid ";`

   This line has been added to the email switch/case block. If the validEmail() function returns false, set the class to be invalid.

2. `var invalidChars = " /:,;";`

   Inside the validEmail() function, create a variable, invalidChars, that contains the five most likely invalid characters in an email address: blank space, slash, colon, comma, and semicolon.

3. `if (email == "") {`
       `return false;`

   This test says, "If the contents of email is nothing (or empty), then the result is false."

   continues on next page

4. `for (var k=0; k<invalidChars.length;`
`→ k++) {`

In this `for` statement, start a loop that scans through the `invalidChars` string. Start by initializing the counter k to zero, then, each time through the loop that k is less than the length of the string, add 1 to k with the ++ increment operator.

5. `var badChar = invalidChars.charAt(k);`
`if (email.indexOf(badChar) > -1) {`
`    return false;`
`}`

The `badChar` variable is set to the invalid character in position k in the `invalidChars` string, and we then check to see if that character is in `email`. If so, `indexOf()` returns the position where it was found; if not, it returns a -1. If we get a value other than -1, we've found a bad character, and so we then return a value of false.

6. `var atPos = email.indexOf("@",1);`
`if (atPos == -1) {`
`    return false;`
`}`

The `atPos` variable holds the position of the @ sign. Using `indexOf`, the script checks for the first @ sign, starting at the second character in the address. If the result is that the position of the @ sign is –1, it means that there is no @ sign in the address, and you've got trouble in Address City.

Script 7.15 *continued*

```
thisTag.className = outClass;

if (outClass.indexOf("invalid") > -1) {
    invalidLabel(thisTag.parentNode);
    thisTag.focus();
    if (thisTag.nodeName == "INPUT") {
        thisTag.select();
    }
    return false;
}
return true;

function validBasedOnClass(thisClass) {
    var classBack = "";

    switch(thisClass) {
        case "":
        case "invalid":
            break;
        case "reqd":
            if (allGood && thisTag.value
→ == "") {
                classBack = "invalid ";
            }
            classBack += thisClass;
            break;
        case "radio":
            if (allGood && !radioPicked
→ (thisTag.name)) {
                classBack = "invalid ";
            }
            classBack += thisClass;
            break;
        case "isNum":
            if (allGood && !isNum
→ (thisTag.value)) {
                classBack = "invalid ";
            }
            classBack += thisClass;
            break;
        case "isZip":
```

(script continues on next page)

Script 7.15 *continued*

```
            if (allGood && !isZip
            → (thisTag.value)) {
               classBack = "invalid ";
            }
            classBack += thisClass;
            break;
         case "email":
            if (allGood && !validEmail
            → (thisTag.value)) {
               classBack = "invalid ";
            }
            classBack += thisClass;
            break;
         default:
            if (allGood && !crossCheck
            → (thisTag,thisClass)) {
               classBack = "invalid ";
            }
            classBack += thisClass;
      }
      return classBack;
}

function crossCheck(inTag,otherFieldID) {
   if (!document.getElementById
   → (otherFieldID)) {
      return false;
   }
   return (inTag.value != "" ||
   → document.getElementById
   → (otherFieldID).value != "");
}

function radioPicked(radioName) {
   var radioSet = "";

   for (var k=0; k<document.forms.
   → length; k++) {
      if (!radioSet) {
         radioSet = document.forms[k]
         → [radioName];
      }
```

(script continues on next page)

7.
```
if (email.indexOf("@",atPos+1)
→ != -1) {
   return false;
}
```

Now the script is making sure that there is only one @ sign and rejecting anything with more than one @, by checking characters beginning at 1 past where we found the first @.

8.
```
var periodPos = email.indexOf
→ (".",atPos);
if (periodPos == -1) {
   return false;
}
```

Now the script checks that there is a period somewhere after the @ sign. If not, we get a false result.

9.
```
if (periodPos+3 > email.length) {
   return false;
}
return true;
```

Finally, the script requires that there be at least two characters after the period in the address. If we made it this far without a false result, then the value of the function validEmail is true, meaning we have a good email address.

✔ Tips

- There's a difference between validating an email address and verifying it. This script validates addresses by making sure that what the user entered is in the proper form for an email address. But it doesn't verify that the address really exists. The only way to do that would be to send an email message to the address and see if the message bounces. Besides the fact that you would probably annoy your users a great deal if you sent such a verifying message, it can take hours for a message to bounce, and the user isn't going to wait patiently at your form in the meantime.

- This script routine doesn't catch every possible incorrect email address, just the most likely errors. A full check for every possible bad email address would take several pages of code. If you think about it a bit, you can probably come up with possible mistakes that fall outside the checks in this script.

Script 7.15 *continued*

```
    }
    if (!radioSet) {
        return false;
    }
    for (k=0; k<radioSet.length; k++) {
        if (radioSet[k].checked) {
            return true;
        }
    }
    return false;
}


function isNum(passedVal) {
    if (passedVal == "") {
        return false;
    }
    for (var k=0; k<passedVal.length;
    → k++) {
        if (passedVal.charAt(k) < "0") {
            return false;
        }
        if (passedVal.charAt(k) > "9") {
            return false;
        }
    }
    return true;
}


function isZip(inZip) {
    if (inZip == "") {
        return true;
    }
    return (isNum(inZip));
}


function validEmail(email) {
    var invalidChars = " /:,;";

    if (email == "") {
        return false;
    }
```

(script continues on next page)

Script 7.15 *continued*

```
                for (var k=0; k<invalidChars.length; k++) {
                    var badChar = invalidChars.charAt(k);
                    if (email.indexOf(badChar) > -1) {
                        return false;
                    }
                }
                var atPos = email.indexOf("@",1);
                if (atPos == -1) {
                    return false;
                }
                if (email.indexOf("@",atPos+1) != -1) {
                    return false;
                }
                var periodPos = email.indexOf(".",atPos);
                if (periodPos == -1) {
                    return false;
                }
                if (periodPos+3 > email.length)  {
                    return false;
                }
                return true;
            }

            function invalidLabel(parentTag) {
                if (parentTag.nodeName == "LABEL") {
                    parentTag.className += " invalid";
                }
            }
        }
    }
}

function doorSet() {
    if (this.checked) {
        document.getElementById("twoDoor").checked = true;
    }
}
```

FORMS AND REGULAR EXPRESSIONS

8

Regular expressions are an amazingly powerful way to validate and format text strings. Using regular expressions, you can write a line or two of JavaScript code that can accomplish tasks that otherwise would have taken several dozen lines.

A *regular expression* (often abbreviated as *RegExp* or called by its synonym *grep*) is a pattern, written using special symbols, which describes one or more text strings. You use regular expressions to match patterns of text, so that your script can easily recognize and manipulate text. Like an arithmetic expression, you create a regular expression by using *operators*, in this case operators that work on text, rather than numbers. There are many regular expression operators, and we'll look at some of the most common in this chapter. By learning and using these operators, you'll be able to save yourself a huge amount of effort whenever you need to detect and manipulate text strings.

continues on next page

Regular expressions are also commonly considered to be one of the geekiest parts of programming. You've gotten to the point where you think that you have a good grasp of JavaScript, and then you'll look at a script that contains a regular expression, and it makes no sense at all. If you don't know the syntax, you don't have any way of even guessing what's going on. What does all that gibberish mean?

But the syntax isn't that hard, so long as you break the gibberish down into small, meaningful pieces (at which point it's no longer gibberish). In this chapter, we'll demystify regular expression syntax and discuss how to make your code tighter and more powerful using regular expressions.

FORMS AND REGULAR EXPRESSIONS

Are You Freaking Out Yet?

If this is the first time that you've been exposed to regular expressions, chances are you're feeling a bit intimidated right about now. We've included this chapter here because it makes the most sense to use regular expressions to validate form entries. But the rest of the material in this book doesn't build on this chapter, so if you want to skip on to the next chapter until you've got a bit more scripting experience under your belt, we won't mind a bit.

On the other hand, regular expressions are well worth the investment of your time. They're not only useful in JavaScript; regular expressions can be used everywhere from other programming languages (such as Perl, Java, Python, and PHP) to Apache configuration files to inside text editors such as BBEdit and TextMate. Even Adobe Dreamweaver and (to a certain extent) Microsoft Word use regular expressions to make search and replace more powerful.

Script 8.1 The HTML for the email validation example.

```
                    script
<!DOCTYPE html PUBLIC "-//W3C//DTD XHTML 1.0
→ Transitional//EN"
        "http://www.w3.org/TR/xhtml1/DTD/
        → xhtml1-transitional.dtd">
<html xmlns="http://www.w3.org/1999/xhtml">
<head>
    <title>Email Validation</title>
    <link type="text/css" rel="stylesheet" href=
    → "script01.css" />
    <script type="text/javascript" src=
    → "script01.js"></script>
</head>
<body>
    <h2 align="center">Email Validation</h2>
    <form action="someAction.cgi">
        <p><label>Email Address:
        <input class="email" type="text"
        → size="50" /></label></p>
        <p><input type="reset" /> <input
        → type="submit" value="Submit" /></p>
    </form>
</body>
</html>
```

Validating an Email Address with Regular Expressions

Back in Chapter 7, one of the tasks was validating an email address. To do the job, the script needed to be relatively long. **Script 8.2**, at its heart, does exactly the same thing as Script 7.15; but by using regular expressions, it takes many fewer lines, and you get a more rigorous result. You'll find the simple HTML in **Script 8.1**, and the CSS is unchanged from Script 7.6.

To validate an email address using regular expressions:

1. `var re = /^\w+([\.-]?\w+)*@\w+` `→ ([\.-]?\w+)*(\.\w{2,3})+$/;`

   Yow! What on earth is this? Don't panic; it's just a regular expression in the `validEmail()` function. Let's break it apart and take it piece by piece. Like any line of JavaScript, you read a regular expression from left to right.

   First, `re` is just a variable. We've given it the name `re` so that when we use it later, we'll remember that it's a regular expression. The line sets the value of `re` to the regular expression on the right side of the equals sign.

   A regular expression always begins and ends with a slash, / (of course, there is still a semicolon here, to denote the end of the JavaScript line, but the semicolon is not part of the regular expression). Everything in between the slashes is part of the regular expression.

   continues on next page

The caret ^ means that we're going to use this expression to examine a string starting at the string's beginning. If the caret was left off, the email address might show as valid even though there was a bunch of garbage at the beginning of the string.

The expression \w means any *one* character, "a" through "z", "A" through "Z", "0" through "9", or underscore. An email address must start with one of these characters.

The plus sign + means *one or more of* whatever the previous item was that we're checking on. In this case, an email address must start with one or more of any combination of the characters "a" through "z", "A" through "Z", "0" through "9", or underscore.

The opening parenthesis (signifies a group. It means that we're going to want to refer to everything inside the parentheses in some way later, so we put them into a group now.

The brackets [] are used to show that we can have any *one* of the characters inside. In this example, the characters \ . - are inside the brackets. We want to allow the user to enter either a period or a dash, but the period has a special meaning to regular expressions, so we need to preface it with a backslash \ to show that we really want to refer to the period itself, not its special meaning. Using a backslash before a special character is called *escaping* that character. Because of the brackets, the entered string can have either a period or a dash here, but not both. Note that the dash doesn't stand for any special character, just itself.

The question mark ? means that we can have *zero or one* of the previous item. So along with it being okay to have either a period or a dash in the first part of the email address (the part before the @), it's also okay to have neither.

Script 8.2 These few lines of JavaScript go a long way to validate email addresses.

```
window.onload = initForms;

function initForms() {
    for (var i=0; i< document.forms.length;
→ i++) {
        document.forms[i].onsubmit =
        → function() {return validForm();}
    }
}

function validForm() {
    var allGood = true;
    var allTags = document.getElementsByTagName
    → ("*");

    for (var i=0; i<allTags.length; i++) {
        if (!validTag(allTags[i])) {
            allGood = false;
        }
    }
    return allGood;

    function validTag(thisTag) {
        var outClass = "";
        var allClasses = thisTag.className.split
        → (" ");

        for (var j=0; j<allClasses.length; j++) {
            outClass += validBasedOnClass
            → (allClasses[j]) + " ";
        }

        thisTag.className = outClass;

        if (outClass.indexOf("invalid") > -1) {
            invalidLabel(thisTag.parentNode);
            thisTag.focus();
            if (thisTag.nodeName == "INPUT") {
                thisTag.select();
            }
            return false;
        }
        return true;
```

(script continues on next page)

Script 8.2 *continued*

```
function validBasedOnClass(thisClass) {
   var classBack = "";

   switch(thisClass) {
      case "":
      case "invalid":
         break;
      case "email":
         if (allGood && !validEmail
         → (thisTag.value)) classBack
         → = "invalid ";
      default:
         classBack += thisClass;
   }
   return classBack;
}

function validEmail(email) {
   var re = /^\w+([\.-]?\w+)*@\w+
   → ([\.-]?\w+)*(\.\w{2,3})+$/;

   return re.test(email);
}

function invalidLabel(parentTag) {
   if (parentTag.nodeName == "LABEL") {
      parentTag.className += " invalid";
   }
}
}
}
```

Following the ?, we once again have \w+, which says that the period or dash must be followed by some other characters.

The closing parenthesis) says that this is the end of the group. That's followed by an asterisk *, which means that we can have *zero or more* of the previous item—in this case, whatever was inside the parentheses. So while "dori" is a valid email prefix, so is "testing-testing-1-2-3".

The @ character doesn't stand for anything besides itself, located between the email address and the domain name.

The \w+ once again says that a domain name must start with one or more of any character "a" through "z", "A" through "Z", "0" through "9", or underscore. That's again followed by ([\.-]?\w+)* which says that periods and dashes are allowed within the suffix of an email address.

We then have another group within a set of parentheses: \.\w{2,3} which says that we're expecting to find a period followed by characters. In this case, the numbers inside the braces mean *either 2 or 3* of the previous item (in this case the \w, meaning a letter, number, or underscore). Following the right parenthesis around this group is a +, which again means that the previous item (the group, in this case) must exist *one or more* times. This will match ".com" or ".edu", for instance, as well as "ox.ac.uk".

And finally, the regular expression ends with a dollar sign $, which signifies that the matched string must end here. This keeps the script from validating an email address that starts off properly but contains garbage characters at the end. The slash closes the regular expression. The semicolon ends the JavaScript statement, as usual.

continues on next page

2. `return re.test(email);`

This single line takes the regular expression defined in the previous step and uses the `test()` method to check the validity of `email`. If the entered string doesn't fit the pattern stored in `re`, `test()` returns false, and the user sees the incorrect field and its label turn red and bold, as shown in **Figure 8.1**. Otherwise, a valid entry returns true (**Figure 8.2**), and the form submits the email address to a CGI, `someAction.cgi` for additional processing.

✔ Tips

■ This code doesn't match every possible legal variation of email addresses, just the ones that you're likely to want to allow a person to enter.

■ Note that in Script 8.2, after we assigned the value of `re`, we used `re` as an object in step 2. Like any other JavaScript variable, the result of a regular expression can be an object.

■ Compare the `validEmail()` functions in Scripts 7.15 and 8.2. The former has 27 lines of code; the latter, only four. They do the same thing, so you can see that the power of regular expressions can save you a lot of coding.

■ In Script 8.1, `someAction.cgi` is just an example name for a CGI—it's literally "some action"—any action that you want it to be. If you want to learn to write CGIs, we recommend Elizabeth Castro's book *Perl and CGI for the World Wide Web, Second Edition: Visual QuickStart Guide*.

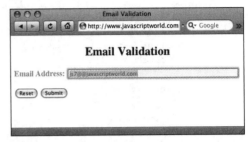

Figure 8.1 Here's the result if the user enters an invalid email address: the label and field turn red and bold.

Figure 8.2 But this address is just fine.

■ You'll see in **Table 8.1** that the special characters (sometimes called *meta characters*) in regular expressions are case-sensitive. Keep this in mind when debugging scripts that use regular expressions.

■ There are characters in regular expressions that modify other operators. We've listed them in **Table 8.2**.

Table 8.1

Regular Expression Special Characters	
CHARACTER	**MATCHES**
\	Toggles between literal and special characters; for example, "\w" means the special value of "\w" (see below) instead of the literal "w", but "\$" means to ignore the special value of "$" (see below) and use the "$" character instead
^	Beginning of a string
$	End of a string
*	Zero or more times
+	One or more times
?	Zero or one time
.	Any character except newline
\b	Word boundary
\B	Non-word boundary
\d	Any digit 0 through 9 (same as `[0-9]`)
\D	Any non-digit
\f	Form feed
\n	New line
\r	Carriage return
\s	Any single white space character (same as `[ \f\n\r\t\v]`)
\S	Any single non-white space character
\t	Tab
\v	Vertical tab
\w	Any letter, number, or the underscore (same as `[a-zA-Z0-9_]`)
\W	Any character other than a letter, number, or underscore
\xnn	The ASCII character defined by the hexadecimal number nn
\onn	The ASCII character defined by the octal number nn
\cX	The control character X
[abcde]	A character set that matches any one of the enclosed characters
[^abcde]	A complemented or negated character set; one that does not match any of the enclosed characters
[a-e]	A character set that matches any one in the range of enclosed characters
[\b]	The literal backspace character (different from \b)
{n}	Exactly *n* occurrences of the previous character
{n,}	At least *n* occurrences of the previous character
{n,m}	Between *n* and *m* occurrences of the previous character
()	A grouping, which is also stored for later use
x|y	Either x or y

Table 8.2

Regular Expression Modifiers	
MODIFIER	**MEANING**
g	Search for all possible matches (globally), not just the first
i	Search without case-sensitivity

Validating a File Name

There are many things that can be done with regular expressions, but one of the most useful is validating entry fields in forms on your Web pages. **Script 8.3** expects the user to enter a valid URL of an image, and the regular expression helps to make sure that users do as you've requested (specifically, that there has to be a suffix that denotes an image file). **Figure 8.3** shows the appearance of the page when an invalid entry was accidentally entered, and **Figure 8.4** shows the result when the image name was typed correctly.

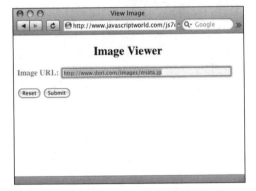

Figure 8.3 If the user enters something that isn't a valid image file name, the page shows an error, thanks to regular expressions.

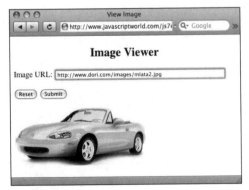

Figure 8.4 When the image name is entered correctly, the image is displayed on the page.

Script 8.3 This script asks for an image location and, if it passes the validation, displays the image on the page.

```
window.onload = initForms;

function initForms() {
    for (var i=0; i< document.forms.length;
    → i++) {
        document.forms[i].onsubmit = function()
        → {return validForm();}
    }
}

function validForm() {
    var allGood = true;
    var allTags = document.getElementsByTagName
    → ("*");

    for (var i=0; i<allTags.length; i++) {
        if (!validTag(allTags[i])) {
            allGood = false;
        }
    }
    return false;

    function validTag(thisTag) {
        var outClass = "";
        var allClasses = thisTag.className.split
        → (" ");

        for (var j=0; j<allClasses.length; j++) {
            outClass += validBasedOnClass
            → (allClasses[j]) + " ";
        }

        thisTag.className = outClass;

        if (outClass.indexOf("invalid") > -1) {
            invalidLabel(thisTag.parentNode);
            thisTag.focus();
            if (thisTag.nodeName == "INPUT") {
                thisTag.select();
            }
            return false;
```

(script continues on next page)

Script 8.3 *continued*

```
                                    script
      }
      return true;

   function validBasedOnClass(thisClass) {
      var classBack = "";

      switch(thisClass) {
         case "":
         case "invalid":
            break;
         case "imgURL":
            if (allGood && !imgURL
            → (thisTag.value)) classBack
            → = "invalid ";
         default:
            classBack += thisClass;
      }
      return classBack;
   }

   function imgURL(newURL) {
      var re = /^(file|http):\/\/\S+
      → \/\S+\.(gif|jpg|jpeg|png)$/i;

      if (re.test(newURL)) {
         document.getElementById
         → ("chgImg").src = newURL;
         return true;
      }
      return false;
   }

   function invalidLabel(parentTag) {
      if (parentTag.nodeName == "LABEL") {
         parentTag.className += " invalid";
      }
   }
}
```

To validate a URL:

◆ `var re = /^(file|http):\/\/\S+\/\S+`
  `→ \.(gif|jpg|jpeg|png)$/i;`

This is in the `imgURL()` function. As in the previous example, we want to check the full field entered, so the regular expression begins with `/^` and ends with `$/`. The input can begin with either the text "http" or "file", so the two are grouped together with a | to show that either one or the other value is acceptable. Whether the user is getting the image off of their hard drive or off the Web, the next characters have to be "://", so that's checked for next. Note that each of the forward slashes must be escaped individually (that's what the two instances of \/ are, escaped forward slashes), because forward slashes are regular expression special characters.

After that, nearly anything goes, so \S+ is used to signify that one or more non–white space characters follow. Then there's another required forward slash (again escaped) to separate the domain from the file name, and then another \S+ to handle the file name.

The file name needs to end with a period and then "gif," "jpg," "jpeg," or "png". The period is escaped, and the suffixes are grouped together to test for any match.

After the regular expression, the modifier i is used, to allow the user input to be either upper- or lowercase. This modifier tells the regular expression not to be case-sensitive.

Extracting Strings

String validation isn't the only useful thing you can do with regular expressions. String *extraction* is also useful; being able to take just part of a string and manipulate it allows you to have more control over the final result. In **Script 8.4**, we'll take a list of names entered in first-name-first order and swap them so that they're in last-name-first order.

To extract strings:

1. `var re = /\s*\n\s*/;`

Here's a new regular expression, which simply searches for a pattern that consists of any white space \s*, followed by a new line character \n, followed again by any white space \s*.

2. `var nameList = inNameList.split(re);`

The string method `split()` takes the regular expression and applies it to the data entered by the user (**Figure 8.5**), stored in `inNameList`. Every new line separates a name, and `split()` cuts up the entered data at each new line. The result is a string array of the entered names, one name per array element, stored in the array `nameList`.

3. `re = /(\S+)\s(\S+)/;`

Next we'll need another regular expression, which splits each name into first and last names. It looks for any non–white space characters (\S+) followed by a single white space character \s, followed by any non–white space characters (\S+). The parentheses are required around each group of characters so that the information can be used later.

Script 8.4 This script rearranges an entered list of names.

```
window.onload = initForms;

function initForms() {
    for (var i=0; i< document.forms.length;
    → i++) {
        document.forms[i].onsubmit = function()
        → {return validForm();}
    }
}

function validForm() {
    var allTags = document.getElementsByTagName
    → ("*");

    for (var i=0; i<allTags.length; i++) {
        validTag(allTags[i]);
    }
    return false;

    function validTag(thisTag) {
        var allClasses = thisTag.className.split
        → (" ");
```

(script continues on next page)

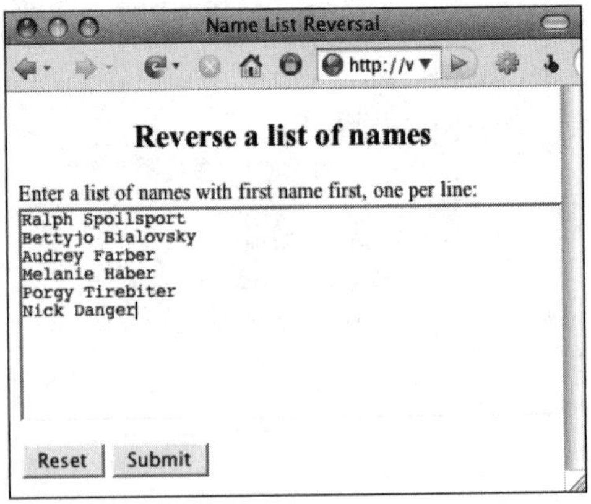

Figure 8.5 Here's the before version of the list.

Script 8.4 *continued*

```
                            script

    for (var j=0; j<allClasses.length; j++) {
        validBasedOnClass(allClasses[j]);
    }

    function validBasedOnClass(thisClass) {
        switch(thisClass) {
            case "":
                break;
            case "nameList":
                thisTag.value = nameList
                → (thisTag.value);
            default:
        }
    }

    function nameList(inNameList) {
        var newNames = new Array;
        var newNameField = "";

        var re = /\s*\n\s*/;
        var nameList = inNameList.split(re);

        re = /(\S+)\s(\S+)/;

        for (var k=0; k<nameList.length;
        → k++) {
            newNames[k] = nameList[k].
            → replace(re, "$2, $1");
        }

        for (k=0; k<newNames.length; k++) {
            newNameField += newNames[k] +
            → "\n";
        }
        return newNameField;
    }
}
}
```

4. `for (var k=0; k<nameList.length;`
   `→ k++) {`

For each name in the `nameList` array, loop through the following line of code.

5. `newNames[k] = nameList[k].replace`
   `→ (re, "$2, $1");`

Remember those parentheses in step 3? When the `replace()` method is executed, the regular expression `re` breaks apart `nameList` into first and last names. Those parentheses tell JavaScript to store the first name in the regular expression property $1 and the last name in the regular expression property $2. The `replace()` method then uses the second parameter passed to it to return the last name $2, followed by a comma, followed by the first name $1. The names, now in last-name-first order, are stored in the new array `newNames`.

6. `for (k=0; k<newNames.length; k++) {`
   `    newNameField += newNames[k] + "\n";`
   `}`

This loop sets up a new variable `newNameField`, which will contain the revised version of the user-entered text. For each name in the `newNames` array, append that name followed by a new line character to `newNameField`.

continues on next page

EXTRACTING STRINGS

7. `return newNameField;`

We pass the result back up to update the Web page. This happens in the `switch/case` section: `thisTag.value = nameList(thisTag.value);`. The result is shown in **Figure 8.6**.

✔ Tips

■ This script, as shown, only handles first and last names that are separated by a space. You'll have to change it if you want it to handle middle names or multi-part last names.

■ In this script, the variable `re` gets used more than once, with different values being assigned to it at different parts of the script. That's perfectly okay to do in JavaScript (and that's why we've done it here as an illustration), but you might want to consider using different variable names in your own scripts. It makes them easier to debug or change when you come back to them in a few months.

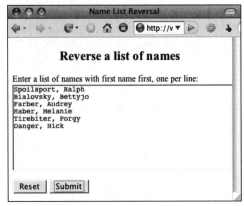

Figure 8.6 Here's the reordered version of the page.

Formatting Strings

Those darn users often enter data in a haphazard fashion. If you want entries to follow a standard format, your best bet is to handle the formatting yourself. **Script 8.5** shows how to take a list of names and convert them to standard capitalization format.

Script 8.5 This script takes a name entered in any format and replaces it with the capitalization you desire.

```
window.onload = initForms;

function initForms() {
    for (var i=0; i< document.forms.length; i++) {
        document.forms[i].onsubmit = function() {return validForm();}
    }
}

function validForm() {
    var allTags = document.getElementsByTagName("*");

    for (var i=0; i<allTags.length; i++) {
        validTag(allTags[i]);
    }
    return false;

    function validTag(thisTag) {
        var allClasses = thisTag.className.split(" ");

        for (var j=0; j<allClasses.length; j++) {
            validBasedOnClass(allClasses[j]);
        }

        function validBasedOnClass(thisClass) {
            switch(thisClass) {
                case "":
                    break;
                case "nameList":
                    thisTag.value = nameList(thisTag.value);
                default:
            }
        }
    }
}
```

(script continues on next page)

FORMATTING STRINGS

To format a string:

1. `re = /^(\S)(\S+)\s(\S)(\S+)$/;`

This regular expression again expects to find names in first name, space, last name order, and separates each name into four parts: the first letter of the first name `^(\S)`, the remainder of the first name `(\S+)`, the first letter of the last name `(\S)`, and the remainder of the last name `(\S+)$`. Note that the `^` and `$` force the string to begin at the beginning and end at the ending—we don't want to leave any parts out.

2. `for (var k=0; k<nameList.length; k++) {`

We want to look at each name in the `nameList` array, shown in **Figure 8.7**.

3. `re.exec(nameList[k]);`

This step uses the `exec()` method to execute the `re` pattern on the string `nameList[k]`, breaking the string into four parts and automatically setting JavaScript's built-in `RegExp` object. These four parts will be stored in `RegExp.$1`, `RegExp.$2`, `RegExp.$3`, and `RegExp.$4` (respectively).

Script 8.5 *continued*

```
function nameList(inNameList) {
    var newNames = new Array;
    var newNameField = "";

    var re = /\s*\n\s*/;
    var nameList = inNameList.split(re);

    re = /^(\S)(\S+)\s(\S)(\S+)$/;

    for (var k=0; k<nameList.length;
    → k++) {
        if (nameList[k]) {
            re.exec(nameList[k]);
            newNames[k] = RegExp.$1.
            → toUpperCase() + RegExp.$2.
            → toLowerCase() + " " +
            → RegExp.$3.toUpperCase() +
            → RegExp.$4.toLowerCase();
        }
    }

    for (k=0; k<newNames.length; k++) {
        newNameField += newNames[k] +
        → "\n";
    }
    return newNameField;
    }
  }
}
```

Figure 8.7 Here's the before version of the names.

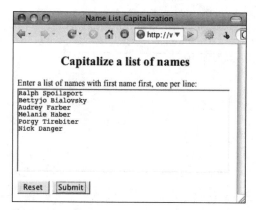

Figure 8.8 And here's how they look afterwards, just the way we wanted them.

4. `newNames[k] = RegExp.$1.`
→ `toUpperCase() + RegExp.$2.`
→ `toLowerCase() + " " + RegExp.$3.`
→ `toUpperCase() + RegExp.$4.`
→ `toLowerCase();`

The new version of the name is stored in the `newNames` array. It consists of the first letter of the first name (`RegExp.$1`), forced to uppercase, then the remainder of the first name (`RegExp.$2`) forced to lowercase, then a space, then the first letter of the last name (`RegExp.$3`) forced to uppercase, and finally the remainder of the last name (`RegExp.$4`) forced to lowercase. The name is then displayed, as shown in **Figure 8.8**.

About the RegExp Object

JavaScript has a built-in `RegExp` object that's automatically set (and reset) every time a script executes a regular expression method (given in **Tables 8.4** and **8.5**). The properties of this object are shown in **Table 8.3** and its methods in **Table 8.4**. The `RegExp` object isn't a variable that contains the result of the regular expression operation, but rather it contains the *pattern* described by the regular expression, in a form that can be used in your scripts via the `RegExp` object's properties and methods.

Table 8.3

Properties of the RegExp Object

PROPERTIES	MEANING
$1 (through $9)	Parenthesized substring matches
$_	Same as `input`
$*	Same as `multiline`
$&	Same as `lastMatch`
$+	Same as `lastParen`
$`	Same as `leftContext`
$'	Same as `rightContext`
constructor	Specifies the function that creates an object's prototype
global	Search globally (g modifier in use)
ignoreCase	Search case-insensitive (i modifier in use)
input	The string to search if no string is passed
lastIndex	The index at which to start the next match
lastMatch	The last matched characters
lastParen	The last parenthesized substring match
leftContext	The substring to the left of the most recent match
multiline	Whether strings are searched across multiple lines
prototype	Allows the addition of properties to all objects
rightContext	The substring to the right of the most recent match
source	The regular expression pattern itself

Table 8.4

Methods of the RegExp Object

METHODS	MEANING
compile(pattern,[, "g" | "i" | "gi"])	Compiles a regular expression
exec(string)	Executes a search for a match
test(string)	Tests for a match
toSource()	Returns a literal representing the object
toString()	Returns a string representing the specified object
valueOf()	Returns the primitive value of the specified object

Table 8.5

String Methods

METHODS	MEANING
match(re)	Finds a match for a regular expression pattern (re) within a string
replace(re,replaceStr)	Using the regular expression (re), performs the desired replacement
search(re)	Searches for a match to the regular expression (re)
split(re)	Splits a string based on a regular expression (re)

Formatting and Sorting Strings

Another typical task you might want to do is to sort a group of names. **Script 8.6** combines the previous two examples and adds a sort. The end result is the list of names in last-name order, properly capitalized, and alphabetized.

Script 8.6 This script takes a bunch of names in any format and order and turns them into a neat and orderly list.

```
                                  script
window.onload = initForms;

function initForms() {
    for (var i=0; i< document.forms.length; i++) {
        document.forms[i].onsubmit = function() {return validForm();}
    }
}

function validForm() {
    var allTags = document.getElementsByTagName("*");

    for (var i=0; i<allTags.length; i++) {
        validTag(allTags[i]);
    }
    return false;

    function validTag(thisTag) {
        var allClasses = thisTag.className.split(" ");

        for (var j=0; j<allClasses.length; j++) {
            validBasedOnClass(allClasses[j]);
        }

        function validBasedOnClass(thisClass) {
            switch(thisClass) {
                case "":
                    break;
                case "nameList":
                    thisTag.value = nameList(thisTag.value);
                default:
            }
        }
    }
```

(script continues on next page)

To format and sort strings:

1. newNames[k] = RegExp.$3.
   → toUpperCase() + RegExp.$4.
   → toLowerCase() + ", " + RegExp.$1.
   → toUpperCase() + RegExp.$2.
   → toLowerCase();

   In this example, we want to sort by last name, so we create the new newNames array by appending the uppercased first letter of the last name, the lowercased remainder of the last name, a comma and space, the uppercased first letter of the first name, and the lowercased remainder of the first name.

2. newNames.sort();

   The array method sort() sorts the elements of an array in place, overwriting the previous contents. **Figure 8.9** shows the "before" version and **Figure 8.10** the "after" version.

Script 8.6 *continued*

```
function nameList(inNameList) {
    var newNames = new Array;
    var newNameField = "";

    var re = /\s*\n\s*/;
    var nameList = inNameList.split(re);

    re = /^(\S)(\S+)\s(\S)(\S+)$/;

    for (var k=0; k<nameList.length;
    → k++) {
        if (nameList[k]) {
            re.exec(nameList[k]);
            newNames[k] = RegExp.$3.
            → toUpperCase() + RegExp.$4.
            → toLowerCase() + ", " +
            → RegExp.$1.toUpperCase() +
            → RegExp.$2.toLowerCase();
        }
    }

    newNames.sort();
    for (k=0; k<newNames.length; k++) {
        newNameField += newNames[k] +
        → "\n";
    }
    return newNameField;
}
}
}
```

Figure 8.9 Here's the version as the user entered it.

Figure 8.10 And here's the sorted and cleaned up list, just the way we want it.

Formatting and Validating Strings

Regular expressions can be used to simultaneously format *and* validate an entered value. In **Script 8.7**, the user enters a phone number in any format. Either the end result will be a formatted phone number or the input box will turn red and the label will turn red and bold.

Script 8.7 This script validates and formats a user-entered phone number.

```
window.onload = initForms;

function initForms() {
    for (var i=0; i< document.forms.length; i++) {
        document.forms[i].onsubmit = function() {return validForm();}
    }
}

function validForm() {
    var allTags = document.getElementsByTagName("*");

    for (var i=0; i<allTags.length; i++) {
        validTag(allTags[i]);
    }
    return false;

    function validTag(thisTag) {
        var outClass = "";
        var allClasses = thisTag.className.split(" ");

        for (var j=0; j<allClasses.length; j++) {
            outClass += validBasedOnClass(allClasses[j]) + " ";
        }

        thisTag.className = outClass;

        if (outClass.indexOf("invalid") > -1) {
            invalidLabel(thisTag.parentNode);
            thisTag.focus();
            if (thisTag.nodeName == "INPUT") {
```

(script continues on next page)

To format and validate a phone number:

1. `var re = /^\(?(\d{3})\)?[\.\-\/ ]?`
   `→ (\d{3})[\.\-\/ ]?(\d{4})$/;`

   This regular expression looks for a string that has:

   ▲ An optional left parenthesis `\(?`

   ▲ 3 digits `(\d{3})`

   ▲ An optional right parenthesis `\)?`

   ▲ An optional period, dash, forward slash, or space `[\.\-\/ ]?`

   ▲ 3 digits `(\d{3})`

   ▲ An optional period, dash, forward slash, or space `[\.\-\/ ]?`

   ▲ 4 digits `(\d{4})`

   This pattern is anchored to both the beginning and ending of the string, so extraneous characters are not valid. The sequences of three digits (the area code), three digits (the prefix), and four digits (the suffix) are saved, if found.

Script 8.7 *continued*

```
          thisTag.select();
        }
      }
    }

    function validBasedOnClass(thisClass) {
      var classBack = "";

      switch(thisClass) {
        case "":
        case "invalid":
          break;
        case "phone":
          if (!validPhone(thisTag.value))
          → classBack = "invalid ";
        default:
          classBack += thisClass;
      }
      return classBack;
    }


    function validPhone(phoneNum) {
      var re = /^\(?(\d{3})\)?[\.\-\/ ]?
      → (\d{3})[\.\-\/ ]?(\d{4})$/;

      var phoneArray = re.exec(phoneNum);
      if (phoneArray) {
        document.getElementById
        → ("phoneField").value =
        → "(" + phoneArray[1] + ") " +
        → phoneArray[2] + "-" +
        → phoneArray[3];
        return true;
      }
      return false;
    }


    function invalidLabel(parentTag) {
      if (parentTag.nodeName == "LABEL") {
        parentTag.className += " invalid";
      }
    }
  }
}
```

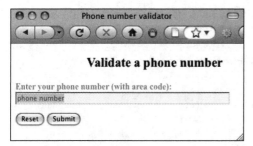

Figure 8.11 Here's the result when an invalid number is entered.

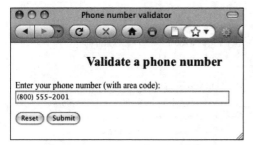

Figure 8.12 And here's what's displayed when the number is entered correctly.

2. `var phoneArray = re.exec(phoneNum);`

The exec() method performs the regular expression stored in re on phoneNum. If the pattern we're searching for isn't found (**Figure 8.11**), phoneArray will be set to null. Otherwise, phoneArray will be an array of the values stored by the regular expression.

3. `if (phoneArray) {`
`    document.getElementById`
`→ ("phoneField").value =`
`→ "(" + phoneArray[1] + ") " +`
`→ phoneArray[2] + "-" +`
`→ phoneArray[3];`

If phoneArray is true, the test was successfully passed, and the array has been initialized. So, we reset the form field on the page to the area code inside parentheses and a space, followed by the prefix, a dash, and the suffix, as shown in **Figure 8.12**.

Replacing Elements using Regular Expressions

You've already seen how useful regular expressions are for finding, matching, and replacing strings. But you can also use them to replace the names of page elements, and this can often save you a bunch of time. In this task, we're going to retrofit a regular expression into a script that you've seen before, Script 4.5. That script built three-state rollovers. It's a useful script, but it has one drawback: it requires you to have tagged every image that you want to manipulate with its own id. That's not too difficult, but you can instead let JavaScript build the names of page elements and save yourself some work.

At this point, you should review Chapter 4's image rollovers (Scripts 4.4 and 4.5) to see what's going on in this example. Go ahead, we'll wait.

Back so soon? Great. In short, instead of creating the _click and _on names of an image on the fly based on the id of each image, we're instead creating the _click and _on names on the fly based on the _off name of the image. That way, we don't even need the image ids. **Script 8.8** shows you the way. There's no change in the way the page looks or acts from changing the JavaScript; but it saves you work in creating the HTML pages.

Script 8.8 Use regular expressions to save you from writing or retrofitting your HTML files.

```
window.onload = rolloverInit;

function rolloverInit() {
    for (var i=0; i<document.images.length;
    → i++) {
        if (document.images[i].parentNode.
        → tagName.toLowerCase() == "a") {
            setupRollover(document.images[i]);
        }
    }
}

function setupRollover(thisImage) {
    var re = /\s*_off\s*/;

    thisImage.outImage = new Image();
    thisImage.outImage.src = thisImage.src;
    thisImage.onmouseout = function() {
        this.src = this.outImage.src;
    }

    thisImage.overImage = new Image();
    thisImage.overImage.src = thisImage.src.
    → replace(re,"_on");
    thisImage.onmouseover = function() {
        this.src = this.overImage.src;
    }

    thisImage.clickImage = new Image();
    thisImage.clickImage.src = thisImage.src.
    → replace(re,"_click");
    thisImage.onclick = function() {
        this.src = this.clickImage.src;
    }

    thisImage.parentNode.childImg = thisImage;
    thisImage.parentNode.onblur = function() {
        this.childImg.src = this.childImg.
        → outImage.src;
    }
    thisImage.parentNode.onfocus = function() {
        this.childImg.src = this.childImg.
        → overImage.src;
    }
}
```

To use a regular expression to replace an element:

1. `var re = /\s*_off\s*/;`

This line sets up a new regular expression pattern that looks for the text _off anywhere in a string.

2. `thisImage.overImage.src =`
`→ thisImage.src.replace(re,"_on");`

The line in Script 4.5 was `thisImage.`
`→ overImage.src = "images/" +`
`→ thisImage.id + "_on.gif";`
The new line uses the re pattern to look for that particular bit of a string and, when it's found, replace it with *this* string. In this case, we're looking for _off and turning it into _on. This allows us to not worry about the id attribute being set on this image—it just doesn't matter any more.

3. `thisImage.clickImage.src = thisImage.`
`→src.replace(re,"_click");`

The line in Script 4.5 was `thisImage.`
`→ clickImage.src = "images/" +`
`→ thisImage.id + "_click.gif";`
In this case, we're looking for _off and turning it into _click.

✔ Tips

■ This can also be handy if your images are a mixture of GIF and JPEG files—now, your JavaScript code doesn't have to ever know what suffix each image has.

■ You may have noticed that there's some code at the end of this script that isn't in Script 4.5. We've added a little bit of extra code here to enhance accessibility--now, for those people who use the keyboard instead of a mouse, tabbing onto an image will give the same effect that a hover does for a mousing user.

REPLACING ELEMENTS

HANDLING EVENTS

Events are actions that the user performs while visiting your page. When the browser detects an event, such as a mouse click or a key press, it can trigger JavaScript objects associated with that event, called *event handlers*. In most of the previous chapters in this book, you've seen examples of how event handlers are used. But event handling is such an important technique to understand—and it encompasses virtually all of your pages' interaction with the user—that it deserves its own chapter.

In this chapter, you'll see how to use event handlers to work with windows, capture mouse movements and clicks, deal with form events, and react when the user presses keys on the keyboard.

Handling Window Events

Window events occur when the user does something affecting an entire browser window. The most common window event is simply loading the window by opening a particular Web page. You can also have events that trigger event handlers when windows are closed, moved, or even sent to the background.

When working with event handlers, you'll often find it useful to connect an event handler to an object using dot syntax, like so:

```
window.onfocus
window.onload
document.onmousedown
```

Note that when you use the event handler as part of an object like this, the event handler is written all in lowercase. Also, keep your event handlers in external scripts, rather than placing them inside the HTML tag—this approach is more standards compliant, it separates out the JavaScript code from the HTML code, and it's easier to edit (or replace) all your JavaScript code in an external file.

Script 9.1 The HTML for the multiple onload example.

```
<!DOCTYPE html PUBLIC "-//W3C//DTD XHTML 1.0
→ Transitional//EN"
        "http://www.w3.org/TR/xhtml1/DTD/
        → xhtml1-transitional.dtd">
<html xmlns="http://www.w3.org/1999/xhtml">
<head>
    <title>Welcome!</title>
    <script type="text/javascript"
    → src="script01.js"></script>
</head>
<body id="pageBody">
    <h1>Welcome to our Web site!</h1>
</body>
</html>
```

Script 9.2 Setting multiple `onload` attributes using our new `addOnload()` function.

```
script
addOnload(initOne);
addOnload(initTwo);
addOnload(initThree);

function addOnload(newFunction) {
    var oldOnload = window.onload;

    if (typeof oldOnload == "function") {
        window.onload = function() {
            if (oldOnload) {
                oldOnload();
            }
            newFunction();
        }
    }
    else {
        window.onload = newFunction;
    }
}

function initOne() {
    document.getElementById("pageBody").style.
    → backgroundColor = "#0000FF";
}

function initTwo() {
    document.getElementById("pageBody").style.
    → color = "#FF0000";
}

function initThree() {
    var allTags = document.getElementsByTagName
    → ("*");

    for (var i=0; i<allTags.length; i++) {
        if (allTags[i].nodeName == "H1") {
            allTags[i].style.border =
            → "5px green solid";
            allTags[i].style.padding = "25px";
            allTags[i].style.backgroundColor =
            → "#FFFFFF";
        }
    }
}
```

The onload event

We have used the `onload` event frequently throughout this book. It is triggered when the user enters your page and all its elements have completed loading. The epidemic of advertising pop-up windows is an example—though not an especially pleasant one—of the `onload` event handler in action.

Although we've shown `onload` repeatedly, up until now we've skipped one important bit of information: what to do when you have multiple things you need to have happen when the page loads. **Scripts 9.1** and **9.2** demonstrate how to do this.

1. `addOnload(initOne);`
`addOnload(initTwo);`
`addOnload(initThree);`

In this script, we want three entirely separate things to happen when the page first loads. Setting `window.onload` three times wouldn't work, because the second time would overwrite the first, and then the third would overwrite the second. Instead, we're calling a new function (defined below), `addOnload()`, which handles the `onload` handler for us. For each call, we're passing one parameter: the name of the function we want to run when an `onload` event is triggered. You can see the result in **Figure 9.1**.

2. `function addOnload(newFunction) {`

This line starts off a new function, much like any other function. What's being passed in is the name of a function.

This can be a bit confusing, so here's an example. Instead of calling

`window.onload = myNewFunction;`

we'll instead call

`addOnload(myNewFunction);`

which works out the same at the end.

3. `var oldOnload = window.onload;`

This line declares a new variable `oldOnload`—if we've already set `window.onload`, we'll store its value here. If we haven't, it doesn't hurt anything.

4. `if (typeof oldOnload == "function") {`

In this line, we check to see what kind of variable `oldOnload` is. If we've previously set `window.onload`, it'll be a function call (otherwise, it'll be nothing at all). If it's a function, do the following.

Figure 9.1 The script is setting multiple `onload` handlers (in this case, for color formatting) to be run when the page loads.

5.
```
window.onload = function() {
    if (oldOnload) {
        oldOnload();
    }
    newFunction();
}
```

These lines of code reset the value of
`window.onload` to do two things: whatever
it was doing before, and our new function. The `window.onload` event handler
is set to be an anonymous function
(one that doesn't have a name). Then, if
`oldOnload` has a value (which it should,
but this works around a bug in Internet
Explorer 7), we tell `window.onload` to do
what it was already doing. But before the
function ends, we add that it needs to *also*
do our `newFunction()` as well.

6.
```
else {
    window.onload = newFunction;
}
```

If `oldOnload` wasn't a function—that is,
it was `undefined`—we tell it do our new
function when the page completes loading. In this fashion, we can call `addOnload()`
multiple times: the first time it assigns its
function to `window.onload`; the second
and later times it creates that anonymous
function, telling JavaScript to do everything it's been told to do previously *and*
the new thing as well.

✔ Tips

- If you want to have an `onload` handler do
  more than one thing, the easiest way is to
  create one function that does everything,
  and then have the `onload` handler call
  that function. But make sure that each
  function returns—if, for example, your
  function contains a `setTimeout()` call to
  itself, it'll never return and therefore never
  go on to the rest of the called functions.

- If you're working with an existing body of
  code, it's easy to accidentally reset `window.`
  `onload`—any given HTML page can call
  multiple external JavaScript files, any of
  which can set the event handler. If one
  place sets `window.onload` directly, but every
  time after that you call `addOnload()`, you're
  fine. But if you set `window.onload` after
  you've set it previously (whether directly or
  via `addOnload()`), you'll have walked on top
  of your handler and lost its original value.

- This script is (very) loosely based on one
  by Simon Willison (`simonwillison.net`)
  and is used with his permission.

The onunload event

The onunload handler is triggered when the user leaves your Web page. The most common use for this is advertising windows that pop up when you leave some commercial sites, especially pornographic sites. If you find yourself on one of the latter, you'll often find that it's almost impossible to leave—every time you close a window or attempt to navigate away from the site, window after window appears, re-opening the same or other pages, all of the same genre.

Consequently, people have come to hate the onunload handler with a passion, so use it sparingly.

The onresize event

Netscape 4.x had a well-known bug where dynamic content wasn't redrawn when a Web page was resized. **Scripts 9.3** and **9.4** force the page to reload its contents to avoid this problem. Thankfully, Netscape versions 6 and later no longer suffer from this bug.

1. `window.onresize = resizeFix;`

The event handler is attached to the window object and calls the `resizeFix` function.

2. `if (document.layers) {`

We only want to do the following if the user has Netscape 4.x, and this is the simplest way to check that. The `document.layers` object only ever existed in this browser.

3. `var origWidth = window.innerWidth;`
`var origHeight = window.innerHeight;`

If we're in Netscape 4.x, we want to save the current height and width of the browser window for later use.

Script 9.3 This HTML includes the JavaScript hidden inside a multi-line comment, since it's meant for use in older browsers.

```
<!DOCTYPE html PUBLIC "-//W3C//DTD XHTML 1.0
→ Transitional//EN"
        "http://www.w3.org/TR/xhtml1/DTD/
        → xhtml1-transitional.dtd">
<html xmlns="http://www.w3.org/1999/xhtml">
<head>
    <title>onResize Netscape fix</title>
    <script type="text/javascript"
    → src="script02.js"></script>
</head>
<body bgcolor="#FFFFFF">
    <h1>
    <script type="text/javascript">
        <!-- Hide code from older browsers

        document.write("This is dynamic content")

        // Stop hiding code -->
    </script>
    </h1>
</body>
</html>
```

Script 9.4 You can fix Netscape 4.x's dynamic content redraw bug with this script.

```
window.onresize = resizeFix;

if (document.layers) {
    var origWidth = window.innerWidth;
    var origHeight = window.innerHeight;
}

function resizeFix() {
    if (document.layers) {
        if (window.innerWidth != origWidth ||
        → window.innerHeight != origHeight) {
            window.location.reload();
        }
    }
}
```

Figure 9.2 The reloaded (but still kind of dull) page.

4. `function resizeFix() {`

Here's where we actually handle the browser being resized.

5. `if (document.layers) {`

Again, check to make sure that this only happens if they are using Netscape 4.x.

6. `if (window.innerWidth != origWidth`
`→ || window.innerHeight !=`
`→ origHeight) {`

If they came in here and either the height or the width of the window has changed, the user resized the window, and we want to force the page to reload. If the browser window size hasn't changed, the `onresize` handler was triggered by Netscape drawing the scrollbars, and it can be ignored.

7. `window.location.reload();`

Reload the page if the user actually did resize the window (**Figure 9.2**).

The onmove event

The `onmove` event handler is triggered when the window is moved.

The onabort event

The `onabort` event handler is triggered when the user cancels an image loading on the Web page. It's not used very often, and not all browsers seem to fully support it.

The onerror event

The `onerror` event may be triggered when a JavaScript error occurs on the page.

✔ Tip

■ It can be polite to set `onerror = null;` in complex pages you put on the Web. With this line of code on your page, *some* error messages will not be displayed to the user in the unfortunate event that there's a problem—but which errors will be hidden depends on the browser.

The onfocus event

The onfocus and onblur handlers are mirror images of each other. While they may sound like what happens when you've been working on JavaScript too late at night, in reality, the onfocus handler triggers when a page becomes the front-most active window. **Scripts 9.5** and **9.6** catch the onfocus handler and force the page to always go to the back (**Figure 9.3**).

1. `window.onfocus = moveBack;`

   Here's another example of the window and event handler object calling a function, in this case moveBack.

2. ```
   function moveBack() {
       self.blur();
   }
   ```

   If the browser window becomes the active window, this function is triggered and forces the window to be blurred (i.e., inactive).

Script 9.5 This HTML is for the page that's in back.

```
<!DOCTYPE html PUBLIC "-//W3C//DTD XHTML 1.0
→ Transitional//EN"
        "http://www.w3.org/TR/xhtml1/DTD/
        → xhtml1-transitional.dtd">
<html xmlns="http://www.w3.org/1999/xhtml">
<head>
    <title>Always in Back</title>
    <script type="text/javascript"
    → src="script03.js"></script>
</head>
<body bgcolor="#FFFFFF">
    <h1>Unimportant content that should never
    → be in front</h1>
</body>
</html>
```

Script 9.6 Using the onfocus handler, you can control window stacking.

```
window.onfocus = moveBack;

function moveBack() {
    self.blur();
}
```

Figure 9.3 The page in the back will stay there.
```

Script 9.7 This HTML is for the page that stays in front.

```
<!DOCTYPE html PUBLIC "-//W3C//DTD XHTML 1.0
→ Transitional//EN"
        "http://www.w3.org/TR/xhtml1/DTD/
        → xhtml1-transitional.dtd">
<html xmlns="http://www.w3.org/1999/xhtml">
<head>
    <title>Always in Front</title>
    <script type="text/javascript"
    → src="script04.js"></script>
</head>
<body bgcolor="#FFFFFF">
    <h1>Important content that should always be
    → in front</h1>
</body>
</html>
```

Script 9.8 This script uses onblur to keep a window in the front (active) position.

```
window.onblur = moveUp;

function moveUp() {
    self.focus();
}
```

The onblur event

If you have a window that you always want to remain in front of all your other windows (a control panel, for instance, that loads in the content of the main page), **Scripts 9.7** and **9.8** are what you need. Any time the user tries to put this page in the background (triggering the onblur handler), it forces its way back up to the front again.

1. `window.onblur = moveUp;`

   Here's another example of the window and event handler object calling a function, in this case moveUp.

2. ```
   function moveUp() {
       self.focus();
   }
   ```

   If the browser window becomes the inactive window, this function is triggered and forces the window to become active.

✔ Tips

■ Be very careful not to accidentally open up two windows that both contain this bit of code. Chances are, your browser will not handle the result gracefully!

■ Instead of using this script on the control panel, you could use Script 9.6 on the main window to always make it go to the back, making the control panel always the front-most window.

■ You may be more familiar with one of the more nefarious uses of the onblur event: advertisers who open ad windows *behind* your current Web page, which you don't discover until you close the window and find a stack of them piled up. Unfortunately, people blame the last Web site they opened, when in fact the ads were likely created by a page browsed much earlier.
   ```

Mouse Event Handling

Many of the user's interactions with your pages come in the form of mouse movements or mouse clicks. JavaScript provides a robust set of handlers for these events.

The onmousedown event

One of the questions most frequently asked by new JavaScripters is, "How do I hide my scripts from anyone coming to my page?" The answer is, simply: you can't. If anyone is determined enough, they can always find out what's in your code.

If you really need to try to hide your code from average surfers, though, **Script 9.9** keeps them from viewing the page source via a mouse-click that would normally bring up the shortcut menu.

1. ```
if (typeof document.oncontextmenu ==
→ "object") {
   if (document.all) {
      document.onmousedown =
      → captureMousedown;
```
   This first block checks to see if this browser is Firefox, which uses `window.oncontextmenu` (and so doesn't know about `document.oncontextmenu`). If it isn't Firefox, we next look for `document.all`, which is an easy way of checking to see if the browser is IE. If it is, we want to set `captureMousedown()` to run whenever `onmousedown` is triggered.

2. ```
else {
   document.oncontextmenu =
   → captureMousedown;
```
   If we're here, it's because your visitor is using Safari, and that browser needs `oncontextmenu` set on the document object.

Script 9.9 This script will deter some inexperienced users from bringing up the shortcut menu on your pages.

```
if (typeof document.oncontextmenu == "object") {
    if (document.all) {
        document.onmousedown = captureMousedown;
    }
    else {
        document.oncontextmenu =
        → captureMousedown;
    }
}
else {
    window.oncontextmenu = captureMousedown;
}

function captureMousedown(evt) {
    if (evt) {
        var mouseClick = evt.which;
    }
    else {
        var mouseClick = window.event.button;
    }

    if (mouseClick==1 || mouseClick==2 ||
    → mouseClick==3) {
        alert("Menu Disabled");
        return false;
    }
}
```

Figure 9.4 This alert box scares off the timid (and annoys the rest).

3. `else {`
    `window.oncontextmenu =`
    → `captureMousedown;`

And finally, if the browser is Firefox, we want `oncontextmenu` events for the window to call the `captureMousedown()` function.

4. `function captureMousedown(evt) {`

The function that handles the `onmousedown` and `oncontextmenu` events begins here. Netscape-based browsers and Safari generate the `evt` parameter being passed in automatically whenever an event is triggered, and this variable contains information about the event.

5. `if (evt) {`
    `var mouseClick = evt.which;`
`}`
`else {`
    `var mouseClick = window.event.`
    → `button;`
`}`

If the `evt` variable exists, we can determine which button the user clicked by checking `evt.which`. If the user has IE, the results of the user's action will be found in `window.event.button`. Either way, we'll store the result in the `mouseClick` variable.

6. `if (mouseClick==1 || mouseClick==2`
`|| mouseClick==3) {`
    `alert("Menu Disabled");`
    `return false;`
`}`

If `mouseClick` is 1, 2, or 3, put up an alert (**Figure 9.4**) saying that that functionality is disabled, and return false. Returning false keeps the menu window from being displayed.

✔ Tips

- Why are we checking for three different mouse clicks? Shouldn't one be enough? In theory, yes, but in practice, no—as shown in **Table 9.1**. Unfortunately, this approach can backfire: you may successfully block left-click and right-click input (to block people from dragging images off Web pages, for example), but it also means that you might be keeping people from clicking any links on your page.

- It's very simple for savvy surfers to work around this: all they have to do is turn JavaScript off in their browser, and their clicking ability returns. Putting your JavaScript code into an external `.js` file seems like a tricky workaround, but users can look in their cache folder on their hard disk. Or they can look at the source of your page, find the name of the external file, and then enter the URL of the external file in their browser, which obediently displays the file's contents. If you really worry about your source code being stolen, the only method that's guaranteed to keep it from being looked at is to never put it on the Web.

- IE understands `document.oncontextmenu`, so you'd think that setting it would cause it to handle those events—but it doesn't. IE is the only browser that needs `document.onmousedown` to be set. And if you set both `window.oncontextmenu` and `document.onmousedown`, Firefox triggers every event twice, once for each action.

The onmouseup event

Similar to the `onmousedown` event, the `onmouseup` event is triggered when the user clicks the mouse and then releases the button.

Table 9.1

Mouse Click Codes	
CODE	**BROWSER/EVENT**
1	Internet Explorer/Left-click All Mac browsers/Control-left-click
2	Internet Explorer/Right-click
3	Firefox/Right-click All Mac browsers/Right-click

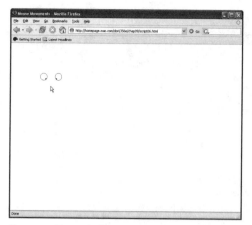

Figure 9.5 The eyeballs will follow the cursor, no matter where it goes.

Script 9.10 The HTML for the following-eyes example.

```
● ● ●                  script
<!DOCTYPE html PUBLIC "-//W3C//DTD XHTML 1.0
→ Transitional//EN"
        "http://www.w3.org/TR/xhtml1/DTD/
        → xhtml1-transitional.dtd">
<html xmlns="http://www.w3.org/1999/xhtml">
<head>
        <title>Mouse Movements</title>
        <link type="text/css" rel="stylesheet"
        → href="script06.css" />
        <script type="text/javascript"
        → src="script06.js"></script>
</head>
<body>
        <img src="images/circle.gif" alt="left eye"
        → width="24" height="25" id="lEye" />
        <img src="images/circle.gif"
        → alt="right eye" width="24" height="25"
        → id="rEye" />
        <img src="images/lilRed.gif"
        → alt="left eyeball" width="4" height="4"
        → id="lDot" />
        <img src="images/lilRed.gif"
        → alt="right eyeball" width="4" height="4"
        → id="rDot" />
</body>
</html>
```

The onmousemove event

The onmousemove event is triggered whenever a visitor to your page moves their mouse. In this example, the user gets the feeling that someone's watching their every move (**Figure 9.5**). **Scripts 9.10**, **9.11**, and **9.12** show how to use JavaScript to display eyeballs that follow your visitor around.

1. `document.onmousemove = moveHandler;`

   For all browsers, if a mousemove event is triggered, call the moveHandler() function.

2. ```
   function moveHandler(evt) {
       if (!evt) {
           evt = window.event;
       }
       animateEyes(evt.clientX,evt.
       → clientY);
   }
   ```

   The moveHandler() function will be triggered whenever a mousemove event occurs. If the visitor has Internet Explorer, we need to initialize evt, and then for all browsers, we call the animateEyes() function and pass it the X and Y cursor coordinates.

3. `function animateEyes(xPos,yPos) {`

   Here's where the actual eyeball movement is done, based on the X and Y coordinates passed in.

4. ```
   var rightEye = document.
   → getElementById("rEye");
   var leftEye = document.
   → getElementById("lEye");
   var rightEyeball = document.
   → getElementById("rDot").style;
   var leftEyeball = document.
   → getElementById("lDot").style;
   ```

   This section assigns variables that match up with the ids of the images of the circles of the eyeballs and the dots of the eyeballs.

   continues on next page

5. `leftEyeball.left = newEyeballPos`
`→ (xPos,leftEye.offsetLeft);`
`leftEyeball.top = newEyeballPos`
`→ (yPos,leftEye.offsetTop);`
`rightEyeball.left = newEyeballPos`
`→ (xPos,rightEye.offsetLeft);`
`rightEyeball.top = newEyeballPos`
`→ (yPos,rightEye.offsetTop);`

This block draws the eyeballs based on the mouse pointer's position, using the results of the `newEyeballPos()` function defined in the next step.

6. `function`
`newEyeballPos(currPos,eyePos) {`
`    return Math.min(Math.max(currPos,`
`    → eyePos+3), eyePos+17) + "px";`
`}`

We never want the eyeball to go outside the eye, do we? So, for each eyeball, we check to make sure that it gets as close to the cursor as possible, while still appearing within the circle of the eye.

Script 9.11 The CSS for the following-eyes example.

```
body {
    background-color: #FFF;
}

#lEye, #rEye {
    position: absolute;
    top: 100px;
}

#lDot, #rDot {
    position: absolute;
    top: 113px;
}

#lEye {
    left: 100px;
}

#rEye {
    left: 150px;
}

#lDot {
    left: 118px;
}

#rDot {
    left: 153px;
}
```

Script 9.12 Keep an eye (OK, two eyes) on your users with this script.

```
document.onmousemove = moveHandler;

function moveHandler(evt) {
    if (!evt) {
        evt = window.event;
    }
    animateEyes(evt.clientX,evt.clientY);
}

function animateEyes(xPos,yPos) {
    var rightEye = document.getElementById
    → ("rEye");
    var leftEye = document.getElementById
    → ("lEye");
    var rightEyeball = document.getElementById
    → ("rDot").style;
    var leftEyeball = document.getElementById
    → ("lDot").style;

    leftEyeball.left = newEyeballPos
    → (xPos,leftEye.offsetLeft);
    leftEyeball.top = newEyeballPos
    → (yPos,leftEye.offsetTop);
    rightEyeball.left = newEyeballPos
    → (xPos,rightEye.offsetLeft);
    rightEyeball.top = newEyeballPos
    → (yPos,rightEye.offsetTop);

    function newEyeballPos(currPos,eyePos) {
        return Math.min(Math.max
        → (currPos,eyePos+3),eyePos+17) + "px";
    }
}
```

✔ Tips

- There's a common JavaScript widget on the Web where the page has a bunch of dots (or whatever the designer wanted) follow the cursor around the page. We didn't want to re-create an already existing effect, so we did the eyeballs instead; but if you want to put tag-along dots on your page, you should be able to just tweak this script.

- Netscape 6 had a bug where both eyeballs were always placed 10 pixels too low. This bug was fixed in Netscape 7.

The onmouseover event

By now, you should be familiar with this event: it's our good buddy from image rollovers. This event will be triggered whenever the mouse is moved into any area for which the onmouseover has been registered.

The onmouseout event

And unsurprisingly by now, where there's an onmouseover, there's usually an onmouseout. This is triggered when the user moves the mouse out of an area for which the event has been registered.

The ondblclick event

One of the drawbacks of the Internet is that the user interface elements that computer users learned how to interact with have all changed on the Web. For instance, one of the first things that new computer users learn how to do is double-click with the mouse, but there's no double-clicking on the Web. Or at least, there hasn't been, but now with **Scripts 9.13** and **9.14**, you'll be able to check for double mouse clicks.

◆ `document.images[i].ondblclick = → newWindow;`

The `newWindow()` event handler gets triggered when a user double-clicks one of the thumbnail images. In that case, a new window pops up (**Figure 9.6**), showing the same image in a larger format.

Script 9.13 This HTML helps you work with double clicks.

```
<!DOCTYPE html PUBLIC "-//W3C//DTD XHTML 1.0
→ Transitional//EN"
        "http://www.w3.org/TR/xhtml1/DTD/
        → xhtml1-transitional.dtd">
<html xmlns="http://www.w3.org/1999/xhtml">
<head>
    <title>Image Popup</title>
    <script type="text/javascript"
    → src="script07.js"></script>
</head>
<body bgcolor="#FFFFFF">
<h3>Double-click on an image to see the
→ full-size version</h3>
    <img src="images/Img0_thumb.jpg"
    → width="160" height="120" hspace="10"
    → border="3" alt="Thumbnail 0" id="Img0" />
    <img src="images/Img1_thumb.jpg"
    → width="160" height="120" hspace="10"
    → border="3" alt="Thumbnail 1" id="Img1" />
    <img src="images/Img2_thumb.jpg"
    → width="160" height="120" hspace="10"
    → border="3" alt="Thumbnail 2" id="Img2" />
</body>
</html>
```

Script 9.14 Capture and handle double clicks with this script.

```
window.onload = initImages;

function initImages() {
    for (var i=0; i<document.images.length;
    → i++) {
        document.images[i].ondblclick =
        → newWindow;
    }
}

function newWindow() {
    var imgName = "images/" + this.id + ".jpg"
    var imgWindow = window.open(imgName,
    → "imgWin", "width=320,height=240,
    → scrollbars=no")
}
```

Figure 9.6 A double-click on a thumbnail opens the larger version of the image.

The onclick event

The `onclick` handler works in a similar fashion to the `ondblclick` handler, except that a single click triggers it instead of a double click. The `onmouseup` handler is also similar, except that the `onclick` requires that the user press the mouse button both down and up in order to be triggered, while the `onmouseup` requires just the latter.

Form Event Handling

You'll want to use form event handling mainly for validating forms. With the events listed below, you can deal with just about any action the user takes with forms.

The onsubmit event

The onsubmit handler (as seen in Chapter 6) is triggered when the user clicks the Submit button to complete a form. In addition, depending on the browser, it can also be triggered when a user exits the last text entry field on a form. If a script contains an onsubmit handler, and the result of the handler is false, the form will not be sent back to the server.

The onreset event

The onreset handler is triggered when the user clicks the Reset button (if one is present) on a form. This can be handy if your form has default values that are set when the page loads—if the user clicks Reset, you'll need to handle this situation with a script that resets the default values dynamically.

The onchange event

As shown in Script 6.2, the onchange event handler is triggered when the user changes a form field. This can be used to verify they entered information immediately, or to respond to the user's choice before they click the Submit button.

The onselect event

The onselect handler is triggered if the user selects text in either an input or a textarea form field.

Script 9.15 This HTML creates the simple form.

```
<!DOCTYPE html PUBLIC "-//W3C//DTD XHTML 1.0
→ Transitional//EN"
        "http://www.w3.org/TR/xhtml1/DTD/
        → xhtml1-transitional.dtd">
<html xmlns="http://www.w3.org/1999/xhtml">
<head>
    <title>Requiring an entry</title>
    <link type="text/css" rel="stylesheet"
    → href="script08.css" />
    <script type="text/javascript"
    → src="script08.js"></script>
</head>
<body>
    <form action="#">
    <h3>
        Email address: <input type="text"
        → class="reqd" /><br /><br />
        Name (optional): <input type="text" />
    </h3>
    </form>
</body>
</html>
```

Script 9.16 A little bit of CSS goes a long way with JavaScript.

```
body {
    background-color: #FFF;
}

.highlight {
    background-color: #FF9;
}
```

The onclick event

While the `onclick` handler is mentioned above under "Mouse Events," it's listed here again because it's most commonly used when dealing with forms. This event is triggered when the user clicks a check box or radio button, as in Script 6.13. Script 2.10 also uses the `onclick` handler; in that case, it allows a single link to do one action for JavaScript-enabled browsers and another, entirely different action, for browsers without JavaScript.

The onblur event

While `onblur` can be used for browser windows (as shown above), it's more common for it to be used in forms. **Scripts 9.15, 9.16,** and **9.17** show the `onblur` handler being used to force the user to enter data into a field.

1. `if (allTags[i].className.`
   `→ indexOf("reqd") > -1) {`

   We're using a class attribute (of `reqd`) to decide on the fly when the `onblur` event handler should be used. Simply adding `class="reqd"` to an input tag triggers the event, instead of having to put the `onblur` handler on fields individually.

2. `allTags[i].onblur = fieldCheck;`

   This event handler on the field causes the `fieldCheck()` function to be called whenever the user leaves a required field.

continues on next page

3.
```
function fieldCheck() {
    if (this.value == "") {
        this.className += " highlight";
        this.focus();
    }
    else {
        this.className = "reqd";
    }
}
```

The `fieldCheck()` function checks to make sure that something (anything) was entered in the current field. If the field has no value, the field's background is colored pale yellow by adding `"highlight"` to its class attribute (**Figure 9.7**), and the cursor gets put back into the form field with `focus()`. When the error is corrected, simply resetting the class attribute back to its initial value resets the background to white.

✔ Tips

- Both the `onblur` and `onchange` events are triggered when the user leaves a field after changing it. If the user leaves a field without changing it, just the `onblur` handler is triggered.

- Some versions of Firefox have had a problem with `focus()`: even though you tell the browser to stay in a field, it doesn't. Changing the background color gives the user a visual cue that something's wrong, though, so they'll still know that there was a problem.

Script 9.17 The `onblur` handler can be used in forms to trigger actions when the user leaves a field.

```
script
window.onload = initForm;

function initForm() {
    var allTags = document.getElementsByTagName
    ➝ ("*");

    for (var i=0; i<allTags.length; i++) {
        if (allTags[i].className.indexOf
        ➝ ("reqd") > -1) {
            allTags[i].onblur = fieldCheck;
        }
    }
}

function fieldCheck() {
    if (this.value == "") {
        this.className += " highlight";
        this.focus();
    }
    else {
        this.className = "reqd";
    }
}
```

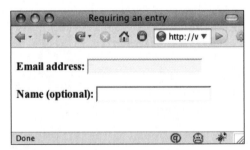

Figure 9.7 When the user tabs out of the Email address field without entering anything, the field turns yellow and remains active until data is present.

Script 9.18 The HTML creates the form, which won't allow entries in the email field.

```
○○○                  script
<!DOCTYPE html PUBLIC "-//W3C//DTD XHTML 1.0
→ Transitional//EN"
        "http://www.w3.org/TR/xhtml1/DTD/
         → xhtml1-transitional.dtd">
<html xmlns="http://www.w3.org/1999/xhtml">
<head>
    <title>Forbidding an entry</title>
    <script type="text/javascript"
    → src="script09.js"></script>
</head>
<body bgcolor="#FFFFFF">
    <form action="#">
    <h3>
        Your message: <textarea rows="5"
        → cols="30">Enter your message
        → here</textarea><br /><br />
        Will be sent to: <input type="text"
        → value="js7@javascriptworld.com"
        → readonly="readonly" />
    </h3>
    </form>
</body>
</html>
```

The onfocus event

Sometimes you'll have a form field on a page with data that you want to display as part of the form, without the user being able to modify that field. You can use the `readonly` HTML attribute to try to keep users out, but not all browsers support it. **Scripts 9.18** and **9.19** show how to use the `onfocus` event to bump users right back out of this field, on the off chance they made it to where they shouldn't be.

◆ `allTags[i].onfocus = function() {`
        `this.blur();`
    `}`

When the user attempts to enter this field, the focus (in this case the active field) will automatically be kicked right back out again (**Figure 9.8**). This happens because the `onfocus` event handler is set to call an anonymous function (one without a name) that does just one thing: call `blur()` on the current field, bouncing the user out.

Script 9.19 Prevent wayward field entries with the onfocus handler in a form.

```
○○○                  script
window.onload = initForm;

function initForm() {
    var allTags = document.getElementsByTagName
    → ("*");

    for (var i=0; i<allTags.length; i++) {
        if (allTags[i].readOnly) {
            allTags[i].onfocus = function() {
                this.blur();
            }
        }
    }
}
```

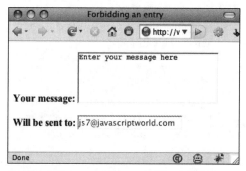

Figure 9.8 The user can't type anything into the bottom field.

Key Event Handling

Besides the mouse, the other main input device is the keyboard, at least until they get that cool computer thought-control device working. Just as with the mouse, JavaScript has the mojo to handle the keyboard.

The onkeydown event

It's handy to allow users to control your Web page via their keyboard as well as via their mouse. With the key event handlers, you can trigger events to happen when the appropriate keys are pressed. In **Scripts 9.20** and **9.21**, a standard slideshow (otherwise identical to the one in Script 4.17) can be viewed by pressing the left and right arrow keys on the keyboard (**Figure 9.9**).

1. `document.onkeydown = keyHit;`

   Here we register the `keyHit()` function as the one to handle `onkeydown` events.

2. `var thisPic = 0;`

   The variable `thisPic` is initialized and set globally, so that it's stored and available for use every time `keyHit()` is called.

3. `function keyHit(evt) {`

   The `keyHit()` function handles the event when keys are hit.

4. `var ltArrow = 37;`
   `var rtArrow = 39;`

   We need to store the appropriate values for when a key is hit. The left arrow key generates a 37, and the right arrow triggers a 39.

Script 9.20 The HTML for the slideshow.

```
<!DOCTYPE html PUBLIC "-//W3C//DTD XHTML 1.0
→ Transitional//EN"
        "http://www.w3.org/TR/xhtml1/DTD/
        → xhtml1-transitional.dtd">
<html xmlns="http://www.w3.org/1999/xhtml">
<head>
    <title>Image Slideshow</title>
    <script type="text/javascript"
    → src="script10.js"></script>
</head>
<body bgcolor="#FFFFFF">
    <h3 align="center">
        <img src="images/callisto.jpg"
        → id="myPicture" width="262"
        → height="262" alt="Slideshow" /><br />
        Use the right and left arrows on your
        → keyboard to view the slideshow
    </h3>
</body>
</html>
```

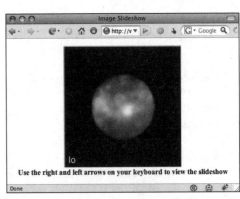

Figure 9.9 This slideshow is controlled with keypresses, rather than mouse clicks on navigation buttons.

Script 9.21 Use the onkeydown handler in this script to trigger a slide change.

```
script
document.onkeydown = keyHit;
var thisPic = 0;

function keyHit(evt) {
    var myPix = new Array("images/callisto.jpg",
    → "images/europa.jpg","images/io.jpg",
    → "images/ganymede.jpg");
    var imgCt = myPix.length-1;
    var ltArrow = 37;
    var rtArrow = 39;

    if (evt) {
        var thisKey = evt.which;
    }
    else {
        var thisKey = window.event.keyCode;
    }

    if (thisKey == ltArrow) {
        chgSlide(-1);
    }
    else if (thisKey == rtArrow) {
        chgSlide(1);
    }
    return false;

    function chgSlide(direction) {
        thisPic = thisPic + direction;
        if (thisPic > imgCt) {
            thisPic = 0;
        }
        if (thisPic < 0) {
            thisPic = imgCt;
        }
        document.getElementById("myPicture").
        → src = myPix[thisPic];
    }
}
```

5.
```
if (evt) {
    var thisKey = evt.which;
}
else {
    var thisKey = window.event.keyCode;
}
```

How we know which key the user hit depends on which browser they're using. If it's Firefox or Safari, we look at `evt.which`, which contains the code for the key hit. If it's IE, that same value will be in `window.event.keyCode`. Either way, the result is saved in `thisKey`.

6.
```
if (thisKey == ltArrow) {
    chgSlide(-1);
}
else if (thisKey == rtArrow) {
    chgSlide(1);
}
```

If the user pressed the left arrow, then go backward through the slideshow. If they pressed the right arrow, go forward. If they chose any other key, don't do anything at all.

7. `return false;`

This line is there to work around a bug in a single browser: Safari. Other browsers handle this just fine, but Safari triggers two keystrokes instead of one (causing `onkeydown` to be triggered twice) every time you press an arrow. If you return a value of `false`, Safari knows that it should stop handling these events, and other browsers don't care one way or another.

The onkeyup event

The onkeyup event handler is identical to the onkeydown handler, except that (big surprise) it gets called when the user has completed pressing the key down and is now letting it come back up again.

The onkeypress event

The onkeypress event is triggered when the user both presses a key down and also lets the key back up again—just for completeness's sake.

✔ Tip

- If you're not sure what the key values are for a particular key, you can find out by putting the line `alert(thiskey);` in between the lines of code in steps 5 and 6, then, press the key for which you want to find the value. The alert box contains the numeric key value.

JavaScript and Cookies

In Web terms, a *cookie* is a unique nugget of information that a Web server gives to your browser when the two first meet and which they then share with each return visit. The remote server saves its part of the cookie and the information it contains about you; your browser does the same, as a plain text file stored on your computer's hard disk.

As a JavaScript author, you can do many useful things with cookies. If your site requires registration, you can set cookies to store your readers' user names and passwords on their hard drives, so they don't need to enter them every time they visit. You can keep track of which parts of your site the user has visited and count the number of visits from that user.

There are many common misconceptions about cookies, so it's important to note what you can't do with them: you can't get any real information about the user such as their email address; you can't use cookies to check out the contents of their hard disks; and cookies can't transmit computer viruses. A cookie is just a simple text file on the user's hard disk where you, the JavaScript programmer, can store some information.

continues on next page

A cookie always includes the address of the server that sent it. That's the primary idea behind cookie technology: identification. Think of it as Caller ID for the Web, with variations on the theme—each Web site using cookies gives your browser a personalized ID of some sort, so that it can recognize you on the next visit. When you return to the Web server that first passed you a particular cookie, the server can query your browser to see if you are one of its many cookie holders. If so, the server can then retrieve the information stored in the cookie the two of you originally exchanged. Keep in mind that cookies just identify the computer being used, not the individual using the computer.

Script 10.1 The HTML for our first cookie page.

```
<!DOCTYPE html PUBLIC "-//W3C//DTD XHTML 1.0
→ Transitional//EN"
        "http://www.w3.org/TR/xhtml1/DTD/
        → xhtml1-transitional.dtd">
<html xmlns="http://www.w3.org/1999/xhtml">
<head>
    <title>Set a cookie based on a form</title>
    <script type="text/javascript"
    → src="script01.js"></script>
</head>
<body bgcolor="#FFFFFF">
    <form id="cookieForm" action="#">
        <h1>Enter your name: <input type="text"
        → id="nameField" /></h1>
    </form>
</body>
</html>
```

Figure 10.1 It doesn't look like much, but the content of the form's text field has just been written to a cookie.

Baking Your First Cookie

A cookie is a text string with a particular format:

```
cookieName=cookieValue;
expires=expirationDateGMT; path=URLpath;
domain=siteDomain
```

Breaking this down, the first part of the string gives the cookie a name and assigns it a value. This is the only mandatory part of a cookie; the rest of the string is optional. Next is the expiration date of the cookie; when this date is reached, the browser automatically deletes the cookie. The expiration date is followed by a URL path, which lets you store a URL in the cookie. Finally, you can store a domain value in the cookie.

Script 10.1, the HTML file, calls the JavaScript in **Script 10.2**, which sets a cookie from a value entered by the user into a form. When you try this one out, it won't appear to do that much (as in **Figure 10.1**), but the cookie is actually being created. Later examples in this chapter build on this one.

To set a cookie:

1. `function nameFieldInit() {`

First, set up the function `nameFieldInit()` to define the value of the cookie. This function is called when the window has completed loading.

2. `var userName = "";`

Next, we initialize the variable `userName` with a null value.

continues on next page

3. `if (document.cookie != "") {`
   `userName = document.cookie.`
   `→ split("=")[1];`

We begin a conditional test by first checking that the object `document.cookie` does not contain a null value. The method `split("=")` splits a cookie into an array, where `cookieField[0]` is the cookie name and `cookieField[1]` is the cookie value. Note that `cookieField` can be any variable that you want to use to store a particular cookie's fields. So you assign `userName` the value returned by `document.cookie.` `split("=")[1]`, that is, the cookie value.

4. `document.getElementById`
   `→ ("nameField").value = userName;`

Setting `getElementById("nameField").` `value` puts the user's name into the text field when the page loads if there's a name stored in the cookie file.

5. `document.getElementById`
   `→ ("nameField").onblur = setCookie;`
   `document.getElementById`
   `→ ("cookieForm").onsubmit =`
   `→ setCookie;`

In the first line, the `onblur` event handler (see Chapter 1) calls the `setCookie()` function when the user leaves the text field. In the second, we do the same thing for the form's `onsubmit` handler. If you press Enter after you've typed your name, Internet Explorer, for some reason, doesn't trigger the `onblur` handler. Adding the `onsubmit` handler catches all the variants.

6. `function setCookie() {`

Now begin a new function, called `setCookie()`.

7. `var expireDate = new Date();`

Get the current date, and put it into the new variable `expireDate`.

Script 10.2 Use this script to set a browser cookie.

```
window.onload = nameFieldInit;

function nameFieldInit() {
    var userName = "";
    if (document.cookie != "") {
        userName = document.cookie.split
        → ("=")[1];
    }

    document.getElementById("nameField").
    → value = userName;
    document.getElementById("nameField").
    → onblur = setCookie;
    document.getElementById("cookieForm").
    → onsubmit = setCookie;
}

function setCookie() {
    var expireDate = new Date();
    expireDate.setMonth(expireDate.
    → getMonth()+6);

    var userName = document.getElementById
    → ("nameField").value;
    document.cookie = "userName=" + userName +
    → ";expires=" + expireDate.toGMTString();

    document.getElementById("nameField").
    → blur();
    return false;
}
```

8. `expireDate.setMonth(expireDate.`
`→ getMonth()+6);`

This line gets the month portion of
`expireDate`, adds 6 to the month,
and then sets the month portion of
`expireDate` to the new value. In other
words, it sets the expiration date of the
cookie we're creating to six months in
the future.

9. `var userName = document.`
`→ getElementById("nameField").value;`

This line creates a new `userName` variable
and assigns it whatever the user typed
into the text field. The `userName` variable
has to be created twice (once inside each
function) because it's not a global; that
is, we're using it inside each function, but
we're not expecting it to keep its value
across functions—it's new each time.

10. `document.cookie = "userName=" +`
`→ userName + ";expires=" +`
`→ expireDate.toGMTString();`

Here's where we write the cookie. We're
setting `document.cookie` (remember, a
cookie is just a text string, so you can
use the same text string techniques to
build it, like using the + sign to combine things) to contain the user's name
and the cookie expiration date. The
`toGMTString()` method converts the
`expireDate` Date object into a text string
so that it can be written into the cookie.

continues on next page

BAKING YOUR FIRST COOKIE

11. `document.getElementById`
`→("nameField").blur();`
`return false;`

Remember when we set up the form so that setCookie() could be called in one of two ways? Here's where we handle the fallout of that choice:

▲ If we're in IE, the first line causes the focus to leave the name field, so it's clear that something has occurred, and the second (returning a value of false) keeps the form from actually submitting.

▲ If we're not in IE, the first line does nothing (that is, we've already left the name field, so leaving it again doesn't matter) and the second line keeps the form submission from being triggered.

✔ Tips

■ This script assumes that the first cookie contains the user name. Later scripts show how to handle multiple cookies and get a cookie by name instead of number.

■ The scripts in this chapter are ordered in such a way that they'll work fine if you run them in the order they appear. If you skip around, though, you may encounter some weird results (such as the browser thinking that your name is a number). If you want to run them out of sequence, try running Script 10.7 ("Deleting Cookies") in between scripts.

A Fistful of Cookies

You can have multiple cookies on a page, and the format for this is:

`"cookieName1=cookieValue1;`
`→expires1=expirationDateGMT1;`
`→path1=sitePath1;`
`→domain1=siteDomain1";`
`"cookieName2=cookieValue2;`
`→expires2=expirationDateGMT2;`
`→path2=sitePath2;`
`→domain2=siteDomain2"`

Again, the only mandatory fields are the name and value pair.

The `split("; ")` command splits the multiple cookie record into an array, with each cookie in a cookie record numbered from 0 on. Note that there is a space after the semicolon in this command. So `cookie-Array[0]` would be the first cookie in the multiple cookie record, `cookieArray[1]` would be next, and so on. For more, see the "Handling Multiple Cookies" example later in this chapter.

Script 10.3 JavaScript uses the id in this HTML page to insert the cookie result.

```
● ● ●                    script
<!DOCTYPE html PUBLIC "-//W3C//DTD XHTML 1.0
→ ransitional//EN"
        "http://www.w3.org/TR/xhtml1/DTD/
        → xhtml1-transitional.dtd">
<html xmlns="http://www.w3.org/1999/xhtml">
<head>
    <title>I know your name!</title>
    <script type="text/javascript"
    → src="script02.js"></script>
</head>
<body bgcolor="#FFFFFF">
    <h1 id="nameField"> </h1>
</body>
</html>
```

Script 10.4 This short script reads a previously set cookie and sends it to the document window.

```
● ● ●                    script
window.onload = nameFieldInit;

function nameFieldInit() {
    if (document.cookie != "") {
        document.getElementById("nameField").
        → innerHTML = "Hello, " + document.
        → cookie.split("=")[1];
    }
}
```

Reading a Cookie

Once you've set a cookie, you'll need to retrieve it in order to do anything useful. The last example set the cookie with the text string "Tom". The very simple **Scripts 10.3** and **10.4** show you how to get that value from the cookie and display it on the screen (of course, you normally would not show off your cookies; this script just displays the cookie as an example).

To read a cookie:

1. if (document.cookie != "") {

   Make sure that the value in the object document.cookie isn't null.

2. document.getElementById
   → ("nameField").innerHTML =
   → "Hello, " + document.cookie.
   → split("=")[1]);

   If the cookie isn't empty, then write a text string (the "Hello," and note the extra space after the comma) and combine it with the split of the cookie value (**Figure 10.2**).

✔ Tip

■ Did you notice that you don't need to specify which of the cookies in the cookie file you are reading? That's because a cookie can only be read by the server that wrote it in the first place. The internal cookie mechanisms in the browser won't let you read or write cookies written by someone else. You only have access to your own cookies.

Figure 10.2 This cookie had my name on it.

Showing Your Cookies

In the previous example, we read the value of one cookie from the server. Now we'll see how to write a script that reads all the cookies that came from your server and displays their names and values. If there are no cookies, the script says, "There are no cookies here" (**Figure 10.3**). If there are cookies, it displays a line per cookie showing what's in the cookie (**Figure 10.4**). **Script 10.5** shows you how.

To show all your cookies:

1. `var outMsg = "";`

   Start by initializing the variable `outMsg`, which will contain the message we want to display.

2. ```
   if (document.cookie == "") {
       outMsg = "There are no cookies
       → here";
   ```

   This conditional test is read, "If the `document.cookie` object is null (that is, empty), then set `outMsg` to "There are no cookies here".

3. ```
   var thisCookie = document.cookie.
   → split("; ");
   ```

   If the previous test failed (i.e., if there was at least one cookie present), then get the values of all of the cookies using `document.cookie.split("; ")` and stuff those values into an array called `thisCookie`. Remember that the `split("; ")` command creates an array of all of the cookies. Later, the script will be able to reference each of the values in that array.

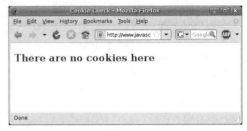

Figure 10.3 If there are no cookies from the server your Web page is on, you'll see this result.

Figure 10.4 If there are one or more cookies, then the script writes them into the document window.

Script 10.5 This script steps through and displays all of the cookies on your machine that have been set by a particular server.

```
●●●                    script
window.onload = showCookies;

function showCookies() {
    var outMsg = "";

    if (document.cookie == "") {
        outMsg = "There are no cookies here";
    }
    else {
        var thisCookie = document.cookie.
        → split("; ");

        for (var i=0; i<thisCookie.length; i++) {
            outMsg += "Cookie name is '" +
            → thisCookie[i].split("=")[0];
            outMsg += "', and the value is '" +
            → thisCookie[i].split("=")[1] +
            → "'<br />";
        }
    }
    document.getElementById("cookieData").
    → innerHTML = outMsg;
}
```

4. `for (var i=0; i<thisCookie.length;`
`→ i++) {`

This line starts a loop by first setting the value of i, the counter variable, to 0. Then, if i is less than the number of cookies in the thisCookie array, increment the value of i by 1.

5. `outMsg += "Cookie name is '" +`
`→ thisCookie[i].split("=")[0]);`
`outMsg += "', and the value is '" +`
`→ thisCookie[i].split("=")[1] +`
`→ "'<br />");`

As the script moves through the array, it puts the text string "Cookie name is '" into outMsg, followed by the name of the cookie. Then it concatenates the text string "', and the value is '" and the value of the cookie. And at the end of each line, we add an HTML break.

6. `document.getElementById.`
`("cookieData").innerHTML = outMsg;`

After setting the variable outMsg, it gets dumped out to the page via innerHTML when all the cookies have been gone through.

Using Cookies as Counters

Because cookies are persistent, that is, because they are available across multiple sessions between a Web server and browser, you can use cookies to store how many times a particular user has accessed a page. But this isn't the same thing as the page counters you see on many Web pages. Because a cookie is specific to a user, you can only tell *that* user how many times he or she has visited; you can't use cookies to tell all users how many times the page has been hit. Still, it's useful to know how to create such an individual counter, and you can adapt **Script 10.6** for other purposes, too (see Tips).

To use a cookie as a counter:

1. `var expireDate = new Date();`
`expireDate.setMonth(expireDate.`
`→ getMonth()+6);`

These two lines are the same as in steps 7 and 8 of the "Baking Your First Cookie" example. Refer there for an explanation.

2. `var hitCt = parseInt(cookieVal`
`→ ("pageHit"));`

The string `pageHit` is the name of the cookie. In a few steps, you'll see the function `cookieVal()`. This line takes the name of the cookie from `cookieVal()`, turns it into a number using the `parseInt()` method, and then stores the result in the variable `hitCt`. The `parseInt()` method changes a string (which is what is in the cookie) into a number (which is what the variable needs to use it as a counter).

Script 10.6 This script counts your cookies.

```
window.onload = initPage;

function initPage() {
    var expireDate = new Date();
    expireDate.setMonth(expireDate.
    → getMonth()+6);

    var hitCt = parseInt(cookieVal("pageHit"));
    hitCt++;

    document.cookie = "pageHit=" + hitCt +
    → ";expires=" + expireDate.toGMTString();
    document.getElementById("pageHits").
    → innerHTML = "You have visited this page "
    → + hitCt + " times.";
}

function cookieVal(cookieName) {
    var thisCookie = document.cookie.
    → split("; ");

    for (var i=0; i<thisCookie.length; i++) {
        if (cookieName == thisCookie[i].
        → split("=")[0]) {
            return thisCookie[i].split("=")[1];
        }
    }
    return 0;
}
```

Figure 10.5 Hard to believe we've visited this dull page this often.

3. `hitCt++;`

Now take the value of `hitCt` and add 1 to it, incrementing the counter.

4. `document.cookie = "pageHit=" +`
`→ hitCt + ";expires=" + expireDate.`
`→ toGMTString();`

This writes back the updated information to the cookie for future use. What's being written is a text string that combines the string `"pageHit="` with the incremented value of `hitCt` and adds `";expires="` with the expiration date, which was incremented by six months back in step 1.

5. `document.getElementById("pageHits").`
`→ innerHTML = "You have visited this`
`→ page " + hitCt + " times.";`

This line displays the user message in the document (**Figure 10.5**). There are extra spaces after "page" and before "times" to make the line look right on screen.

6. `function cookieVal(cookieName) {`

This line begins a new function called `cookieVal()`. It is passed some data, which can then be referenced inside the function as the variable `cookieName`.

7. `var thisCookie = document.cookie.`
`→ split("; ");`

The variable `thisCookie` is set to the array generated by the `split("; ")` method.

8. `for (var i=0; i<thisCookie.length;`
`→ i++) {`

Here we're beginning a loop, just as in step 4 of the "Showing Your Cookies" example.

continues on next page

USING COOKIES AS COUNTERS

9. `if (cookieName == thisCookie[i].`
`→ split("=")[0]) {`

This conditional checks to see if
`cookieName` is the same as the `i`th
element of the cookie array.

10. `return thisCookie[i].split("=")[1];`

If the test in step 9 succeeded, then
return the cookie's value.

11. `return 0;`

If we've looked at all the items in the array
and found no match, return a 0 value.

✔ Tips

■ When you load the HTML page that calls
this script, press the Reload button in your
browser to see the counter increment.

■ As mentioned earlier, you can adapt Script
10.6 for other purposes. One possibility
would be to use a cookie to track when a
particular user had last visited your site
and display different pages depending on
when that was. For example, some online
magazines have a cover page with artwork
and the names of the stories in the day's
issue. If the user visits the site more than
once in a 24-hour period, they only see the
cover page the first time; subsequent visits
jump the user directly to the site's Table of
Contents page.

■ If you want a true page hit counter, one
that tells how many times a page has been
loaded by all users, you'll need to use a
counter program that is installed on your
Web server. Check with your Web hosting
company to see if they have counters
available, or put "Web page hit counter"
into your favorite search engine.

Script 10.7 This script deletes cookies.

```
window.onload = cookieDelete;

function cookieDelete() {
    var cookieCt = 0;

    if (document.cookie != "" && confirm
→ ("Do you want to delete the cookies?")) {
        var thisCookie = document.cookie.
        → split("; ");
        cookieCt = thisCookie.length;

        var expireDate = new Date();
        expireDate.setDate(expireDate.
        → getDate()-1);

        for (var i=0; i<cookieCt; i++) {
            var cookieName = thisCookie[i].
            → split("=")[0];
            document.cookie = cookieName +
            → "=;expires=" + expireDate.
            → toGMTString();
        }
    }
    document.getElementById("cookieData").
    → innerHTML = "Number of cookies deleted: "
    → + cookieCt;
}
```

Figure 10.6 It's good interface design to confirm with the user whenever you are going to erase or delete anything.

Deleting Cookies

At some point, you're going to want to delete a cookie or many cookies in a cookie record. It's fairly easy to do; one technique that works well is to simply set the cookie's expiration date to a date in the past, which causes the browser to delete it automatically. **Script 10.7** shows how to force your cookies to become stale.

To delete cookies:

1. `var cookieCt = 0;`

   This script is going to keep track of how many cookies we've deleted, so we start off by creating the `cookieCt` variable and setting it to zero.

2. `if (document.cookie != "" && confirm`
   `→ ("Do you want to delete the`
   `→ cookies?")) {`

   This test first checks to make sure that the cookie doesn't contain a null value, that is, there are some cookies. If the test shows that the cookie is empty, then the script will do nothing. The second part of the test tells the browser to put up a confirmation dialog with the included text (**Figure 10.6**). If `confirm()` returns `true`, then we know the user wants to delete their cookies. If `false`, then we skip down to step 9.

3. `var thisCookie = document.cookie.`
   `→ split("; ");`

   This line splits the contents of the cookie into an array with the `split("; ")` method and assigns that array to the variable `thisCookie`.

4. `cookieCt = thisCookie.length;`

   We now know how many cookies we're going to be deleting, so that's stored in `cookieCt`.

continues on next page

DELETING COOKIES

5. `var expireDate = new Date();`
`expireDate.setDate(expireDate.`
`→ getDate()-1);`

Here we create a new date object, `expireDate`, which is then set to the current date minus 1—in other words, to yesterday.

6. `for (var i=0; i<cookieCt; i++) {`

Now begin a `for` loop, so that we can delete all the cookies, not just one. First set the value of i to 0; then, as long as i is less than the number of cookies, increment i by 1.

7. `var cookieName = thisCookie[i].`
`→ split("=")[0];`

Use `split("=")[0]` to get the name of the ith cookie in the array, which is then stored in the variable `cookieName`.

8. `document.cookie = cookieName +`
`→ "=;expires=" + expireDate.`
`→ toGMTString();`

Here's where the cookie with the changed expiration date gets written back out.

9. `document.getElementById`
`→ ("cookieData").innerHTML = "Number`
`→ of cookies deleted: " + cookieCt;`

The script is out of the `for` loop now, and this line sets the number of cookies deleted in the HTML document (**Figure 10.7**).

✔ Tip

■ In some previous editions of this book, this script showed nothing at all if no cookies existed, or if the user cancelled the deletion. Setting `innerHTML` to a value will now show the actual number of cookies deleted in those cases (always zero) as well.

Figure 10.7 Users should also get feedback that events have occurred as expected.

Script 10.8 Use an array to deal with multiple cookies in a single script.

```
window.onload = initPage;

function initPage() {
    var now = new Date();
    var expireDate = new Date();
    expireDate.setMonth(expireDate.getMonth()+6);

    var hitCt = parseInt(cookieVal("pageHit"));
    hitCt++;

    var lastVisit = cookieVal("pageVisit");
    if (lastVisit == 0) {
        lastVisit = "";
    }

    document.cookie = "pageHit=" + hitCt +
    → ";expires=" + expireDate.toGMTString();
    document.cookie = "pageVisit=" + now +
    → ";expires=" + expireDate.toGMTString();

    var outMsg = "You have visited this page
    → " + hitCt + " times.";
    if (lastVisit != "") {
        outMsg += "<br />Your last visit was
        → " + lastVisit;
    }
    document.getElementById("cookieData").
    → innerHTML = outMsg;
}

function cookieVal(cookieName) {
    var thisCookie = document.cookie.
    → split("; ");

    for (var i=0; i<thisCookie.length; i++) {
        if (cookieName == thisCookie[i].
        → split("=")[0]) {
            return thisCookie[i].split("=")[1];
        }
    }
    return 0;
}
```

Handling Multiple Cookies

You will often want to deal with more than one cookie at a time, and **Script 10.8** shows you how to read from more than one cookie and display the information. This example shares a fair amount of code with the "Using Cookies as Counters" example.

To handle multiple cookies:

1. `var lastVisit = cookieVal`
   `→ ("pageVisit");`

   We start off by looking for a cookie named `pageVisit` by passing that string to the `cookieVal()` function. It returns a value, which is then stored in `lastVisit`.

2. `if (lastVisit == 0) {`
   `    lastVisit = "";`
   `}`

   If the value of `lastVisit` is zero, then put a null value into `lastVisit`. We now know the user has never been here before.

continues on next page

3.
```
document.cookie = "pageHit=" +
→ hitCt + ";expires=" + expireDate.
→ toGMTString();
document.cookie = "pageVisit=" +
→ now + ";expires=" + expireDate.
→ toGMTString();
```

These two lines write the two cookies back to disk with an updated hit number and visit date.

4.
```
var outMsg = "You have visited this
→ page " + hitCt + " times.";
if (lastVisit != "") {
  outMsg += "<br />Your last visit
  → was " + lastVisit;
}
```

The outMsg variable stores the outgoing message for our site's visitor and starts off by being set to tell them how many times they've been here. The next lines check if the user has been here before (in code: if lastVisit isn't null) and if they have, we remind them when.

5.
```
document.getElementById
→ ("cookieData").innerHTML = outMsg;
```

And finally, outMsg is displayed on the screen, telling the user what they've done before. The result of this script is shown in **Figure 10.8**.

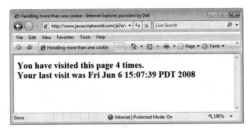

Figure 10.8 The two cookies, written to the screen (along with some other text).

Script 10.9 The HTML of this page applies the next script's results to the page.

```
<!DOCTYPE html PUBLIC "-//W3C//DTD XHTML 1.0
→ Transitional//EN"
        "http://www.w3.org/TR/xhtml1/DTD/
        → xhtml1-transitional.dtd">
<html xmlns="http://www.w3.org/1999/xhtml">
<head>
    <title>New for You</title>
    <link type="text/css" rel="stylesheet"
    → href="script07.css" />
    <script type="text/javascript"
    → src="script07.js"></script>
</head>
<body>
    <p>Negrino and Smith's most recent books:
    → </p>
    <p id="New-20080901"><a href="http://www.
    → javascriptworld.com/">JavaScript &amp;
    → Ajax for the Web: Visual QuickStart
    → Guide, 7th Edition</a></p>
    <p id="New-20081027"><a href="http://
    → www.dreamweaverbook.com/">Adobe
    → Dreamweaver for Windows &amp; Macintosh:
    → Visual QuickStart Guide</a></p>
</body>
</html>
```

Script 10.10 The CSS combined with the JavaScript and HTML makes things personal.

```
body {
    background-color: #FFF;
}

p.newImg {
    padding-left: 35px;
    background-image: url(images/new.gif);
    background-repeat: no-repeat;
}
```

Displaying "New to You" Messages

You can use cookies and JavaScript to alert frequent visitors to your site to items that are new to them. This gives the user a more personalized experience when they visit your site, making it a smarter and friendlier place. **Scripts 10.9**, **10.10**, and **10.11** add a little "New!" image to the beginning of lines when the cookie says that a line has been added since the last time the visitor was there (**Figure 10.9**). Again, you'll see familiar code from previous examples in this chapter.

To display a "New to You" message:

1. ```
   p.newImg {
       padding-left: 35px;
       background-image:
       → url(images/new.gif);
       background-repeat: no-repeat;
   }
   ```

   In Script 10.10, we use CSS to specify that anything on the page marked as a paragraph (within a <p> tag) which also has a class of newImg will have 35 pixels of padding added to the left and a "New!" image put in the background. However, since the padding ensures that nothing appears in front of the paragraph contents, the image won't look like a background pattern.

   continues on next page

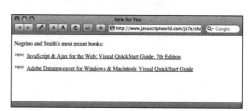

Figure 10.9 JavaScript can ask a cookie when you've last visited a site and flag new items for you.
   ```

2. ```
   <p id="New-20080901"><a href=
   → "http://www.javascriptworld.
   → com/">JavaScript &amp; Ajax for
   → the Web: Visual QuickStart Guide,
   → 7th Edition</a></p>
   <p id="New-20081027"><a href=
   → "http://www.dreamweaverbook.
   → com/">Adobe Dreamweaver for
   → Windows &amp; Macintosh: Visual
   → QuickStart Guide</a></p>
   ```

   In Script 10.9, the id attributes on these two paragraphs will signal to the JavaScript (as we'll see shortly) that they contain dates that get compared against the information set up in the following steps.

3. ```
   var lastVisit = new Date(cookieVal
   → ("pageVisit"));
   var expireDate = new Date();
   expireDate.setMonth(expireDate.
   → getMonth()+6);
   ```

   In Script 10.11, this section initializes the lastVisit, and expireDate dates. The first is the saved date of the surfer's last visit to the site and the second will be the expiration date of the cookie when it's rewritten.

4. ```
   document.cookie = "pageVisit=" +
   → now + ";expires=" + expireDate.
   → toGMTString();
   ```

   This line writes the cookie, putting the current date into the pageVisit value and the value of expireDate into expires.

5. ```
   var allGrafs = document.
   → getElementsByTagName("p");
   ```

   This line creates an array of all the <p> elements on the page, which allows us to go through each of them one by one looking for just the ones we care about.

Script 10.11 This script can help you personalize your site by alerting the user to new content.

```
window.onload = initPage;

function initPage() {
    var now = new Date();
    var lastVisit = new Date(cookieVal
    → ("pageVisit"));
    var expireDate = new Date();
    expireDate.setMonth(expireDate.
    → getMonth()+6);

    document.cookie = "pageVisit=" + now +
    → ";expires=" + expireDate.toGMTString();
    var allGrafs = document.
    → getElementsByTagName("p");

    for (var i=0; i<allGrafs.length; i++) {
        if (allGrafs[i].id.indexOf("New-")
        → != -1) {
            newCheck(allGrafs[i],allGrafs[i].
            → id.substring(4));
        }
    }
}

function newCheck(grafElement,dtString) {
    var yyyy = parseInt(dtString.
    → substring(0,4),10);
    var mm = parseInt(dtString.
    → substring(4,6),10);
    var dd = parseInt(dtString.
    → substring(6,8),10);
    var lastChgd = new Date(yyyy,mm-1,dd);

    if (lastChgd.getTime() > lastVisit.
    → getTime()) {
        grafElement.className += " newImg";
    }
}
```

(script continues on next page)

Script 10.11 *continued*

```
function cookieVal(cookieName) {
    var thisCookie = document.cookie.
    → split("; ");

    for (var i=0; i<thisCookie.length; i++) {
        if (cookieName == thisCookie[i].
        → split("=")[0]) {
            return thisCookie[i].split("=")[1];
        }
    }
    return "1 January 1970";
}
```

6. `for (var i=0; i<allGrafs.length;`
`→ i++) {`

Here, we start a loop to go through the array, looking at each paragraph element in turn.

7. `if (allGrafs[i].id.indexOf("New-")`
`→ != -1) {`

If this paragraph has an `id` attribute that contains the text "New-", then we know that this is a paragraph we care about, so do the following.

8. `newCheck(allGrafs[i], allGrafs[i].`
`→ id.substring(4));`

We want to check to see if this paragraph has something in it that will be new to the visitor. The `newCheck()` function will do that, and it's passed two parameters: the current paragraph element (`allGrafs[i]`) and the second part of the `id` attribute. The `substring()` grabs the part of the string from the fifth character on to the end, and as that's all we care about here, that's all we'll pass. (Remember that JavaScript strings are zero-relative, which is why the fifth character of the string is found at position 4.)

9. `function newCheck(grafElement,`
`→ dtString) {`

This function is expecting two parameters to be passed in, which will be referred to internally as `grafElement` (that paragraph element) and `dtString` (the second part of the `id` attribute).

continues on next page

10.
```
var yyyy = parseInt(dtString.
→ substring(0,4),10);
var mm = parseInt(dtString.
→ substring(4,6),10);
var dd = parseInt(dtString.
→ substring(6,8),10);
```

Here, the date is parsed out of a string; so, for example, "20060901" is 1 September 2006.

The yyyy variable gets the first 4 digits (starting at digit 0 and ending just before digit 4), with the result of "2006". The mm variable gets the fourth and fifth digits, and the dd variable gets the sixth and seventh digits. In each case, we also do a parseInt() on the result, which forces the value returned by substring() into an integer.

11.
```
var lastChgd = new Date(yyyy, mm-1,
→ dd);
```

Finally, we can set lastChgd, because we've got a year, month, and day. But wait! JavaScript and its bizarre dates now hit us, and we have to subtract 1 from the month to get the correct result—just the month, mind you, not the year or day. Really. Months are zero-relative, years and days are one-relative. (See Chapter 12, "Making Your Pages Dynamic," for more on dates and their oddities.)

12. `if (lastChgd.getTime() > lastVisit.`
`→ getTime()) {`

Now we can compare the two dates, and only do the following line if the date that the information last changed is after the date the surfer last visited.

13. `grafElement.className += " newImg";`

Now, here's the slick part: we know that this is a paragraph that should display the "New!" image. So, if we add a class attribute of `newImg` to the `<p>` tag, that style (declared on the HTML page) automatically then applies to that paragraph, resulting in the display of the image.

That is, we can use JavaScript to add an attribute (and its associated value) to an element. In this case, the element is a `<p>`, the attribute is `class`, and the value of the attribute is `newImg`. As the element may already have an existing class, this code takes care to add the value and not just overwrite what's currently there.

Once this new attribute has been added, it triggers the browser's rendering engine to immediately and automatically apply the style to the element, causing the image to appear.

continues on next page

More about substring()

The command `substring(to,from)` returns the characters in a string, starting with the **to** position and ending with the character just before the **from** position, zero-relative. So, if the string contains "20060807", and you want characters 5 and 6, you want to use `substring(4,6)`. Your result is the string "08".

The **from** parameter is optional; leaving it off means you'll get the string starting from the **to** position all the way to the end.

DISPLAYING "NEW TO YOU" MESSAGES

```
14. function cookieVal(cookieName) {
        var thisCookie = document.cookie.
        → split("; ");

        for (var i=0; i<thisCookie.
        → length; i++) {
          if (cookieName ==
          → thisCookie[i].
          → split("=")[0]) {
            return thisCookie[i].
            → split("=")[1];
          }
        }
        return "1 January 1970";
    }
```

This is the now-familiar cookieVal() function. The only difference here is that it has been changed to return "1 January 1970" instead of zero if no cookie with that name was found, which makes the code a bit simpler elsewhere. The oddity of that date is that JavaScript thinks that is when time began, so everything should be after that. That date won't appear to the user; it's just an internal reference date for JavaScript.

✔ Tip

■ You're probably more familiar with parseInt() being passed only a single parameter. Here, two are passed: the string to be converted, and 10. That last parameter tells parseInt() to always return a decimal number. Otherwise, when parseInt() is passed a string starting with 0, it may try to turn the result into octal (base 8 numbering), with incorrect results. In this case, a call to parseInt("09") doesn't return the same result as parseInt("09",10), and the latter is what we want. It's just a weird JavaScript thing that you need to be aware of.

OBJECTS
AND THE DOM

Node manipulation is the W3C-recommended way for standards-compliant browsers to support Web pages that act more like applications than the standard, static pages that you're used to. For instance, you can have pages that change based on entries the user makes, without hitting the server, and you can update pages under script control. Although you can use techniques like `innerHTML`, as we've done elsewhere in this book, here we show the officially supported approach. While this can also be done with server-side CGIs, it's only with JavaScript that we can provide this functionality without the user having to go from page to page to page.

In this chapter, you'll learn a bit more about nodes and the DOM; add, delete, and work with specific nodes; and insert and replace nodes on your pages.

About Node Manipulation

This chapter is about the deepest that this book goes into JavaScript and the DOM, so we'll first need to cover a little bit of history and terminology.

DOM-2 and the W3C

The W3C (as mentioned in Chapter 1) has released specifications for how browsers should handle the Document Object Model (also known as the DOM). The DOM Level 2 specification, which became an official recommendation in November 2000, goes into more depth as to how browsers should be able to refer to and manage the content on their pages. You can find out more details about the specification at `http://www.w3.org/TR/DOM-Level-2-Core/`.

Although this specification has been around for years, there are still plenty of browsers in use that have incomplete or partial DOM-2 support. Before using any of these scripts, make sure that your intended audience is able to run them, or that you offer another way for older browsers to achieve the same results. Thankfully, the majority of surfers today use Internet Explorer 6+, Firefox, or Safari, which should all work just fine with these scripts.

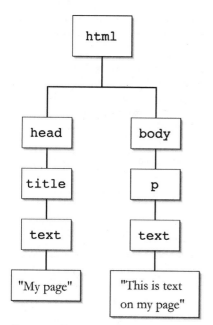

Figure 11.1 The tree structure, showing nodes, is just another way of looking at how an HTML page is organized.

DOM-2 terminology

At the beginning of this book, we referred to JavaScript as "the snap-together language," because of the way that you can put objects, properties, and methods together to build JavaScript applications. There's a different way to look at HTML pages that we've only briefly mentioned before: as a tree structure with *nodes*. For example, this simple Web page

```
<html>
<head>
    <title>My page</title>
</head>
<body>
    <p>This is text on my page</p>
</body>
</html>
```

can be displayed as seen in **Figure 11.1**.

We can use JavaScript to modify any aspect of this tree, including the ability to add, access, change, and delete nodes on the tree. Each box on the tree is a node. If the node contains an HTML tag, it's referred to as an *element node*. Otherwise, it's referred to as a *text node*. Of course, element nodes can contain text nodes.

DOM-3

Level 3 of the DOM standard became an official recommendation in April 2004. That specification is at http://www.w3.org/TR/DOM-Level-3-Core/. As with so many other parts of the W3C process, we're still a long ways off from true support in shipping browsers, so this chapter sticks to discussing DOM-2. However, if you're interested in learning more about DOM-3, the best place to look is at ECMAScript bindings, which can be found at http://www.w3.org/TR/DOM-Level-3-Core/ecma-script-binding.html.

ABOUT NODE MANIPULATION

Adding Nodes

The easiest way to learn about nodes is to start off by simply appending an element node (one which will contain a text node) to the end of your document. **Scripts 11.1** (the HTML) and **11.2** allow the user to enter some data and click a button, and voila! a new paragraph is added to your page (**Figure 11.2**).

To add nodes:

1. `var newText = document.createTextNode`
   `→ (inText);`

   We start by creating a new text node (called `newText`) using the `createTextNode()` method, which will contain whatever text was found in `textArea`.

2. `var newGraf = document.createElement`
   `→ ("p");`

   Next, we create a new element node using the `createElement()` method. While the node we're creating here is a paragraph tag, it could be any HTML container (`div`, `span`, etc.). The name of the new element is `newGraf`.

3. `newGraf.appendChild(newText);`

   In order to put the new text into the new paragraph, we have to call `appendChild()`. That's a method of `newGraf`, which, when passed `newText`, puts the text node into the paragraph.

Script 11.1 This HTML creates the text area and submit button that allow the user to add a text node.

```
<!DOCTYPE html PUBLIC "-//W3C//DTD XHTML 1.0
→ Transitional//EN"
         "http://www.w3.org/TR/xhtml1/DTD/
         → xhtml1-transitional.dtd">
<html xmlns="http://www.w3.org/1999/xhtml">
<head>
    <title>Adding Nodes</title>
    <script type="text/javascript"
    → src="script01.js"></script>
</head>
<body>
    <form action="#">
        <p><textarea id="textArea" rows="5"
        → cols="30"></textarea></p>
        <input type="submit" value="Add some
        → text to the page" />
    </form>
</body>
</html>
```

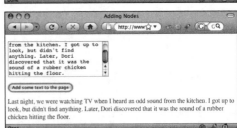

Figure 11.2 To add a node, enter the text in the field (top), and then click the button. The text appears on the page (bottom).

ADDING NODES

Script 11.2 With this script, the user can add any text they want to the page.

```
window.onload = initAll;

function initAll() {
    document.getElementsByTagName("form")[0].
    → onsubmit = addNode;
}

function addNode() {
    var inText = document.getElementById
    → ("textArea").value;
    var newText = document.createTextNode
    → (inText);

    var newGraf = document.createElement
    → ("p");
    newGraf.appendChild(newText);

    var docBody = document.
    → getElementsByTagName("body")[0];
    docBody.appendChild(newGraf);

    return false;
}
```

4. `var docBody = document.`
   `→ getElementsByTagName("body")[0];`

   In order to add a new node into the body of our document, we need to figure out where the body is. The `getElementsByTagName()` method gives us every body tag on our page. If our page is standards-compliant, there should only be one. The `[0]` property is that first body tag, and we store that in `docBody`.

5. `docBody.appendChild(newGraf);`

   And finally, appending `newGraf` onto `docBody` (using `appendChild()` again) puts the user's new text onto the page.

✔ Tip

- Wondering why you'd bother to go through all the hassle of creating a text node, creating an element node, and appending a child to each just to do what you could have done with a simple assignment to `innerHTML`? Here's one reason: with this approach, you cannot make your page invalid. For example, every <p> or <div> tag that's added is automatically closed. With `innerHTML`, on the other hand, it's very easy (almost too easy) to create tag soup—and once you do, your page's DOM becomes difficult to work with. You can't read the contents of an element if it has a beginning but no ending tag, for instance.

Deleting Nodes

If you want to add content to your page, you're also likely to want to delete content from your page. **Scripts 11.3** (the HTML) and **11.4** delete the last paragraph on the page, as shown in **Figure 11.3**.

To delete nodes:

1. `var allGrafs = document.`
   `→ getElementsBy TagName("p");`

   This line uses the `getElementsByTagName` method to collect all the paragraph tags in our page and store them in the `allGrafs` array.

2. `if (allGrafs.length > 1) {`

   Before doing anything we regret, we have to check first that the `allGrafs` array has a `length` greater than one. We don't want to try to delete something that doesn't exist, and the `length` will always be at least one (as Script 11.3's `textarea` form field is inside a `<p>` tag).

Script 11.3 This script adds a link, rather than a button, to delete a text node.

```
<!DOCTYPE html PUBLIC "-//W3C//DTD XHTML 1.0
    Transitional//EN"
        "http://www.w3.org/TR/xhtml1/DTD/
        → xhtml1-transitional.dtd">
<html xmlns="http://www.w3.org/1999/xhtml">
<head>
    <title>Deleting Nodes</title>
    <script type="text/javascript"
    → src="script02.js"></script>
</head>
<body>
    <form action="#">
        <p><textarea id="textArea" rows="5"
        → cols="30"></textarea></p>
        <input type="submit" value="Add some
        → text to the page" />
    </form>
    <a id="deleteNode" href="#">Delete last
    → paragraph</a>
</body>
</html>
```

Figure 11.3 The last paragraph on this page needed a little revision (left), so it's good that it can be deleted using the "Delete last paragraph" link (right).

Script 11.4 Now the user can both add and delete text.

```
window.onload = initAll;

function initAll() {
    document.getElementsByTagName("form")[0].
    → onsubmit = addNode;
    document.getElementById("deleteNode").
    → onclick = delNode;
}

function addNode() {
    var inText = document.
    → getElementById("textArea").value;
    var newText = document.createTextNode
    → (inText);

    var newGraf = document.createElement
    → ("p");
    newGraf.appendChild(newText);

    var docBody = document.
    → getElementsByTagName("body")[0];
    docBody.appendChild(newGraf);

    return false;
}

function delNode() {
    var allGrafs = document.
    → getElementsByTagName("p");

    if (allGrafs.length > 1) {
        var lastGraf = allGrafs.item
        → (allGrafs.length-1);
        var docBody = document.
        → getElementsByTagName("body")[0];
        docBody.removeChild(lastGraf);
    }
    else {
        alert("Nothing to remove!");
    }

    return false;
}
```

3. `var lastGraf = allGrafs.item`
`→ (allGrafs.length-1);`

If there are paragraphs, get the last one on the page by subtracting one from `length` and using that as our index array. Remember that `length` is one-relative while arrays are zero-relative, so subtracting one from the `length` gives us the last paragraph on the page.

4. `var docBody = document.`
`→ getElementsBy TagName("body")[0];`
`docBody.removeChild(lastGraf);`

Just like the last task, in order to modify the document we need to get the contents of the `body`. Once we've got that, it's simply a matter of calling the `docBody.removeChild()` method and passing it `lastGraf`, which tells JavaScript which paragraph we want to delete. Our page should immediately show one less paragraph.

✔ Tip

■ Once again, remember that you can delete element nodes other than paragraphs. To do this, you need to change the script so that `getElementsByTagName()` is passed something other than a `p`.

DELETING NODES

273

Deleting Specific Nodes

While always deleting the last paragraph might be interesting, you'll sometimes want to delete something that's not at the end of the page. **Scripts 11.5** (the HTML) and **11.6** make our code considerably more flexible, allowing the user to decide which paragraph is history, as shown in **Figures 11.4** and **11.5**.

To delete a particular node:

1. `nodeChgArea = document.`
   `→ getElementById("modifiable");`

   As our HTML page now has multiple paragraphs, it could be confusing to keep track of which can and can't be deleted. Instead, we now set up an entirely new area: a div with the id of modifiable. Here, we set the global variable nodeChgArea to that element node.

   continues on page 276

Script 11.5 Radio buttons let you offer your visitors the choice of adding or deleting text.

```
<!DOCTYPE html PUBLIC "-//W3C//DTD XHTML 1.0
→ Transitional//EN"
        "http://www.w3.org/TR/xhtml1/DTD/
        → xhtml1-transitional.dtd">
<html xmlns="http://www.w3.org/1999/xhtml">
<head>
    <title>Deleting Selected Nodes</title>
    <script type="text/javascript"
    → src="script03.js"></script>
</head>
<body>
    <form action="#">
        <p><textarea id="textArea" rows="5"
        → cols="30"></textarea></p>
        <p><label><input type="radio"
        → name="nodeAction" />Add node</label>
        <label><input type="radio"
        → name="nodeAction"
        → />Delete node</label></p>
        Paragraph #: <select id="grafCount">
        → </select>
        <input type="submit" value="Submit" />
    </form>
    <div id="modifiable"> </div>
</body>
</html>
```

Script 11.6 This script allows users to choose which paragraph they want to delete.

```
window.onload = initAll;
var nodeChgArea;

function initAll() {
    document.getElementsByTagName("form")[0].onsubmit = nodeChanger;
    nodeChgArea = document.getElementById("modifiable");
}

function addNode() {
    var inText = document.getElementById("textArea").value;
    var newText = document.createTextNode(inText);

    var newGraf = document.createElement("p");
    newGraf.appendChild(newText);

    nodeChgArea.appendChild(newGraf);
}

function delNode() {
    var grafChoice = document.getElementById("grafCount").selectedIndex;
    var allGrafs = nodeChgArea.getElementsByTagName("p");
    var oldGraf = allGrafs.item(grafChoice);

    nodeChgArea.removeChild(oldGraf);
}

function nodeChanger()  {
    var actionType = -1;
    var pGrafCt = nodeChgArea.getElementsByTagName("p").length;
    var radioButtonSet = document.getElementsByTagName("form")[0].nodeAction;

    for (var i=0; i<radioButtonSet.length; i++) {
      if (radioButtonSet[i].checked) {
          actionType = i;
      }
    }

    switch(actionType) {
      case 0:
          addNode();
          break;
```

(script continues on next page)

2. `var grafChoice = document.`
`→ getElementById("grafCount").`
`→ selectedIndex;`
`var allGrafs = nodeChgArea.`
`→ getElementsByTagName("p");`
`var oldGraf = allGrafs.item`
`→ (grafChoice);`

When the user chose to delete a paragraph, they also had to pick which paragraph to delete. We read that number from the `grafCount` field and store it in `grafChoice`. The `allGrafs` variable is then set to be all the paragraphs within `nodeChangingArea`, and the paragraph to be deleted is then stored in `oldGraf`.

3. `nodeChgArea.removeChild(oldGraf);`

This step is just like that in the previous task, except that when it's run we'll see paragraphs disappear from the middle of our page.

Script 11.6 *continued*

```
case 1:
    if (pGrafCt > 0) {
        delNode();
        break;
    }
default:
    alert("No valid action was chosen");
}

document.getElementById("grafCount").
→ options.length = 0;

for (i=0; i<nodeChgArea.
→ getElementsByTagName("p").length; i++) {
    document.getElementById("grafCount").
    → options[i] = new Option(i+1);
}

return false;
}
```

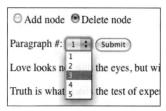

Figure 11.4 After adding nodes, the Paragraph # pop-up menu contains a list of paragraph numbers.

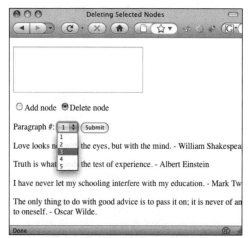

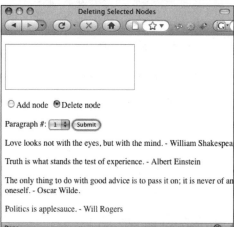

Figure 11.5 First, you click the Delete node radio button, and then you choose a paragraph to delete from the pop-up menu (top). Clicking the Submit button wipes out the selected paragraph (the Mark Twain quote) and moves up the following paragraph (bottom).

✔ Tips

- Having trouble figuring out some of the other code? The nodeChanger() function combines (in order of appearance) functionality from Scripts 7.12, 2.15, and 7.4. It's very common in programming to have a library of simple routines, which, when put together, can create a single, much more complex whole.

- Note that in the code above we're using nodeChgArea where we previously used docBody—when you're working with nodes, it's straightforward to swap out code that works with one element node for another. Here, we're looking at just one part of the page instead of the whole, but the overall way to accomplish our task is identical.

- Instead of declaring nodeChgArea as a global variable and initializing it in initAll(), we could have created and initialized it locally inside every function in which it's used. Each choice has its pros and cons; here, we went with the global so that we didn't have to initialize it over and over again.

Inserting Nodes

Along with wanting to delete nodes other than at the end of the document, you're likely to want to add nodes somewhere other than the end. With **Scripts 11.7** (the HTML) and **11.8**, you'll be able to choose where you want your new nodes to appear. In **Figure 11.6**, you can see how the new node gets inserted.

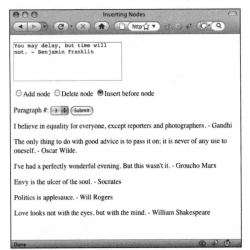
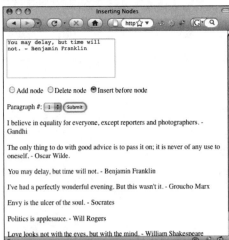

Figure 11.6 To insert a paragraph, click the Insert before node radio button, select the desired paragraph you want for the insertion point (top), enter your text, and then click Submit (bottom).

Script 11.7 Another radio button and some script changes allow a third option—inserting text before another paragraph.

```
<!DOCTYPE html PUBLIC "-//W3C//DTD XHTML 1.0
→ Transitional//EN"
        "http://www.w3.org/TR/xhtml1/DTD/
        → xhtml1-transitional.dtd">
<html xmlns="http://www.w3.org/1999/xhtml">
<head>
    <title>Inserting Nodes</title>
    <script type="text/javascript"
    → src="script04.js"></script>
</head>
<body>
    <form action="#">
        <p><textarea id="textArea" rows="5"
        → cols="30"></textarea></p>
        <p><label><input type="radio"
        → name="nodeAction" />Add node</label>
        <label><input type="radio"
        → name="nodeAction"
        → />Delete node</label>
        <label><input type="radio"
        → name="nodeAction" />Insert before
        → node</label></p>
        Paragraph #: <select id="grafCount"></
        → select>
        <input type="submit" value="Submit" />
    </form>
    <div id="modifiable"> </div>
</body>
</html>
```

Script 11.8 The user can now add text anywhere on the page.

```
                                    script
window.onload = initAll;
var nodeChgArea;

function initAll() {
    document.getElementsByTagName("form")[0].onsubmit = nodeChanger;
    nodeChgArea = document.getElementById("modifiable");
}

function addNode() {
    var inText = document.getElementById("textArea").value;
    var newText = document.createTextNode(inText);

    var newGraf = document.createElement("p");
    newGraf.appendChild(newText);

    nodeChgArea.appendChild(newGraf);
}

function delNode() {
    var grafChoice = document.getElementById("grafCount").selectedIndex;
    var allGrafs = nodeChgArea.getElementsByTagName("p");
    var oldGraf = allGrafs.item(grafChoice);

    nodeChgArea.removeChild(oldGraf);
}

function insertNode() {
    var grafChoice = document.getElementById("grafCount").selectedIndex;
    var inText = document.getElementById("textArea").value;

    var newText = document.createTextNode(inText);
    var newGraf = document.createElement("p");
    newGraf.appendChild(newText);

    var allGrafs = nodeChgArea.getElementsByTagName("p");
    var oldGraf = allGrafs.item(grafChoice);

    nodeChgArea.insertBefore(newGraf,oldGraf);
}
```

(script continues on next page)

INSERTING NODES

To insert a node:

1. `var grafChoice = document.`
`→ getElementById("grafCount").`
`→ selectedIndex;`
`var inText = document.getElementById`
`→ ("textArea").value;`

In order to insert a paragraph, we need to know two things: the place where the user wants it inserted (`grafChoice`) and the text they want inserted (`inText`).

2. `var newText = document.`
`→ createTextNode(inText);`
`var newGraf = document.`
`→ createElement("p");`
`newGraf.appendChild(newText);`

Here's our by-now standard way of creating a new paragraph node and filling it with the user's text.

3. `var allGrafs = nodeChgArea.`
`→ getElementsByTagName("p");`
`var oldGraf = allGrafs.item`
`→ (grafChoice);`

Once again, we get all the p tags in our region, and then we store the target paragraph (the one we'll be inserting our new paragraph in front of) in `oldGraf`.

4. `nodeChgArea.insertBefore`
`→ (newGraf,oldGraf);`

The new paragraph is inserted by calling the `insertBefore()` method and passing it two parameters: the new node and the existing node that we want the new node to be inserted before (hence the name).

✔ Tip

■ While you might think that if there's an `insertBefore()` there ought to be an `insertAfter()`, but that's not the case. If you want to add something to the end of the page, you need to use `appendChild()`.

INSERTING NODES

Script 11.8 *continued*

```
function nodeChanger() {
    var actionType = -1;
    var pGrafCt = nodeChgArea.
    → getElementsByTagName("p").length;
    var radioButtonSet = document.
    → getElementsByTagName("form")[0].
    → nodeAction;

    for (var i=0; i<radioButtonSet.length;
    → i++) {
        if (radioButtonSet[i].checked) {
            actionType = i;
        }
    }

    switch(actionType) {
        case 0:
            addNode();
            break;
        case 1:
            if (pGrafCt > 0) {
                delNode();
                break;
            }
        case 2:
            if (pGrafCt > 0) {
                insertNode();
                break;
            }
        default:
            alert("No valid action was chosen");
    }

    document.getElementById("grafCount").
    → options.length = 0;

    for (i=0; i<nodeChgArea.
    → getElementsByTagName("p").length; i++) {
        document.getElementById("grafCount").
        → options[i] = new Option(i+1);
    }

    return false;
}
```

Script 11.9 Adding the Replace node radio button to the HTML rounds out our node manipulation examples.

```
● ● ●                    script
<!DOCTYPE html PUBLIC "-//W3C//DTD XHTML 1.0
→ Transitional//EN"
        "http://www.w3.org/TR/xhtml1/DTD/
        → xhtml1-transitional.dtd">
<html xmlns="http://www.w3.org/1999/xhtml">
<head>
    <title>Replacing Nodes</title>
    <script type="text/javascript"
    → src="script05.js"></script>
</head>
<body>
    <form action="#">
        <p><textarea id="textArea" rows="5"
        → cols="30"></textarea></p>
        <p><label><input type="radio"
        → name="nodeAction" />Add node</label>
        <label><input type="radio"
        → name="nodeAction" />Delete
        → node</label>
        <label><input type="radio"
        → name="nodeAction" />Insert before
        → node</label>
        <label><input type="radio"
        → name="nodeAction" />Replace
        → node</label></p>
        Paragraph #: <select
        → id="grafCount"></select>
        <input type="submit" value="Submit" />
    </form>
    <div id="modifiable"> </div>
</body>
</html>
```

Replacing Nodes

While you can always delete existing nodes and insert new nodes, it's simpler to just replace nodes if that's what you want. **Scripts 11.9** (the HTML) and **11.10** show how you can replace one node with another. **Figure 11.7** shows the replacement process.

Script 11.10 And now, the user can add, delete, and replace any text on the page.

```
window.onload = initAll;
var nodeChgArea;

function initAll() {
    document.getElementsByTagName("form")[0].onsubmit = nodeChanger;
    nodeChgArea = document.getElementById("modifiable");
}

function addNode() {
    var inText = document.getElementById("textArea").value;
    var newText = document.createTextNode(inText);

    var newGraf = document.createElement("p");
    newGraf.appendChild(newText);

    nodeChgArea.appendChild(newGraf);
}

function delNode() {
    var grafChoice = document.getElementById("grafCount").selectedIndex;
    var allGrafs = nodeChgArea.getElementsByTagName("p");
    var oldGraf = allGrafs.item(grafChoice);

    nodeChgArea.removeChild(oldGraf);
}

function insertNode() {
    var grafChoice = document.getElementById("grafCount").selectedIndex;
    var inText = document.getElementById("textArea").value;

    var newText = document.createTextNode(inText);
    var newGraf = document.createElement("p");
    newGraf.appendChild(newText);

    var allGrafs = nodeChgArea.getElementsByTagName("p");
    var oldGraf = allGrafs.item(grafChoice);

    nodeChgArea.insertBefore(newGraf,oldGraf);
}
```

(script continues on next page)

Script 11.10 *continued*

```
○ ○ ○                              script
function replaceNode() {
    var grafChoice = document.getElementById("grafCount").selectedIndex;
    var inText = document.getElementById("textArea").value;

    var newText = document.createTextNode(inText);
    var newGraf = document.createElement("p");
    newGraf.appendChild(newText);

    var allGrafs = nodeChgArea.getElementsByTagName("p");
    var oldGraf = allGrafs.item(grafChoice);

    nodeChgArea.replaceChild(newGraf,oldGraf);
}

function nodeChanger()  {
    var actionType = -1;
    var pGrafCt = nodeChgArea.getElementsByTagName("p").length;
    var radioButtonSet = document.getElementsByTagName("form")[0].nodeAction;

    for (var i=0; i<radioButtonSet.length; i++) {
        if (radioButtonSet[i].checked) {
            actionType = i;
        }
    }

    switch(actionType) {
        case 0:
            addNode();
            break;
        case 1:
            if (pGrafCt > 0) {
                delNode();
                break;
            }
        case 2:
            if (pGrafCt > 0) {
                insertNode();
                break;
            }
        case 3:
            if (pGrafCt > 0) {
```

(Script continues on next page)

To replace nodes:

◆ `nodeChgArea.replaceChild`
  `→ (newGraf,oldGraf);`

  The only line in this script that should be new to you is this one (see the rest of this chapter for explanations about the rest of the script). And in a similar fashion to the last task, all we need to do is call `replaceChild()` with two parameters: the paragraph we want to swap in and the paragraph we want to swap out.

Script 11.10 *continued*

```
            replaceNode();
            break
        }
    default:
        alert("No valid action was chosen");
}

document.getElementById("grafCount").
→ options.length = 0;

for (i=0; i<nodeChgArea.
→ getElementsByTagName("p").length; i++) {
    document.getElementById("grafCount").
    → options[i] = new Option(i+1);
}

return false;
}
```

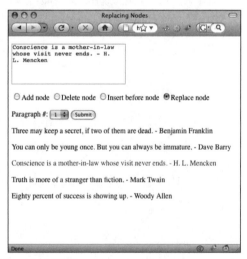

Figure 11.7 Here, we've replaced the third paragraph (left) with new text (right).

Writing Code with Object Literals

As covered in the sidebar, *About Object Literals*, there's more than one way to write any given JavaScript. **Script 11.11** is an example of how Script 11.10 can be rewritten to use object literals.

About Object Literals

Standard procedural JavaScript, like what you've seen so far, has been in the dot notation format:

```
var myCat = new Object;
myCat.name = "Pixel";
myCat.breed = "Tuxedo";
myCat.website = "www.pixel.mu";

function allAboutMyCat() {
    alert("Can I tell you about my cat?");
    tellMeMore = true;
}
```

Where in object literal format, that same code would be something like this:

```
var myCat = {
    name : "Pixel",
    breed : "Tuxedo",
    website: "www.pixel.mu",
    allAbout : function() {
        alert("Can I tell you about my cat?");
        tellMeMore = true;
    }
}
```

With either format, you can refer to a property of `myCat` as `myCat.name` (for instance). However, with object literal format, the function becomes `myCat.allAbout()` instead of `allAboutMyCat()`.

If at this point you're thinking that this looks sort of familiar, pat yourself on the back—it's very similar, in many ways, to CSS. At its most basic level, it's a list of property and value pairs, with the colon in between and a separator around each pair.

Some differences to remember when using object literals:

◆ Properties are set using : not =.

◆ Lines end with , instead of ;.

◆ No comma is needed on the last statement inside the object.

To use an object literal:

1. `document.getElementsByTagName`
`→ ("form")[0].onsubmit =`
`→ nodeChanger;`
`chgNodes.init();`

Just as with code you've seen before, we have to start off by doing our initializations. The first line is the same as what you've seen previously, but the second is a little different: it calls the `init()` function that's inside the `chgNodes` object.

2. `function nodeChanger() {`
`    return chgNodes.doAction();`
`}`

The `nodeChanger()` function here doesn't do much at all—all it does is call `chgNodes.doAction()`. Why that function couldn't have been called directly will be covered shortly.

3. `var chgNodes = {`

Here's the beginning of the `chgNodes` object. All we had to do to create it is start the line off as if we're setting a simple variable, but then end with a set of statements between braces.

Script 11.11 This brief script shows many of the useful features of the object literal.

```
window.onload = initAll;

function initAll() {
    document.getElementsByTagName("form")[0].
    → onsubmit = nodeChanger;
    chgNodes.init();
}

function nodeChanger() {
    return chgNodes.doAction();
}

var chgNodes = {
    actionType : function() {
        var radioButtonSet = document.
        → getElementsByTagName("form")[0].
        → nodeAction;
        for (var i=0; i<radioButtonSet.length;
        → i++) {
            if (radioButtonSet[i].checked) {
                return i;
            }
        }
        return -1;
    },

    allGrafs : function() {
        return this.nodeChgArea.
        → getElementsByTagName("p");
    },
    pGrafCt : function() {
        return this.allGrafs().length;
    },
    inText : function() {
        return document.getElementById
        → ("textArea").value;
    },
    newText : function() {
        return document.createTextNode
        → (this.inText());
    },
```

(script continues on next page)

Script 11.11 *continued*

```
                    script
  grafChoice : function() {
    return document.getElementById
    → ("grafCount").selectedIndex;
  },
  newGraf : function() {
    var myNewGraf = document.createElement
    → ("p");
    myNewGraf.appendChild(this.newText());
    return myNewGraf;
  },
  oldGraf : function () {
    return this.allGrafs().item
    → (this.grafChoice());
  },

  doAction : function() {
    switch(this.actionType()) {
      case 0:
        this.nodeChgArea.appendChild
        → (this.newGraf());
        break;
      case 1:
        if (this.pGrafCt() > 0) {
          this.nodeChgArea.removeChild
          → (this.oldGraf());
          break;
        }
      case 2:
        if (this.pGrafCt() > 0) {
          this.nodeChgArea.
          → insertBefore
          → (this.newGraf(),
          → this.oldGraf());
          break;
        }
      case 3:
        if (this.pGrafCt() > 0) {
          this.nodeChgArea.replaceChild
          → (this.newGraf(),
          → this.oldGraf());
          break;
        }
```

(script continues on next page)

4.
```
actionType : function() {
  var radioButtonSet = document.
  → getElementsByTagName("form")[0].
  → nodeAction;
  for (var i=0; i<radioButtonSet.
  → length; i++) {
    if (radioButtonSet[i].checked) {
      return i;
    }
  }
  return -1;
},
```

In the previous version of the script, the first part of the nodeChanger() function was spent setting the actionType variable. Here, actionType() is a method of chgNodes. While the style of the code is different, the end result should be identical.

5.
```
allGrafs : function() {
  return this.nodeChgArea.
  → getElementsByTagName("p");
},
pGrafCt : function() {
  return this.allGrafs().length;
},
```

Here's an example of two simple functions inside chgNodes: allGrafs() and pGrafCt(). Because they return values, they can be used anywhere they're needed for adding, replacing, or deleting nodes.

continues on next page

6.
```
doAction : function() {
    switch(this.actionType()) {
        case 0:
            this.nodeChgArea.appendChild
            → (this.newGraf());
            break;
```

The doAction() function handles most of the heavy lifting needed in chgNodes—this small bit is just the start. Just as with the prior version, we look at the radio button to see which action we want to do, and that action is done by means of a switch statement.

7.
```
init : function() {
    this.nodeChgArea = document.
    → getElementById("modifiable");
}
```

And finally, we end up with our init() function, and all it does is initialize nodeChgArea for later use. What's most important is that we do *not* have a comma at the end of this routine—every statement except the last should end with a comma (and yes, a function is basically an extended statement).

Script 11.11 *continued*

```
                    default:
                        alert("No valid action was
                        → chosen");
                }

            document.getElementById("grafCount").
            → options.length = 0;

            for (var i=0; i<this.pGrafCt(); i++) {
                document.getElementById
                → ("grafCount").options[i] =
                → new Option(i+1);
            }
            return false;
        },

    init : function() {
        this.nodeChgArea = document.
        → getElementById("modifiable");
    }
}
```

✔ Tips

- In steps 1 and 2, you may have been wondering why we couldn't just write:

```
document.getElementsByTagName
→ ("form")[0].onsubmit =
→ chgNodes.doAction();
```

Or maybe you're wondering why we've used this so often in the code? Here's the trick: it's the same answer for both.

Inside an object literal, you can reference every other property and method of the object just by referring to this. If we use a var command, as in the case of myNewGraf or radioButtonSet, it's a normal variable that can't be accessed outside the parent object. By not using var, and instead always referring to it as this.whatever, those properties become part of the object itself.

However, this for object literals has to abide by the same rules that this does everywhere in JavaScript—what it evaluates to depends on from where it was called. If chgNodes.doAction() is called directly from the form, than this refers to the form object—which isn't what we want. Calling chgNodes.doAction() from nodeChanger() lets us work around this.

- If you're considering switching from procedural JavaScript, but haven't made a firm decision, here's one more reason to think about using object literals instead: note that Script 11.11 does the exact same thing as Script 11.10—but it's about 20% shorter.

- This chapter is not by any means a thorough discussion of node manipulation—it's just a sample to get you started. If you want more documentation of all the available properties and methods, check out the W3C specification mentioned at the beginning of the chapter.

Why Object Literals?

By this point in the book, you've more than likely been looking through other people's code. And if you're looking at code that's longer than a page, or code from a company where many people work together on a site, it's very likely that you've noticed that theirs looks a tad...shall we say, different? That's very likely because they use the *object literal*, a different (although equally valid) way of writing JavaScript.

There are several reasons why a programmer might want to use the object literal versus procedural approach to JavaScript:

◆ Because each object (including methods and properties) is contained within one parent object, you never run into a problem with overwriting other people's code. If you and your co-worker both have a variable called `myText` in your respective `.js` files, and some page brings in both files, then whichever page loads last takes precedence—one is going to write directly over the other, and it will be as if that code never loaded. The solution: make sure you don't use global variables, and the simplest way to do that is to tuck all of yours away neatly inside an object literal.

◆ A subset of the object literal has been dubbed *JavaScript Object Notation*, better known as JSON (pronounced like the name "Jason"). JSON is one of the most common data formats for Ajax, and as such, you're likely to see a lot of it when you start working with Ajax.

◆ And finally, like everything else, programming languages have styles that go in and out of fashion. JavaScript itself is on its second upswing, and as part of the renewed interest in scripting, the current trend is towards increased use of object literals—so it helps to get used to seeing them.

MAKING YOUR PAGES DYNAMIC

Effective Web pages are a result of many different factors, including compelling content, good design, and attention to details, such as how fast the page loads. One of the ways to speed up page loads, while still providing the user with an interesting and interactive experience, is to use JavaScript to make individual page elements update within the user's browser. In other words, instead of your Web server pushing the page experience to the user, the server pushes the script over the Internet. The script then uses the power of the user's computer to make the page come alive. Pages with scripts like these can be called *dynamic pages*.

By moving the processing from the server side to the client (user) side, you get better performance and you can personalize the user experience to some extent.

In this chapter, you'll learn how to use JavaScript to display the local date and time on your Web pages; customize a greeting by the time of day where your user is; convert between different time formats; and move an object across the user's page under script control.

Putting the Current Date into a Web Page

JavaScript can determine the current date and time from your computer (which it gets as a number) and then manipulate that figure in many ways. Your script has to handle the conversion from a number the computer uses into a textual date you can understand, however. **Script 12.1** shows how to get the current date, convert it from a number into a standard date, and then write the result to a document window.

To put the current date into a Web page:

1. `window.onload = initDate;`

   When the document loads, call `initDate()`.

2. ```
   var dayName = new Array("Sunday",
   → "Monday", "Tuesday", "Wednesday",
   → "Thursday", "Friday", "Saturday");
   ```

   First, we need to create a new array that contains the days of the week. Make sure to use commas to separate the items in the array; and because they are text strings, each item must be enclosed in quotes. The array gets assigned to the variable *dayName*.

3. ```
   var monName = new Array("January",
   → "February", "March", "April",
   → "May", "June", "July", "August",
   → "September", "October",
   → "November", "December");
   ```

   In this step, we're doing the same thing with month names; and assigning them to the brilliantly named *monName* variable.

Script 12.1 This script writes the current date to the document window.

```
window.onload = initDate;

function initDate() {
    var dayName = new Array("Sunday",
    → "Monday", "Tuesday", "Wednesday",
    → "Thursday", "Friday", "Saturday");
    var monName = new Array("January",
    → "February", "March", "April", "May",
    → "June", "July", "August", "September",
    → "October", "November", "December");

    var now = new Date();
    var dtString = dayName[now.getDay()] + ",
    → " + monName[now.getMonth()] + " " +
    → now.getDate();

    document.getElementById("dtField").
    → innerHTML = dtString;
}
```

Figure 12.1 JavaScript dynamically displays the current date in the window.

JavaScript's Inconsistent Handling of Time

As mentioned earlier in this book, JavaScript begins numbering at zero in most cases, so numbering begins with 0, 1, 2, 3, etc. But this isn't consistent with dates, which begin with the number 1. So if you have an array that deals with the days of the week, you'll have this:

Sunday = 0

Monday = 1

Tuesday = 2

Wednesday = 3

Thursday = 4

Friday = 5

Saturday = 6

In much the same way, the 12 months of the year are numbered from 0 through 11.

On the other hand, when you're dealing with the date of the month, it makes no sense to start at zero (personally, I've never heard of April 0), so JavaScript starts at 1.

Hours are dealt with from 0 (midnight) to 23 (11 P.M.), using a 24-hour clock. Later in this chapter we'll show you how to convert from a 24-hour clock to a 12-hour clock.

4. `var now = new Date();`

    The last thing to do in this first section is to tell JavaScript to create a new `Date` object, call it `now`, and fill it with the current date.

5. `var dtString = dayName[now.getDay()]`
    `→ + ", " + monName[now.getMonth()] +`
    `→ " " + now.getDate();`

    The object `dayName[now.getDay()]` is read from right to left; `getDay()` is the JavaScript method that gets the day of the week, and asking `now` for it gets today's day of the week. The numerical result references one of the entries in the array `dayName`.

    Next, we concatenate a comma and a space to the text string that we're building, and then we concatenate the next expression, which is the month name, expressed by the object `monName[now.getMonth()]`. This gets the month in much the same fashion as getting the day name; and references one of the entries in the array `monName`.

    A space is concatenated next, and we end with the object `now.getDate()`, which returns the date of the month. All of this is assigned to the `dtString` variable.

6. `document.getElementById("dtField").`
    `→ innerHTML = dtString;`

    The `id` `dtField` is in the HTML page (the HTML is trivial, so we haven't included it here); it's within a `<span>` tag, like so:

    `<h1>Today is <span id="dtField">`
    `→ </span>.</h1>`

    The JavaScript sets the `innerHTML` property of `dtField` to the value of `dtString`. The result is shown in **Figure 12.1**.

Working with Days

You might want to display a different message to your users if it's a weekend. **Script 12.2** tells you how to do it.

To figure out if it is a weekend:

1. `var now = new Date();`

   Fill the variable now with the current date.

2. `if (now.getDay() > 0 && now.`
   `→ getDay() < 6) {`

   This extracts the numerical day of the week from the now variable and asks if it is greater than 0 (remember that Sunday is 0). Next the line uses the && operator, which is a logical *and* (i.e., both parts have to be true), and asks if now is less than 6, which is the number for Saturday.

3. `dtString = "Sorry, it's a weekday.";`

   If the result of the last expression is greater than 0 and less than 6, it has to be between 1 and 5, which is to say, from Monday to Friday, so the script puts a string to that effect into dtString.

4. `else {`
   `    dtString = "Hooray, it's a`
   `    → weekend!";`

   If we failed the test in the step 2, it must be a weekend, and we put a string with the happy news in dtString.

5. `document.getElementById("dtField").`
   `→ innerHTML = dtString;`

   Finally, we set the innerHTML property of dtField to the value of dtString, just as in the previous example. The result is shown in **Figure 12.2**.

Script 12.2 This script figures out if it is a weekday or weekend.

```
window.onload = initDate;

function initDate() {
    var now = new Date();

    if (now.getDay() > 0 && now.getDay() < 6) {
        var dtString = "Sorry, it's a
        → weekday.";
    }
    else {
        var dtString = "Hooray, it's a
        → weekend!";
    }

    document.getElementById("dtField").
    → innerHTML = dtString;
}
```

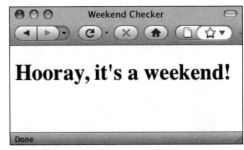

Figure 12.2 The happy news gets written to the window.

Script 12.3 Scripts can be used to check what time of day it is and react appropriately.

```
script
window.onload = initDate;

function initDate() {
    var now = new Date();
    document.getElementById("dtField").
    → innerHTML = timeString(now.getHours());

    function timeString(theHour) {
        if (theHour < 5) {
            return "What are you doing up so
            → late?";
        }
        if (theHour < 9) {
            return "Good Morning!";
        }
        if (theHour < 17) {
            return "No surfing during working
            → hours!";
        }
        return "Good Evening!";
    }
}
```

Figure 12.3 It was definitely too late at night when we wrote this.

Customizing a Message for the Time of Day

You can take the technique used in the last example and use it again to customize a message for the user, depending on the time of day. This could be used, for instance, as a friendly greeting when a user enters a site. **Script 12.3** shows how it is done, and **Figure 12.3** shows how we were up writing way past our usual bedtime.

To customize messages for the time of day:

◆ if (theHour < 5) {
      return "What are you doing up
      → so late?";

  We begin the new code in this script by starting a conditional test. Earlier in this script, the getHours() method extracted theHour from the now variable and here we test to see if that number is less than 5 (which corresponds to 5 A.M., since numbering in JavaScript starts at midnight).

  If it is before 5 A.M., the script scolds the user by writing this message to the document window, as shown in Figure 12.3.

  The rest of the script repeats the above line, adjusting it for the time of day and writing out a different message. If it is between 5 A.M. and 9 A.M., the script says "Good Morning!"; between 9 A.M. and 5 P.M., it says "No surfing during working hours!"; and after 5 P.M., it says "Good Evening!"

Displaying Dates by Time Zone

By default, the dates and times that are displayed are those on the user's machine (assuming that they are set correctly). If you want to display a date somewhere else, you need to calculate it based on UTC, Coordinated Universal Time. UTC is essentially a different name for Greenwich Mean Time (GMT); UTC also goes under the names "universal time" (UT) and "world time." **Script 12.4** shows the HTML for the page; **Script 12.5**, with the JavaScript, shows you how to calculate dates in other time zones.

To display dates by time zone:

1. `var allTags = document.`
   `→ getElementsByTagName("*");`

   Inside the `initDate()` function, create the `allTags` variable. The command `document.getElementsByTagName("*")` is a handy trick—that asterisk tells JavaScript to return an array containing every tag on the page. Then, we can just loop through it looking for things of interest.

   continues on page 298

Script 12.4 The HTML for the time zone script uses classes to tag the different offices with the time zone for that office.

```
● ● ●                    script
<!DOCTYPE html PUBLIC "-//W3C//DTD XHTML 1.0
→ Transitional//EN"
        "http://www.w3.org/TR/xhtml1/DTD/
         → xhtml1-transitional.dtd">
<html xmlns="http://www.w3.org/1999/xhtml">
<head>
    <title>Time Zones</title>
    <script type="text/javascript"
    → src="script04.js"></script>
</head>
<body bgcolor="#FFFFFF">
    <h3>Our office hours are 9:00 am to
    → 5:00 pm, Monday through Friday, at each
    → of our locations. It is now</h3><ul>
    <li><span class="tz-8"> </span> in
    → San Francisco</li>
    <li><span class="tz-5"> </span> in
    → New York</li>
    <li><span class="tz-0"> </span> in
    → London</li>
    <li><span class="tz+7"> </span> in
    → Hong Kong</li></ul>
</body>
</html>
```

Script 12.5 You can adapt this script to display any time zone you wish.

```
window.onload = initDate;

function initDate() {
    var allTags = document.getElementsByTagName("*");

    for (var i=0;i<allTags.length; i++) {
        if (allTags[i].className.indexOf("tz")==0) {
            showTheTime(allTags[i],allTags[i].className.substring(2));
        }
    }
}

function showTheTime(currElem,tzOffset) {
    var dayName = new Array ("Sunday ","Monday ","Tuesday ","Wednesday ","Thursday ","Friday ",
    → "Saturday ");

    var thatTZ = new Date();
    var dateStr = thatTZ.toUTCString();

    dateStr = dateStr.substr(0,dateStr.length - 3);
    thatTZ.setTime(Date.parse(dateStr));
    thatTZ.setHours(thatTZ.getHours() + parseInt(tzOffset));

    currElem.innerHTML = showTheHours(thatTZ.getHours()) + showZeroFilled(thatTZ.getMinutes()) +
    → showAmPm(thatTZ.getHours()) + dayName[thatTZ.getDay()];

    function showTheHours(theHour) {
        if (theHour == 0) {
            return 12;
        }
        if (theHour < 13) {
            return theHour;
        }
        return theHour-12;
    }

    function showZeroFilled(inValue) {
        if (inValue > 9) {
            return ":" + inValue;
        }
        return ":0" + inValue;
    }

    function showAmPm(thatTime) {
        if (thatTime < 12) {
            return " AM ";
        }
        return " PM ";
    }
}
```

2.
```
for (var i=0;i<allTags.length; i++) {
    if (allTags[i].className.
    → indexOf("tz")==0) {
        showTheTime(allTags[i],
        → allTags[i].className.
        → substring(2));
    }
}
```

We begin a loop so we can walk through the page elements, represented by allTags. The allTags[i].className. indexOf("tz")==0 bit just means, "does the *i*th tag have an attribute class that starts with "tz"—if so, call showTheTime()."

The showTheTime() function is passed two parameters: first, the *i*th tag element, and second, the part of the class attribute (seen in Script 12.4) that is *after* the "tz", represented by substring(2). Yes, we could figure out the second part from the first, but why bother? It makes the showTheTime() function much simpler, as that second parameter turns into the time zone offset.

3.
```
function showTheTime(currElem,
→ tzOffset) {
```

This function takes in the two parameters that were passed to showTheTime() in the previous step. Inside the function, they'll be called currElem and tzOffset, respectively.

4.
```
var thatTZ = new Date();
var dateStr = thatTZ.toUTCString();
```

We create a new date variable, thatTZ. The next line turns that date and time (based on UT) into a string (see **Table 12.1** at the end of the chapter), saving the result in dateStr.

5. `dateStr = dateStr.substr`
   `→ (0,dateStr.length - 3);`

What we're trying to do in this section is reset `thatTZ` to be based on UT instead of local time, so that we can then add the passed offset for the desired result. Unfortunately, JavaScript doesn't make this simple. We now have the universal time in string format, but if we just try to reset the time based on it, it'll outsmart us, knowing that we *really* want local time. What we need to do is take the string version of the date and time and strip off the last three characters, which are UTC.

6. `thatTZ.setTime(Date.parse(dateStr));`

Once we've stripped off the last three characters, we can use the `parse` method to turn the date into milliseconds and then the `setTime` method to set `thatTZ` to our desired time.

7. `thatTZ.setHours(thatTZ.getHours() +`
   `→ parseInt(tzOffset));`

Now that we've finally got the UT date stored, we need to add the passed number of hours that our desired time is off UT. As the time zone can be anywhere from +12 to -12, the time zone that was passed in can be anything from `"-12"` to `"+12"`. We use `parseInt()` to turn that string into a number from -12 to 12, and we then add it to the current UT time. The result gives us our desired value: the correct date and time in that time zone.

continues on next page

8.
```
currElem.innerHTML =
→ showTheHours(thatTZ.getHours()) +
→ showZeroFilled(thatTZ.
→ getMinutes()) + showAmPm
→ (thatTZ.getHours()) +
→ dayName[thatTZ.getDay()];
```

This looks scary, but all it is doing is building the time value that goes into the document by concatenating the result from all of the other functions and then setting the innerHTML property of currElem, thereby putting the result of the calculation into the document. The final result is shown in **Figure 12.4**.

The next three functions, showTheHours(), showZeroFilled(), and showAmPm() are within the showTheTime() function so that they can share variables. As it turns out, they don't in this task, but they will in the next.

9.
```
function showTheHours(theHour) {
    if (theHour == 0) {
        return 12;
    }
```

First, set up a function called showTheHours, which is passed the variable theHour. Then, if theHour is zero, return the result 12 (meaning the hour is 12 A.M.); otherwise continue with the function.

10.
```
if (theHour < 13) {
    return theHour;
}
return theHour-12;
```

If the result of the hour portion of the time is less than 13, then simply put that number into the variable theHour. Otherwise, return theHour minus 12 (which converts hours 13 and higher to their 12-hour-clock counterparts).

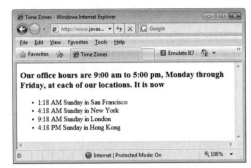

Figure 12.4 The script calculates the time in each office, based on its time zone.

11.
```
function showZeroFilled(inValue) {
    if (inValue > 9) {
        return ":" + inValue;
    }
    return ":0" + inValue;
}
```

This function is used to pretty up the output; when the minutes or seconds figure is 9 or under, it pads the figure with a leading zero.

12.
```
function showAmPm(thatTime) {
    if (thatTime < 12) {
        return " AM ";
    }
    return " PM ";
}
```

This function adds AM or PM to the time. If the passed variable thatTime is less than 12, then the returned value of the function is " AM"; otherwise it is " PM". Note that there is a leading space in the AM or PM text string so things look nice.

✔ Tips

- There's no simple and straightforward way to deal with Daylight Savings Time. Some browsers just don't handle it correctly. And unfortunately, you're also at the mercy of computer users knowing how to set up their computers to be aware when it's happening. Luckily, both Windows and Mac OS X have the ability to automatically set the time based on an Internet time server, which does take Daylight Savings into account, so it's less of a problem than it used to be. The bad news: JavaScript doesn't have a way to get at that information from the OS, so it can't tell if you're in a time and place for it to apply.

- It's easy to add another city to the HTML without touching a single line of JavaScript—and it will all just work.

Converting 24-Hour to 12-Hour Time

JavaScript provides the time in 24-hour format, also known as military time. Many people are unfamiliar or uncomfortable with this format, so you'll want to know how to convert it to 12-hour format. In the next two scripts, you see one way to go about the task, which needs a bit of explanation. Our page (**Script 12.6**) has two important elements: an h2 tag and a form. The script will write the time into the former. The latter contains two radio buttons, which let us switch the time from 24-hour format into 12-hour format. The JavaScript behind this is in **Script 12.7**. The result is shown in **Figure 12.5**.

To convert 24-hour to 12-hour time:

1. `document.getElementById`
   `("showTime").innerHTML =`
   → `showTheHours(now.getHours()) +`
   → `showZeroFilled(now.getMinutes()) +`
   → `showZeroFilled(now.getSeconds()) +`
   → `showAmPm();`

   As in the previous task, this may look daunting, but all it is doing is building the time value displayed on the page by concatenating the result of the other functions (covered below). The result gets put into the `innerHTML` property of `showTime`.

2. `setTimeout(showTheTime,1000);`

   This bit of code tells the display to update every second.

3. `function showTheHours(theHour) {`

   Next, set up a function called `showTheHours`, containing the variable `theHour`.

Script 12.6 This HTML uses `ids` to identify each radio button.

```
<!DOCTYPE html PUBLIC "-//W3C//DTD XHTML 1.0
→ Transitional//EN"
        "http://www.w3.org/TR/xhtml1/DTD/
        → xhtml1-transitional.dtd">
<html xmlns="http://www.w3.org/1999/xhtml">
<head>
    <title>JavaScript Clock</title>
    <script type="text/javascript"
    → src="script05.js"></script>
</head>
<body bgcolor="#FFFFFF">
<div align="center">
    <h2 id="showTime"> </h2>
    <form action="#">
        Display 24-hour Clock?
        <input type="radio" name="timeClock"
        → id="show24" checked="checked"
        → /><label for="show24">Yes</label>
        →   
        <input type="radio" name="timeClock"
        → id="show12" /><label for=
        → "show12">No</label>
    </form>
</div>
</body>
</html>
```

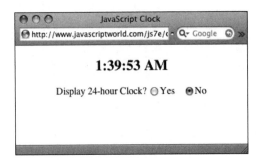

Figure 12.5 The script in action.

Script 12.7 This script converts between 24-hour and 12-hour time.

```
script
window.onload = showTheTime;

function showTheTime() {
    var now = new Date();

    document.getElementById("showTime").
    → innerHTML = showTheHours
    → (now.getHours()) +
    → showZeroFilled(now.getMinutes()) +
    → showZeroFilled(now.getSeconds()) +
    → showAmPm();
    setTimeout(showTheTime,1000);

    function showTheHours(theHour) {
        if (show24Hour() || (theHour > 0 &&
        → theHour < 13)) {
            return theHour;
        }
        if (theHour == 0) {
            return 12;
        }
        return theHour-12;
    }

    function showZeroFilled(inValue) {
        if (inValue > 9) {
            return ":" + inValue;
        }
        return ":0" + inValue;
    }

    function show24Hour() {
        return (document.getElementById
        → ("show24").checked);
    }

    function showAmPm() {
        if (show24Hour()) {
            return "";
        }
        if ((now.getHours() < 12)) {
            return " AM";
        }
        return " PM";
    }
}
```

4.
```
if (show24Hour() ||
→ (theHour > 0 && theHour < 13)) {
    return theHour;
}
if (theHour == 0) {
    return 12;
}
return theHour-12;
```

These conditionals say that if the user wants to show 24-hour time, or if the result of the hour portion of the time is greater than zero but less than 13, then simply return the variable theHour. Remember that the || operator means a logical *or*, as you first saw in Chapter 1. Otherwise, if theHour is zero, then return with the result 12 (when the hour is 12 A.M.); otherwise return theHour minus 12 (which converts hours 13 and higher to their 12-hour counterparts).

5.
```
function show24Hour() {
    return (document.getElementById
    → ("show24").checked);
```

This function returns a value based on which radio button on the page the user has checked. If show24 is selected, then it should return a true result; otherwise it returns a false result.

6.
```
if (show24Hour()) {
    return "";
}
if ((now.getHours() < 12)) {
    return " AM";
}
return " PM";
```

The showAmPm() function adds the AM or PM to the 12-hour time. If the function show24Hour is true, it returns nothing, and goes to the next function. If the hours portion of the now variable is less than 12, then the value of the function is AM; otherwise it is PM. Again, there is a leading space in the AM or PM text string, so things look nice.

Creating a Countdown

Sooner or later, you'll want to put a count-down on your pages that tells the user how many days or hours until a particular event. **Script 12.8** (HTML) and **Script 12.9** (JavaScript) lets one of the authors know his responsibilities, in no uncertain terms, as you can see in **Figure 12.6**.

To create a countdown:

1. var allTags = document.
   → getElementsByTagName("*");

Create a new allTags array, and fill it with every tag on the page.

2. for (var i=0;i<allTags.length; i++) {
   if (allTags[i].className.
   → indexOf("daysTill") > -1) {
      allTags[i].innerHTML =
      → showTheDaysTill(allTags[i].id);
   }
}

This loop scans through allTags to see if the string daysTill is found in the class attribute of any tags on the page. Remember that a tag could have multiple class attributes (i.e., class="firstClass daysTill somethingElse fourthThing").

If we found daysTill, we call the showTheDaysTill() function, which is passed one parameter: that tag's id (which stores what date to put up on the page). That function returns a value that is then put into innerHTML.

continues on page 306

Script 12.8 The HTML for the countdown script.

```
●●●                    script
<!DOCTYPE html PUBLIC "-//W3C//DTD XHTML 1.0
→ Transitional//EN"
        "http://www.w3.org/TR/xhtml1/DTD/
        → xhtml1-transitional.dtd">
<html xmlns="http://www.w3.org/1999/xhtml">
<head>
     <title>Dynamic Countdown</title>
     <script type="text/javascript"
     → src="script06.js"></script>
</head>
<body bgcolor="#FFFFFF">
     <p>Dori says:</p>
     <p>It's only <span class="daysTill"
     → id="bday"> </span> days until my
     → birthday and <span class="daysTill"
     → id="xmas"> </span> days until
     → Christmas, so you'd better start
     → shopping now!</p>
     <p>And it's only <span class="daysTill"
     → id="anniv"> </span> days until our
     → anniversary...</p>
</body>
</html>
```

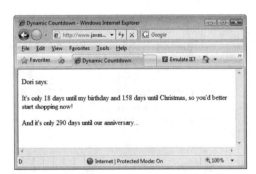

Figure 12.6 Loading this page gives one of the authors his marching orders.

Script 12.9 This script counts down the number of days Tom stays out of the doghouse.

```
window.onload = showDays;

function showDays() {
    var allTags = document.getElementsByTagName("*");

    for (var i=0;i<allTags.length; i++) {
        if (allTags[i].className.indexOf("daysTill") > -1) {
            allTags[i].innerHTML = showTheDaysTill(allTags[i].id);
        }
    }

    function showTheDaysTill(thisDate) {
        var theDays;

        switch(thisDate) {
            case "anniv":
                theDays = daysTill(5,6);
                break;
            case "bday":
                theDays = daysTill(8,7);
                break;
            case "xmas":
                theDays = daysTill(12,25);
                break;
            default:
        }
        return theDays + " ";
    }

    function daysTill(mm,dd) {
        var now = new Date();
        var inDate = new Date(now.getFullYear(),mm-1,dd);

        if (inDate.getTime() < now.getTime()) {
            inDate.setYear(now.getFullYear()+1);
        }

        return (Math.ceil(dayToDays(inDate) - dayToDays(now)));
    }

    function dayToDays(inTime) {
        return (inTime.getTime() / (1000 * 60 * 60 * 24));
    }
}
```

3.
```
switch(thisDate) {
    case "anniv":
        theDays = daysTill(5,6);
        break;
    case "bday":
        theDays = daysTill(8,7);
        break;
    case "xmas":
        theDays = daysTill(12,25);
        break;
    default:
```

If you don't remember the switch/case multi-level conditionals, you can review the discussion in Chapter 3. Here, we are using the value of thisDate to test against the three case statements. For the anniv case, we're setting theDays to May 6 (5,6 is the numerical representation, much like you would write it in the real world); for bday, we're setting it to August 7; and for xmas, theDays gets set to December 25.

4.
```
return theDays + " ";
```

The showTheDays() function ends by returning the number of days followed by a space. This is to work around a problem in IE: it eats the spaces in the HTML. If the script doesn't return a space at the end, the number runs into the word "days". If you just stuck the word "days" into this function, then there'd need to be a space after that, and so on.

5.
```
function daysTill(mm,dd) {
    var now = new Date();
    var inDate = new Date
    → (now.getFullYear(),mm-1,dd);
```

This step shows the daysTill() function, which receives the dates from the case statements in step 3. Then, we create the now and inDate variables. The latter variable is filled with the current year, but with the month (with 1 subtracted from it to get it right; see the "More Weird Time Stuff" sidebar) and the day that were passed in.

More Weird Time Stuff

Month numbering in JavaScript begins with 0 and day numbering with 1, and JavaScript deals inconsistently with years prior to 1970, depending on the version of JavaScript your browser is using.

Navigator 2 (using JavaScript 1.0) couldn't deal with years before 1970 at all and had a Year 2000 Problem, as it returned the wrong answer for dates in or after 2000. Navigator 3 (which used JavaScript 1.1) supposedly changed the value returned by the getYear() method to be two digits if the year is in the 1900s and four digits if the year was before 1900 or after 2000. However, this is not true for all versions of Netscape; for example, Netscape Navigator 4 for Mac returns 100 for the year 2000. And to make things even worse, this still occurs in Firefox—the current version (3) still returns numbers in the hundreds (versus in the 2000s) for getYear().

JavaScript 1.2 (in Navigator 4, and also in ECMAScript-compatible browsers such as Internet Explorer 4 and later) introduced a new method, getFullYear(), which always returns four-digit years. We recommend that you use getFullYear() any time you know that you'll only be working with version 4 and later browsers, so that's what we're using throughout this book.

The getTime() method in JavaScript, for reasons probably best left unexplored, returns a number that is the number of milliseconds since January 1, 1970. Luckily, we hardly ever have to look at that number, as there have been a whopping number of milliseconds in the past four decades.

6.
```
if (inDate.getTime() <
now.getTime()) {
    inDate.setYear
    → (now.getFullYear()+1);
}
```
We then check that date against today. If that date in this year has already passed, we increment the year, going for next year's instead.

7.
```
return (Math.ceil(dayToDays(inDate)
→ - dayToDays(now)));
```
Here, we're calculating the number of days between inDate and the current date. The Math.ceil() method makes sure that our result is a whole number.

8.
```
function dayToDays(inTime) {
    return (inTime.getTime() /
    → (1000 * 60 * 60 * 24));
```
JavaScript stores dates in milliseconds since January 1, 1970. In order to compare two dates, change this to be the number of days since January 1, 1970. First, get the number of milliseconds in a day by multiplying 1000 (the number of milliseconds in a second) by 60 (number of seconds in a minute), by 60 again (number of minutes in an hour), and then by 24 (number of hours in a day). Dividing the number of milliseconds returned by getTime() by this number gives the number of days since January 1, 1970.

CREATING A COUNTDOWN

Hiding and Displaying Layers

Although your HTML, CSS, and JavaScript combine to make a single document, it's sometimes useful to make it appear as if you actually have multiple documents—that is, using a combination of CSS and JavaScript, you can have something like a pop-up window display inside—or on top of—your current HTML page. No, this doesn't use the obsolete Netscape layer tag; it just appears to be a separate layer so far as the user is concerned.

This requires three documents: the HTML document (**Script 12.10**), the CSS style sheet (**Script 12.11**), and the JavaScript file (**Script 12.12**). We're using JavaScript to manipulate an image using the id assigned in the HTML, and CSS to set the positioning for our annoying advertisement on the page: in particular, its *z-index*, which is an indicator of which object is shown on top of another object. The object with the higher-numbered z-index is shown when two objects occupy the same space.

Script 12.10 The HTML for the advertisement example uses `id`s to tag the elements we want to manipulate.

```
<!DOCTYPE html PUBLIC "-//W3C//DTD XHTML 1.0 Transitional//EN"
        "http://www.w3.org/TR/xhtml1/DTD/xhtml1-transitional.dtd">
<html xmlns="http://www.w3.org/1999/xhtml">
<head>
    <title>Layered Divs</title>
    <link type="text/css" href="script07.css" rel="stylesheet" />
    <script type="text/javascript" src="script07.js"></script>
</head>
<body>
    <div id="annoyingAdvert">
        This is an incredibly annoying ad of the type you might find on some web sites.
        <div id="closeBox">&otimes;</div>
    </div>
    <p>Lorem ipsum dolor sit amet, consectetuer adipiscing elit. Aenean lacus elit, volutpat vitae,
→ egestas in, tristique ut, nibh. Donec congue lacinia magna. Duis tortor justo, dapibus vel,
→ vulputate sed, mattis sit amet, leo. Cras purus quam, semper quis, dignissim id,
→ hendrerit eget, ante. Nulla id lacus eget nulla bibendum venenatis. Duis faucibus adipiscing
→ mauris. Integer augue. In vulputate purus eget enim. Nam odio eros, porta vitae,
→ bibendum sit amet, iaculis nec, elit. Cras egestas scelerisque pede. Donec a tellus.
→ Nullam consectetuer fringilla nunc.</p>

    <p>Nam varius metus congue ligula. In hac habitasse platea dictumst. In ut ipsum a pede rhoncus
→ convallis. Sed at enim. Integer sed metus quis est egestas vestibulum. Quisque mattis tortor
→ a lorem. Nam diam. Integer consequat lectus. Donec molestie elementum nisl. Donec ligula
→ sapien, volutpat eget, dictum quis, mollis a, odio. Aliquam augue enim, gravida nec,
→ tempor ac, interdum in, urna. Aliquam mauris. Duis massa urna, ultricies id, condimentum ac,
→ gravida nec, dolor. Morbi et est quis enim gravida nonummy. Cum sociis natoque penatibus et
→ magnis dis parturient montes, nascetur ridiculus mus. Mauris nisl quam, tincidunt ultrices,
→ malesuada eget, posuere eu, lectus. Nulla a arcu. Sed consectetuer arcu et velit. Quisque
→ dignissim risus vel elit.</p>

    <p>Nunc massa mauris, dictum id, suscipit non, accumsan et, lorem. Suspendisse non lorem quis
→ dui rutrum vestibulum. Quisque mauris. Curabitur auctor nibh non enim. Praesent tempor aliquam
→ ligula. Fusce eu purus. Vivamus ac enim eget urna pulvinar bibendum. Integer porttitor,
→ augue et auctor volutpat, lectus dolor sagittis ipsum, sed posuere lacus pede eget wisi.
→ Proin vel arcu ac velit porttitor pellentesque. Maecenas mattis velit scelerisque tellus.
→ Cras eu tellus quis sapien malesuada porta. Nunc nulla. Nullam dapibus malesuada lorem.
→ Duis eleifend rutrum tellus. In tempor tristique neque. Mauris rhoncus. Aliquam purus.</p>

    <p>Morbi felis quam, placerat sed, gravida a, bibendum a, mauris. Aliquam porta diam.
→ Nam consequat feugiat diam. Fusce luctus, felis ut gravida mattis, ante mi viverra sapien,
→ a vestibulum tellus lectus ut massa. Duis placerat. Aliquam molestie tellus. Suspendisse
→ potenti. Fusce aliquet tellus a lectus. Proin augue diam, sollicitudin eget, hendrerit non,
→ semper at, arcu. Sed suscipit tincidunt nibh. Donec ullamcorper. Nullam faucibus euismod
→ augue. Cras lacinia. Aenean scelerisque, lorem sed gravida varius, nunc tortor gravida odio,
→ sed sollicitudin pede augue ut metus. Maecenas condimentum ipsum et enim. Sed nulla. Ut neque
→ elit, varius a, blandit quis, facilisis sed, velit. Suspendisse aliquam odio sed nibh.</p>
</body>
</html>
```

To display and hide an object:

1. document.getElementById
   → ("annoyingAdvert").style.display =
   → "block";

   If you look at Script 12.10, you'll see that
   the layer that we want to show has an id
   of annoyingAdvert. Script 12.11 tells that
   layer it should start off hidden, so that it's
   not seen. However, once the page loads,
   our script tells it to appear by setting the
   display property to block.

2. document.getElementById("closeBox").
   → onclick = function() {
      document.getElementById
      → ("annoyingAdvert").style.display
      → = "none";
   }

   There's a reason why annoyingAdvert has
   that name: you can't read what's underneath it! (as you can see in **Figure 12.7**).
   We'll be nice, though, and let the user
   close the layer (that is, hide it) by clicking
   what looks like a close widget. Setting the
   display property to none turns the layer
   back off again.

Figure 12.7 The advertisement starts on the left,
looking like a layer that can be closed.

Script 12.11 The CSS styles the layer to make it look
different from the rest of the document.

```
body {
    background-color: #FFF;
}


#annoyingAdvert {
    position: absolute;
    z-index: 2;
    display: none;
    width: 100px;
    background-color: #FFC;
    padding: 10px;
    margin: 10px;
    border: 5px solid yellow;
}


#closeBox {
    position: absolute;
    color: red;
    font-size: 1.5em;
    top: 0;
    right: 0;
}
```

Script 12.12 The JavaScript shows the layer and then
(thankfully) lets you hide it again.

```
window.onload = initAdvert;


function initAdvert() {
    document.getElementById
    → ("annoyingAdvert").style.display =
    → "block";
    document.getElementById
    → ("closeBox").onclick = function() {
        document.getElementById
        → ("annoyingAdvert").style.display =
        → "none";
    }
}
```

Script 12.13 The JavaScript gets the advertisement moving.

```
script
window.onload = initAdvert;

function initAdvert() {
    document.getElementById("annoyingAdvert").
    → style.display = "block";
    document.getElementById("annoyingAdvert").
    → onmouseover = slide;
    document.getElementById("closeBox").
    → onclick = function() {
        document.getElementById
        → ("annoyingAdvert").style.display =
        → "none";
    }
}

function slide() {
    if (currPos("annoyingAdvert") <
    → (document.body.clientWidth-150)) {
        document.getElementById
        → ("annoyingAdvert").style.left =
        → currPos("annoyingAdvert") + 1 + "px";
        setTimeout(slide,100);
    }

    function currPos(elem) {
        return document.getElementById(elem).
        → offsetLeft;
    }
}
```

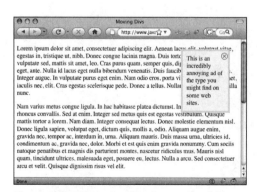

Figure 12.8 In this version, it ends up on the right, where you can finally close it.

Moving an Object in the Document

It's possible to use JavaScript to move an object (an image, or text, or whatever) around your screen. In fact, you can make an object appear to move in three dimensions, so that it looks as through it passes behind other objects in the document. In this example, you'll see how that annoying advertisement in the previous task can be made even more annoying.

This again requires three documents; however, the HTML and CSS are identical to that in the previous version. Here, we'll just show the JavaScript file (**Script 12.13**). Now, as soon as the user wants to close the advertisement layer, it starts to move away from them. Thankfully, it will stop before it goes off the screen (**Figure 12.8**), allowing them to finally close it!

To move an object:

1. `document.getElementById`
   → `("annoyingAdvert").onmouseover =`
   → `slide;`

   In order to start the movement, we add an `onmouseover` event handler to our advertisement, which tells it to trigger the `slide()` function.

2. `if (currPos("annoyingAdvert") <`
   → `(document.body.clientWidth-150)) {`

   Before we move the layer, we need to figure out if it's within the restrictions that we've placed on it—that's done by checking its current position (using the `currPos()` function, which we'll describe below) and comparing it to the width of the document window. If it's less than that (minus another 150 pixels, to take the width of the layer itself into account), then we want to move it some more.

continues on next page

3. ```
document.getElementById
→ ("annoyingAdvert").style.left
→ = currPos("annoyingAdvert") + 1
→ + "px";
```

To move the layer (in a way that works cross-browser), we have to change its `style.left` property. Here, we change it by getting the object's current position, incrementing it by 1, and finally adding `px` to the end to put it in the correct format. Changing `style.left` is all that's needed to move it to its new location.

4. ```
setTimeout(slide,100);
```

Here's where we tell JavaScript to keep on moving, by calling `setTimeout()` to call `slide()` again in one hundred milliseconds (one-tenth of a second).

5. ```
function currPos(elem) {
```

Two places above needed to get the current position of an element, and here's where we'll do it. All we need is the `id` of that element.

6. ```
return document.getElementById
→ (elem).offsetLeft;
```

Given the `id` of the object, we can get the object. And given that, all we need is its `offsetLeft` property, which is the object's left position. The `offsetLeft` property contains a numeric value, so we can just return it as-is.

✔ Tip

■ You might be wondering: if `offsetLeft` is numeric, why jump through all those hoops to instead change the `style.left` property? We have to do that because `offsetLeft` is read-only; that is, you can read its value, but you can't change it. There aren't any cross-browser, writeable, numeric positioning elements.

Date Methods

Because you'll often need to deal with dates, here's a table of all of the methods of the Date object. In **Table 12.1**, you'll see a reference to UTC, which stands for Coordinated Universal Time, which replaced Greenwich Mean Time (GMT) as the world standard for time in 1986. Any of the methods that contain UTC are available only in JavaScript 1.2 or later.

Table 12.1

Date Methods

METHOD	DESCRIPTION	RETURNED VALUES	SUPPORTING BROWSERS
getDate() getUTCDate()	The day of the month	1–31	JavaScript 1.0 JavaScript 1.2
getDay() getUTCDay()	The integer value of the day of the week	0–6	JavaScript 1.0 JavaScript 1.2
getFullYear() getUTCFullYear()	The full four-digit year	1900+	JavaScript 1.2
getHours() getUTCHours()	The integer hour of the day	0–23	JavaScript 1.0 JavaScript 1.2
getMilliseconds() getUTCMilliseconds()	The number of milliseconds since the last second	0–999	JavaScript 1.2
getMinutes() getUTCMinutes()	The number of minutes since the last hour	0–59	JavaScript 1.0 JavaScript 1.2
getMonth() getUTCMonth()	The month of the year	0–11	JavaScript 1.0 JavaScript 1.2
getSeconds() getUTCSeconds()	The number of seconds since the last minute	0–59	JavaScript 1.0 JavaScript 1.2
getTime()	The number of milliseconds since midnight 1 January 1970		JavaScript 1.0
getTimezoneOffset()	The difference between local time and GMT in minutes	0–1439	JavaScript 1.0
getYear()	The year field of the date	0–99 for the years 1900–1999, four-digit year thereafter	JavaScript 1.0
parse()	Given a date/time string, return the number of milliseconds since midnight 1 January 1970		JavaScript 1.0
setDate() setUTCDate()	Set the day, given a number between 1–31	Date in milliseconds (as of JavaScript 1.2)	JavaScript 1.0 JavaScript 1.2
setFullYear() setUTCFullYear()	Set the year, given a four-digit year	Date in milliseconds	JavaScript 1.2

continues on next page

Table 12.1 *continued*

Date Methods

METHOD	DESCRIPTION	RETURNED VALUES	SUPPORTING BROWSERS
setHours() setUTCHours()	Set the hour, given a number between 0–23	Date in milliseconds (as of JavaScript 1.2)	JavaScript 1.0 JavaScript 1.0
setMilliseconds() setUTCMilliseconds()	Set the milliseconds, given a number between 0–999	Date in milliseconds	JavaScript 1.2
setMinutes() setUTCMinutes()	Set the minutes, given a number between 0–59	Date in milliseconds (as of JavaScript 1.2)	JavaScript 1.0 JavaScript 1.2
setMonth() setUTCMonth()	Set the month, given a number between 0–11	Date in milliseconds (as of JavaScript 1.2)	JavaScript 1.0 JavaScript 1.2
setSeconds() setUTCSeconds()	Set the seconds, given a number between 0–59	Date in milliseconds (as of JavaScript 1.2)	JavaScript 1.0 JavaScript 1.2
setTime()	Set a date, given the number of milliseconds since 1 January 1970	Date in milliseconds	JavaScript 1.0
setYear()	Set the year, given either a two- or four-digit value	Date in milliseconds (as of JavaScript 1.2)	JavaScript 1.0
toGMTString() toUTCString()	The GMT date and time in string format	day dd mm yyyy hh:mm:ss GMT	JavaScript 1.0 JavaScript 1.2
toLocaleString()	The local date and time in string format	Varies based on OS, locale, and browser	JavaScript 1.0
toString()	The local date and time in string format	Varies based on OS and browser	JavaScript 1.0
UTC()	Given a date in year, month, day (and optional hours, minutes, seconds, and milliseconds) format, return the number of milliseconds since 1 January 1970	Date in milliseconds	JavaScript 1.0
valueOf()	The number of milliseconds since midnight 1 January 1970	Date in milliseconds	JavaScript 1.2

DATE METHODS

13

INTRODUCING AJAX

The Web is always changing, and for Web and JavaScript developers the ground shifted under their feet beginning in early 2005. New and immediately popular Web applications appeared, some of them from Google, such as Gmail and Google Maps, and some from others, such as Flickr and the My Yahoo! portal. The common denominator of all of these new sites was that they acted more like desktop applications, with fast, responsive user interfaces. Instead of the traditional Web application, where the user clicked, waited some number of seconds for the server to respond and refresh the page, and then repeated the process, these new sites were more reactive, updating pages right away, providing superior interaction, and making for a better user experience.

There was something new (actually not so new, as we'll see) powering these sites, and it's called *Ajax*. You can use Ajax techniques to make your sites more responsive and attractive, which makes your site's users happier in the process. Best of all, you don't have to learn a completely new technology, because Ajax is made from building blocks that you already know (and that we've covered earlier in this book).

continues on next page

In this chapter, you'll learn how to request information from the server in the background and turn it into a form your Ajax application can use; automatically refresh the information from the server; build a cool previewing effect for objects on your page; and build an Ajax application that auto-completes form fields, just like a desktop application. Let's get to it.

Figure 13.1 This is the article that launched a zillion Ajax sites.

Ajax: Pinning It Down

One of the interesting things about Ajax is that there is some confusion and even a little disagreement as to what Ajax really is. We know that it is important and that it's very popular; heck, we even changed the name of this book from previous editions to hitch onto Ajax's popularity. So here is our take on what Ajax is and isn't, and what we mean when we use the term.

First, a little history: In February 2005, Jesse James Garrett, a founder of Adaptive Path (a Web interface and design shop in San Francisco), coined the term Ajax in an article on their site. He said Ajax was shorthand (but *not* an acronym) for "Asynchronous JavaScript and XML." You can read the article for yourself at www.adaptivepath.com/ideas/essays/archives/000385.php (**Figure 13.1**).

According to Garrett, Ajax is not in itself a new technology; it's a technique that combines several long-standing Web technologies:

◆ Using XHTML and CSS for structure and presentation

◆ Displaying and manipulating pages using the Document Object Model

◆ Using the browser's XMLHttpRequest object to transfer data between the client and the server

◆ Using XML as the format for the data flowing between the client and server

◆ And finally, using JavaScript to dynamically display and interact with all of the above

An Ajax application places an intermediary between the user and the server. This *Ajax engine* (also known as the JavaScript part of a Web page) provides an interface to the user (in concert, of course, with XHTML and CSS), and if a user action doesn't require a request to the server (for example, displaying data that is already local), the Ajax engine responds. This allows the browser to react immediately to many user actions and makes the Web page act with the snappiness we've come to expect from our desktop programs. If the user action does require a server call, the Ajax engine performs it *asynchronously*, that is, without making the user wait for the server response; the user can continue to interact with the application, and the engine updates the page when the requested data arrives. The important part is that the user's actions don't come to a screeching halt while waiting for the server.

As the technique evolved, not all of the pieces had to be in place to call something an Ajax application, and this is where the confusion and disagreements set in. In fact, even the authors disagree about this:

Tom says, "I'm fine with just manipulating the page with the DOM, XHTML and CSS, and JavaScript and calling it Ajax. There are tons of effects that people are referring to as Ajax, and the whole look of modern sites has changed because of this approach. The change from the static Web to the dynamic Web page, which is sometimes called Web 2.0, owes its look and feel to the Ajax approach, whether or not there's a server call behind the scenes. Maybe calling it Ajax won't please the purists, but it's good enough for me."

Dori, who's the real JavaScript programmer in the family, says: "To call it Ajax, you need to transfer some data between the client and server. Otherwise, what's so new about it?"

Dori's writing the code, so for the most part in this chapter we're sticking to her sensibilities as to what an Ajax application is and what it should do. But in later chapters, we'll show you how to add some great (but still useful, not just flashy) Web 2.0–style eye candy to your sites.

Now, let's talk a little about what's not Ajax. Because you can do some cool visual effects on Web pages using Ajax, some people think that Ajax is *anything* you can do that looks good on a page, leading them to refer to things like interfaces made in Flash as "Ajax." But just saying it doesn't make it so. Ajax is not about loading up your sites with cute user interface widgets and adding user interface tweaks that are cool but that change or break behaviors that people are used to with Web pages.

That leads us to problems with Ajax, and they can be significant. For example, to work correctly, an Ajax site needs to be running in a modern browser (for a list, see the back cover of this book). It also requires JavaScript. So what do you do about people using older browsers or who have turned JavaScript off? Or what about disabled users, or people who may be browsing your site with limited-capability handheld devices such as mobile phones or PDAs? The answer is that you must write your sites to degrade gracefully, meaning that users with less-capable browsers get a subset of your site's functionality, or, at the minimum, get a meaningful error message explaining why they can't use your site.

continues on next page

Ajax: Pinning It Down

Another potential problem with Ajax applications is that they may break the expected behavior of the browser's back button. With a static page, users expect that clicking the back button will move the browser to the last page it loaded. But because Ajax-enabled pages are dynamically updated, that might not be a valid expectation. There are solutions for the "back button problem," and before you dive wholeheartedly into Ajax, you should take the problem and its solutions into account.

Additionally, Ajax is not dependent on specific server-side technologies. There are a number of companies that are using the Ajax boom to try to sell their own server-side solutions, and that's what they're in business to do—but there's no reason why their products are required. So long as what's on the back end is something that your JavaScript can read (XML, ideally), you're fine. Just because the guys in the snappy suits (*cough* IBM *cough* Sun *cough*) want to hitch their buzzword-compliant products to Ajax's success in order to get you to buy doesn't mean that you have to fall for it.

Script 13.1 The HTML for the text and XML file request example.

```
<!DOCTYPE html PUBLIC "-//W3C//DTD XHTML 1.0
→ Transitional//EN"
        "http://www.w3.org/TR/xhtml1/DTD/
        → xhtml1-transitional.dtd">
<html xmlns="http://www.w3.org/1999/xhtml">
<head>
    <title>My First Ajax Script</title>
    <script type="text/javascript"
    → src="script01.js"></script>
</head>
<body>
    <p><a id="makeTextRequest"
    → href="gAddress.txt">Request a text
    → file</a><br />
    <a id="makeXMLRequest"
    → href="us-states.xml">Request an XML
    → file</a></p>
    <div id="updateArea"> </div>
</body>
</html>
```

Script 13.2 This JavaScript gets the files from the server.

```
window.onload = initAll;
var xhr = false;

function initAll() {
    document.getElementById("makeTextRequest").
    → onclick = getNewFile;
    document.getElementById("makeXMLRequest").
    → onclick = getNewFile;
}

function getNewFile() {
    makeRequest(this.href);
    return false;
}

function makeRequest(url) {
    if (window.XMLHttpRequest) {
```

(script continues on next page)

Reading Server Data

We begin our exploration of Ajax with the basics: using the XMLHttpRequest object to retrieve and display information from a server.

To get the job done, we'll use **Scripts 13.1** (HTML) and **13.2** (JavaScript). There are two possible files that can be read: the XML file that is shown in **Script 13.3** and the plain text file that is **Script 13.4**.

To request server data:

1. `var xhr = false;`

   In Script 13.2, the xhr variable is one that you'll be seeing a lot of in this chapter. It's an XMLHttpRequest object (or it will be later, after it's initialized). At this point, we just need to create it outside any functions in order to make it globally available.

2. ```
   function initAll() {
       document.getElementById
       → ("makeTextRequest").onclick =
       → getNewFile;
       document.getElementById
       → ("makeXMLRequest").onclick =
       → getNewFile;
   }
   ```

   When the page is first loaded, it knows to call the initAll() function. Here, we set two onclick handlers so that when a user clicks either of the links, the getNewFile() function is triggered.

   continues on next page
   ```

3.
```
function getNewFile() {
    makeRequest(this.href);
    return false;
}
```

Someone's clicked a link, so it's time to do something. Here, that something is to call makeRequest()—but that function needs to know which file was requested. Thankfully, we know that that information is tucked away in this.href, so we can pass it along. When we come back, we know we're done, so we return a value of false, telling the browser that no, we don't really want to load up a new Web page.

4.
```
if (window.XMLHttpRequest) {
    xhr = new XMLHttpRequest();
}
```

Now, we're inside makeRequest(), and it's here that things get interesting. Modern browsers support a native XMLHttpRequest object as a property of window. So, we check to see if that property exists, and if it does, we create a new XMLHttpRequest object.

5.
```
if (window.ActiveXObject) {
    try {
        xhr = new ActiveXObject
        → ("Microsoft.XMLHTTP");
    }
    catch (e) { }
}
```

However, there's a browser that supports XMLHttpRequest that doesn't have a native version of the object, and that's Microsoft Internet Explorer (versions 5.5 and 6). In that case, we have to check to see if the browser supports ActiveX. If it does, we then check (using a try/catch error check) to see if we can create an XMLHttpRequest object based on ActiveX. If we can, great.

continues on page 324

Script 13.2 *continued*

```
xhr = new XMLHttpRequest();
}
else {
    if (window.ActiveXObject) {
        try {
            xhr = new ActiveXObject
            → ("Microsoft.XMLHTTP");
        }
        catch (e) { }
    }
}

if (xhr) {
    xhr.onreadystatechange = showContents;
    xhr.open("GET", url, true);
    xhr.send(null);
}
else {
    document.getElementById("updateArea").
    → innerHTML = "Sorry, but I couldn't
    → create an XMLHttpRequest";
}
}

function showContents() {
    if (xhr.readyState == 4) {
        if (xhr.status == 200) {
            if (xhr.responseXML && xhr.
            → responseXML.contentType==
            → "text/xml") {
                var outMsg = xhr.responseXML.
                → getElementsByTagName
                → ("choices")[0].textContent;
            }
            else {
                var outMsg = xhr.responseText;
            }
        }
        else {
            var outMsg = "There was a problem
            → with the request " + xhr.status;
        }
        document.getElementById("updateArea").
        → innerHTML = outMsg;
    }
}
```

READING SERVER DATA

Script 13.3 This is the XML file that is requested.

```
                                    script
<?xml version="1.0"?>
<choices xml:lang="EN">
    <item><label>Alabama</label><value>AL</value></item>
    <item><label>Alaska</label><value>AK</value></item>
    <item><label>Arizona</label><value>AZ</value></item>
    <item><label>Arkansas</label><value>AR</value></item>
    <item><label>California</label><value>CA</value></item>
    <item><label>Colorado</label><value>CO</value></item>
    <item><label>Connecticut</label><value>CT</value></item>
    <item><label>Delaware</label><value>DE</value></item>
    <item><label>Florida</label><value>FL</value></item>
    <item><label>Georgia</label><value>GA</value></item>
    <item><label>Hawaii</label><value>HI</value></item>
    <item><label>Idaho</label><value>ID</value></item>
    <item><label>Illinois</label><value>IL</value></item>
    <item><label>Indiana</label><value>IN</value></item>
    <item><label>Iowa</label><value>IA</value></item>
    <item><label>Kansas</label><value>KS</value></item>
    <item><label>Kentucky</label><value>KY</value></item>
    <item><label>Louisiana</label><value>LA</value></item>
    <item><label>Maine</label><value>ME</value></item>
    <item><label>Maryland</label><value>MD</value></item>
    <item><label>Massachusetts</label><value>MA</value></item>
    <item><label>Michigan</label><value>MI</value></item>
    <item><label>Minnesota</label><value>MN</value></item>
    <item><label>Mississippi</label><value>MS</value></item>
    <item><label>Missouri</label><value>MO</value></item>
    <item><label>Montana</label><value>MT</value></item>
    <item><label>Nebraska</label><value>NE</value></item>
    <item><label>Nevada</label><value>NV</value></item>
    <item><label>New Hampshire</label><value>NH</value></item>
    <item><label>New Jersey</label><value>NJ</value></item>
    <item><label>New Mexico</label><value>NM</value></item>
    <item><label>New York</label><value>NY</value></item>
    <item><label>North Carolina</label><value>NC</value></item>
    <item><label>North Dakota</label><value>ND</value></item>
    <item><label>Ohio</label><value>OH</value></item>
    <item><label>Oklahoma</label><value>OK</value></item>
    <item><label>Oregon</label><value>OR</value></item>
    <item><label>Pennsylvania</label><value>PA</value></item>
    <item><label>Rhode Island</label><value>RI</value></item>
```

(sctipt continues on next page)

READING SERVER DATA

6. `if (xhr) {`
    `xhr.onreadystatechange =`
    → `showContents;`
    `xhr.open("GET", url, true);`
    `xhr.send(null);`
`}`

Either way, we should have a new `xhr` object, and if we do, we need to do something (in fact, three somethings) with it. Here are the three things that we always do with `xhr`:

▲ Set the `xhr`'s `onreadystatechange` event handler. Any time the `xhr.readyState` property changes its value, this handler is triggered.

▲ We call `open()` and pass in three parameters: an HTTP request method (e.g., `"GET"`, `"POST"`, or `"HEAD"`), a URL to a file on the server, and a Boolean telling the server if the request is asynchronous (that is, if we're sitting around waiting for it).

▲ And finally, we `send()` the request we just created. If we were requesting a `POST`, the parameters would be passed here.

7. `else {`
    `document.getElementById`
    → `("updateArea").innerHTML =`
    → `"Sorry, but I couldn't create an`
    → `XMLHttpRequest";`
`}`

If we end up here, we couldn't create an `XMLHttpRequest` for some reason, and there's nothing else that can be done.

Script 13.3 *continued*

```
○ ○ ○                    script
    <item><label>South Carolina</label>
 → <value>SC</value></item>
    <item><label>South Dakota</label>
 → <value>SD</value></item>
    <item><label>Tennessee</label><value>
 → TN</value></item>
    <item><label>Texas</label><value>
 → TX</value></item>
    <item><label>Utah</label><value>
 → UT</value></item>
    <item><label>Vermont</label><value>
 → VT</value></item>
    <item><label>Virginia</label><value>
 → VA</value></item>
    <item><label>Washington</label><value>
 → WA</value></item>
    <item><label>West Virginia</label><value>
 → WV</value></item>
    <item><label>Wisconsin</label><value>
 → WI</value></item>
    <item><label>Wyoming</label><value>
 → WY</value></item>
</choices>
```

Script 13.4 The requested text file.

```
⊖ ⊙ ⊙                    script
Four score and seven years ago our fathers
 ⟶ brought forth on this continent, a new
 ⟶ nation, conceived in Liberty, and dedicated
 ⟶ to the proposition that all men are created
 ⟶ equal.

Now we are engaged in a great civil war,
 ⟶ testing whether that nation, or any nation
 ⟶ so conceived and so dedicated, can long
 ⟶ endure. We are met on a great battle-field
 ⟶ of that war. We have come to dedicate a
 ⟶ portion of that field, as a final resting
 ⟶ place for those who here gave their lives
 ⟶ that that nation might live. It is
 ⟶ altogether fitting and proper that we should
 ⟶ do this.

But, in a larger sense, we can not dedicate --
 ⟶ we can not consecrate -- we can not hallow --
 ⟶ this ground. The brave men, living and dead,
 ⟶ who struggled here, have consecrated it,
 ⟶ far above our poor power to add or detract.
 ⟶ The world will little note, nor long
 ⟶ remember what we say here, but it can never
 ⟶ forget what they did here. It is for us the
 ⟶ living, rather, to be dedicated here to the
 ⟶ unfinished work which they who fought here
 ⟶ have thus far so nobly advanced. It is
 ⟶ rather for us to be here dedicated to the
 ⟶ great task remaining before us -- that from
 ⟶ these honored dead we take increased
 ⟶ devotion to that cause for which they gave
 ⟶ the last full measure of devotion -- that
 ⟶ we here highly resolve that these dead shall
 ⟶ not have died in vain -- that this nation,
 ⟶ under God, shall have a new birth of
 ⟶ freedom -- and that government of the
 ⟶ people, by the people, for the people, shall
 ⟶ not perish from the earth.
```

8. `if (xhr.readyState == 4) {`
　　`if (xhr.status == 200) {`

Now we're down in the showContents() function. The readyState property can have one of several values (see **Table 13.1**), and every time the server changes its value, the showContents() function is triggered. However, we don't actually want to do anything (at least not here) until the request is finished, so we start off by checking to see if readyState is 4. If it is, we're good to go, and we can check to see what the request returned.

The first thing to check is the request's status, which will be a result code returned by the server (servers routinely return these codes behind the scenes for every file served, although browsers only show them to you if there's an error). A status code of 200 means that everything's fine. The status here is the same status that is returned by any server call; for instance, if you ask for a file that doesn't exist you'll get a 404 error from the Web server.

continues on next page

Table 13.1

readyState Property Values	
VALUE	WHAT IT MEANS
0	Uninitialized; object contains no data
1	Loading; object is currently loading its data
2	Loaded; object has finished loading its data
3	Interactive; user may interact with the object even though it is not fully loaded
4	Complete; object has finished initializing

9.
```
if (xhr.responseXML &&
→ xhr.responseXML.contentType
→ =="text/xml") {
    var outMsg = xhr.responseXML.
    → getElementsByTagName("choices")
    → [0].textContent;
}
else {
    var outMsg = xhr.responseText;
}
```

If we're here, that means that everything is fine, and we want to look at what the server actually gave us. There were two different types of files we could be reading, so we need to check what type of data we got back. The `responseXML` property contains the data if it's XML. If the `contentType` property (which can also be referred to as the MIME type) contains "text/xml", then we know that we've got a properly formatted DOM object back, and we can use commands we've seen before (such as `getElementsByTagName()`) to traverse its nodes. But here, we're just trying to see if it worked, so we'll take everything and dump it all into `outMsg`.

If what we got back isn't valid XML, then it's our text file. In that case, we want to put xhr's `responseText` property into `outMsg`.

10.
```
else {
    var outMsg = "There was a problem
    → with the request " + xhr.status;
}
```

If what we got back had a `status` other than 200, we've got a problem, so we set `outMsg` to say that and append the status error so we can try to figure out what the problem is.

11.
```
document.getElementById
→ ("updateArea").innerHTML = outMsg;
```

And finally, we take `outMsg` and dump it onto the screen, as shown in **Figure 13.2**.

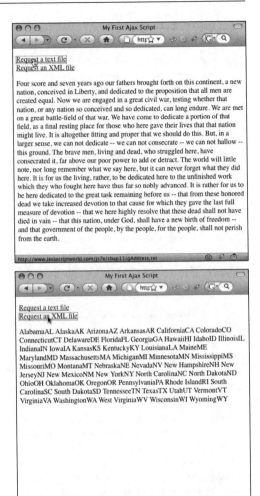

Figure 13.2 By clicking the appropriate link, you can fetch either a text file of the Gettysburg Address (top) or an XML file of U.S. states and their abbreviations (bottom).

READING SERVER DATA

✔ Tips

■ Because of the way that Ajax works, when you are doing your development and testing, the files that you're reading must reside on a server; they can't just be local files.

■ Back in step 5, we said that IE 5.5 and 6 used an ActiveX control to create the XMLHttpRequest object. Thankfully, IE versions 7 and up have a native object so that's no longer required. However, this means that you always have to check for the existence of a native object first—if you check for window.ActiveXObject first, that will be true for IE7+, and then you'll be going down the wrong path. A considerable amount of older, pre-IE7 Ajax code has this problem.

■ If it matters deeply to your code which version of Microsoft's ActiveX object you actually get, here's a code snippet for you to use instead:

```
if (window.ActiveXObject) {
  try {
    xhr = new ActiveXObject
    → ("Msxml2.XMLHTTP");
  }
  catch (e) {
    try {
      xhr = new ActiveXObject
      ("Microsoft.XMLHTTP");
    }
    catch (e) { }
  }
}
```

This approach attempts to use the IE6 version (Msxml2.XMLHTTP) of the XMLHttpRequest object first and only falls back to the older version if it can't find it. However, the Microsoft.XMLHTTP version should always give you the latest version available on the PC, so we'll just be using that in this chapter—because eventually, the older code will be going away.

✔ Tips

- One drawback of Ajax calls is that they can be cached; that is, it looks like your application is contacting the server and getting new data, but it's really just looking at stuff it read previously. If that's the case, setting the headers of the request can help. Adding one or more of these can help force recalcitrant servers to fork over the goods:

```
xhr.setRequestHeader
→ ("If-Modified-Since", "Wed, 15 Jan
→ 1995 01:00:00 GMT");
xhr.setRequestHeader
→ ("Cache-Control","no-cache");
xhr.setRequestHeader
→ ("Cache-Control",
"must-revalidate");
xhr.setRequestHeader
→ ("Cache-Control","no-store");
xhr.setRequestHeader
→ ("Pragma","no-cache");
xhr.setRequestHeader("Expires","0");
```

- You can force the call to return XML data by overriding the MIME type:

```
xhr.overrideMimeType("text/xml");
```

However, this may cause problems with certain browsers and configurations, so use it with care.

Script 13.5 This simple HTML page will be much more impressive with the addition of some JavaScript.

```
● ● ●                script
<!DOCTYPE html PUBLIC "-//W3C//DTD XHTML 1.0
→ Transitional//EN"
        "http://www.w3.org/TR/xhtml1/DTD/
        → xhtml1-transitional.dtd">
<html xmlns="http://www.w3.org/1999/xhtml">
<head>
    <title>My Second Ajax Script</title>
    <link type="text/css" rel="stylesheet"
    → href="script02.css" />
    <script type="text/javascript"
    → src="script02.js"></script>
</head>
<body>
    <div id="pictureBar"> </div>
</body>
</html>
```

Script 13.6 Only a little bit of CSS, but it's needed to make the page look good.

```
● ● ●                script
img {
    border-width: 0;
    margin: 5px;
}
```

Parsing Server Data

Now that we have data from the server, we need to find the exact information we need and make sure that it is in a format that our Ajax application can use. To do that, we'll first need to examine the information. Because the data is a nicely structured XML document, our script walks the XML document tree to find and extract the particular data we need and store it in variables. Then, if needed, the script can reformat the data for later use.

The HTML and CSS that are in **Scripts 13.5** and **13.6** couldn't be much simpler, so we're only going to look at the code in the JavaScript file, **Script 13.7**. For this task, the XML file is data about photographs stored on Flickr; a portion of the XML can be seen in **Script 13.8**.

To parse information from the server:

1. `xhr.onreadystatechange =`
   `→ showPictures;`
   `xhr.open("GET", "flickrfeed.xml",`
   `→ true);`

   Every time `readyState` changes, we want to call the `showPictures()` function. The file name we want to read off the server is `flickrfeed.xml`. Both those values are set here.

2. `var tempDiv = document.`
   `→ createElement("div");`
   `var tempText = document.`
   `→ createElement("div");`

   Down in `showPictures()` is where the real work is done. We start by creating variables to store two elements: `tempDiv` and `tempText`, both of which are temporary `div` placeholders.

   continues on next page

3. `var allImages = xhr.responseXML.`
`→ getElementsByTagName("content");`

The response back from the server contained XML, so we're taking that response and looking for every `content` node. If you take a look at the XML in Script 13.8, you'll see that there's a lot of stuff there that we don't care about at all—in fact, all we want is what's in the *<a>* tags (and really, only half of those). Here, we've started to narrow down to just what we want.

4. `for (var i=0; i<allImages.length;`
`→ i++) {`

Now we need to loop through all the nodes that we found to get the actual data we want.

5. `tempText.innerHTML = allImages[i].`
`→ textContent;`
`tempDiv = tempText.`
`→ getElementsByTagName("p");`

Because we've got XML data, we can use its `textContent` property to get the text of the node. Given that, we want to find all the paragraphs inside it—and there should be two of them.

continues on page 334

Script 13.7 The additional JavaScript in this script allows you to parse the data you previously requested.

```
script
window.onload = initAll;
var xhr = false;

function initAll() {
    if (window.XMLHttpRequest) {
        xhr = new XMLHttpRequest();
    }
    else {
        if (window.ActiveXObject) {
            try {
                xhr = new ActiveXObject("Microsoft.XMLHTTP");
            }
            catch (e) { }
        }
    }

    if (xhr) {
        xhr.onreadystatechange = showPictures;
        xhr.open("GET", "flickrfeed.xml", true);
        xhr.send(null);
    }
    else {
        alert("Sorry, but I couldn't create an XMLHttpRequest");
    }
}

function showPictures() {
    var tempDiv = document.createElement("div");
    var tempText = document.createElement("div");

    if (xhr.readyState == 4) {
        if (xhr.status == 200) {
            var allImages = xhr.responseXML.getElementsByTagName("content");

            for (var i=0; i<allImages.length; i++) {
                tempText.innerHTML = allImages[i].textContent;
                tempDiv = tempText.getElementsByTagName("p");

                var theText = tempDiv[1].innerHTML;
                theText = theText.replace(/240/g,"75");
                theText = theText.replace(/180/g,"75");
                theText = theText.replace(/_m/g,"_s");
                document.getElementById("pictureBar").innerHTML += theText;
            }
        }
        else {
            alert("There was a problem with the request " + xhr.status);
        }
    }
}
```

Script 13.8 This is an edited and shortened version of the XML file that Flickr provides; the original was approximately 500 lines long!

```
                                    script
<?xml version="1.0" encoding="utf-8" standalone="yes"?>
<feed xmlns="http://www.w3.org/2005/Atom"
        xmlns:dc="http://purl.org/dc/elements/1.1/"  xmlns:flickr="urn:flickr:" xmlns:media=
     → "http://search.yahoo.com/mrss/">


    <title>Content from Paradise Ridge Sculpture Grove</title>
    <link rel="self" href="http://api.flickr.com/services/feeds/photoset.gne?set=
     → 72157600976524175&amp;nsid=23922109@N00&amp;lang=en-us" />
    <link rel="alternate" type="text/html" href="http://www.flickr.com/photos/dorismith/sets/
     → 72157600976524175"/>
    <id>tag:flickr.com,2005:http://www.flickr.com/photos/23922109@N00/sets/72157600976524175</id>
    <icon>http://farm2.static.flickr.com/1335/882568164_72eee9b41f_s.jpg</icon>
    <subtitle>The &lt;a href=&quot;http://www.paradiseridgewinery.com/&quot;&gt;
     → Paradise Ridge Winery&lt;/a&gt; not only has great wines, but they also have a sculpture
     → garden. We visited on 22 July 2007.</subtitle>
    <updated>2007-07-24T05:19:08Z</updated>
    <generator uri="http://www.flickr.com/">Flickr</generator>


    <entry>
        <title>IMG_0045.JPG</title>
        <link rel="alternate" type="text/html" href="http://www.flickr.com/photos/dorismith/
         → 882590644/in/set-72157600976524175/"/>
        <id>tag:flickr.com,2005:/photo/882590644/in/set-72157600976524175</id>
        <published>2007-07-24T05:19:08Z</published>
        <updated>2007-07-24T05:19:08Z</updated>
            <dc:date.Taken>2007-07-22T13:42:49-08:00</dc:date.Taken>
        <content type="html">&lt;p&gt;&lt;a href=&quot;http://www.flickr.com/people/dorismith/
         → &quot;&gt;Dori Smith&lt;/a&gt; posted a photo:&lt;/p&gt;
&lt;p&gt;&lt;a href=&quot;http://www.flickr.com/photos/dorismith/882590644/&quot; title=
 → &quot;IMG_0045.JPG&quot;&gt;&lt;img src=&quot;http://farm2.static.flickr.com/1063/
 → 882590644_5a4a0d89f3_m.jpg&quot; width=&quot;240&quot; height=&quot;180&quot; alt=&quot;
 → IMG_0045.JPG&quot; /&gt;&lt;/a&gt;&lt;/p&gt;


</content>
        <author>
            <name>Dori Smith</name>
            <uri>http://www.flickr.com/people/dorismith/</uri>
            </author>
        <link rel="enclosure" type="image/jpeg" href="http://farm2.static.flickr.com/1063/
         → 882590644_5a4a0d89f3_m.jpg" />
```

(script continues on next page)

Script 13.8 *continued*

```
         <category term="winery" scheme="http://www.flickr.com/photos/tags/" />
         <category term="sonomacounty" scheme="http://www.flickr.com/photos/tags/" />
         <category term="sculptures" scheme="http://www.flickr.com/photos/tags/" />
         <category term="dorismith" scheme="http://www.flickr.com/photos/tags/" />
         <category term="paradiseridge" scheme="http://www.flickr.com/photos/tags/" />
         <category term="paradiseridgesculptures" scheme="http://www.flickr.com/photos/tags/" />
                 </entry>
      <entry>
         <title>IMG_0032.JPG</title>
         <link rel="alternate" type="text/html" href="http://www.flickr.com/photos/dorismith/
         ⇥ 882568164/in/set-72157600976524175/"/>
         <id>tag:flickr.com,2005:/photo/882568164/in/set-72157600976524175</id>
         <published>2007-07-24T05:15:14Z</published>
         <updated>2007-07-24T05:15:14Z</updated>
                 <dc:date.Taken>2007-07-22T13:35:09-08:00</dc:date.Taken>
         <content type="html">&lt;p&gt;&lt;a href=&quot;http://www.flickr.com/people/dorismith/
         ⇥ &quot;&gt;Dori Smith&lt;/a&gt; posted a photo:&lt;/p&gt;
&lt;p&gt;&lt;a href=&quot;http://www.flickr.com/photos/dorismith/882568164/&quot; title=
⇥ &quot;IMG_0032.JPG&quot;&gt;&lt;img src=&quot;http://farm2.static.flickr.com/1335/
⇥ 882568164_72eee9b41f_m.jpg&quot; width=&quot;240&quot; height=&quot;180&quot; alt=&quot;
⇥ IMG_0032.JPG&quot; /&gt;&lt;/a&gt;&lt;/p&gt;

</content>
         <author>
            <name>Dori Smith</name>
            <uri>http://www.flickr.com/people/dorismith/</uri>
                 </author>
         <link rel="enclosure" type="image/jpeg" href="http://farm2.static.flickr.com/1335/
         ⇥ 882568164_72eee9b41f_m.jpg" />

         <category term="winery" scheme="http://www.flickr.com/photos/tags/" />
         <category term="sonomacounty" scheme="http://www.flickr.com/photos/tags/" />
         <category term="sculptures" scheme="http://www.flickr.com/photos/tags/" />
         <category term="dorismith" scheme="http://www.flickr.com/photos/tags/" />
         <category term="paradiseridge" scheme="http://www.flickr.com/photos/tags/" />
         <category term="paradiseridgesculptures" scheme="http://www.flickr.com/photos/tags/" />
                 </entry>

</feed>
```

PARSING SERVER DATA

6. `var theText = tempDiv[1].innerHTML;`
`theText = theText.replace`
`→ (/240/g,"75");`
`theText = theText.replace`
`→ (/180/g,"75");`
`theText = theText.replace`
`→ (/_m/g,"_s");`

As previously mentioned, we only want half the <a> nodes, so we winnow out the ones here that we don't want. In a file with information about 20 photos, there will be 20 <content> nodes, each of which contains two paragraphs. Each <content> node contains the photographer's name (linked to their Flickr page), followed by an image that links to the Flickr-hosted version. We want just the latter, so we can just take the innerHTML from the second item in the tempDiv array, which gives us the <a> inside the paragraph (and the <img> tag it contains, as well).

Next, we're using regular expressions to tweak the results. Flickr has sent us the tags for medium-sized version of the image, but we only want the thumbnail version. Because our images are either 240 wide by 180 tall or 180 wide by 240 tall (that is, they're either horizontal or vertical), and we know the thumbnails are always 75 x 75, we just find any use of the numbers 240 or 180 in the text and change them to 75. We finish up by changing the image name itself; Flickr gives the medium-sized version a name that ends with _m, while the small version ends with _s, so we can just swap one for the other.

7. `document.getElementById`
`→ ("pictureBar").innerHTML += theText;`

Inside the loop, we take the now-modified node that we want and then append it onto the HTML page's pictureBar. The end result is as we see it in **Figure 13.3**, where every thumbnail image on the page is a link back to the full-sized version.

Figure 13.3 These thumbnail images were read from Flickr.

Getting Your Data

One of the things people want to do when they first hear about Ajax is write JavaScript that reads in all kinds of XML files (including RSS and Atom feeds), mash them up, and then put the results on their own Web page.

The bad news: it doesn't quite work that way—a script can only read a file that comes from the same server as the one that the script is on itself. If you think about it for a while, you'll start to figure out why; after all, if a script could read anything, then that would open up all kinds of possible security scams and fake sites.

The sort-of good news: you can have a program on your server that goes out periodically, grabs an XML file, and then stores it locally. Once you've done that, your Ajax application will have no problems reading it. In this example and the next, it's assumed that you've got something running that grabs the Flickr data file of your choice periodically and saves it on your server. How to do that, though, is beyond the scope of this book.

The better news, though, is that you can (in some cases) use a script that's hosted by the destination server itself—which can then read its own files, and report the results back to you. We'll see an example of that shortly.

✔ Tips

■ While you can't read a data file that's stored on another server (see the "Getting Your Data" sidebar for more about why that's the case), you can always have your HTML file load information from another server. Here, your Web page, no matter where it is, is able to display images from Flickr's servers.

■ One of the best things about the Web 2.0 dot-coms is that they understand that people want access to data—and not just their own data, but other people's data (when they've agreed to make it public) as well. For instance, it's possible to search Flickr for all the photographs containing the tags "Hawaii" and "sunset," and then get the result as an XML file. Combine that with this script or the next, and you'll always have new and lovely photos on your page.

Refreshing Server Data

Our Ajax application has fetched information from the server and then parsed the data and acted upon it. Now we'll show you how to make the application retrieve a new version of the data from the server, which automatically refreshes the page. **Script 13.9** contains the necessary JavaScript.

To refresh server information:

1.
```
function getPix() {
    xhr.open("GET", "flickrfeed.xml",
    → true);
    xhr.onreadystatechange =
    → showPictures;
    xhr.send(null);

    setTimeout(getPix,5 * 1000);
}
```

Where the previous script did the `xhr` call inside `initAll()`, this script pushes it down into its own function, `getPix()`. There's one addition: the `setTimeout()` afterwards. Five seconds after the script has grabbed a random image, it goes and gets another.

Script 13.9 Use this script to automatically refresh server information.

```
window.onload = initAll;
var xhr = false;

function initAll() {
    if (window.XMLHttpRequest) {
        xhr = new XMLHttpRequest();
    }
    else {
        if (window.ActiveXObject) {
            try {
                xhr = new ActiveXObject
                → ("Microsoft.XMLHTTP");
            }
            catch (e) { }
        }
    }

    if (xhr) {
        getPix();
    }
    else {
        alert("Sorry, but I couldn't create an
        → XMLHttpRequest");
    }
}

function getPix() {
    xhr.open("GET", "flickrfeed.xml", true);
    xhr.onreadystatechange = showPictures;
    xhr.send(null);

    setTimeout(getPix,5 * 1000);
}

function showPictures() {
    var tempText = document.
createElement("div");
    var allLinks = new Array;
```

(script continues on next page)

Script 13.9 *continued*

```
                    script
  if (xhr.readyState == 4) {
    if (xhr.status == 200) {
      var allImages = xhr.responseXML.
      → getElementsByTagName("content");

      for (var i=0; i<allImages.length;
      → i++) {
        tempText.innerHTML =
        → allImages[i].textContent;
        allLinks[i] = tempText.
        → getElementsByTagName("p")[1];
      }

      var randomImg = Math.floor
      → (Math.random() * allLinks.length);
      document.getElementById
      → ("pictureBar").innerHTML =
      → allLinks[randomImg].innerHTML;
    }
    else {
      alert("There was a problem with the
      → request " + xhr.status);
    }
  }
}
```

2.
```
for (var i=0; i<allImages.length;
→ i++) {
  tempText.innerHTML = allImages[i].
  → textContent;
  allLinks[i] = tempText.
  → getElementsByTagName("p")[1];
}
```

This is almost the same loop that's in the previous task, with one difference: instead of appending the nodes to the Web page, it adds them to a temporary array.

3.
```
var randomImg = Math.floor
→ (Math.random() * allLinks.length);
document.getElementById
→ ("pictureBar").innerHTML =
→ allLinks[randomImg].innerHTML;
```

When the loop completes, we want to figure out one random image out of all of them to display. We start by calculating a random number between zero and one less than the number of images, using `Math.random()` and `Math.floor()` as we did back in Chapter 4 in "Displaying a Random Image." And finally, we use that random number as an index into the `allLinks` array to grab the one image, and we put that into our Web page (**Figure 13.4**).

✔ Tips

- You might wonder why this script bothers to read from the same XML file every time—after all, if the file isn't changing, why not just keep the data in variables after the first time through? If you keep in mind the technique referred to in the previous sidebar ("Getting Your Data"), you'll then realize that the XML file could be changing at any point. Say your server-side program grabs a new version of the XML file every few minutes—why should anyone have to wait to see the latest pictures? This way, your site's visitors always get the latest possible version.

- If you take the approach just mentioned, you're likely to run into the Ajax drawback covered earlier in this chapter: caching. Different browsers (and different versions, and different platforms) all have their own unique caching peculiarities, most of which are solved by modifying the headers as discussed earlier. Another solution many recommend is to change the GET to a POST. But here's what we've found that works: instead of the order they're seen in Script 13.2, we've swapped the order of the open() and onreadystatechange in Script 13.9, as shown above in step 1.

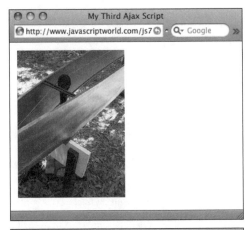

Figure 13.4 The script fetches one image after another.

Script 13.10 The trick to your JavaScript is adding the remote script tag to this HTML page.

```
script
<!DOCTYPE html PUBLIC "-//W3C//DTD XHTML 1.0
→ Transitional//EN"
        "http://www.w3.org/TR/xhtml1/DTD/
        → xhtml1-transitional.dtd">
<html xmlns="http://www.w3.org/1999/xhtml">
<head>
    <title>Using JSON Data</title>
    <link type="text/css" rel="stylesheet"
    → href="script02.css" />
    <script type="text/javascript"
    → src="script04.js"></script>
    <script type="text/javascript" src="http:
    → //api.flickr.com/services/feeds/
    → photoset.gne?nsid=23922109@N00&set=
    → 72157600976524175&format=
    → json"></script>
</head>
<body>
    <div id="pictureBar"> </div>
</body>
</html>
```

Script 13.11 Our JavaScript file can be short because most of the work is being done by the remote server.

```
script
window.onload = initAll;
var imgDiv = "";

function initAll() {
    document.getElementById("pictureBar").
    → innerHTML = imgDiv;
}

function jsonFlickrFeed(flickrData) {
    for (var i=0; i<flickrData.items.length;
    → i++) {
        imgDiv += "<img src='";
        imgDiv += flickrData.items[i].
        → media.m.replace(/_m/g,"_s");
        imgDiv += "' alt='" + flickrData.
        → items[i].title + "' />";
    }
}
```

Getting Data From a Server

As mentioned in the earlier sidebar, "Getting Your Data," Ajax limits from where you can read data. After all, you don't want everyone in the world reading any file you have, right? But there are some cases where a company may want people to read files and then be able to create their own content on their own sites. For instance, Flickr (as seen in the previous examples) lets your server get their XML files and what you do next is only up to your imagination.

But sometimes you don't have that kind of access to a server—so Flickr has made files available in another format: JavaScript Object Notation, known as JSON (pronounced like the name Jason). The neat trick here is in the HTML file, **Script 13.10**; the JavaScript file (**Script 13.11**) just takes advantage of it.

To read and parse server data:

1. ```
<script type="text/javascript"
→ src="http://api.flickr.com/
→ services/feeds/photoset.gne?nsid=
→ 23922109@N00&set=72157600976524175
→ &format=json"></script>
```

   Remember how we said earlier that a script can only read files from the same server on which it resides? That's still true—but there's nothing that says that you can't call a script file that itself is on another server. In this case, the script is on the api.flickr.com machine, and therefore, it can read in data from that server.

*continues on next page*
```

2. `document.getElementById`
`→ ("pictureBar").innerHTML = imgDiv;`

Back over in the JavaScript file, this single line of code puts all the images onto the page when it loads, as seen in **Figure 13.5**.

3. `function jsonFlickrFeed(flickrData) {`

By now, you're surely wondering where all the code is that sets up the images, and here's the other part of the slick functionality: it's mostly in the data file itself (**Script 13.12**). What JSON gets you is a data file that contains code that JavaScript recognizes. In this case, the data file says that it's expecting to find a function named `jsonFlickrFeed()`, so here we've created one. Whatever name we give the parameter coming in is where the data itself is stored.

Figure 13.5 Not only do the images come from Flickr's servers, but so does the data used to create the page.

4. `for (var i=0; i<flickrData.items.`
`→ length; i++) {`
`    imgDiv += "<img src='";`
`    imgDiv += flickrData.items[i].`
`    → media.m.replace(/_m/g,"_s");`
`    imgDiv += "' alt='" + flickrData.`
`    → items[i].title + "' />";`
`}`

Because we have the data in a format that JavaScript already understands, we don't have much work to do. Here, we loop through all the images in the `items` array, building one large text string that will (in step 2, above) be displayed on the screen. Each element in items has a variety of information about an image, but all we want is the URL, which is stored in `media.m`. And once again, a little bit of regular expression magic turns our medium-sized image into a thumbnail.

Script 13.12 An excerpt of the JSON file—note that it's about half the size of the XML file, while including all the same data.

```
○ ○ ○                                    script
jsonFlickrFeed({
        "title": "Content from Paradise Ridge Sculpture Grove",
        "link": "http://www.flickr.com/photos/dorismith/sets/72157600976524175",
        "description": "The &lt;a href=&quot;http://www.paradiseridgewinery.com/&quot;&gt;
     → Paradise Ridge Winery&lt;/a&gt; not only has great wines, but they also have a sculpture
     → garden. We visited on 22 July 2007.",
        "modified": "2007-07-24T05:19:08Z",
        "generator": "http://www.flickr.com/",
        "items": [
        {
           "title": "IMG_0045.JPG",
           "link": "http://www.flickr.com/photos/dorismith/882590644/in/set-72157600976524175/",
           "media": {"m":"http://farm2.static.flickr.com/1063/882590644_5a4a0d89f3_m.jpg"},
           "date_taken": "2007-07-22T13:42:49-08:00",
           "description": "&lt;p&gt;&lt;a href=&quot;http://www.flickr.com/people/dorismith/
     → &quot;&gt;Dori Smith&lt;/a&gt; posted a photo:&lt;/p&gt; &lt;p&gt;&lt;a
     → href=&quot;http://www.flickr.com/photos/dorismith/882590644/&quot;
     → title=&quot;IMG_0045.JPG&quot;&gt;&lt;img src=&quot;http://farm2.static.flickr.com/
     → 1063/882590644_5a4a0d89f3_m.jpg&quot; width=&quot;240&quot; height=&quot;180&quot;
     → alt=&quot;IMG_0045.JPG&quot; /&gt;&lt;/a&gt;&lt;/p&gt; ",
           "published": "2007-07-24T05:19:08Z",
           "author": "nobody@flickr.com (Dori Smith)",
           "author_id": "23922109@N00",
           "tags": "winery sonomacounty sculptures dorismith paradiseridge paradiseridgesculptures"
        },
        {
           "title": "IMG_0032.JPG",
           "link": "http://www.flickr.com/photos/dorismith/882568164/in/set-72157600976524175/",
           "media": {"m":"http://farm2.static.flickr.com/1335/882568164_72eee9b41f_m.jpg"},
           "date_taken": "2007-07-22T13:35:09-08:00",
           "description": "&lt;p&gt;&lt;a href=&quot;http://www.flickr.com/people/dorismith/
     → &quot;&gt;Dori Smith&lt;/a&gt; posted a photo:&lt;/p&gt; &lt;p&gt;&lt;a
     → href=&quot;http://www.flickr.com/photos/dorismith/882568164/&quot;
     → title=&quot;IMG_0032.JPG&quot;&gt;&lt;img src=&quot;http://farm2.static.flickr.com/
     → 1335/882568164_72eee9b41f_m.jpg&quot; width=&quot;240&quot; height=&quot;180&quot;
     → alt=&quot;IMG_0032.JPG&quot; /&gt;&lt;/a&gt;&lt;/p&gt; ",
           "published": "2007-07-24T05:15:14Z",
           "author": "nobody@flickr.com (Dori Smith)",
           "author_id": "23922109@N00",
           "tags": "winery sonomacounty sculptures dorismith paradiseridge paradiseridgesculptures"
        }
        ]
})
```

GETTING DATA FROM A SERVER

✔ Tips

- If you're wondering why JSON sounds slightly familiar, we introduced it when covering Object Literals in Chapter 11. The JSON format itself is a subset of the object literal. And if JSON doesn't sound familiar, you might want to go back and review that section to learn more.

- You won't always use exactly the URL that's in step one; in fact, if you do, you'll just get the same results shown on this page. Flickr allows you to put in many combinations of tags, sets, and groups so that you'll get personalized results. Go to Flickr, find the Web page that matches what you want in your images file, and find the feed directions on that page. Once you've got that, just add `&format=json` to the end of the URL, and you should be set.

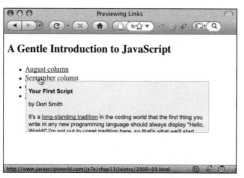

Figure 13.6 When you hover over a link, this script reads the HTML file on the server and gives you an overlay containing a preview of the first few lines of the file.

Script 13.13 This HTML builds the page for the preview example.

```
<!DOCTYPE html PUBLIC "-//W3C//DTD XHTML 1.0
→ Transitional//EN"
        "http://www.w3.org/TR/xhtml1/DTD/
        → xhtml1-transitional.dtd">
<html xmlns="http://www.w3.org/1999/
→ xhtml"><head>
    <title>Previewing Links</title>
    <link type="text/css" rel="stylesheet"
    → href="script05.css" />
    <script type="text/javascript"
    → src="script05.js"></script>
</head>
<body>
    <h2>A Gentle Introduction to JavaScript
    → </h2>
    <ul>
        <li><a href="jsintro/2000-08.html">
        → August column</a></li>
        <li><a href="jsintro/2000-09.html">
        → September column</a></li>
        <li><a href="jsintro/2000-10.html">
        → October column</a></li>
        <li><a href="jsintro/2000-11.html">
        → November column</a></li>
    </ul>
    <div id="previewWin"> </div>
</body>
</html>
```

Previewing Links with Ajax

There's a handy and great-looking visual effect that many sites are using now, where, when you hover the mouse pointer over a link, the first few lines of the page that is the link's destination appear in a floating window under the cursor (**Figure 13.6**). This turns out to be a fairly easy-to-create Ajax application. You'll find the HTML in **Script 13.13**, the CSS in **Script 13.14**, and the JavaScript in **Script 13.15**.

To use Ajax to preview links:

1. ```
   var allLinks = document.
   → getElementsByTagName("a");
   for (var i=0; i< allLinks.length;
   → i++) {
       allLinks[i].onmouseover =
       → showPreview;
       allLinks[i].onmouseout =
       → hidePreview;
   }
   ```

   Here's our `initAll()` function, which simply plows through all the links on the page and adds `onmouseover` and `onmouseout` event handlers to each. The former event handler will (as you'll see, below) read the destination page and display a preview for the (possible) visitor.

2. ```
   function showPreview(evt) {
       getPreview(evt);
       return false;
   }
   ```

   The `showPreview()` event handler function passes the event triggering the function call to `getPreview()`. That's where the real work will be done.

   continues on next page

PREVIEWING LINKS WITH AJAX

3.
```
function hidePreview() {
    document.getElementById
    → ("previewWin").style.visibility
    → = "hidden";
}
```
If we have a showPreview() function, we
need a hidePreview(), right? Here's ours,
and all it does is set the preview window
back to its hidden level of visibility.

4.
```
if (evt) {
    var url = evt.target;
}
else {
    evt = window.event;
    var url = evt.srcElement;
}
xPos = evt.clientX;
yPos = evt.clientY;
```
Here in getPreview(), the first thing
we need to do is figure out what file we
want to read, and that's done by looking at the event's properties. Depending
on which browser your visitor is using,
the URL is in either evt.target or
window.event.srcElement. Once we've
got that, we can grab the x and y positions
of the mouse for later use.

5.
```
var prevWin = document.
→ getElementById("previewWin");

if (xhr.readyState == 4) {
```
Having used Ajax to read the file, we're
now down in the showContents() function. We store the previewWin element
for later use in prevWin, and when
xhr.readyState is 4, it's time to show off.

PREVIEWING LINKS WITH AJAX

Script 13.14 This CSS styles the preview pop-up.
```
#previewWin {
    background-color: #FF9;
    width: 400px;
    height: 100px;
    font: .8em arial, helvetica, sans-serif;
    padding: 5px;
    position: absolute;
    visibility: hidden;
    top: 10px;
    left: 10px;
    border: 1px #CC0 solid;
    clip: auto;
    overflow: hidden;
}

#previewWin h1, #previewWin h2 {
    font-size: 1.0em;
}
```

Script 13.15 The JavaScript that allows the server
request and the appearance of the pop-up.
```
window.onload = initAll;
var xhr = false;
var xPos, yPos;

function initAll() {
    var allLinks = document.
    → getElementsByTagName("a");

    for (var i=0; i< allLinks.length; i++) {
        allLinks[i].onmouseover = showPreview;
        allLinks[i].onmouseout = hidePreview;
    }
}

function showPreview(evt) {
    getPreview(evt);
    return false;
}
```
(script continues on next page)

Script 13.15 *continued*

```
function hidePreview() {
    document.getElementById("previewWin").
    → style.visibility = "hidden";
}

function getPreview(evt) {
    if (evt) {
        var url = evt.target;
    }
    else {
        evt = window.event;
        var url = evt.srcElement;
    }
    xPos = evt.clientX;
    yPos = evt.clientY;

    if (window.XMLHttpRequest) {
        xhr = new XMLHttpRequest();
    }
    else {
        if (window.ActiveXObject) {
            try {
                xhr = new ActiveXObject
                → ("Microsoft.XMLHTTP");
            }
            catch (e) { }
        }
    }

    if (xhr) {
        xhr.onreadystatechange = showContents;
        xhr.open("GET", url, true);
        xhr.send(null);
    }
    else {
        alert("Sorry, but I couldn't create an
        → XMLHttpRequest");
    }
}
```

(script continues on next page)

6.
```
if (xhr.status == 200){
    prevWin.innerHTML =
    → xhr.responseText;
}
else {
    prevWin.innerHTML = "There was a
    → problem with the request " +
    → xhr.status;
}
prevWin.style.top = parseInt(yPos)+2
→ + "px";
prevWin.style.left =
→ parseInt(xPos)+2 + "px";
prevWin.style.visibility =
→ "visible";
prevWin.onmouseout = hidePreview;
```

If everything's fine, then xhr.status is 200 and the data we want to put into prevWin. innerHTML is in xhr.responseText. If not, we put the error message there instead.

Once that's done, it's simply a matter of figuring out where to place the preview window, and that's where those x and y mouse coordinates come in handy. It's a pop-up, so we put it just below and to the right (2 pixels over and 2 down) of the cursor position that triggered this call.

Lastly, we set prevWin to be visible, and we let JavaScript know that prevWin should be hidden when the cursor moves off the preview.

✔ Tips

■ The data being read is in HTML format. Putting `xhr.responseText` into `innerHTML` tells the browser that when the preview window displays, it should interpret the HTML as, well, HTML. If you wanted something else to display (say, for instance, that you wanted to see the actual source of the page), you could modify what's in `innerHTML` before displaying the preview.

■ Ajax requires that the file being read reside on the same server—but it doesn't require that it be in the same directory. If the page you're reading in is in a different directory, and the page contains relative links, then those links will not work. If your pages refer to a particular CSS file, or images, or JavaScript, you won't be able to preview those particular parts of the file. The same solution applies here as well: modify `prevWin.innerHTML` before displaying it.

Script 13.15 *continued*

```
function showContents() {
    var prevWin = document.getElementById
    → ("previewWin");

    if (xhr.readyState == 4) {
        if (xhr.status == 200){
            prevWin.innerHTML =
            → xhr.responseText;
        }
        else {
            prevWin.innerHTML = "There was a
            → problem with the request " +
            → xhr.status;
        }
        prevWin.style.top = parseInt(yPos)+2
        → + "px";
        prevWin.style.left = parseInt(xPos)+2
        → + "px";
        prevWin.style.visibility = "visible";
        prevWin.onmouseout = hidePreview;
    }
}
```

Script 13.16: This simple HTML provides the form field that will be auto-completed.

```
script
<!DOCTYPE html PUBLIC "-//W3C//DTD XHTML 1.0
→ Transitional//EN"
        "http://www.w3.org/TR/xhtml1/DTD/
        → xhtml1-transitional.dtd">
<html xmlns="http://www.w3.org/1999/
→ xhtml"><head>
    <title>Auto-fill Form Fields</title>
    <link type="text/css" rel="stylesheet"
    → href="script06.css" />
    <script type="text/javascript"
    → src="script06.js"></script>
</head>
<body>
    <form action="#">
        Please enter your state:<br />
        <input type="text" id="searchField"
        → autocomplete="off" /><br />
        <div id="popups"> </div>
    </form>
</body>
</html>
```

Auto-Completing Form Fields

A first-rate way to help your site's visitors is to lessen the drudgery of data entry into fields. Helping them fill out forms that have a large number of choices saves them time and effort, and additionally helps provide your site with valid data.

For this example, **Script 13.16** (HTML), **Script 13.17** (CSS), and **Script 13.18** (JavaScript) automatically show a list of U.S. states that match the letters the user types into a form field (**Figure 13.7**). As the user continues typing, the list shrinks until there is only one state left; this is then automatically put into the entry field, and the list goes away.

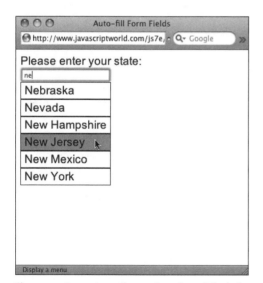
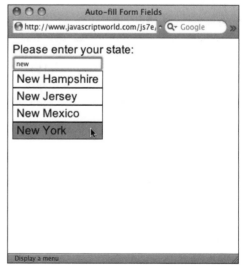

Figure 13.7 As you type, the number of possible choices narrows.

To build auto-completing form fields:

1. Please enter your state:
   → <input type="text" id="searchField"
   → autocomplete="off" />
   → <div id="popups"> </div>

   Here's the bit of HTML that we care about. It's the one tricky (and non-standards compliant) part: that autocomplete attribute. It tells browsers not to do any auto-completion on this field, as we'll be handling it with the script. While it isn't part of any W3C recommendations, autocomplete, like XMLHttpRequest itself, has excellent cross-browser support.

2. document.getElementById
   → ("searchField").onkeyup =
   → searchSuggest;

   In order to grab and process each keystroke, we need an event handler, and here's ours, set in initAll().

3. xhr.onreadystatechange =
   → setStatesArray;
   xhr.open("GET", "us-states.xml",
   → true);
   xhr.send(null);

   Unlike those photographs earlier in this chapter, the names of the United States aren't likely to change. We can read the XML file (Script 13.3) in once, initialize our array, and safely assume that our list will still be valid at the end of this session.

Script 13.17 The CSS here styles the search field and the pop-up menu.

```
body, #searchfield {
    font: 1.2em arial, helvetica, sans-serif;
}


.suggestions {
    background-color: #FFF;
    padding: 2px 6px;
    border: 1px solid #000;
}


.suggestions:hover {
    background-color: #69F;
}


#popups {
    position: absolute;
}


#searchField.error {
    background-color: #FFC;
}
```

Script 13.18 This JavaScript handles the server request and the pop-up display.

```
                    script
window.onload = initAll;
var xhr = false;
var statesArray = new Array();

function initAll() {
    document.getElementById("searchField").
    → onkeyup = searchSuggest;

    if (window.XMLHttpRequest) {
        xhr = new XMLHttpRequest();
    }
    else {
        if (window.ActiveXObject) {
            try {
                xhr = new ActiveXObject
                → ("Microsoft.XMLHTTP");
            }
            catch (e) { }
        }
    }

    if (xhr) {
        xhr.onreadystatechange =
        → setStatesArray;
        xhr.open("GET", "us-states.xml", true);
        xhr.send(null);
    }
    else {
        alert("Sorry, but I couldn't create an
        → XMLHttpRequest");
    }
}

function setStatesArray() {
    if (xhr.readyState == 4) {
        if (xhr.status == 200) {
            if (xhr.responseXML) {
                var allStates = xhr.responseXML.
                → getElementsByTagName("item");
                for (var i=0; i<allStates.
                → length; i++) {
```

(script continues on next page)

4.
```
if (xhr.responseXML) {
    var allStates = xhr.responseXML.
    → getElementsByTagName("item");
    for (var i=0; i<allStates.length;
    → i++) {
        statesArray[i] = allStates[i].
        → getElementsByTagName("label")
        → [0].firstChild;
    }
}
```

Here's where we read that file in, looking at each `item` node, finding the `label` node inside, and then storing `label`'s `firstChild`—the name of the state itself. Each of them goes into a slot in the `statesArray` array.

5.
```
var str = document.getElementById
→ ("searchField").value;
document.getElementById
→ ("searchField").className = "";
```

When you start typing in the field, you'll end up here, in the `searchSuggest()` event handler function. We start off by getting the value of `searchField`, which is whatever has been typed so far. Next, we clear that field's `class` attribute.

6.
```
if (str != "") {
    document.getElementById("popups").
    → innerHTML = "";
```

If nothing's been entered, we don't want to do anything, so there's a check here to make sure that the user's entry has a value before we start popping up possibilities. If there's something there, we then blank out the previous list of possibilities.

7.
```
for (var i=0; i<statesArray.length;
→ i++) {
    var thisState = statesArray[i].
    → nodeValue;
```

Now, we loop through the list of states, storing the current state we're looking at in `thisState`.

continues on next page

8. `if (thisState.toLowerCase().indexOf`
`→ (str.toLowerCase()) == 0) {`

We want to see if what they've entered so far is part of a state name—but that alone isn't sufficient; we also have to make sure that what they've entered is at the beginning of the name. If you type in Kansas, you don't want to see a drop-down box asking if you want Arkansas or Kansas, after all. And so long as we're doing that check, we'll also force the comparison to be lowercase on both sides before checking `indexOf()`.

If `indexOf()` returns 0—that is, the entered string was found starting at position 1 of `thisState`—then we know we have a hit.

9. `var tempDiv = document.`
`→ createElement("div");`
`tempDiv.innerHTML = thisState;`
`tempDiv.onclick = makeChoice;`
`tempDiv.className = "suggestions";`
`document.getElementById("popups").`
`→ appendChild(tempDiv);`

Because this state is a possibility, we want to add it to the list that will display. That's done by creating a temporary `div`, setting its `innerHTML` to the name of the state, adding an `onclick` handler and `className`, and then appending the whole to the `popups` `div`. Adding each state as a separate `div` allows us to manipulate each using JavaScript and CSS.

Script 13.18 *continued*

```
                    statesArray[i] = allStates[i].
                    getElementsByTagName
                    → ("label")[0].firstChild;
                }
            }
        }
        else {
            alert("There was a problem with the
            → request " + xhr.status);
        }
    }
}

function searchSuggest() {
    var str = document.getElementById
    → ("searchField").value;
    document.getElementById("searchField").
    → className = "";
    if (str != "") {
        document.getElementById("popups").
        → innerHTML = "";

        for (var i=0; i<statesArray.length;
        → i++) {
            var thisState = statesArray[i].
            → nodeValue;

            if (thisState.toLowerCase().
            → indexOf(str.toLowerCase()) == 0) {
                var tempDiv = document.
                → createElement("div");
                tempDiv.innerHTML = thisState;
                tempDiv.onclick = makeChoice;
                tempDiv.className =
                → "suggestions";
                document.getElementById
                → ("popups").appendChild
                → (tempDiv);
            }
        }
        var foundCt = document.getElementById
        → ("popups").childNodes.length;
```

(script continues on next page)

Script 13.18 *continued*

```
                    script
        if (foundCt == 0) {
            document.getElementById
            → ("searchField").className =
            → "error";
        }
        if (foundCt == 1) {
            document.getElementById
            → ("searchField").value = document.
            → getElementById("popups").
            → firstChild.innerHTML;
            document.getElementById("popups").
            → innerHTML = "";
        }
    }
}


function makeChoice(evt) {
    if (evt) {
        var thisDiv = evt.target;
    }
    else {
        var thisDiv = window.event.srcElement;
    }
    document.getElementById("searchField").
    → value = thisDiv.innerHTML;
    document.getElementById("popups").
    → innerHTML = "";
}
```

10. ```
    var foundCt = document.
    → getElementById("popups").
    → childNodes.length;
    ```

    When we've looped through all the states, we're done setting up the pop-ups—but how many do we have? We calculate that, the foundCt, here.

11. ```
    if (foundCt == 0) {
        document.getElementById
        → ("searchField").className =
        → "error";
    }
    ```

    If foundCt is 0, they've entered something unexpected. We let them know that by setting the className to "error", which causes the entry field to display with a pale yellow background (based on a CSS style rule in Script 13.12).

12. ```
    if (foundCt == 1) {
        document.getElementById
        → ("searchField").value =
        → document.getElementById
        → ("popups").firstChild.
        → innerHTML;
        document.getElementById
        → ("popups").innerHTML = "";
    }
    ```

    If foundCt is one, however, we know that they've got a unique hit, so we can then put that state into the entry field. If they've typed in ca, they shouldn't have to type in lifornia also; we already know which state they want. We give them the full state by using the single div in popups to fill in the entry field, and then we blank out the popups div.

    continues on next page
    ```

13.
```
function makeChoice(evt) {
    if (evt) {
        var thisDiv = evt.target;
    }
    else {
        var thisDiv = window.event.
        → srcElement;
    }
    document.getElementById
    → ("searchField").value =
    → thisDiv.innerHTML;
    document.getElementById
    → ("popups").innerHTML = "";
}
```

Another way the user can enter a state name is to click one from the pop-up list. In that case, the `makeChoice()` event handler function is called. First, we figure out which state the user clicked by looking at the target of the event, and that gives us a particular `div`. Looking at the `innerHTML` for that `div` gives us the state name, and we put that into the entry field. And finally, we clear out the pop-up list of possibilities.

✔ Tips

- You can see an advanced example of this technique at Google Suggest (`labs.google.com/suggest/`). As you type into what looks like the usual Google search field, a pop-up list appears with search results. As you type, the search results are continually filtered in the list.

- You may have noticed that this task and the last spent a lot more time and effort making things look good than actually demonstrating Ajax, XML, and server-side technologies. That's because much of what has come to be known (or at least thought of by some) as Ajax involves not just the underlying technology but also the way the technology works. How to make that all much simpler is covered in the next few chapters.

14

Ajax Toolkits

Here's what we didn't tell you in the last chapter: writing Ajax applications can be difficult. They often require a great deal of knowledge of working with the DOM, CSS, JavaScript, and server resources. Since this is a book for beginning scripters, we've shown you how to do some easy things with Ajax, so you can see that learning Ajax techniques is well within your reach. But many books have been written that are completely devoted to showing intermediate-to-advanced scripters how to create Ajax applications, and our Ajax chapters are no substitute for that kind of in-depth exploration.

Does that mean that you can't make good use of Ajax on your sites, even though you're not yet a total JavaScript wizard? Not at all! This chapter shows you how to take advantage of *Ajax toolkits*: prewritten, already-programmed libraries of functions that make it easy for you to bring the power of Ajax to your projects.

continues on next page

There are many Ajax toolkits available for download, and most of them are free. For this chapter, we're using the Yahoo! User Interface Library (YUI) (`developer.yahoo.com/yui/`). YUI is a freely downloadable, open-source set of utilities and controls that help you build interactive Web applications. We think it's one of the best. In this chapter, we'll show you how to use YUI to enable the user to drag-and-drop page elements; add calendar objects; create overlays and pop-up windows; add cool animation effects to your pages; and finally, embed a light-weight debugger right in your page to help you create your applications.

Understanding the Yahoo! User Interface Library

All of the examples in this chapter require you to download the entire Yahoo! User Interface Library, which is available as a downloadable ZIP archive from Sourceforge (`sourceforge.net/projects/yui`). When you download and unpack the archive, you'll get a folder with subfolders containing all of the library components (`build`), documentation files (`docs`), and an `examples` folder. You'll need to upload the particular JavaScript and CSS files you'll be using from the `build` folder to your server, and in the `<link>` and `<script>` tags in your XHTML pages, you'll need to specify the paths to those files.

The files you'll need to upload will vary, depending on the library components that you'll be using. You'll also want to keep in mind that most of their JavaScript files come in three formats:

◆ `libName.js`: the standard version of the library.

◆ `libName-min.js`: a "minimized" version of the library; everything's in here except for line feeds, comments, and white space. Don't try to read it, but it's great for keeping down the number of bytes you're serving.

◆ `libName-debug.js`: everything that's in the standard version, plus logging statements to help you track down what is (and isn't) going on in the code. Not recommended for production use (obviously) but invaluable when trying to track something down.

Figure 14.1 You can drag modules around on your personalized Google home page.

Dragging and Dropping Page Elements

One of the nicest Ajax effects is the ability to drag and drop page elements to suit your preferences. You see this implemented on the personalized My Yahoo! and Google pages, which allow you to move around customizable modules (**Figure 14.1**).

In this example, we've created a virtual light-table page for a Web-based slideshow (**Figure 14.2**). You can drag and drop the images into a particular order on the page. If this was a complete Web application, you could then click the Build it! button to create and play the slideshow in the order you chose. The HTML for the page is in **Script 14.1**, the CSS in **Script 14.2**, and the JavaScript in **Script 14.3**.

Serving the Yahoo! User Interface Library

It used to be that if you downloaded a JavaScript framework (framework being an interchangeable term with library) you'd then have to serve the files from your own server. A surfer who goes to several high-end websites regularly could end up downloading large parts of various libraries (or multiple copies of them) in a day.

YUI came up with a solution to this: they host stable versions of all their code—the same versions they use themselves—and you're encouraged to link to them directly. This means that if someone visiting your site has already been to (for instance) my.yahoo.com that day, they may already have some of these files cached, making your site appear to be amazingly fast. And even if they haven't, it's almost guaranteed that Yahoo! has better Internet connectivity than you do, so they can get these files served faster than you can.

While we haven't showed you examples of this in this chapter, if you go to the YUI developer site, you'll see that all their examples recommend that you link to their files at yui.yahooapis.com—feel free to take their recommendation.

Script 14.1 This HTML creates the Slideshow Builder page and calls three YUI files and three of our own.

```
● ● ●                              script
<!DOCTYPE html PUBLIC "-//W3C//DTD XHTML 1.0 Transitional//EN"
        "http://www.w3.org/TR/xhtml1/DTD/xhtml1-transitional.dtd">
<html xmlns="http://www.w3.org/1999/xhtml">
<head>
    <title>Drag and Drop</title>
    <link type="text/css" rel="stylesheet" href="script01.css" />
    <script type="text/javascript" src="yui/yahoo-dom-event.js"></script>
    <script type="text/javascript" src="yui/animation.js"></script>
    <script type="text/javascript" src="yui/dragdrop.js"></script>
    <script type="text/javascript" src="ddlist.js"></script>
    <script type="text/javascript" src="script01.js"></script>
</head>
<body>
    <h1>Slideshow Builder</h1>
    <ul id ="ul1" class="draglist">
        <li id="li0" class="sortList"><img src="images/IMG_1225.jpg" alt="IMG_1225.jpg" width="128"
        ↦ height="96" /></li>
        <li id="li1" class="sortList"><img src="images/IMG_1213.jpg" alt="IMG_1213.jpg" width="128"
        ↦ height="96" /></li>
        <li id="li2" class="sortList"><img src="images/IMG_1368.jpg" alt="IMG_1368.jpg" width="128"
        ↦ height="96" /></li>
        <li id="li3" class="sortList"><img src="images/IMG_1251.jpg" alt="IMG_1251.jpg" width="128"
        ↦ height="96" /></li>
        <li id="li4" class="sortList"><img src="images/IMG_1260.jpg" alt="IMG_1260.jpg" width="128"
        ↦ height="96" /></li>
        <li id="li5" class="sortList"><img src="images/IMG_1234.jpg" alt="IMG_1234.jpg" width="128"
        ↦ height="96" /></li>
        <li id="li6" class="sortList"><img src="images/IMG_1267.jpg" alt="IMG_1267.jpg" width="128"
        ↦ height="96" /></li>
    </ul>
    <br clear="all" />
    <div>
        <form action="#">
            <input id="build" type="submit" value="Build it!" />
            <input id="revert" type="reset" value="Revert" />
        </form>
    </div>
</body>
</html>
```

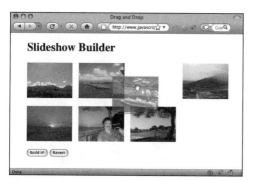

Figure 14.2 Drag the images around to arrange them in the Slideshow Builder.

Script 14.2 This CSS file handles the styling for the Slideshow Builder.

```
h1, form {
    margin-left: 40px;
}

li {
    list-style-type: none;
    float: left;
    margin: 0 16px 16px 0;
}

.sortList {
    width: 130px;
}

ul {
    width: 600px;
}
```

To enable drag and drop for page elements:

1. ```
<script type="text/javascript"
→ src="yui/yahoo-dom-event.js">
→ </script>
<script type="text/javascript"
→ src="yui/animation.js"></script>
<script type="text/javascript"
→ src="yui/dragdrop.js"></script>
<script type="text/javascript"
→ src="ddlist.js"></script>
<script type="text/javascript"
→ src="script01.js"></script>
```

   Most of the work done by YUI is handled almost entirely just by including links to its files in our HTML page. Here in Script 14.1, we've added a link to several YUI script files, which are then followed by links to our files. Here, we're bringing in `yahoo-dom-event.js`, `animation.js`, and `dragdrop.js` before ending with our own files, `ddlist.js` and `script01.js`.

   What's in each of those files? One of the best parts of using a toolkit is that you don't have to learn all the details—follow Yahoo!'s examples and directions, and your code should work.

2. ```
<li id="li0" class="sortList"><img
→ src="images/IMG_1225.jpg"
→ alt="IMG_1225.jpg" width="128"
→ height="96" /></li>
```

   Here's one of the images on our page. It's inside a list tag, because we're using YUI's drag-and-drop list handler (see `dragdrop.js`, above) to handle our dragging and dropping needs.

continues on next page

DRAGGING AND DROPPING PAGE ELEMENTS

3. ```li {
    list-style-type: none;
    float: left;
    margin: 0 16px 16px 0;
}```

Inside Script 14.2, we set the list style to not display as a list. While it needs to be one internally, there's no reason for it to look like one on the screen.

4. ```var Dom = YAHOO.util.Dom;
var Event = YAHOO.util.Event;
var DDM = YAHOO.util.DragDropMgr;```

The code in Script 14.3 may look a little different than what you've seen previously in this book, but it's all a matter of coding style. Here, we're setting up some variables to be initialized when the page first loads. You'll notice that all of the functions and variables start with YAHOO; that's to allow them to coexist with other code and be sure that neither steps on or overwrites the other.

5. ```YAHOO.DDApp = {
    init: function() {
        new YAHOO.util.DDTarget("ul1");
        for (var i=0; i<7; i++) {
            new YAHOO.DDList("li" + i);
        }
    }
};```

When the page loads, we need to tell YUI and the browser what it is we want to drag. In this case, it's the `<ul>` and all the `<li>` tags inside it, so we set the former to be a `DDTarget` and set the latter to all be instances of `DDList`.

6. ```Event.onDOMReady(YAHOO.DDApp.init,
→ YAHOO.DDApp, true);```

`Event.onDOMReady`, here, is a custom YUI event that's triggered when the DOM is ready for manipulation. When it is, we want to start initializing our new framework.

Script 14.3 This JavaScript calls the YUI libraries and makes the drag and drop work.

```
var Dom = YAHOO.util.Dom;
var Event = YAHOO.util.Event;
var DDM = YAHOO.util.DragDropMgr;

YAHOO.DDApp = {
    init: function() {
        new YAHOO.util.DDTarget("ul1");
        for (var i=0; i<7; i++) {
            new YAHOO.DDList("li" + i);
        }
    },
};


Event.onDOMReady(YAHOO.DDApp.init,
→ YAHOO.DDApp, true);
```

DRAGGING AND DROPPING PAGE ELEMENTS

Learning More about YUI

The Yahoo! folks want you to use their toolkit, and they've created a few different places where you can learn about the package and interact with the growing community of users and developers that Yahoo! is building. Check out these resources:

◆ The main Yahoo! User Interface Library page (developer.yahoo.com/yui/) has links to all of the components in the library, with extensive documentation, sample code, and running examples. This should be your first stop.

◆ The YUI developers have a weblog where they explain how to use the components and highlight innovative uses they've run across. You'll find the blog at yuiblog.com.

◆ If you need a bit more interactivity, there's a Yahoo! Group that allows you to ask and answer questions about YUI. Like all Yahoo! Groups, you can read the discussions on the Web or receive them in your email program as a mailing list. The address for the group is groups.yahoo.com/group/ydn-javascript/.

✔ Tips

■ In this example, the Build it! button is non-functional; all that works is the drag-and-drop capability. For examples of building slideshows, see Chapters 4 and 15.

■ You should also take the time to check out the YUI Library CSS Tools, which are on the same page as the rest of the YUI Library. The CSS Tools include the Grids CSS component, which is a suite of Web page templates that allow you to create grids of one to four columns in each template. This gives you access to more than a thousand CSS-based page layouts, with a CSS library that is less than 4K in size. There are also the CSS Fonts and CSS Reset components, which give you greater control over font display and HTML rendering, respectively.

■ When you download the YUI files, you'll find that they're grouped into various directories depending on what task they're associated with. You don't have to keep them that way, though—you can move them around in whatever way works best for your own style. In this chapter, we've moved them all into a yui directory of their own, one level below our HTML, CSS, and script pages.

Other Ajax Toolkits

Back in the late 1990s, when Dynamic HTML was the latest rage, there were a variety of DHTML toolkits people wrote and made available. Some of the best were (in effect) written by a couple of guys in a garage somewhere. When the dot-com boom dot-bombed, the toolkits' authors had to get day jobs, and the packages were abandoned and not maintained. So when we looked for Ajax toolkits for an earlier edition of this book, we were a bit wary.

We chose to discuss the Yahoo! User Interface Library in this chapter, because it is documented, high quality, open source, and actively supported by a large company, which makes it more likely to stay available for the lifetime of this book. But there are many other good Ajax toolkits available. There are even sites that rate the different toolkits; at press time, our favorite is Wikipedia's, at `wikipedia.org/wiki/Comparison_of_JavaScript_frameworks`.

We think that the most important thing you should look for in a toolkit is that it does a great job of supporting Web standards. That means that it should fully support the most popular browsers, cross-platform. To us, that list includes Firefox, Safari, and Opera for Windows and Mac, and Internet Explorer 7 and up for Windows. It's also important that the toolkit be thoroughly debugged and that it have good documentation.

We suggest that you also take a look at these other toolkits, all of which are popular, well supported, well documented, and have great demos on their sites so you can see if they meet your needs:

◆ Dojo (`www.dojotoolkit.org`)

◆ jQuery (`jquery.com`)

◆ Prototype (`prototypejs.org`)

While this chapter focuses on YUI, Chapter 16 (*Designing with Ajax*) uses jQuery for its examples.

Figure 14.3 When you hover over a future date, the date highlights.

Adding a Calendar to Your Page

Many Web applications need a calendar that the user can refer to and interact with. Reservation forms, to-do lists, navigation for posts on weblogs—the list goes on and on. The YUI library has a good calendar widget that is easy to implement (**Figure 14.3**).

The simple HTML for our calendar appears in **Script 14.4**. The CSS is in **Script 14.5**, and **Script 14.6** shows you how to add the JavaScript for an interactive, one-up calendar (where only one month appears).

To add a one-up calendar:

1. ```
<link type="text/css"
→ rel="stylesheet"
→ href="yui/calendar.css" />
```
   For a calendar, all we need to include is Yahoo!'s calendar.css files in Script 14.4.

2. ```
<script type="text/javascript"
→ src="yui/yahoo-dom-event.js">
→ </script>
<script type="text/javascript"
→ src="yui/calendar.js"></script>
```
   For scripts, we need yahoo-dom-event.js and calendar.js. That's in addition to our own CSS and JavaScript files, of course.

3. ```
YAHOO.namespace("calendar");
```
   This line of code that starts off Script 14.6 tells the browser that we're going to be working with variables and objects that have to do with YUI's calendar. This way, we not only can't step on non-YUI code, we can't even interfere with code from YUI's other modules.

*continues on next page*
```

4. YAHOO.calendar.cal1 = new YAHOO.
→ widget.Calendar("cal1Container");
resetCal();

document.getElementById("resetCal").
→ onclick = resetCal;
document.getElementById
→ ("getSelectedDate").onclick =
→ showSelected;

function resetCal() {
    YAHOO.calendar.cal1.cfg.
    → setProperty("pagedate",
    → new Date());
    YAHOO.calendar.cal1.cfg.
    → setProperty("selected","");
    YAHOO.calendar.cal1.render();
}

This code, inside the init() function, is all called when the page is first loaded. We start off by creating a new calendar object: cal1. We also set the event handlers for two links: resetCal, which resets the dates on the calendar, and getSelectedDate, which allows a user to choose a date on the calendar. We end up by defining our reset function, which will set the date back to its default value and render the calendar.

Script 14.4 This relatively simple HTML mostly calls external files for the Calendar example.

```
script
<!DOCTYPE html PUBLIC "-//W3C//DTD XHTML 1.0
→ Transitional//EN"
        "http://www.w3.org/TR/xhtml1/DTD/
        → xhtml1-transitional.dtd">
<html xmlns="http://www.w3.org/1999/xhtml">
<head>
    <title>Yahoo! Calendar Control:
    → 1 up</title>
    <link type="text/css" rel="stylesheet"
    → href="yui/calendar.css" />
    <link type="text/css" rel="stylesheet"
    → href="script02.css" />
    <script type="text/javascript"
    → src="yui/yahoo-dom-event.js"></script>
    <script type="text/javascript"
    → src="yui/calendar.js"></script>
    <script type="text/javascript"
    → src="script02.js"></script>
</head>
<body>
    <div class="column left">
        <h1>Make a Reservation</h1>
        <p>Use the calendar to your right to
        → pick your preferred date to visit:
        → </p>
        <p id="datePicked"> </p>
    </div>
    <div class="column right yui-skin-sam">
        <div id="cal1Container"></div>
        <a class="navLink"
        → id="resetCal">Reset</a>|
        <a class="navLink"
        → id="getSelectedDate">Choose Date</a>
    </div>
</body>
</html>
```

Script 14.5 The Calendar style sheet.

```
script
a.navLink {
    font-size: 12px;
    text-decoration: underline;
    padding: 5px;
    color: #000;
    cursor:pointer;
}

div.right div {
    margin-left: auto;
    margin-right: auto;
    width: 150px;
}

h1 {
    font-size: 1.5em;
}

.column p {
    margin: 10px 0px;
    font: normal 12px verdana, sans-serif;
    line-height: 15px;
}

.column.right {
    text-align: center;
    background-color: #C2C2D7;
    float: left;
    margin-left: 10px;
    width: 200px;
    padding: 50px 0 50px 25px;
    height: 425px;
    font-size: .8em;
}

.column.left {
    float: left;
    display: inline;
    margin-left: 80px;
    width: 300px;
}
```

5.
```
var dateString = "Please select a
→ date";
var pickedDate = YAHOO.calendar.
→ cal1.getSelectedDates()[0];
if (pickedDate) {
  var outDate =  YAHOO.calendar.
  → cal1.Locale.WEEKDAYS_LONG
  → [pickedDate.getDay()] + ", " +
  → YAHOO.calendar.cal1.Locale.
  → MONTHS_LONG[pickedDate.
  → getMonth()] + " " + pickedDate.
  → getDate() + ".";
  dateString = "We're looking
  → forward to seeing you on " +
  → outDate;
}
document.getElementById
→ ("datePicked").innerHTML =
→ dateString;
```

Sometimes, you'll want your Web application to do something that isn't already built in to YUI, and that's what's happening here. We want our picked date to display in a friendly manner on the screen after the user selects a date.

Because users can do all kinds of wacky things, we want to make sure that they actually did choose a date. On the off chance they didn't, we set our default output to prompt them to try again.

In step 4, we told the showSelected() function that it was to handle when the user was done, and here's the code. The YUI toolkit has the date we want stored in YAHOO.calendar.cal1. getSelectedDates()[0]. That's not the friendliest (or the shortest, or most memorable) variable, so we put it into the pickedDate variable instead.

continues on next page

If `pickedDate` exists, they chose a date, so we set `outdate` to be the string that we want displayed on the screen. We could use the date methods you learned in Chapter 12, but it's simpler to use the ones built into YUI: `YAHOO.calendar.cal1.Locale.WEEKDAYS_LONG` and `YAHOO.calendar.cal1.Locale.MONTHS_LONG` are arrays that contain the names of the days of the week and the months of the year, respectively. And to finish, we set `datePicked`'s `innerHTML` to display our message (**Figure 14.4**).

✔ Tip

- It's so simple to do a single calendar with YUI that you'd expect writing a standard 2-up calendar would be similar. Unfortunately, while it's still much easier than writing it from scratch, there's no simple, "just add this" method to go from one to another—which is why it's a task of its own, next.

Figure 14.4 Clicking the Choose Date link adds a message to the text and locks the date into the calendar.

Script 14.6 The JavaScript can get a bit long for the calendar, but it isn't too complex.

```
YAHOO.namespace("calendar");

YAHOO.calendar.init = function() {
    YAHOO.calendar.cal1 = new YAHOO.widget.
    → Calendar("cal1Container");
    resetCal();

    document.getElementById("resetCal").
    → onclick = resetCal;
    document.getElementById
    → ("getSelectedDate").onclick =
    → showSelected;

    function resetCal() {
        YAHOO.calendar.cal1.cfg.setProperty
        → ("pagedate",new Date());
        YAHOO.calendar.cal1.cfg.setProperty
        → ("selected","");
        YAHOO.calendar.cal1.render();
    }
}

YAHOO.util.Event.onDOMReady
→ (YAHOO.calendar.init);

function showSelected() {
    var dateString = "Please select a date";
    var pickedDate = YAHOO.calendar.cal1.
    → getSelectedDates()[0];
    if (pickedDate) {
        var outDate = YAHOO.calendar.cal1.
        → Locale.WEEKDAYS_LONG[pickedDate.
        → getDay()] + ", " + YAHOO.calendar.
        → cal1.Locale.MONTHS_LONG[pickedDate.
        → getMonth()] + " " + pickedDate.
        → getDate() + ".";
        dateString = "We're looking forward to
        → seeing you on " + outDate;
    }
    document.getElementById("datePicked").
    → innerHTML = dateString;
}
```

Figure 14.5 Click the small calendar icon next to the first set of pop-up menus to bring up the dual calendar, allowing you to choose the first date.

Script 14.7 This HTML sets up the pop-up menus and the library calls.

```
script
<!DOCTYPE html PUBLIC "-//W3C//DTD XHTML 1.0
→ Transitional//EN"
        "http://www.w3.org/TR/xhtml1/DTD/
        → xhtml1-transitional.dtd">
<html xmlns="http://www.w3.org/1999/xhtml">
<head>
    <title>Yahoo! Calendar Control:
    → 2 up</title>
    <link type="text/css" rel="stylesheet"
    → href="yui/calendar.css" />
    <link type="text/css" rel="stylesheet"
    → href="script03.css" />
    <script type="text/javascript"
    → src="yui/yahoo-dom-event.js"></script>
    <script type="text/javascript"
    → src="yui/calendar.js"></script>
    <script type="text/javascript"
    → src="script03.js"></script>
</head>
<body>
<h1>Select your check-in and check-out dates:
→ </h1>
<div class="yui-skin-sam" id="sel1">
    <select id="selMonth1" name="selMonth1">
        <option value="Jan">Jan</option>
        <option value="Feb">Feb</option>
```

(script continues on next page)

Adding a 2-up Calendar to Your Page

Sometimes you only need one calendar: appointments, restaurant reservations, what have you. But 2-up calendars are also seen frequently; they're used for events that begin and end on different dates. You'll often see them used when making hotel reservations and purchasing plane tickets, for instance. **Script 14.7** (HTML), **Script 14.8** (CSS), and **Script 14.9** (JavaScript) show you how to do a two-up calendar (**Figure 14.5**).

To add a two-up calendar:

1. ```
   <select id="selMonth1" name=
   → "selMonth1">
       <option value="Jan">Jan</option>
       <option value="Feb">Feb</option>
       <option value="Mar">Mar</option>
       <option value="Apr">Apr</option>
       <option value="May">May</option>
       <option value="Jun">Jun</option>
       <option value="Jul">Jul</option>
       <option value="Aug">Aug</option>
       <option value="Sep">Sep</option>
       <option value="Oct">Oct</option>
       <option value="Nov">Nov</option>
       <option value="Dec">Dec</option>
   </select>
   ```

   Script 14.7 needs to allow the user to pick a date, so we have two pop-up menus: one for the month and one for the day of the month.

   Here, as we're doing throughout this task, we're showing the steps for just the first calendar, but the code itself handles both.

continues on next page
   ```

2. `<img id="dateLink1"`
   → `src="images/pdate.gif"`
   → `alt="cal button" border="0" />`

But along with picking a date from pop-ups, it's also possible to click a button and see an actual calendar that lets users pick from a visual display of dates.

3. `YAHOO.calendar.cal1 =`
   → `new YAHOO.widget.CalendarGroup`
   → `("cal1Container");`
   `YAHOO.calendar.cal1.cfg.setProperty`
   → `("pagedate",new Date());`
   `YAHOO.calendar.cal1.cfg.setProperty`
   → `("selected","");`
   `YAHOO.calendar.cal1.cfg.setProperty`
   → `("title","Select your desired`
      → `check-in date:");`
   `YAHOO.calendar.cal1.render();`
   `YAHOO.calendar.cal1.selectEvent.`
   → `subscribe(handleSelect1,`
   → `YAHOO.calendar.cal1, true);`

A lot of variables are set in Script 14.9's `init()` routine when the page is loaded, but we're concerned with the ones that handle our new calendars. Here, we create `cal1` (the first of the two 2-up calendars) to be of type `CalendarGroup` and initialized to display in the `cal1Container` div. When it's first displayed, the current month will be shown, so we need to pass today's date, but we tell the calendar to not select a default. Next we set the title, and render the calendar. Finally, we set the calendar's `selectEvent` handler to call the `handleSelect1` function when a selection is made.

Script 14.7 *continued*

```
            <option value="Mar">Mar</option>
            <option value="Apr">Apr</option>
            <option value="May">May</option>
            <option value="Jun">Jun</option>
            <option value="Jul">Jul</option>
            <option value="Aug">Aug</option>
            <option value="Sep">Sep</option>
            <option value="Oct">Oct</option>
            <option value="Nov">Nov</option>
            <option value="Dec">Dec</option>
         </select>
         <select name="selDay1" id="selDay1">
            <option value="1">1</option>
            <option value="2">2</option>
            <option value="3">3</option>
            <option value="4">4</option>
            <option value="5">5</option>
            <option value="6">6</option>
            <option value="7">7</option>
            <option value="8">8</option>
            <option value="9">9</option>
            <option value="10">10</option>
            <option value="11">11</option>
            <option value="12">12</option>
            <option value="13">13</option>
            <option value="14">14</option>
            <option value="15">15</option>
            <option value="16">16</option>
            <option value="17">17</option>
            <option value="18">18</option>
            <option value="19">19</option>
            <option value="20">20</option>
            <option value="21">21</option>
            <option value="22">22</option>
            <option value="23">23</option>
            <option value="24">24</option>
            <option value="25">25</option>
            <option value="26">26</option>
            <option value="27">27</option>
            <option value="28">28</option>
            <option value="29">29</option>
            <option value="30">30</option>
            <option value="31">31</option>
         </select><img id="dateLink1"
   → src="images/pdate.gif"
   → alt="cal button" border="0" />
```

(script continues on next page)

Script 14.7 *continued*

```
                                                script
        <div id="cal1Container"></div>
</div>
<div id="sel2">
    <select id="selMonth2" name="selMonth2">
        <option value="Jan">Jan</option>
        <option value="Feb">Feb</option>
        <option value="Mar">Mar</option>
        <option value="Apr">Apr</option>
        <option value="May">May</option>
        <option value="Jun">Jun</option>
        <option value="Jul">Jul</option>
        <option value="Aug">Aug</option>
        <option value="Sep">Sep</option>
        <option value="Oct">Oct</option>
        <option value="Nov">Nov</option>
        <option value="Dec">Dec</option>
    </select>
    <select name="selDay2" id="selDay2">
        <option value="1">1</option>
        <option value="2">2</option>
        <option value="3">3</option>
        <option value="4">4</option>
        <option value="5">5</option>
        <option value="6">6</option>
        <option value="7">7</option>
        <option value="8">8</option>
        <option value="9">9</option>
        <option value="10">10</option>
        <option value="11">11</option>
        <option value="12">12</option>
        <option value="13">13</option>
        <option value="14">14</option>
        <option value="15">15</option>
        <option value="16">16</option>
        <option value="17">17</option>
        <option value="18">18</option>
        <option value="19">19</option>
        <option value="20">20</option>
        <option value="21">21</option>
        <option value="22">22</option>
        <option value="23">23</option>
        <option value="24">24</option>
        <option value="25">25</option>
        <option value="26">26</option>
        <option value="27">27</option>
        <option value="28">28</option>
```

(script continues on next page)

4.
```
function handleSelect1
→ (type,args,obj) {
    handleSelect(args[0],1);
}
```

We end up in the handleSelect1() function when the user picks a date off the calendar. When that happens, we figure out what date was selected using the automatically passed in args parameter, and then send that to handleSelect().

5.
```
var date = dates[0];
var monthString = "selMonth" +
→ calNo;
var dayString = "selDay" + calNo;
document.getElementById
→ (monthString).selectedIndex =
→ date[1]-1;
document.getElementById(dayString).
→ selectedIndex = date[2]-1;

if (calNo==1) {
    YAHOO.calendar.cal1.hide();
}
else {
    YAHOO.calendar.cal2.hide();
}
```

Here inside handleSelect(), we set the month and day pop-ups to match (**Figure 14.6**) and then hide the calendar.

continues on next page

Figure 14.6 When you click the date in the calendar, it changes the pop-up menus to reflect your choice.

6.
```
var month = document.getElementById
→ (monthString).selectedIndex;
var day = document.getElementById
→ (dayString).selectedIndex + 1;

thisCal.select((month+1) + "/" + day
→ + "/" + today.getFullYear());
thisCal.setMonth(month);
thisCal.render();
```

The changeDate() function does the reverse of the handleSelect() function: given a new pop-up selected date, it changes what will display on the calendar when it's next displayed. The month and day variables are set based on the pop-ups, the year is always set to the current year, and then select() and setMonth() are set to change the dates. Finally, render() is called to render the calendar display for future use.

Script 14.7 *continued*

```
⊝ ⊙ ⊙                    script
            <option value="29">29</option>
            <option value="30">30</option>
            <option value="31">31</option>
        </select><img id="dateLink2"
    → src="images/pdate.gif"
    → alt="cal button" border="0" />

        <div class="column right yui-skin-sam">
            <div id="cal2Container"></div>
        </div>
    </div>
    </body>
    </html>
```

Script 14.8 The CSS for the 2-up calendar.

```
⊝ ⊙ ⊙                    script
#sel1 {
    position: absolute;
    left: 148px;
    top: 75px;
}

#sel2 {
    position: absolute;
    left: 303px;
    top: 75px;
}

#selMonth1, #selDay1, #selMonth2, #selDay2 {
    vertical-align: middle;
}

#dateLink1, #dateLink2 {
    vertical-align: middle;
    margin: 5px;
}

#cal1Container, #cal2Container {
    position: absolute;
    display: none;
    width: 380px;
    font-size: .8em;
}

h1 {
    font-size: 1.5em;
    margin: 50px 0 0 50px;
}
```

Script 14.9 This JavaScript is where the action happens for the 2-up calendar.

```
                                  script
YAHOO.namespace("calendar");

YAHOO.calendar.init = function() {
    var today = new Date();

    document.getElementById("selMonth1").selectedIndex = today.getMonth();
    document.getElementById("selDay1").selectedIndex = today.getDate()-1;
    document.getElementById("selMonth2").selectedIndex = today.getMonth();
    document.getElementById("selDay2").selectedIndex = today.getDate()-1;

    document.getElementById("selMonth1").onchange = function() {changeDate(1)};
    document.getElementById("selDay1").onchange = function() {changeDate(1)};
    document.getElementById("selMonth2").onchange = function() {changeDate(2)};
    document.getElementById("selDay2").onchange = function() {changeDate(2)};

    YAHOO.calendar.cal1 = new YAHOO.widget.CalendarGroup("cal1Container");
    YAHOO.calendar.cal1.cfg.setProperty("pagedate",new Date());
    YAHOO.calendar.cal1.cfg.setProperty("selected","");
    YAHOO.calendar.cal1.cfg.setProperty("title","Select your desired check-in date:");
    YAHOO.calendar.cal1.render();
    YAHOO.calendar.cal1.selectEvent.subscribe(handleSelect1, YAHOO.calendar.cal1, true);

    YAHOO.calendar.cal2 = new YAHOO.widget.CalendarGroup("cal2Container");
    YAHOO.calendar.cal2.cfg.setProperty("pagedate",new Date());
    YAHOO.calendar.cal2.cfg.setProperty("selected","");
    YAHOO.calendar.cal2.cfg.setProperty("title","Select your desired check-out date:");
    YAHOO.calendar.cal2.render();
    YAHOO.calendar.cal2.selectEvent.subscribe(handleSelect2, YAHOO.calendar.cal2, true);

    document.getElementById("dateLink1").onclick = showCalendar1;
    document.getElementById("dateLink2").onclick = showCalendar2;
}

function showCalendar1() {
    YAHOO.calendar.cal2.hide();
    YAHOO.calendar.cal1.show();
}

function showCalendar2() {
    YAHOO.calendar.cal1.hide();
    YAHOO.calendar.cal2.show();
}
```

(script continues on next page)

Script 14.9 *continued*

```
                                              script
function handleSelect1(type,args,obj) {
    handleSelect(args[0],1);
}

function handleSelect2(type,args,obj) {
    handleSelect(args[0],2);
}

function handleSelect(dates,calNo) {
    var date = dates[0];
    var monthString = "selMonth" + calNo;
    var dayString = "selDay" + calNo;

    document.getElementById(monthString).selectedIndex = date[1]-1;
    document.getElementById(dayString).selectedIndex = date[2]-1;

    if (calNo==1) {
        YAHOO.calendar.cal1.hide();
    }
    else {
        YAHOO.calendar.cal2.hide();
    }
}

function changeDate(calNo) {
    var today = new Date();
    var monthString = "selMonth" + calNo;
    var dayString = "selDay" + calNo;
    if (calNo==1) {
        var thisCal = YAHOO.calendar.cal1;
    }
    else {
        var thisCal = YAHOO.calendar.cal2;
    }

    var month = document.getElementById(monthString).selectedIndex;
    var day = document.getElementById(dayString).selectedIndex + 1;

    thisCal.select((month+1) + "/" + day + "/" + today.getFullYear());
    thisCal.setMonth(month);
    thisCal.render();
}

YAHOO.util.Event.onDOMReady(YAHOO.calendar.init);
```

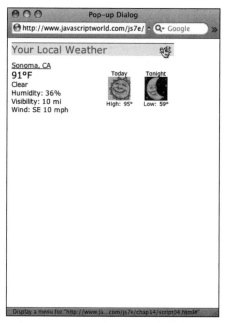

Figure 14.7 The Weather module on this page has an edit link to bring up a preferences dialog.

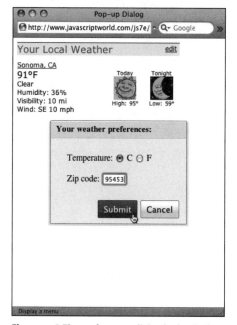

Figure 14.8 The preferences dialog looks similar to those used by real applications.

Using the Container Utility

In the parlance of the Yahoo! User Interface Library, a *container* is an object that encloses any kind of content. There are two basic types of containers: *Module* and *Overlay*. The first can appear anywhere on your page, and the user treats it as a single unit (if you allow it to be manipulated). Overlay is an extension of Module that floats above the document's inline content and does not affect the flow of text and images on the page.

There are four other container types related to Overlay. *Tooltip* creates small floating boxes similar to the ones that provide contextual help in operating systems like Windows and Mac OS X. *Panel* mimics an operating system window. *Dialog* creates a standard dialog that can look like a system dialog. And *Simple Dialog* behaves like an operating system alert, with dual choices (Yes/No, OK/Cancel, etc.).

In this example, we've created a new Dialog to act as the preferences for a weather application (**Figures 14.7** and **14.8**). **Script 14.10** shows the HTML, **Script 14.11** the CSS, and **Script 14.12** the JavaScript.

Script 14.10 In this case, we've hard-coded the HTML for the Weather module; in a production application, this would be dynamically generated.

```
<!DOCTYPE html PUBLIC "-//W3C//DTD XHTML 1.0 Transitional//EN"
        "http://www.w3.org/TR/xhtml1/DTD/xhtml1-transitional.dtd">
<html xmlns="http://www.w3.org/1999/xhtml">
<head>
    <title>Pop-up Dialog</title>
    <link type="text/css" rel="stylesheet" href="yui/container.css" />
    <link type="text/css" rel="stylesheet" href="yui/button.css" />
    <link type="text/css" rel="stylesheet" href="script04.css" />
    <script type="text/javascript" src="yui/yahoo-dom-event.js"></script>
    <script type="text/javascript" src="yui/dragdrop.js"></script>
    <script type="text/javascript" src="yui/element-beta.js"></script>
    <script type="text/javascript" src="yui/button.js"></script>
    <script type="text/javascript" src="yui/container.js"></script>
    <script type="text/javascript" src="script04.js"></script>
</head>
<body class="yui-skin-sam">
<div id="WeatherWidget">
    <div id="header">
        <a href="#" id="loadDialog">edit</a>
        <span>Your Local Weather</span>
    </div>
    <a href="#">Sonoma, CA</a><br />
    <div class="weatherFig">
        Tonight<br />
        <img src="images/nt_clear.gif" alt="nt_clear.gif" width="42" height="42" /><br />
        Low: 59&deg;
    </div>
    <div class="weatherFig">
        Today<br />
        <img src="images/clear.gif" alt="clear.gif" width="42" height="42" /><br />
        High: 95&deg;
    </div>
    <span class="big">91&deg;F</span><br />
    Clear<br />
    Humidity: 36%<br />
    Visibility: 10 mi<br />
    Wind: SE 10 mph
</div>
<div id="dlg">
    <div class="hd">Your weather preferences:</div>
    <div class="bd">
        <form name="dlgForm" action="#">
            <p><label for="radiobuttons">Temperature:</label>
            <input type="radio" name="radiobuttons[]" value="C" checked="checked" /> C
            <input type="radio" name="radiobuttons[]" value="F" /> F</p>
            <p><label for="zip">Zip code:</label> <input type="text" name="zip" size="5" /></p>
        </form>
    </div>
</div>
</body>
</html>
```

Script 14.11 This CSS styles the main page and the pop-up dialog.

```
⊖ ⊖ ⊖              script
#WeatherWidget {
    font-family: verdana, arial, sans-serif;
    font-size: 12px;
    width: 300px;
}


#header {
    background-color: #E4ECF9;
    border-top: 1px blue solid;
    margin-bottom: 10px;
    color: #36C;
    font-size: 18px;
}


#loadDialog {
    float: right;
    padding: 2px 5px 0 0;
    font-size: 12px;
}


.big {
    font-size: 16px;
}


div.weatherFig {
    float: right;
    text-align: center;
    padding: 0 10px;
    font-size: 10px;
}


form p {
    margin-left: 20px;
}
```

To add a dialog container:

1. ```
   <link type="text/css"
   → rel="stylesheet" href="yui/
   → container.css" />
   <link type="text/css"
   → rel="stylesheet" href="yui/button.
   → css" />
   ```

   A container has to look like a certain type of container, so here in Script 14.10 is where we bring in container.css and button.css to handle the style requirements. We'll also bring in container.js and button.js in the script section.

2. ```
   <div id="dlg">
       <div class="hd">Your weather
       → preferences:</div>
       <div id="bd">
         <form name="dlgForm"
         → action="#">
           <p><label for="radiobuttons">
           → Temperature:</label>
           <input type="radio"
           → name="radiobuttons[]"
           → value="C" checked=
           → "checked" /> C
           <input type="radio"
           → name="radiobuttons[]"
           → value="F" /> F</p>
           <p><label for="zip">Zip code:
           → </label> <input type="text"
           → name="zip" size="5" /></p>
         </form>
       </div>
   </div>
   ```

   This div doesn't look like much when the page first loads—in fact, it doesn't look like anything at all. It's hidden until the user clicks the edit link.

   continues on next page

3.
```
YAHOO.container.dialog1 =
→ new YAHOO.widget.Dialog("dlg",
  { width: "250px",
    fixedcenter: true,
    visible: false,
    constraintoviewport: true,
    buttons:[
      {text:"Submit", handler:
      → handleSubmit, isDefault:true},
      {text:"Cancel", handler:
      → handleCancel}
    ]
  }
);
```

Parts of Script 14.12 may look a little odd, but it really is JavaScript, and it's worth getting used to. To be more precise, it's Object Literal format, as previously discussed back in Chapter 11. It's a way of treating JavaScript objects as if they were data; that is, they can be passed back and forth as if they were XML. In our standard format, the code above would have been expressed as something like:

```
YAHOO.container.dlg =
→ new YAHOO.widget.Dialog();
YAHOO.container.dlg.width="250px";
YAHOO.container.dlg.fixedcenter=
→ true;YAHOO.container.dlg.visible=
→ false;
YAHOO.container.dlg.
→ constraintoviewports=true;
```
and so on.

Script 14.12 The JavaScript for the container.

```
YAHOO.namespace("container");

function init() {
    var handleSubmit = function() {
        this.hide();
    }
    var handleCancel = function() {
        this.hide();
    }

    YAHOO.container.dialog1 =
    → new YAHOO.widget.Dialog("dlg",
        { width: "250px",
            fixedcenter: true,
            visible: false,
            constraintoviewport: true,
            buttons:[
                {text:"Submit", handler:
                → handleSubmit, isDefault:true},
                {text:"Cancel", handler:
                → handleCancel}
            ]
        }
    );

    YAHOO.container.dialog1.render();

    document.getElementById("loadDialog").
    → onclick = function() {
        YAHOO.container.dialog1.show();
    }
}

YAHOO.util.Event.onDOMReady(init);
```

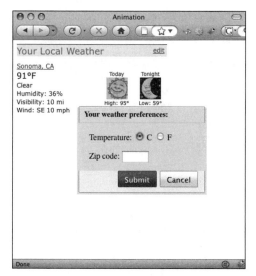

Figure 14.9 We haven't figured out how to add animation on the printed page, but this dialog really did fade in.

4. ```
document.getElementById
→ ("loadDialog").onclick =
→ function() {
    YAHOO.container.dialog1.show();
}
```

When the edit link is clicked, its `onclick` event handler is triggered, which brings us here. The `show()` method simply tells the browser to show the dialog, as seen in **Figure 14.9**.

### ✔ Tip

■ As we said way back in Chapter 2: there's no one right way to write JavaScript. Some programmers (like the YUI folks) prefer Object Literals because it's compact and because (in its JSON flavor) it works well as a transport method. JSON can also be somewhat complex and convoluted, so for the most part we have avoided its use in this book.
```

Adding Animation Effects

The Yahoo! User Interface Library's Animation Utility allows you to add many sorts of animated effects to YUI objects. You can make graphics and other objects bigger or smaller; fade them in or out; animate colors; move objects across the page; move them along a specified path; and scroll text fields horizontally, vertically, or both. And of course, the combinations and possibilities are almost endless.

In this example, we're going to show you how to animate the dialog we used in the previous task. The additions to the HTML are in **Script 14.13**, and the ones to the JavaScript are in **Script 14.14**.

Script 14.13 This HTML has a different title and calls additional libraries than Script 14.10, but it is otherwise identical.

```
● ● ●                  script
<!DOCTYPE html PUBLIC "-//W3C//DTD XHTML 1.0
→ Transitional//EN"
        "http://www.w3.org/TR/xhtml1/DTD/
        → xhtml1-transitional.dtd">
<html xmlns="http://www.w3.org/1999/xhtml">
<head>
    <title>Animation</title>
    <link type="text/css" rel="stylesheet"
    → href="yui/container.css" />
    <link type="text/css" rel="stylesheet"
    → href="yui/button.css" />
    <link type="text/css" rel="stylesheet"
    → href="script04.css" />
    <script type="text/javascript"
    → src="yui/yahoo-dom-event.js"></script>
    <script type="text/javascript"
    → src="yui/dragdrop.js"></script>
    <script type="text/javascript"
    → src="yui/element-beta.js"></script>
    <script type="text/javascript"
    → src="yui/animation.js"></script>
    <script type="text/javascript"
    → src="yui/button.js"></script>
    <script type="text/javascript"
    → src="yui/container.js"></script>
    <script type="text/javascript"
    → src="script05.js"></script>
</head>
<body class="yui-skin-sam">
<div id="WeatherWidget">
    <div id="header">
        <a href="#" id="loadDialog">edit</a>
        <span>Your Local Weather</span>
    </div>
    <a href="#">Sonoma, CA</a><br />
    <div class="weatherFig">
        Tonight<br />
        <img src="images/nt_clear.gif"
        → alt="nt_clear.gif" width="42"
        → height="42" /><br />
        Low: 59&deg;
```

(script continues on next page)

Script 14.13 *continued*

```
                                    script
        </div>
        <div class="weatherFig">
            Today<br />
            <img src="images/clear.gif" alt="clear.gif" width="42" height="42" /><br />
            High: 95&deg;
        </div>
        <span class="big">91&deg;F</span><br />
        Clear<br />
        Humidity: 36%<br />
        Visibility: 10 mi<br />
        Wind: SE 10 mph
    </div>
    <div id="dlg">
        <div class="hd">Your weather preferences:</div>
        <form name="dlgForm" action="#">
            <p><label for="radiobuttons">Temperature:</label>
            <input type="radio" name="radiobuttons[]" value="C" checked="checked" /> C
            <input type="radio" name="radiobuttons[]" value="F" /> F</p>
            <p><label for="zip">Zip code:</label> <input type="text" name="zip" size="5" /></p>
        </form>
    </div>
    </body>
    </html>
```

To add animation to an object:

1. `<script type="text/javascript"`
   → `src="yui/animation.js"></script>`

   This may be why so much of Web 2.0 is about animating objects such as fade-ins and fade-outs: the only change that needed to be made to Script 14.10 was to bring in YUI's animation.js file.

2. `effect:{effect:YAHOO.widget.`
   → `ContainerEffect.FADE,`
   → `duration:0.25}`

   In Script 14.14, this really is all we have to add to our code to make it fade in and out (**Figure 14.9**). It's not even a line of code; it's just one more set of parameters passed to YAHOO.widget.Dialog when we create our dialog.

Script 14.14 The JavaScript that makes the animation happen.

```
script
YAHOO.namespace("container");

function init() {
    var handleSubmit = function() {
        this.hide();
    }
    var handleCancel = function() {
        this.hide();
    }

    YAHOO.container.dialog1 =
    → new YAHOO.widget.Dialog("dlg",
        { width: "250px",
            fixedcenter: true,
            visible: false,
            constraintoviewport : true,
            buttons:[
                {text:"Submit", handler:
                → handleSubmit, isDefault:true},
                {text:"Cancel", handler:
                → handleCancel}
            ],
            effect:{effect:YAHOO.widget.
            → ContainerEffect.FADE,duration:
            → 0.25}
        }
    );

    YAHOO.container.dialog1.render();

    document.getElementById("loadDialog").
    → onclick = function() {
        YAHOO.container.dialog1.show();
    }
}

YAHOO.util.Event.onDOMReady(init);
```

Implementing the Logger Control for Debugging

When you're doing Ajax development, the browser is doing a lot of work behind the scenes, and you can use as much information about what's going on as you can get. That's why we like the Logger control in the Yahoo! User Interface Library. It allows you to see messages about the inner workings of any of the YUI components as they are doing their work. And you can *pipe* (that is, you can write) the output of the Logger to either FireBug (a debugging extension for Firefox) or Safari's JavaScript Console. It's a good tool to help you figure out what's going on when things aren't working exactly as expected.

You can choose to show the Logger on your page if you want instant feedback (**Figure 14.10**), or you can leave it running invisibly in memory and send the output to your external debugger. The HTML in **Script 14.15** and the JavaScript in **Script 14.16** show you how to use the Logger on your development pages.

Figure 14.10 The Logger control can be shown on the page, as here, or it can be hidden to unobtrusively send messages to your debugger.

Script 14.15 Again, we're calling additional libraries in this HTML page.

```
<!DOCTYPE html PUBLIC "-//W3C//DTD XHTML 1.0 Transitional//EN"
        "http://www.w3.org/TR/xhtml1/DTD/xhtml1-transitional.dtd">
<html xmlns="http://www.w3.org/1999/xhtml">
<head>
    <title>Event Logger</title>
    <link type="text/css" rel="stylesheet" href="yui/container.css" />
    <link type="text/css" rel="stylesheet" href="yui/button.css" />
    <link type="text/css" rel="stylesheet" href="yui/logger.css" />
    <link type="text/css" rel="stylesheet" href="script04.css" />
    <script type="text/javascript" src="yui/yahoo-dom-event.js"></script>
    <script type="text/javascript" src="yui/dragdrop.js"></script>
    <script type="text/javascript" src="yui/element-beta.js"></script>
    <script type="text/javascript" src="yui/animation.js"></script>
    <script type="text/javascript" src="yui/button.js"></script>
    <script type="text/javascript" src="yui/container.js"></script>
    <script type="text/javascript" src="yui/logger.js"></script>
    <script type="text/javascript" src="script06.js"></script>
</head>
<body class="yui-skin-sam">
<div id="WeatherWidget">
    <div id="header">
        <a href="#" id="loadDialog">edit</a>
        <span>Your Local Weather</span>
    </div>
    <a href="#">Sonoma, CA</a><br />
    <div class="weatherFig">
        Tonight<br />
        <img src="images/nt_clear.gif" alt="nt_clear.gif" width="42" height="42" /><br />
        Low: 59&deg;
    </div>
    <div class="weatherFig">
        Today<br />
        <img src="images/clear.gif" alt="clear.gif" width="42" height="42" /><br />
        High: 95&deg;
    </div>
    <span class="big">91&deg;F</span><br />
    Clear<br />
    Humidity: 36%<br />
    Visibility: 10 mi<br />
    Wind: SE 10 mph
</div>
<div id="dlg">
    <div class="hd">Your weather preferences:</div>
    <form name="dlgForm" action="#">
        <p><label for="radiobuttons">Temperature:</label>
        <input type="radio" name="radiobuttons[]" value="C" checked="checked" /> C
        <input type="radio" name="radiobuttons[]" value="F" /> F</p>
        <p><label for="zip">Zip code:</label> <input type="text" name="zip" size="5" /></p>
    </form>
</div>
<div id="logArea"></div>
</body>
</html>
```

Script 14.16 You can specify which messages go to the Logger, as in this JavaScript.

```
script
YAHOO.namespace("container");

function init() {
    var handleSubmit = function() {
        YAHOO.log("Dialog submitted","warn");
        this.hide();
    }
    var handleCancel = function() {
        YAHOO.log("Dialog cancelled","warn");
        this.hide();
    }

    YAHOO.container.dialog1 =
    → new YAHOO.widget.Dialog("dlg",
        { width: "250px",
            fixedcenter: true,
            visible: false,
            constraintoviewport : true,
            buttons:[
                {text:"Submit", handler:
                → handleSubmit, isDefault:true},
                {text:"Cancel", handler:
                → handleCancel}
            ],
            effect:{effect:YAHOO.widget.
            → ContainerEffect.FADE,duration:
            → 0.25}
        }
    );

    YAHOO.container.dialog1.render();

    document.getElementById("loadDialog").
    → onclick = function() {
        YAHOO.log("Animation starting now");
        YAHOO.container.dialog1.show();
    }

    var myLogReader = new YAHOO.widget.
    → LogReader("logArea");
}

YAHOO.util.Event.onDOMReady(init);
```

To add the Logger window to your page:

1. `<script type="text/javascript"` → `src="yui/logger.js"></script>`

By now, you're probably unsurprised that the only changes we need to make to Script 14.13 are to add references to the `logger.css` and `logger.js` files, and to add a dummy `<div>` at the end (named `logArea`).

2. `YAHOO.log("Dialog submitted","warn");`

When you want to write out information to the log file, just call `YAHOO.log()`. Here in Script 14.16, we've written a note to ourselves to show that we've hit the code that submits the dialog.

There are five types of messages that the Logger knows about: info, warn, error, time, and window. This one is a "warn".

3. `YAHOO.log("Animation starting now");`

If we don't include a second parameter at all, the Logger will assume that it's an "info" message, and here's one in the `onclick` handler noting that the animation is starting.

4. `var myLogReader = new YAHOO.widget.` → `LogReader("logArea");`

The code above has used the Logger, but we haven't seen the code yet to set it up. Here's where we create the Logger: we just tell `YAHOO.widget.LogReader()` the name of the dummy `<div>` in the HTML page where we want it to go.

✔ Tips

■ Everyone has their own style of working, and how they like their logs to appear (and even if they like them at all) is a personal choice. What works for us is to create a log file as shown above, but remember: that log file is a movable widget. As such, you can move it almost off the Web page, so you can see what's going on inside your page without the Logger blocking anything. But then when there's a problem, it's right there, and it's easy to bring it back and view its history.

■ Now that you've seen a small fraction of what's included in YUI, are you starting to wonder how you'll keep it all straight in your head? The answer is: don't. Instead, grab the downloadable "Cheat Sheets" at `developer.yahoo.com/yui/docs/assets/cheatsheets.zip`, and you'll have a collection of single-page PDFs suitable for printing and referring to regularly.

IMPLEMENTING THE LOGGER CONTROL

Grading the Browsers

Earlier, we said that an important factor in choosing a toolkit is its support for Web standards and for working cross-browser. Here's how YUI does it:

◆ **A grade**: These browsers are the most popular and are known and tested by Yahoo!'s QA team. If YUI bugs are found that apply to these browsers, the YUI bugs are fixed.

◆ **C grade**: These browsers are on the old side and aren't seen much—or at least not currently. Their capabilities are known, and they're not up to snuff to handle the cool modern stuff. They get the "core" experience; that is, they get the content but not the style.

◆ **X grade**: These browsers are the weird ones. There's always someone out there trying to write their own browser, and Yahoo! can't guarantee what their libraries might do in unknown situations. Because they could be testing versions of new browsers, YUI code serves them as if they're A grade—meaning that if they can handle the cutting-edge features, they're fine.

Overall, the breakdown of YUI browser support is at about 96% A grade, 3% C grade, and 1% X grade.

Because Yahoo! has documented its goals and its support requirements, we're comfortable recommending its tools—after all, you don't want to find yourself in a situation when Firefox 4.0 comes out where your Web application doesn't work and your toolkit's development team is too busy with finals and their high school prom to bring it up to speed to match.

Want to read what Yahoo! said for yourself? You can find the original article at `developer.yahoo.com/yui/articles/gbs/gbs.html` and Yahoo!'s table of graded browsers at `developer.yahoo.com/yui/articles/gbs/`.

15

Applied JavaScript

In earlier chapters in this book, you've learned how to use dozens of JavaScript techniques to accomplish many specific tasks. On many Web pages that you build, you'll often need just one technique, and you'll be able to use a script from this book (usually with some minor modifications) to get the job done.

But sometimes you'll need to use more than one technique to get the job done on your pages. That's where this chapter comes in. The tasks you'll find here require a variety of approaches and are similar (in spirit, if not specifically) to what you'll need to do on your own Web sites.

In this chapter, you'll learn to improve your site's user interface with outline-style sliding and fly-out menus; create a slideshow; process text by crunching it with JavaScript; let JavaScript do the hard work of displaying data in an easy-to-understand graphical manner; and switch between different style sheets under script control.

Using Sliding Menus

A sliding menu is a simple user interface widget that lets you put a lot of information on a page without cluttering it all up. The user can view just as much (or as little) of the extra information as they want to see at a time. **Script 15.1** contains the HTML, **Script 15.2** the CSS, and **Script 15.3** the JavaScript, as shown below.

Script 15.1 Here's a straightforward HTML page with a lot of links.

```
<!DOCTYPE html PUBLIC "-//W3C//DTD XHTML 1.0 Transitional//EN"
        "http://www.w3.org/TR/xhtml1/DTD/xhtml1-transitional.dtd">
<html xmlns="http://www.w3.org/1999/xhtml">
<head>
    <title>Shakespeare's Plays</title>
    <link type="text/css" rel="stylesheet" href="script01.css" />
    <script type="text/javascript" src="script01.js"></script>
</head>
<body>
    <h1>Shakespeare's Plays</h1>
    <div>
        <a href="menu1.html" class="menuLink">Comedies</a>
        <ul class="menu" id="menu1">
            <li><a href="pg1.html">All's Well That Ends Well</a></li>
            <li><a href="pg2.html">As You Like It</a></li>
            <li><a href="pg3.html">Love's Labour's Lost</a></li>
            <li><a href="pg4.html">The Comedy of Errors</a></li>
        </ul>
    </div>
    <div>
        <a href="menu2.html" class="menuLink">Tragedies</a>
        <ul class="menu" id="menu2">
            <li><a href="pg5.html">Anthony &amp; Cleopatra</a></li>
            <li><a href="pg6.html">Hamlet</a></li>
            <li><a href="pg7.html">Romeo &amp; Juliet</a></li>
        </ul>
    </div>
    <div>
        <a href="menu3.html" class="menuLink">Histories</a>
        <ul class="menu" id="menu3">
            <li><a href="pg8.html">Henry IV, Part 1</a></li>
            <li><a href="pg9.html">Henry IV, Part 2</a></li>
        </ul>
    </div>
</body>
</html>
```

Script 15.2 It doesn't take much CSS to pull off this effect.

```
●●●                script
body {
    background-color: white;
    color: black;
}

div {
    margin-bottom: 10px;
}

ul.menu {
    display: none;
    list-style-type: none;
    margin-top: 5px;
}

a.menuLink {
    font-size: 16px;
    font-weight: bold;
}
```

Script 15.3 Text (and links) can appear and disappear with this script.

```
●●●                script
window.onload = initAll;

function initAll() {
    var allLinks = document.getElementsByTag
    → Name("a");

    for (var i=0; i<allLinks.length; i++) {
        if (allLinks[i].className.indexOf
        → ("menuLink") > -1) {
            allLinks[i].onclick = toggleMenu;
        }
    }
}

function toggleMenu() {
    var startMenu = this.href.lastIndexOf
    → ("/")+1;
```

(script continues on next page)

To use sliding menus:

1. `var allLinks = document.getElements`
   `→ ByTagName("a");`

   When the page loads, the `initAll()` function is called, and it begins by creating an array of all the links on the page.

2. `for (var i=0;i<allLinks.length;i++) {`
   `    if (allLinks[i].className.indexOf`
   `→ ("menuLink") > -1) {`
   `        allLinks[i].onclick =`
   `        → toggleMenu;`
   `    }`
   `}`

   Once we have all the links, we loop through them, looking for those links with a class of `menuLink` and adding an `onclick` handler to just those links. Here, that `onclick` handler is set to call the `toggleMenu()` function when they're clicked.

3. `var startMenu = this.href.`
   `→ lastIndexOf("/")+1;`
   `var stopMenu = this.href.`
   `→ lastIndexOf(".");`

   Inside `toggleMenu()`, JavaScript has given us `this`. Here, `this` is the link object that the user clicked, which means that `this.href` is the full link URL. But we only want the part between the last forward slash and the last period (that is, if the link was to `http://www.javascriptworld.com/index.html`, we'd only want "index"), so we create and set `startMenu` and `stopMenu` to be the locations in `this.href` where we want to start and stop finding the string that will end up being our menu name.

   continues on next page

continues on next page

USING SLIDING MENUS

4. `var thisMenuName = this.href.`
`→ substring(startMenu,stopMenu);`

The menu name we want begins and ends at these two positions, so here's where we set it.

5. `var thisMenu = document.`
`→ getElementById(thisMenuName).`
`→ style;`

The variable `thisMenu` is set to the desired menu using the `getElementById()` method.

6.
```
if (thisMenu.display == "block") {
   thisMenu.display = "none";
}
else {
   thisMenu.display = "block";
}
```

If the `display` property of `thisMenu` is `block`, then this code changes it to `none`. Alternatively, if it's `none`, it's changed to `block`. This is what toggles the menu display, as shown in **Figures 15.1** and **15.2**.

7. `return false;`

And finally, we return a value of `false`—that's because the `toggleMenu()` function was called due to an `onclick` event handler on a link. When we return false, the `href` attribute never gets loaded into the browser window, so the viewer stays on the same page.

Script 15.3 *continued*

```
var stopMenu = this.href.lastIndexOf(".");
var thisMenuName = this.href.substring
→ (startMenu,stopMenu);

var thisMenu = document.getElementById
→ (thisMenuName).style;
if (thisMenu.display == "block") {
   thisMenu.display = "none";
}
else {
   thisMenu.display = "block";
}

return false;
}
```

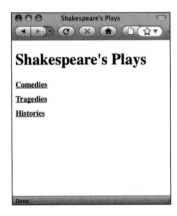

Figure 15.1
The initial view of the sliding menus.

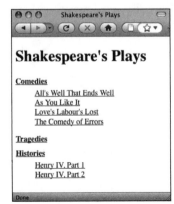

Figure 15.2
After a click, the menu expands and the additional choices appear.

Script 15.4 A little more CSS and a little more JavaScript give your menus a more traditional look.

```
●  ●  ●                script
body {
      background-color: white;
      color: black;
}


div {
      margin-bottom: 10px;
      width: 20em;
      background-color: #9CF;
}


ul.menu {
      display: none;
      list-style-type: none;
      margin: 0;
      padding: 0;
}


ul.menu li {
      font: 1em arial, helvetica, sans-serif;
      padding-left: 10px;
}


a.menuLink, li a {
      text-decoration: none;
      color: #006;
}


a.menuLink {
      font-size: 1.2em;
      font-weight: bold;
}


ul.menu li a:hover {
      background-color: #006;
      color: white;
      padding-right: 10px;
}
```

Adding Pull-Down Menus

You may have looked at the sliding menus in the previous task and said to yourself, that's nice, but what I really want are those pull-down menus that make Web pages look like applications. Here's the secret: there's not a lot of difference between the previous task and this one. In fact, the HTML is identical (just refer back to Script 15.1); the CSS is in **Script 15.4**, and the JavaScript is in **Script 15.5**.

Script 15.5 This script turns your everyday links into pull-down menus.

```
                                          script
window.onload = initAll;

function initAll() {
    var allLinks = document.getElementsByTagName("a");

    for (var i=0; i<allLinks.length; i++) {
        if (allLinks[i].className.indexOf("menuLink") > -1) {
            allLinks[i].onmouseover = toggleMenu;
            allLinks[i].onclick = function() {
                return false;
            }
        }
    }
}

function toggleMenu() {
    var startMenu = this.href.lastIndexOf("/")+1;
    var stopMenu = this.href.lastIndexOf(".");
    var thisMenuName = this.href.substring(startMenu,stopMenu);

    document.getElementById(thisMenuName).style.display = "block";

    this.parentNode.className = thisMenuName;
    this.parentNode.onmouseout = function() {
        document.getElementById(this.className).style.display = "none";
    }
    this.parentNode.onmouseover = function() {
        document.getElementById(this.className).style.display = "block";
    }
}
```

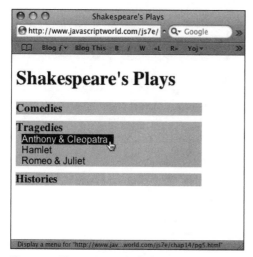

Figure 15.3 The menus expand when you roll the mouse over them, highlighting the choice under the mouse pointer.

To add a pull-down menu:

1. `allLinks[i].onmouseover =`
   `→ toggleMenu;`
   `allLinks[i].onclick = function() {`
   `   return false;`
   `}`

   Instead of adding an `onclick` handler to call `toggleMenu()` as we did previously, here, we set `onclick` to always return false—we don't want it to do anything at all. Instead, we'll have `onmouseover` call `toggleMenu()`, which means that the menu will open up whenever we move the mouse over it (**Figure 15.3**).

2. `document.getElementById`
   `→ (thisMenuName).style.display =`
   `→ "block";`

   Down in `toggleMenu()`, we're not toggling quite the same way any more. Instead, we're now just going to set this menu to always display.

   continues on next page

3. `this.parentNode.className =`
`→ thisMenuName;`

Once we've set the menu to display, we have to figure out how to hide it again. The secret to a pull-down menu is that you don't want it to close when you move the mouse off the triggering link; you want it to close when you move the mouse off the entire `div`. That is, if you're anywhere on the menu, you want it to stay open. Here, we assign a `class` to the parent of the current link (that's the `div` around the link) so that we can keep track of what menu triggered the initial toggle.

Here's the trick: if we got here, then by definition, the cursor is inside the `div`. And consequently, just setting the parent div's `onmouseover` event handler causes it to immediately trigger.

4. `this.parentNode.onmouseout =`
`→ function() {`
`   document.getElementById`
`   → (this.className).style.display =`
`   → "none";`
`}`

We still need to tell the parent `div` when to open and close, and the latter is done here. Instead of setting the `div` to always display, we set it to hide—but only when the cursor moves off the entire `div` area.

5. `this.parentNode.onmouseover =`
`→ function() {`
`   document.getElementById`
`   → (this.className).style.display =`
`   → "block";`
`}`

Here we tell the entire `div` to (again) display. Yes, we did it above in step 2, but we need to do it again here; otherwise, the moment we moved off the link, the menu would snap shut again.

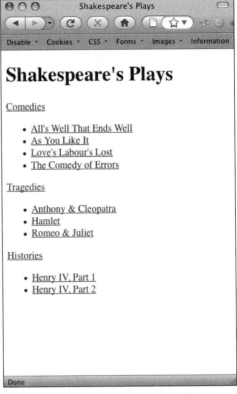

Figure 15.4 When you turn off the CSS display, as we have done here in Firefox, the menus are revealed for what they really are: just a simple unordered list.

✔ Tip

■ Here's some of what's going on inside these menus: if you take a close look at the HTML, the links are actually inside `<ul>` and `<li>` tags—that is, they're unordered lists and list items. If a user has a browser that doesn't support CSS, they'll just see a list of items on the page (**Figure 15.4**). If the browser is capable, though, we can use CSS to style how we want those lists to look, with a result that looks nothing like a plain list.

Script 15.6 Add one line of CSS, and you get an entirely new look to your menus.

```
○ ○ ○                    script
body {
        background-color: white;
        color: black;
}

div {
        margin-bottom: 10px;
        width: 20em;
        background-color: #9CF;
        float: left;
}

ul.menu {
        display: none;
        list-style-type: none;
        margin: 0;
        padding: 0;
}

ul.menu li {
        font: 1em arial, helvetica, sans-serif;
        padding-left: 10px;
}
```

(script continues on next page)

Enhancing Pull-down Menus

Maybe you've looked at the previous example, and now you're saying, "I don't want a vertical menu; I want a horizontal menu!" That's straightforward (and doesn't even require any changes to the JavaScript!). Or maybe you want it to be a little more compatible for people who navigate using the keyboard? Here's how to do it. Once again, there's no change to the HTML, so you can refer back to Script 15.1 if you need to see it.

To enhance pull-down menus:

1. `float: left;`

   Here's the sneaky trick: just add `float: left;` to the CSS for each menu `div`, as shown in **Script 15.6** and **Figure 15.5**. Yes, that's all it takes to turn a vertical menu into one that's horizontal—no JavaScript required.

   continues on next page

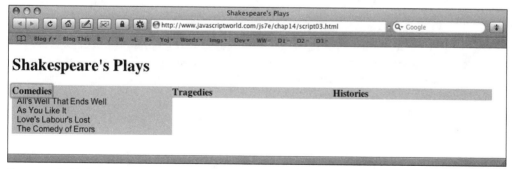

Figure 15.5 A simple change to the CSS makes the menus appear across the page, rather than down the left side.

391

2. `allLinks[i].onclick = clickHandler;`

If you want to make your menus more accessible, however, you need to add a little more JavaScript, as you see in **Script 15.7**. In particular, we'll need to add more code to the `onclick` event handler, so we're giving it a function of its own, `clickHandler`.

3. `function clickHandler(evt) {`

And here's that event handler, being passed the `evt` parameter. If you recall from earlier examples, some browsers pass an event object and some don't.

4.
```
if (evt) {
    if (typeof evt.target == "string") {
        toggleMenu(evt,evt.target);
    }
    else {
        toggleMenu(evt,evt.target.
        → toString());
    }
}
else {
    toggleMenu(evt,window.event.
    → srcElement.href);
}
return false;
```

Here's the code to handle those darn browsers that can pass in all kinds of different things. First off, we check to see if we have an event object—if we do, `evt` exists. Next, once we know we've got it, we check to see if its `target` property is a string, because we're going to need it to be one. If it is, we pass both the event and its target to `toggleMenu()`.

If `target` isn't a string, we force it to be one, by calling the `toString()` method, and use that (along with `evt`) as our parameters to `toggleMenu()`.

Script 15.6 *continued*

```
a.menuLink, li a {
    text-decoration: none;
    color: #006;
}


a.menuLink {
    font-size: 1.2em;
    font-weight: bold;
}


ul.menu li a:hover {
    background-color: #006;
    color: white;
    padding-right: 10px;
}
```

Script 15.7 A little more JavaScript lets the menu work without a mouse.

```
window.onload = initAll;

function initAll() {
    var allLinks = document.getElementsByTag
    → Name("a");

    for (var i=0; i<allLinks.length; i++) {
        if (allLinks[i].className.indexOf
        → ("menuLink") > -1) {
            allLinks[i].onmouseover =
            → toggleMenu;
            allLinks[i].onclick = clickHandler;
        }
    }
}

function clickHandler(evt) {
    if (evt) {
        if (typeof evt.target == "string") {
            toggleMenu(evt,evt.target);
        }
```

(script continues on next page)

Script 15.7 *continued*

```
                                  script
      else {
         toggleMenu(evt,evt.target.toString
         → ());
      }
   }
   else {
      toggleMenu(evt,window.event.srcElement.
      → href);
   }
   return false;
}


function toggleMenu(evt,currMenu) {
   if (toggleMenu.arguments.length < 2) {
      var currMenu = this.href;
   }

   var startMenu = currMenu.lastIndexOf
   → ("/")+1;
   var stopMenu = currMenu.lastIndexOf(".");
   var thisMenuName = currMenu.substring
   → (startMenu,stopMenu);

   var thisMenu = document.getElementById
   → (thisMenuName);
   thisMenu.style.display = "block";

   thisMenu.parentNode.className =
   → thisMenuName;
   thisMenu.parentNode.onmouseout =
   → function() {
      document.getElementById(this.className)
      → .style.display = "none";
   }
   thisMenu.parentNode.onmouseover =
   → function() {
      document.getElementById(this.className)
      → .style.display = "block";
   }
}
```

And finally, if there wasn't any event object, we'll send `toggleMenu()` a dummy `evt` object and `window.event.srcElement.href`—which is where IE stores the value we need.

5. ```
   function toggleMenu(evt,currMenu) {
      if (toggleMenu.arguments.length <
      → 2) {
         var currMenu = this.href;
      }
   ```

Here's where the menu gets toggled, and because both a click and a mouse movement can trigger the display, `toggleMenu()` needs to be a little more complex to handle things. We start off the function with two parameters, but here's an important thing about JavaScript: just because a function is expecting to be passed two arguments, doesn't mean that it always *must* be passed both. In fact, the way we've written `toggleMenu()`, it can get:

▲ zero arguments, when the browser is IE and `toggleMenu()` was triggered via the mouse,

▲ one argument (the event object), when the browser isn't IE and `toggleMenu()` was triggered via the mouse, or

▲ two arguments (the event object and the menu name) when `toggleMenu()` was called by `clickHandler()`.

If we come in here with zero or one arguments (which we can check by looking at `toggleMenu.arguments.length`), we know that we can find the menu name by looking at `this.href`—in other words, it should work just the way it used to. But because we need the value in `currMenu`, that's where we'll store it.

continues on next page
   ```

6. `var startMenu = currMenu.lastIndexOf`
`→ ("/")+1;`
`var stopMenu = currMenu.lastIndexOf`
`→ (".");`
`var thisMenuName = currMenu.substring`
`→ (startMenu,stopMenu);`

Once again, we calculate `startMenu`, `stopMenu`, and `thisMenuName`, but now it's based off of `currMenu`.

7. `var thisMenu = document.`
`→ getElementById(thisMenuName);`
`thisMenu.style.display = "block";`

Because we can't always just refer to `this` (as it's not accurate if we clicked to get here), we'll store the current menu in `thisMenu`, and then as before, we set it to display.

8. `thisMenu.parentNode.className =`
`→ thisMenuName;`

And finally, we have to change the parent class name to match the menu's id, and that's handled here.

✔ Tips

■ It's not just blind users that need keyboard access to menu items. Some people prefer to use the keyboard in general, and some browsers (such as the ones in mobile browsers) don't handle mouseovers in the way that menus need. Accessibility is always a good idea, and you should never use JavaScript or fancy features as an excuse to not consider everyone's needs.

■ In this example, clicking on a menu item expands the menu, but a mouse is required to close it again.

A Slideshow with Captions

While a slideshow (like the one shown in Script 4.17) can be handy, it's likely to be more useful if you can also show captions that change along with the images. **Scripts 15.8** (HTML), **15.9** (CSS), and **15.10** (JavaScript) show an example of such a slideshow (with pictures of our summer vacation!). In this task, we'll show you how to blend together different techniques you've seen in earlier chapters into one script.

Script 15.8 Our slideshow HTML page.

```
<!DOCTYPE html PUBLIC "-//W3C//DTD XHTML 1.0 Transitional//EN"
        "http://www.w3.org/TR/xhtml1/DTD/xhtml1-transitional.dtd">
<html xmlns="http://www.w3.org/1999/xhtml">
<head>
     <title>Our Summer Vacation!</title>
     <link type="text/css" rel="stylesheet" href="script04.css" />
     <script type="text/javascript" src="script04.js"></script>
</head>
<body>
     <h1>Our Summer Vacation Slideshow</h1>
     <img height="240" width="320" src="images/slideImg0.jpg" alt="Our Vacation Pix" id="slideshow" />
     <div id="imgText">   </div>
     <br clear="all" />
     <form action="#">
        <input type="button" id="prevLink" value="&laquo; Previous" />
        <input type="button" id="nextLink" value="Next &raquo;" />
     </form>
</body>
</html>
```

Script 15.9 The external Cascading Style Sheet called by Script 15.8.

```
body {
    background-color: white;
    color: black;
    font: 12px verdana, arial, helvetica, geneva, sans-serif;
}

h1 {
    font: 24px "trebuchet ms", verdana, arial, helvetica, geneva, sans-serif;
    margin-left: 100px;
}

form {
    margin-left: 100px;
}

#slideshow {
    padding: 0 10px 10px 10px;
    float: left;
}

#imgText {
    padding: 10px 0 0 10px;
    float: left;
    width: 200px;
    height: 150px;
    border-color: black;
    border-width: 1px 0 0 1px;
    border-style: solid;
}
```

Script 15.10 The slideshow script displays the photo and the caption.

```
window.onload = initAll;

var currImg = 0;
var captionText = new Array(
    "Our ship, leaving Vancouver.",
    "We took a helicopter ride at our first port, Juneau.",
    "The helicopter took us to Mendenhall Glacier.",
    "The happy (and chilly) couple, on the glacier.",
    "Here's what our second stop, Ketchikan, looked like from the ship.",
    "We got to cruise through Glacier Bay. It was absolutely breathtaking!",
    "In Skagway, we took a train up into the mountains, all the way to the Canadian Border.",
    "Looking back down at Skagway from the train.",
    "On a trip this romantic, I shouldn't have been surprised by a proposal, but I was (obviously, I
said yes).",
    "It's nice to go on vacation, but it's nice to be home again, too."
)

function initAll() {
    document.getElementById("imgText").innerHTML = captionText[0];
    document.getElementById("prevLink").onclick = function() {
        newSlide(-1);
    }
    document.getElementById("nextLink").onclick = function() {
        newSlide(1);
    }
}

function newSlide(direction) {
    var imgCt = captionText.length;

    currImg = currImg + direction;
    if (currImg < 0) {
        currImg = imgCt-1;
    }
    if (currImg == imgCt) {
        currImg = 0;
    }
    document.getElementById("slideshow").src = "images/slideImg" + currImg + ".jpg";
    document.getElementById("imgText").innerHTML = captionText[currImg];
}
```

A SLIDESHOW WITH CAPTIONS

To create a slideshow with captions:

1. `document.getElementById("imgText").`
`→ innerHTML = captionText[0];`

Our `initAll()` function needs to set three
things: the photo caption for the first slide
(in the `imgText` area), and the `onclick`
handlers for the forward and back buttons (in the following step).

2. `document.getElementById("prevLink").`
`→ onclick = function() {`
`    newSlide(-1);`
`}`
`document.getElementById("nextLink").`
`→ onclick = function() {`
`    newSlide(1);`
`}`

Yes, this really is all that these two functions do—well, mostly. We could rig up
some convoluted code to know whether
or not we want to go forward or backward
based on which button was clicked, but
instead, we'll just have two functions,
both of which call `newSlide()`. The difference: one passes it a value of 1, and
the other a value of -1, letting `newSlide()`
know in which direction to move.

3. `document.getElementById`
`→ ("slideshow").src =`
`→ "images/slideImg" + currImg +`
`→ ".jpg";`

`document.getElementById("imgText").`
`→ innerHTML = captionText[currImg];`

This step changes both the image and its
corresponding caption at the same time.
Figure 15.6 shows the result.

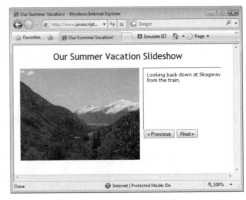

Figure 15.6 The script calculates which photo and
caption to display.

Script 15.11 The Web page where you can enter your real name and get your silly name.

```
<!DOCTYPE html PUBLIC "-//W3C//DTD XHTML 1.0
→ Transitional//EN"
        "http://www.w3.org/TR/xhtml1/DTD/
        → xhtml1-transitional.dtd">
<html xmlns="http://www.w3.org/1999/xhtml">
<head>
    <title>Silly Name Generator</title>
    <script type="text/javascript"
    → src="script05.js"></script>
</head>
<body bgcolor="#FFFFFF">
<h1>What's your silly name?</h1>
<form action="#">
<table>
    <tr>
        <td align="right">First Name:</td>
        <td><input type="text" id="fName"
        → size="30" /></td>
    </tr>
    <tr>
        <td align="right">Last Name:</td>
        <td><input type="text" id="lName"
        → size="30" /></td>
    </tr>
    <tr>
        <td> </td>
        <td><input type="submit" value="Submit"
        → /> <input type="reset" /></td>
    </tr>
</table>
</form>
<p id="msgField"> </p>
</body>
</html>
```

A Silly Name Generator

You may have seen Web-based toys before that take your name and transform it into a new name, like "Your Superhero Name," or "Your Name if You Were a Character in *The Sopranos*." We've settled for simply being ridiculous, so **Scripts 15.11** and **15.12** can show you how to get your own, new, silly name. In the process, you can see how to combine string handling, arrays, error checking, and form validation into one darned silly script.

To combine JavaScript techniques:

1. `document.getElementById("msgField").`
   `→ innerHTML = getSillyName();`
   `return false;`

   When the page first loads, the form's onsubmit handler is set to call a function, and this is its entire content. First, we call getSillyName(). That function returns a string value (either the silly name or an error message), which we then write out to the page. Then we return false, so that the onsubmit doesn't actually try to submit the form to the server.

2. `var firstNm = document.`
   `→ getElementById("fName").value.`
   `→ toUpperCase();`
   `var lastNm = document.`
   `→ getElementById("lName").value.`
   `→ toUpperCase();`

   Anyone visiting this page will be asked to enter their first and last names into form fields. When the form is submitted, we start off the getSillyName() function by converting both names to all uppercase and storing the result in the variables firstNm and lastNm.

Script 15.12 This script generates a silly name from three arrays, based on characters from the first and last names entered by the user.

```
window.onload = initAll;

function initAll() {
    document.forms[0].onsubmit = function() {
        document.getElementById("msgField").
        → innerHTML = getSillyName();
        return false;
    }
}

function getSillyName() {
    var firstName = new Array("Runny",
    → "Buttercup", "Dinky", "Stinky",
    → "Crusty", "Greasy", "Gidget",
    → "Cheesypoof", "Lumpy", "Wacky",
    → "Tiny", "Flunky", "Fluffy", "Zippy",
    → "Doofus", "Gobsmacked", "Slimy", "Grimy",
    → "Salamander", "Oily", "Burrito", "Bumpy",
    → "Loopy", "Snotty", "Irving", "Egbert");
    var lastName1 = new Array("Snicker",
    → "Buffalo", "Gross", "Bubble", "Sheep",
    → "Corset", "Toilet", "Lizard", "Waffle",
    → "Kumquat", "Burger", "Chimp", "Liver",
    → "Gorilla", "Rhino", "Emu", "Pizza",
    → "Toad", "Gerbil", "Pickle", "Tofu",
    → "Chicken", "Potato", "Hamster", "Lemur",
    → "Vermin");
    var lastName2 = new Array("face", "dip",
    → "nose", "brain", "head", "breath",
    → "pants", "shorts", "lips", "mouth",
    → "muffin", "butt", "bottom", "elbow",
    → "honker", "toes", "buns", "spew",
    → "kisser", "fanny", "squirt", "chunks",
    → "brains", "wit", "juice", "shower");

    var firstNm = document.getElementById
    → ("fName").value.toUpperCase();
    var lastNm = document.getElementById
    → ("lName").value.toUpperCase();
    var validName = true;
```

(script continues on next page)

Script 15.12 *continued*

```
                    script
if (firstNm == "") {
    validName = false;
}
else {
    var firstNum = firstNm.charCodeAt(0)
    → - 65;
    if (firstNum < 0 || firstNum > 25) {
        validName = false;
    }
}

if (!validName) {
    document.getElementById("fName").
    → focus();
    document.getElementById("fName").
    → select();
    return "That's not a valid first name";
}

if (lastNm == "") {
    validName = false;
}
else {
    var lastNum1 = lastNm.charCodeAt(0)
    → - 65;
    var lastNum2 = lastNm.charCodeAt
    → ((lastNm.length-1)) - 65;

    if (lastNum1 < 0 || lastNum1 > 25 ||
    → lastNum2 < 0 || lastNum2 > 25) {
        validName = false;
    }
}

if (!validName) {
    document.getElementById("lName").
    → focus();
    document.getElementById("lName").
    → select();
    return "That's not a valid last name";
}
```

(script continues on next page)

3. ```
if (firstNm == "") {
    validName = false;
}
```

It's required that a visitor enter at least one character for the first name, so that check is done here. Remember, the expression is read as "if firstNm is equal to nothing, then." If that's the case, we set validName to false.

4. ```
var firstNum = firstNm.charCodeAt(0)
→ - 65;
```

Otherwise, the charCodeAt() method takes a single character from a string. That single character in the string is based on the number passed to the method; in this case, it is the character in the 0th place, which means the first character in the string (remember, JavaScript starts counting at 0) and returns the ASCII value for that character. The uppercase alphabet starts with "A" having an ASCII value of 65 and ends with "Z" having a value of 90. We then subtract 65 to get a result between 0 and 25, and this result is saved as firstNum.

continues on next page

A SILLY NAME GENERATOR

5. `if (firstNum < 0 || firstNum > 25) {`
  `validName = false;`
`}`

If the user enters a first name that doesn't start with a character between "A" and "Z", there won't be an equivalent silly name. Here, we make sure that it's within this range before checking the last name. If it isn't, we set validName to false.

6. `if (!validName) {`
  `document.getElementById("fName").`
  `→ focus();`
  `document.getElementById("fName").`
  `→ select();`
  `return "That's not a valid first`
  `→ name";`
`}`

At this point, we know that if validName is false, it means that the user didn't enter a valid first name. When this happens, we put the cursor in the field, select anything that's in that field, and return an error message.

7. `if (lastNm == "") {`
  `validName = false;`
`}`

Just as with the first name, they have to enter something in the last name field.

8. `var lastNum1 = lastNm.charCodeAt(0)`
  `→ - 65;`
  `var lastNum2 = lastNm.charCodeAt`
  `→ ((lastNm.length-1)) - 65;`

To figure out the visitor's new silly last name, we'll need to calculate the ASCII values of both the first and last characters of the last name. The first is found in the same fashion as in step 4. The last character in the string is found by taking the length of lastNm, subtracting 1, and then passing that number to charCodeAt().

Script 15.12 *continued*

```
                    script
    return "Your silly name is " +
    → firstName[firstNum] + " " +
    → lastName1[lastNum1] +
    → lastName2[lastNum2];
}
```

Table 15.1

Chart of Silly Names			
	First Letter of First Name	**First Letter of Last Name**	**Last Letter of Last Name**
A	runny	snicker	face
B	buttercup	buffalo	dip
C	dinky	gross	nose
D	stinky	bubble	brain
E	crusty	sheep	head
F	greasy	corset	breath
G	gidget	toilet	pants
H	cheesypoof	lizard	shorts
I	lumpy	waffle	lips
J	wacky	kumquat	mouth
K	tiny	burger	muffin
L	flunky	chimp	butt
M	fluffy	liver	bottom
N	zippy	gorilla	elbow
O	doofus	rhino	honker
P	gobsmacked	emu	toes
Q	slimy	pizza	buns
R	grimy	toad	spew
S	salamander	gerbil	kisser
T	oily	pickle	fanny
U	burrito	tofu	squirt
V	bumpy	chicken	chunks
W	loopy	potato	brains
X	snotty	hamster	wit
Y	irving	lemur	juice
Z	egbert	vermin	shower

9.
```
if (lastNum1 < 0 || lastNum1 > 25 ||
→ lastNum2 < 0 || lastNum2 > 25) {
    validName = false;
}
```
As with the first name field, we have to make sure that both the first and last letter of the last name contain a character between "A" and "Z", so once again, we set validName to false if there's a problem.

10.
```
if (!validName) {
    document.getElementById("lName").
    → focus();
    document.getElementById("lName").
    → select();
    return "That's not a valid last
    → name";
}
```
Just as we did in step 6, if the name isn't valid, we want to let the user know.

continues on next page

Your Silly Name

Your silly name is found by taking the first letter of your first name, the first letter of your last name, and the last letter of your last name, and looking each up on the chart in **Table 15.1**. The first letter of your first name gives you your new first name, and the two letters from your last name give you the first and second parts of your new silly last name.

For example, the "T" in Tom gives a new first name of "Oily," and the "N" and "O" from Negrino produce a new last name of "Gorillahonker." The "D" in Dori turns into "Stinky," and the "S" and "H" from Smith turn into "Gerbilshorts." Consequently, the silly names of this book's authors are Oily Gorillahonker and Stinky Gerbilshorts.

A Silly Name Generator

11.
```
return "Your silly name is
  → " + firstName[firstNum] +
  → " " + lastName1[lastNum1] +
  → lastName2[lastNum2];
```

If we've passed all the tests, it's time to calculate the new silly name. Because we turned the characters into numbers between 0 and 25, we can use the results as indices into the name arrays firstName, lastName1, and lastName2. The result of each array lookup is concatenated to the next, with a blank space between the first name and the last name. Notice that the two parts of the last name are concatenated without a space. When we're done, that name is returned and put into the document, as shown in **Figure 15.7**.

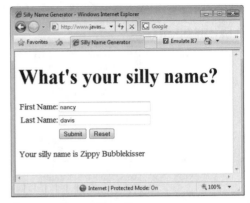

Figure 15.7 The resulting silly name.

Script 15.13 The HTML page for the bar chart generator.

```
<!DOCTYPE html PUBLIC "-//W3C//DTD XHTML 1.0
→ Transitional//EN"
        "http://www.w3.org/TR/xhtml1/DTD/
        → xhtml1-transitional.dtd">
<html xmlns="http://www.w3.org/1999/xhtml">
<head>
    <title>Bar Chart Display</title>
    <link type="text/css" rel="stylesheet"
    → href="script06.css" />
    <script type="text/javascript"
    → src="script06.js"></script>
</head>
<body>
<form action="#">
    Choose a chart<br />
    <input type="radio" name="type"
    → value="browser" checked="checked"
    → /> Browser Usage<br />
    <input type="radio" name="type"
    → value="platform" /> JavaScript Usage<br />
    <p><br /></p>
    Choose a color<br />
    <input type="radio" name="color"
    → value="lilRed.gif" checked="checked"
    → /> Red<br />
    <input type="radio" name="color"
    → value="lilGreen.gif" /> Green<br />
    <input type="radio" name="color"
    → value="lilBlue.gif" /> Blue<br />
    <p><br /></p>
    Choose a direction<br />
    <input type="radio" name="direction"
    → value="horizontal" checked="checked"
    → /> Horizontal<br />
    <input type="radio" name="direction"
    → value="vertical" /> Vertical
</form>
<div id="chartArea"> </div>
</body>
</html>
```

A Bar Graph Generator

Graphs are excellent ways to display visual information. You can create bar graphs by drawing them in Adobe Photoshop or by calculating them in Microsoft Excel, but for dynamic data that might need to change on a regular basis, why not have JavaScript do it instead on the fly? While we've said throughout this book that JavaScript is object-oriented (and therefore buzzword-compliant), and we've used objects throughout the book, we've only briefly shown you how to create your own custom objects. Here's a more in-depth example of how objects work, as seen in **Scripts 15.13** (HTML), **15.14** (CSS), and **15.15** (JavaScript).

To generate a bar graph:

1. `var radioButtons = document.`
`→ getElementsByTagName("input");`

```
for (var i=0; i<radioButtons.length;
→ i++) {
  if (radioButtons[i].type ==
  → "radio") {
    radioButtons[i].onclick =
    → chgChart;
  }
}
chgChart();
```

As we've done so many times, the `initAll()` function starts the ball rolling. Here, we get all the radio buttons and loop through them, setting each to call `chgChart()` when they're clicked. When that's done, we call `chgChart()` manually to display the default view of the page.

2. `var bChart = new Object();`

Here inside `chgChart()` is where we create our first custom object, `bChart` (short for "browser chart"). Yep, that's all there is to it.

continues on next page

3. `bChart.name = "Browser usage by year";`
`bChart.years = new Array("1998",`
`→ "1999","2000","2001","2002",`
`→ "2003","2004","2005","2006",`
`→ "2007","2008");`
`bChart.fieldnames = new Array`
`→ ("Netscape","MSIE","Other");`
`bChart.field1 = new Array(38.9,31.9,`
`→ 21.2,12.4,6.6,5.1,3,1,6,11,14);`
`bChart.field2 = new Array(60.6,67.4,`
`→ 78.3,85.6,92.5,94.0,92,89,90,84,`
`→ 79);`
`bChart.field3 = new Array(0.5,0.5,`
`→ 0.5,2.1,0.9,1.0,4,9,3,5,5);`

The properties for a custom object are created and initialized simply by assigning values to them. Here, we set up the name, years, fieldnames, field1, field2, and field3 properties of bChart. Those fields are, respectively, the name of the chart, the years covered by the chart, the three labels for the chart values, and the sets of values for each year and each label (in this case, each browser).

Note that we're not using the var keyword before each of these; that's because they aren't new variables. Instead, they're new properties that we're adding to an existing variable (albeit one we just created).

4. `bChart.fields = new Array(bChart.`
`→ field1,bChart.field2,bChart.`
`→ field3);`

Here we create the fields property. It's actually an array of arrays and will make it easier to get at the data inside.

Script 15.14 This script contains the styles for the bar chart example.

```
body {
        background-color: white;
        color: black;
        font-size: 12px;
}

form {
        float: left;
        width: 200px;
}

.vert {
        text-align: center;
        vertical-align: bottom;
}

.horiz {
        padding: 5px;
}

th.vert {
        border-left: 1px black solid;
        border-bottom: 1px black solid;
        vertical-align: middle;
        text-align: left;
        font-size: 16px;
}

th.horiz {
        border-right: 1px black solid;
        vertical-align: middle;
        text-align: left;
        font-size: 16px;
}
```

A BAR GRAPH GENERATOR

Script 15.15 And here's the code that draws the bar chart.

```
                    script
window.onload = initAll;

function initAll() {
    var radioButtons = document.
    → getElementsByTagName("input");

    for (var i=0; i<radioButtons.length; i++) {
        if (radioButtons[i].type == "radio") {
            radioButtons[i].onclick = chgChart;
        }
    }
    chgChart();
}


function chgChart() {
    var bChart = new Object();
    bChart.name = "Browser usage by year";
    bChart.years = new Array("1998","1999",
    → "2000","2001","2002","2003","2004",
    → "2005","2006","2007","2008");
    bChart.fieldnames = new Array("Netscape",
    → "MSIE","Other");
    bChart.field1 = new Array(38.9,31.9,21.2,
    → 12.4,6.6,5.1,3,1,6,11,14);
    bChart.field2 = new Array(60.6,67.4,78.3,
    → 85.6,92.5,94.0,92,89,90,84,79);
    bChart.field3 = new Array(0.5,0.5,0.5,2.1,
    → 0.9,1.0,4,9,3,5,5);
    bChart.fields = new Array(bChart.field1,
    → bChart.field2,bChart.field3);

    var jsChart = new Object();
    jsChart.name = "JavaScript usage by year";
    jsChart.years = new Array("1998","1999",
    → "2000","2001","2002","2003","2004",
    → "2005","2006","2007","2008");
    jsChart.fieldnames = new Array("1.2 or
    → later","1.0 - 1.1","No JavaScript");
    jsChart.field1 = new Array(63.4,66.5,78.4,
    → 80.2,88.1,89.1,94,89,96,95,94);
```

(script continues on next page)

5.
```
var jsChart = new Object();
jsChart.name = "JavaScript usage by
→ year";
jsChart.years = new Array "1998",
→ "1999","2000","2001","2002",
→ "2003","2004","2005","2006",
→ "2007","2008");
jsChart.fieldnames = new Array("1.2
→ or later","1.0 - 1.1","No
→ JavaScript");
jsChart.field1 = new Array(63.4,
→ 66.5,78.4,80.2,88.1,89.1,94,89,
→ 96,95,94);
jsChart.field2 = new Array(18.7,
→ 12.6,2.8,0.8,0.3,0.3,0,0,0,0,0);
jsChart.field3 = new Array(17.9,
→ 21.0,18.8,19.0,11.6,10.6,4,9,3,4,5);
jsChart.fields = new Array(jsChart.
→ field1,jsChart.field2,jsChart.
→ field3);
```

In the same way that we created the bChart object, we now create the jsChart (JavaScript chart) object and assign its properties. For the JavaScript chart, we again have the years, but this time we're displaying what percentage of browsers had which version of JavaScript.

continues on next page

A BAR GRAPH GENERATOR

6.
```
var radioButtons = document.
→ getElementsByTagName("input");
var currDirection = getButton
→ ("direction");
var imgSrc = "images/" + getButton
→ ("color");
```

Before we draw our chart, we need to know which radio buttons have been selected. The `radioButtons` array contains all the input elements on the page, and once we've got that, we can call the `getButton()` function. The `getButton()` function is passed a string (the name of the radio set), and it returns a string (the current value of that set).

We could have written `getButton()` to set up `radioButtons` instead of doing it here, but this way means that it's only initialized once instead of three times (once for every time `getButton()` is called).

7.
```
if (getButton("type")=="browser") {
    var thisChart = bChart;
}
else {
    var thisChart = jsChart;
}
```

When the user clicks any of the radio buttons to change the chart, the `chgChart()` function is called. When that happens, if the browser chart is the one that's wanted, the entire `bChart` object gets stored in `thisChart`. Otherwise, it's the JavaScript chart for us, so `thisChart` is assigned the `jsChart` object.

Script 15.15 *continued*

```
jsChart.field2 = new Array(18.7,12.6,2.8,
→ 0.8,0.3,0.3,0,0,0,0);
jsChart.field3 = new Array(17.9,21.0,18.8,
→ 19.0,11.6,10.6,4,9,3,4,5);
jsChart.fields = new Array(jsChart.field1,
→ jsChart.field2,jsChart.field3);

var radioButtons = document.getElementsBy
→ TagName("input");
var currDirection = getButton("direction");
var imgSrc = "images/" + getButton("color");

if (getButton("type")=="browser") {
    var thisChart = bChart;
}
else {
    var thisChart = jsChart;
}

var chartBody = "<h2>"+thisChart.name+
→ "</h2><table>";

for (var i=0; i<thisChart.years.length;
→ i++) {
    if (currDirection=="horizontal") {
        chartBody += "<tr><th rowspan='4'
        → class='horiz'>"+thisChart.years[i];
        chartBody += "</th><td
        → colspan='2'></td></tr>";
        for (var j=0; j<thisChart.
        → fieldnames.length; j++) {
            chartBody += "<tr><td
            → class='horiz'>"+thisChart.
            → fieldnames[j];
            chartBody += "</td><td><img
            → src='"+imgSrc+"' height='15'
            → width='";
            chartBody += thisChart.
            → fields[j][i]*3 + "' alt='horiz
            → bar' />";
```

(script continues on next page)

Script 15.15 *continued*

```
script

        chartBody += "  "
        → +thisChart.fields[j][i]+
        → "</td></tr>";
    }
}
else {
    chartBody += "<tr><th rowspan='2'
    → class='vert'>"+thisChart.years[i]+
    → "</th>";
    for (var j=0; j<thisChart.
    → fieldnames.length; j++) {
        chartBody += "<td
        → class='vert'><img src='" +
        → imgSrc;
```

(script continues on next page)

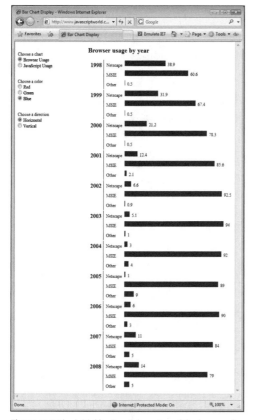

Figure 15.8 The initial horizontal version of the bar graph.

8. `var chartBody = "<h2>"+thisChart.`
`→ name+"</h2><table>";`

Here's the start of the actual drawing code. First, we write out the name of the chart (stored in `thisChart.name` and displayed inside an <h2> tag), and then we open up a <table> tag. From here on out, we're adding to the `chartBody` variable, and when we're done, we'll write it out to the page.

9. `for (var i=0; i<thisChart.years.`
`→ length; i++) {`

Here's the first of two loops that we'll be going through (remember that pseudo two-dimensional array from step 4?). This external loop uses i as the index variable, and how many times it loops around is based on the number of years covered by the chart.

10. `if (currDirection=="horizontal") {`

If the user wants to see the horizontal version of the chart (**Figure 15.8**), run the following code.

11. `chartBody += "<tr><th rowspan='4'`
`→ class='horiz'>"+thisChart.`
`→ years[i];`
`chartBody += "</th><td colspan=`
`→ '2'></td></tr>";`

The first row of each horizontal chart contains the ith year label.

12. `for (var j=0; j<thisChart.`
`→ fieldnames.length; j++) {`

Here's the horizontal version of the second of the two loops. This internal loop uses j as its index, and how many times it loops around is based on the number of fieldnames that we stored.

continues on next page

13. `chartBody += "<tr><td class=`
`→ 'horiz'>"+thisChart.`
`→ fieldnames[j];`

The detail row of the table is started here, and we first write out the value label (either the browser type or the JavaScript version), which is stored in the jth element of `fieldnames`.

14. `chartBody += "</td><td><img src=`
`→ '"+imgSrc+"' height='15'`
`→ width='";`
`chartBody += thisChart.fields`
`→ [j][i]*3 + "' alt='horiz bar' />";`

Next, we close the previous cell and calculate the bar image. The color of the bar is based on `imgSrc`, the height is always 15 pixels, and the width is the value of the jth by ith index in the array, multiplied by 3. For example, if `imgSrc` is `lilBlue.gif` and `thisChart.fields[3][4]` is 30, this would write out an image tag to draw a blue rectangle, 15 pixels high by 90 pixels wide.

15. `chartBody += "  "+`
`→ thisChart.fields[j][i]+"</td>`
`→ </tr>";`

A couple of blank characters (the ` `) are written out, followed by the actual data value to the right of the bar to finish off this row. This is the end of the interior loop for the horizontal section of the code.

16. `chartBody += "<tr><th rowspan=`
`→ '2' class='vert'>"+thisChart.`
`→ years[i]+"</th>";`

If the user wants to see the chart drawn vertically (**Figure 15.9**), we start by writing the initial row of the chart. The vertical version of the chart is somewhat more complex and requires two internal (but separate) j loops. Here we write out the label for the chart.

Script 15.15 *continued*

```
                 script
            chartBody += "' alt='vert bar'
            → hspace='10' width='15' height='";
            chartBody += thisChart.
            → fields[j][i]*3 +"' /></td>";
        }
        chartBody += "</tr><tr>";
        for (j=0; j<thisChart.fieldnames.
        → length; j++) {
            chartBody += "<td class='vert'>"
            → + thisChart.fields[j][i] +
            → "<br />";
            chartBody += thisChart.
            → fieldnames[j] + "<br /><br />
            → </td>";
        }
        chartBody += "</tr>";
    }
}

chartBody += "</table>";
document.getElementById("chartArea").
→ innerHTML = chartBody;

function getButton(buttonSet) {
    for (var i=0; i<radioButtons.
    → length; i++) {
        if (radioButtons[i].name ==
        → buttonSet && radioButtons[i].
        → checked) {
            return radioButtons[i].value;
        }
    }
    return -1;
}
}
```

A BAR GRAPH GENERATOR

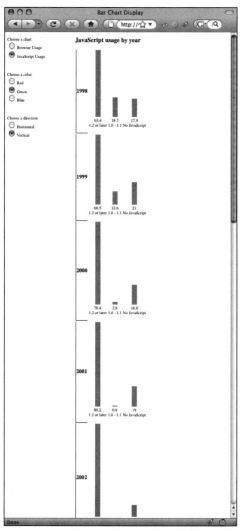

Figure 15.9 The vertical version of the bar graph.

17. `for (var j=0; j<thisChart.`
`→ fieldnames.length; j++) {`

Here's the first internal loop. This one writes out each vertical bar on the graph in a row.

18. `chartBody += "<td class='vert'>`
`→ <img src='" + imgSrc;`
`chartBody += "' alt='vert bar'`
`→ hspace='10' width='15' height='";`
`chartBody += thisChart.fields`
`→ [j][i]*3 +"' /></td>";`

And here's the image tag being written on the fly. This time, the width is fixed at 15 pixels, but the height varies based on the value found in the array of arrays. For example, if imgSrc is `lilGreen.gif` and `thisChart.fields[3][4]` is 30, this would write out an image tag to draw a green rectangle, 90 pixels high by 15 pixels wide.

19. `chartBody += "</tr><tr>";`

When all the bars on the graph have been written out, close that table row and start the next row.

20. `for (j=0; j<thisChart.fieldnames.`
`→ length; j++) {`

Here's the second internal loop. This one writes the value of each data point, under its corresponding bar, followed by the y-axis label.

21. `chartBody += "<td class='vert'>" +`
`→ thisChart.fields[j][i] +`
`→ "<br />";`
`chartBody += thisChart.fieldnames`
`→ [j] + "<br /><br /></td>";`

Here's the information being written out for each bar. The variable `thisChart.fields[j][i]` is the value of that bar, and `thisChart.fieldnames[j]` is the data label for that bar.

continues on next page

22. `chartBody += "</tr>";`

After the last internal loop is complete, we need to write out a final end row tag.

23. `chartBody += "</table>";`
`document.getElementById`
`→ ("chartArea").innerHTML =`
`→ chartBody;`

At this point, both the horizontal and vertical sections are done, and the external loop has completed, so we write out the final table tag to end our script and then put the entire thing into the `innerHTML` property of the `chartArea` section of the page.

✔ Tips

■ This code uses three images: `lilRed.gif`, `lilBlue.gif`, and `lilGreen.gif`. Each of these is a single-pixel GIF in its corresponding color. HTML allows you to set the height and width regardless of the image's actual physical dimensions, so a single pixel allows us to create bars of any size and shape.

■ This chart can be changed to graph almost anything simply by changing the array values in steps 3 and 5. No matter what you set the arrays to, you shouldn't have to change the loops that create the graphs.

■ The statistics on these charts are based on those found at The Counter's Global Statistics, at `http://www.thecounter.com/stats/`. Unfortunately, they only started keeping track of these figures in September 1998, so the 1998 figures begin in September. Figures for all other years begin in January.

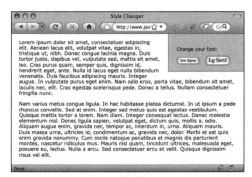

Figure 15.10 Some visitors prefer to read smaller, sans-serif text that can get more text on the page.

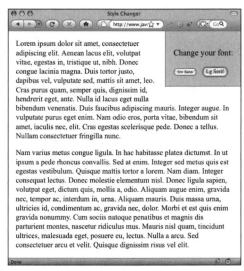

Figure 15.11 Other visitors will be glad to choose larger, serif text that they find more readable.

Style Sheet Switcher

One of the most powerful uses of JavaScript is the ability to modify, on the fly, which style sheet is being used. For example, you can offer your site's visitors the ability to choose the style and size of the text on your site. Some people like to read tiny, sans-serif text that gets lots of words on the screen (**Figure 15.10**), while others prefer larger, serif text that's a bit more readable (**Figure 15.11**). Now you can make both kinds of visitors happy. And to make it even more useful, this script also uses cookies to store the user's choice for future visits.

To allow the user to switch between style sheets:

1. ```
   <link type="text/css"
   → href="sansStyle.css"
   → rel="stylesheet"
   → title="default" />
   ```

   Script 15.16 shows a standard `link` to bring in an external style sheet, with one new twist: it has a `title` attribute, "default". That comes into play later.

continues on page 415
   ```

Script 15.16 This page has the content for the page and the user controls, and it calls the external style sheets that the user can choose.

```
● ● ●                              script
<!DOCTYPE html PUBLIC "-//W3C//DTD XHTML 1.0 Transitional//EN"
        "http://www.w3.org/TR/xhtml1/DTD/xhtml1-transitional.dtd">
<html xmlns="http://www.w3.org/1999/xhtml">
<head>
    <title>Style Changer</title>
    <link type="text/css" href="script07.css" rel="stylesheet" />
    <link type="text/css" href="sansStyle.css" rel="stylesheet" title="default" />
    <link type="text/css" href="serifStyle.css" rel="alternate stylesheet" title="serif" />
    <script type="text/javascript" src="script07.js"></script>
</head>
<body>
    <div class="navBar"><p>Change your font:</p>
        <form action="#">
            <input type="button" class="typeBtn" value="Sm Sans" id="default" />  
            <input type="button" class="typeBtn2" value="Lg Serif" id="serif" />
        </form>
        <br clear="all" />
    </div>
    <p>Lorem ipsum dolor sit amet, consectetuer adipiscing elit. Aenean lacus elit, volutpat vitae,
    → egestas in, tristique ut, nibh. Donec congue lacinia magna. Duis tortor justo, dapibus vel,
    → vulputate sed, mattis sit amet, leo. Cras purus quam, semper quis, dignissim id, hendrerit eget,
    → ante. Nulla id lacus eget nulla bibendum venenatis. Duis faucibus adipiscing mauris. Integer
    → augue. In vulputate purus eget enim. Nam odio eros, porta vitae, bibendum sit amet, iaculis nec,
    → elit. Cras egestas scelerisque pede. Donec a tellus. Nullam consectetuer fringilla nunc.</p>

    <p>Nam varius metus congue ligula. In hac habitasse platea dictumst. In ut ipsum a pede rhoncus
    → convallis. Sed at enim. Integer sed metus quis est egestas vestibulum. Quisque mattis tortor a
    → lorem. Nam diam. Integer consequat lectus. Donec molestie elementum nisl. Donec ligula sapien,
    → volutpat eget, dictum quis, mollis a, odio. Aliquam augue enim, gravida nec, tempor ac, interdum
    → in, urna. Aliquam mauris. Duis massa urna, ultricies id, condimentum ac, gravida nec, dolor.
    → Morbi et est quis enim gravida nonummy. Cum sociis natoque penatibus et magnis dis parturient
    → montes, nascetur ridiculus mus. Mauris nisl quam, tincidunt ultrices, malesuada eget, posuere eu,
    → lectus. Nulla a arcu. Sed consectetuer arcu et velit. Quisque dignissim risus vel elit.</p>

    <p>Nunc massa mauris, dictum id, suscipit non, accumsan et, lorem. Suspendisse non lorem quis dui
    → rutrum vestibulum. Quisque mauris. Curabitur auctor nibh non enim. Praesent tempor aliquam
    → ligula. Fusce eu purus. Vivamus ac enim eget urna pulvinar bibendum. Integer porttitor, augue et
    → auctor volutpat, lectus dolor sagittis ipsum, sed posuere lacus pede eget wisi. Proin vel arcu
    → ac velit porttitor pellentesque. Maecenas mattis velit scelerisque tellus. Cras eu tellus quis
    → sapien malesuada porta. Nunc nulla. Nullam dapibus malesuada lorem. Duis eleifend rutrum tellus.
    → In tempor tristique neque. Mauris rhoncus. Aliquam purus.</p>
```

(script continues on next page)

Script 15.16 *continued*

```
🔴 🟡 🟢              script
  <p>Morbi felis quam, placerat sed, gravida
→ a, bibendum a, mauris. Aliquam porta
→ diam. Nam consequat feugiat diam.
→ Fusce luctus, felis ut gravida mattis,
→ ante mi viverra sapien, a vestibulum
→ tellus lectus ut massa. Duis placerat.
→ Aliquam molestie tellus. Suspendisse
→ potenti. Fusce aliquet tellus a lectus.
→ Proin augue diam, sollicitudin eget,
→ hendrerit non, semper at, arcu. Sed
→ suscipit tincidunt nibh. Donec
→ ullamcorper. Nullam faucibus euismod
→ augue. Cras lacinia. Aenean scelerisque,
→ lorem sed gravida varius, nunc tortor
→ gravida odio, sed sollicitudin pede augue
→ ut metus. Maecenas condimentum ipsum
→ et enim. Sed nulla. Ut neque elit,
→ varius a, blandit quis, facilisis sed,
→ velit. Suspendisse aliquam odio sed
→ nibh.</p>
</body>
</html>
```

2.
```
<link type="text/css"
→ href="serifStyle.css"
→ rel="alternate stylesheet"
→ title="serif" />
```

Here's another style sheet, again using the link tag. However, the rel attribute isn't set to the usual stylesheet; instead, it's set to alternate stylesheet. This is because this style sheet isn't actually in use—instead, it'll only be used if the user chooses it.

3.
```
<input type="button" class="typeBtn"
→ value="Sm Sans" id="default"
→ />  <input type="button"
→ class="typeBtn2" value="Lg Serif"
→ id="serif" />
```

There are two buttons: Sm Sans and Lg Serif. Clicking the former puts all the text on the page into a small sans-serif font, while clicking the latter puts all the text on the page into a larger, serif font. If supported by the browser, the styles in **Script 15.17** cause the buttons to themselves appear in the destination font, giving the user a signal as to what they will see if they choose that button.

continues on next page

STYLE SHEET SWITCHER

4. body, p, td, ol, ul, select, span,
→ div, input {
    font: .9em/1.1em verdana, geneva,
    → arial, helvetica, sans-serif;
}

Script 15.18 (better known as sansStyle.css), just tells the browser that when it's loaded, every tag that it covers should be displayed in .9em Verdana (or one of the other sans-serif fonts on the user's computer).

Script 15.17 This Cascading Style Sheet contains the styles that always load, no matter which font style you've picked.

```
⊙ ⊙ ⊙                    script
body {
    margin: 0 20px;
    padding: 0;
    background-color: white;
    color: black;
}

div.navBar {
    background-color: #CCC;
    width: 175px;
    position: relative;
    top: -1.0em;
    right: -20px;
    float: right;
    padding: 20px 0 0 20px;
    border-left: 2px groove #999;
    border-bottom: 2px groove #999;
}

.typeBtn {
    font: 9px/10px verdana, geneva, arial,
    → helvetica, sans-serif;
}

.typeBtn2 {
    font: 14px/15px "Times New Roman", Times,
    → serif;
}
```

Script 15.18 This style sheet, sansStyle.css, changes all the text to a smaller, sans-serif font.

```
⊙ ⊙ ⊙                    script
body, p, td, ol, ul, select, span, div, input {
    font: .9em/1.1em verdana, geneva, arial,
    → helvetica, sans-serif;
}
```

Script 15.19 This style sheet, serifStyle.css, changes the page text to a larger serif font.

```
● ● ●              script
body, p, td, ol, ul, select, span, div, input {
    font: 1.1em/1.2em "Times New Roman", Times,
    → serif;
}
```

Script 15.20 This script handles setting the active style sheet.

```
● ● ●              script
window.onload = initStyle;
window.onunload = unloadStyle;

function initStyle() {
    var thisCookie = cookieVal("style");
    if (thisCookie) {
        var title = thisCookie;
    }
    else {
        var title = getPreferredStylesheet();
    }
    setActiveStylesheet(title);

    var allButtons = document.
    → getElementsByTagName("input");
    for (var i=0; i<allButtons.length; i++) {
        if (allButtons[i].type == "button") {
            allButtons[i].onclick =
            → setActiveStylesheet;
        }
    }
}

function unloadStyle() {
    var expireDate = new Date();
    expireDate.setYear(expireDate.getFullYear
    → ()+1);
    document.cookie = "style=" +
    → getActiveStylesheet() + ";expires=" +
    → expireDate.toGMTString() + ";path=/";
}
```

(script continues on next page)

5. ```
   body, p, td, ol, ul, select, span,
   → div, input {
       font: 1.1em/1.2em "Times New
       → Roman", Times, serif;
   }
   ```

In a complementary way, **Script 15.19** (also better known as serifStyle.css) tells the browser that every tag that *it* covers should be displayed in 1.1em Times New Roman (or again, any other serif font the browser can find).

6. ```
   var thisCookie = cookieVal("style");
   if (thisCookie) {
       var title = thisCookie;
   }
   else {
       var title =
       → getPreferredStylesheet();
   }
   setActiveStylesheet(title);
   ```

The initStyle() function in **Script 15.20** is loaded when the page runs, and its goal is to initialize everything that the page needs. Here, we're checking to see if the user has a cookie already set that saved their preferred style. Our old buddy the cookieVal() function comes back from Chapter 9 to read the cookies and see if there's one called "style". If there is, its value is the style sheet we want; if not, getPreferredStylesheet() is called. Once the desired style sheet is known, setActiveStylesheet() is called to set the wanted appearance.

continues on next page

7.
```
var allButtons = document.
→ getElementsByTagName("input");
for (var i=0; i<allButtons.length;
→ i++) {
  if (allButtons[i].type ==
  → "button") {
    allButtons[i].onclick =
    → setActiveStylesheet;
  }
}
```

The initStyle() function also needs to add event handlers to our buttons. Here, we tell them both to call setActiveStylesheet() when they're clicked.

8.
```
function unloadStyle() {
  var expireDate = new Date();
  expireDate.setYear(expireDate.
  → getFullYear()+1);
  document.cookie = "style=" +
  → getActiveStylesheet() +
  → ";expires=" + expireDate.
  → toGMTString() + ";path=/";
}
```

When the page is unloaded, we need to set the cookie for the future. The cookie's expiration date is set to one year from today, getActiveStylesheet() is called to establish what the user currently has, and the cookie is written out for future use.

9.
```
function getPreferredStylesheet() {
  var thisLink, relAttribute;
  var linksFound = document.
  → getElementsByTagName("link");
```

If, when the page is loaded, there's no cookie saying which style the user has previously chosen, our script needs to be able to figure out what the preferred style sheet is. That's the goal of the getPreferredStylesheet() function in this step and the next.

```
function getPreferredStylesheet() {
    var thisLink, relAttribute;
    var linksFound = document.
    → getElementsByTagName("link");

    for (var i=0; i<linksFound.length; i++) {
        thisLink = linksFound[i];
        relAttribute = thisLink.getAttribute
        → ("rel");
        if (relAttribute.indexOf("style") >
        → -1 && relAttribute.indexOf("alt") ==
        → -1 && thisLink.getAttribute("title")) {
            return thisLink.getAttribute
            → ("title");
        }
    }
    return "";
}

function getActiveStylesheet() {
    var thisLink;
    var linksFound = document.
    → getElementsByTagName("link");

    for (var i=0; i<linksFound.length; i++) {
        thisLink = linksFound[i];
        if (thisLink.getAttribute("rel").
        → indexOf("style") > -1 && thisLink.
        → getAttribute("title") && !thisLink.
        → disabled) {
            return thisLink.getAttribute
            → ("title");
        }
    }
    return "";
}

function setActiveStylesheet(inVal) {
    var thisLink;
    var linksFound = document.
    → getElementsByTagName("link");
```

(script continues on next page)

Script 15.20 *continued*

```
                    script
    if (inVal) {
        if (typeof inVal == "string") {
            var title = inVal;
        }
        else {
            var title = inVal.target.id;
        }
    }
    else {
        var title = window.event.srcElement.id;
    }

    for (var i=0; i<linksFound.length; i++) {
        thisLink = linksFound[i];
        if (thisLink.getAttribute("rel").
        → indexOf("style") > -1 && thisLink.
        → getAttribute("title")) {
            thisLink.disabled = true;
            if (thisLink.getAttribute("title")
            → == title) {
                thisLink.disabled = false;
            }
        }
    }
}

function cookieVal(cookieName) {
    var thisCookie = document.cookie.split("; ");
    for (var i=0; i<thisCookie.length; i++) {
        if (cookieName == thisCookie[i].split
        → ("=")[0]) {
            return thisCookie[i].split("=")[1];
        }
    }
    return "";
}
```

10. ```
    for (var i=0; i<linksFound.length;
    → i++) {
        thisLink = linksFound[i];
        relAttribute = thisLink.
        → getAttribute("rel");
        if (relAttribute.indexOf
        → ("style") > -1 && relAttribute.
        → indexOf("alt") == -1 &&
        → thisLink.getAttribute("title")) {
            return thisLink.getAttribute
            → ("title");
        }
    }
}
```

This function loops through each `link` tag, looking to see if each has a `rel` attribute, if that attribute has a value that contains "style", if that attribute has a value that does *not* contain "alt", and if the tag has a `title` attribute. If one is found that matches all these criteria, that's the preferred style sheet, and its `title` attribute is returned.

To see which of the actual tags in our code is the preferred style sheet, look at the `link` tags in our HTML file. While there are three `link` tags, only two of them have `title` attributes. And of those two, one has a `rel` attribute of "stylesheet", while the other is "alternate stylesheet". Consequently, the preferred style sheet has to be `default`.

*continues on next page*
```

11.
```
for (var i=0; i<linksFound.length;
→ i++) {
   thisLink = linksFound[i];
   if (thisLink.getAttribute
   → ("rel").indexOf("style") >
   → -1 && thisLink.getAttribute
   → ("title") && !thisLink.
   → disabled) {
      return thisLink.getAttribute
      → ("title");
   }
}
```

As mentioned above, we're going to want to use a cookie to store the user's chosen style sheet when they leave this site, so that they'll be greeted with their favorite font when they return. While we could write out a cookie every time they click the style button, it's a better idea to only write it out once when they leave the site. Here, the getActiveStylesheet() function (which is called when the page is unloaded, as we saw above) looks through all the link tags, chooses the one that's currently enabled, and returns the title of that style.

12.
```
var thisLink;
var linksFound = document.
→ getElementsByTagName("link");

if (inVal) {
   if (typeof inVal == "string") {
      var title = inVal;
   }
   else {
      var title = inVal.target.id;
   }
}
else {
   var title = window.event.
   → srcElement.id;
}
```

As seen above, when the user loads this page, the `setActiveStylesheet()` function is called and passed a parameter that's referred to inside the function as `inVal`. When `setActiveStylesheet()` is called after a button is clicked, however, there may or may not be a parameter passed, depending on which browser is being used and how it handles events. Here's where we do a little checking to figure out how we got here and what the user wants to do. There are three possibilities:

▲ `initStyle()` called this function and passed it a string containing the preferred stylesheet. In this case, `inVal` exists and it's a string, so `title` is set to `inVal`.

▲ A style button was clicked in a browser that supports W3C style events. In this case, `inVal` is automatically set to the event that triggered the function, so `inVal` will exist but it won't be a string. When that happens, we know that the `target` of the event (what caused the event to trigger) is the button that was clicked, and the `id` of that button stores the style desired.

▲ A style button was clicked in a browser that doesn't support W3C standards but does support the IE event model. If that's the case, the `inVal` variable won't exist, so we instead grab the style desired from `window.event.srcElement.id`.

continues on next page

STYLE SHEET SWITCHER

13.
```
thisLink = linksFound[i];
if (thisLink.getAttribute("rel").
→ indexOf("style") > -1 &&
→ thisLink.getAttribute("title")) {
   thisLink.disabled = true;
   if (thisLink.getAttribute
   → ("title") == title) {
      thisLink.disabled = false;
   }
}
```

The `setActiveStylesheet()` function loops through all the link tags in the document, checking each one to make sure that it has both a `rel` attribute that contains "style" and an existing `title` attribute. If both of these are true, the link is first disabled and then (and only then) re-enabled if the `title` attribute is set to the `title` value.

So, if the current style sheet being used has the `title` attribute of "default", and the user clicks the Lg Serif button, JavaScript sees that it should load the `serif` style sheet. There's one link tag with a `title` of "serif", so all others (i.e., the `default` style sheet, in this case) are disabled, and only the `serif` style sheet is turned on.

Designing with Ajax

Ajax, as mentioned earlier in this book, is "officially" JavaScript's `XMLHttpRequest()` combined with XML—but in practice the name is used so often with certain other types of JavaScript and CSS functionality that, in order for a site to appear "Web 2.0"-ish, it's got to have a certain look and *feel*.

In this chapter, we'll be talking about that Web look and feel: both how it's created and why it's used. In order to demonstrate these elements, we'll be using another JavaScript library—jQuery—and you'll get a brief introduction to its advantages and uses. You'll learn how to highlight elements, create accordion-like menus, and display modal dialogs (with accompanying visual effects). We'll finish off with smarter tables, including both zebra-striping (for ease of reading) and sorting by any column.

Highlighting New Elements

The "yellow fade" has become almost a cliché of Ajax: when something new materializes on the page, viewers expect to see it appear with a yellow background, which then slowly fades to white (or whatever the site's usual background color is). It's a handy way to let visitors know that something has changed without the overhead of having to keep track of what's new versus newer versus newest.

It's also a good introduction to jQuery, as you'll be able to see how much can be done with only a few lines of code.

To highlight an element's display:

1. ```
<script type="text/javascript"
→ src="jquery/jquery.js"></script>
<script type="text/javascript"
→ src="jquery/effects.core.js">
→ </script>
<script type="text/javascript"
→ src="jquery/effects.highlight.js">
→ </script>
<script type="text/javascript"
→ src="script01.js"></script>
```

   In order for **Script 16.1** (our HTML page) to be jQuery-savvy, it needs to have access to three files: jquery.js, effects. core.js, and effects.highlight.js, all of which come with the standard jQuery download. We've put them all into a jQuery folder to keep them separate from our usual development scripts. The fourth file needed is our own local script file, which here is called script01.js.

**Script 16.1.** Adding jQuery to a page starts with adding just a few <script> tags.

```
● ● ●   script
<!DOCTYPE html PUBLIC "-//W3C//DTD XHTML 1.0
→ Transitional//EN"
        "http://www.w3.org/TR/xhtml1/DTD/
        → xhtml1-transitional.dtd">
<html xmlns="http://www.w3.org/1999/xhtml">
<head>
    <title>Show/Hide Text</title>
    <script type="text/javascript"
    → src="jquery/jquery.js"></script>
    <script type="text/javascript"
    → src="jquery/effects.core.js"></script>
    <script type="text/javascript"
    → src="jquery/effects.highlight.js">
    → </script>
    <script type="text/javascript"
    → src="script01.js"></script>
</head>
<body>
    <a href="#" id="textToggle">show/hide
    → text</a>
    <div id="bodyText">Lorem ipsum dolor sit
    → amet, consectetuer adipiscing elit.
    → Nulla viverra aliquet mi. Cras
    → urna. Curabitur diam. Curabitur eros
    → nibh, condimentum eu, tincidunt at,
    → commodo vitae, nisi. Duis nulla lectus,
    → feugiat et, tincidunt nec, iaculis
    → vehicula, tortor. Sed tortor felis,
    → viverra vitae, posuere et, ullamcorper
    → a, leo. Suspendisse euismod libero at
    → orci. Pellentesque odio massa,
    → condimentum at, pellentesque sed,
    → lacinia quis, mauris. Proin ultricies
    → risus cursus mi. Cras nibh quam,
    → adipiscing vel, tincidunt a, consequat
    → ut, mi. Aenean neque arcu, pretium
    → posuere, tincidunt non, consequat sit
    → amet, enim. Duis fermentum. Donec eu
    → augue. Mauris sit amet ligula.</div>
</body>
</html>
```
```

Script 16.2 This JavaScript (using jQuery) makes highlighting a new page element easy.

```
script
$(document).ready(function() {
    $("#bodyText").hide();

    $("#textToggle").toggle(
        function() {
            $("#bodyText").show("slow");
            $("#bodyText").effect("highlight",
            ⇢ {}, 2000);
        },
        function() {
            $("#bodyText").hide();
        }
    );
});
```

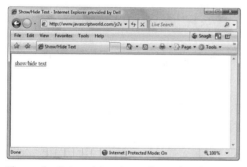

Figure 16.1 Not much is going on here when this page first loads.

2. `$(document).ready(function() {`

In **Script 16.2**, we start our JavaScript routines. This looks different from other code we've used elsewhere, in that we're not starting off with `document.onload`—or are we?

Actually we still are; this is just jQuery's way of saying virtually the same thing.

The dollar sign, **$**, is jQuery's way of referring to itself (as opposed to some other JavaScript object). We're passing jQuery the `document` object, which, as you might guess, is the current document. We're then using a method built into jQuery called `ready()`, which is automatically triggered when JavaScript is ready to start handling events. Everything you want to happen when the document loads must be passed into `$(document).ready()`. In this case, we're passing in an anonymous function, shown in the rest of the steps.

3. `$("#bodyText").hide();`

One of jQuery's most useful features is the way you tell it what object you want to do something with—it's virtually just like CSS. With CSS, if we want a rule to hide to an element with an id of `bodyText`, we might write something like this:

`#bodyText { display:none; }`

And as you can see, that CSS is much shorter than the equivalent JavaScript command:

`document.getElementById("bodyText").`
`⇢ style.display = "none";`

The line of code in this step does the same thing as both the standard JavaScript and the CSS rule above: it tells the browser not to display this particular element, as seen in **Figure 16.1**. It uses jQuery's built in `hide()` method, which needs no parameters.

continues on next page

HIGHLIGHTING NEW ELEMENTS

4. `$("#textToggle").toggle(`

Here, we want to call another method built into jQuery: `toggle()`. Unlike the code in the previous step (which is run when the document loads), this line is triggered by a particular event—it runs whenever the element with the id of `textToggle` is clicked.

The `toggle()` method is passed two functions as parameters, each of which contains the code for one of `toggle()`'s two states. The `toggle()` method remembers its current state, so when it's triggered it automatically switches to the other state (i.e., runs the code in the other function).

Why jQuery?

Whatever your personal programming preferences, there's probably a JavaScript framework to match. In other words, while there are large variations in libraries including some that aren't quite as good as others, there are many libraries that are top-notch, but which have different strengths and weaknesses.

Some of jQuery's strengths are:

◆ **Lightweight**: It's considerably smaller than many of its competitors, which means sites using it load more quickly.

◆ **Active development community**: If you have a question, you can join the mailing list and get a fast response, or you can search the list's archives to see if it's a FAQ.

◆ **Plug-in architecture**: If you need a feature that isn't in jQuery, there's a good chance that someone's written it as a plug-in. An additional benefit of plug-ins is that you're only adding them to your site when they're needed—that is, you don't have their added weight on every page.

◆ **Speed**: Even in tests created by its competition, jQuery comes out ahead (see `http://mootools.net/ slickspeed`, for instance).

◆ **Ease of use for non-geeks**: Because its selection queries are based on CSS, someone who isn't a full-time professional programmer can easily drop into jQuery, add some functionality to their site, and have it work the way they expect.

Due to all of the above, jQuery has become one of the most popular JavaScript frameworks available.

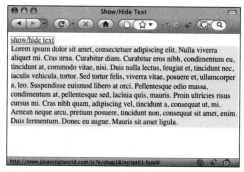

Figure 16.2 But click on the link, and text appears with a brief yellow highlight that then fades out.

Figure 16.3 Here's the final display of the page.

5.
```
function() {
    $("#bodyText").show("slow");
    $("#bodyText").effect("highlight",
    ⟶ {}, 2000);
},
```

Here's the first function passed to toggle(). We start by letting jQuery find the element with the id of bodyText; that's the bit that's going to be displayed when show() is called. The show() method is passed one parameter: the string "slow", which tells jQuery to slowly make the new element visible.

Once that's done, the effect() method is called and passed three parameters:

▲ "highlight": the effect we want.

▲ {}: the options desired on that effect. The yellow fade technique is so prevalent that yellow is the default color, so we don't need to modify any options here.

▲ 2000: the speed at which we want the effect to display. This is set in milliseconds, so we're saying that we want the fade out to last two seconds. **Figure 16.2** shows the brief fade, and **Figure 16.3** shows the final result.

continues on next page

HIGHLIGHTING NEW ELEMENTS

6.
```
function() {
    $("#bodyText").hide();
}
```

Here's the alternate state of the toggle, and all it does is tell the `bodyText` element to hide again, just as we did at the beginning of the code.

✔ Tip

■ If we wanted the text to slowly disappear (in the same way that it slowly appeared), we could pass `"slow"` as a string to `hide()` in the last step. And if we took out the `"slow"` parameter being passed into `show()`, the element would display immediately instead of slowly.

Learning More About jQuery

If this brief coverage whets your appetite to learn more about jQuery, here are some resources:

◆ The main jQuery site is at `http://www.jquery.com/`

◆ To download jQuery (in any of a number of formats), go to `http://docs.jquery.com/Downloading_jQuery`

◆ The jQuery documentation wiki is at `http://docs.jquery.com/`. If you feel that anything's missing, they invite you to add it.

◆ The jQuery discussion lists are available via Web, email, and RSS, and can be found at `http://docs.jquery.com/Discussion`

◆ If you want tutorials, there are a number of them (including screencasts) at `http://docs.jquery.com/Tutorials`

◆ On its own, jQuery is mostly about adding functionality. If what you want to do primarily affects the appearance of your page, you'll want to check out jQuery UI, at `http://ui.jquery.com/`

◆ If what you want doesn't appear to be included in jQuery, chances are there's a plug-in, and those can be found at `http://plugins.jquery.com/`

◆ And last but not least, the jQuery blog is located at `http://jquery.com/blog/`

And it wouldn't be proper to discuss jQuery and not give some credit to its creator and lead developer, John Resig `http://www.ejohn.org`

Script 16.3 The links in this outline will, via jQuery, be seen in a browser as an accordion menu.

```
● ● ●                    script
<!DOCTYPE html PUBLIC "-//W3C//DTD XHTML 1.0
Transitional//EN"
        "http://www.w3.org/TR/xhtml1/DTD/
    → xhtml1-transitional.dtd">
<html xmlns="http://www.w3.org/1999/xhtml">
<head>
    <title>Accordion Menus</title>
    <link type="text/css" rel="stylesheet"
    → href="jquery/theme/flora/flora.
    → accordion.css" />
    <link type="text/css" rel="stylesheet"
    → href="script02.css" />
    <script type="text/javascript"
    → src="jquery/jquery.js"></script>
    <script type="text/javascript"
    → src="jquery/ui.core.js"></script>
    <script type="text/javascript"
    → src="jquery/ui.accordion.js"></script>
    <script type="text/javascript"
    → src="script02.js"></script>
</head>
<body>
    <h1>Shakespeare's Plays</h1>
    <ul id="theMenu">
      <li><a href="menu1.html"
    → class="menuLink">Comedies</a>
        <ul>
            <li><a href="pg1.html">All's
            → Well That Ends Well</a></li>
            <li><a href="pg2.html">As You
            → Like It</a></li>
            <li><a href="pg3.html">Love's
            → Labour's Lost</a></li>
            <li><a href="pg4.html">The
            → Comedy of Errors</a></li>
        </ul>
      </li>
      <li><a href="menu2.html"
    → class="menuLink">Tragedies</a>
        <ul>
            <li><a href="pg5.html">Anthony
            → &amp; Cleopatra</a></li>
```

script continues on next page

Creating Accordion Menus

One way to choose a framework is to pick a common thing you want to add to a site, and then see how much that framework helps you to accomplish that task. Here, we want an *accordion* menu—a type of menu where, when one section is opened, any others automatically close. Similar to a tabbed interface, it's a common design element.

To create accordion menus:

1. ```
   <link type="text/css"
   → rel="stylesheet"
   → href="jquery/theme/flora/flora.
   → accordion.css" />
   <link type="text/css"
   → rel="stylesheet"
   → href="script02.css" />
   ```

   Script 16.3 needs two CSS files: one provided by jQuery (using one of its built-in themes, Flora) and ours (script02.css, seen in **Script 16.4**) that adds on the little bit of CSS needed to make things look just the way we want.

   continues on next page
   ```

2. `<script type="text/javascript"`
`→ src="jquery/ui.core.js"></script>`
`<script type="text/javascript"`
`→ src="jquery/ui.accordion.js">`
`→ </script>`
`<script type="text/javascript"`
`→ src="script02.js"></script>`

Both Script 16.1 and this script need jquery.js, as it's required. But while Script 16.1 needed effects.core.js and effects.highlight.js, this script needs ui.core.js and ui.accordion.js. Here's where we bring them in, along with script02.js, as seen in **Script 16.5**, below.

3. `$(document).ready(function() {`

As before, if we want something to run when the page loads, it needs to be inside this function.

4. `$("#theMenu").accordion({`

In Script 16.3, our menu is structured as an outline, using unordered list items as the contents of each menu. Here's an example of the simplicity of jQuery: all Script 16.5 needs to do is take the id from the top-level ul (in this case, theMenu) and then apply the built-in accordion() method to it.

5. `alwaysOpen: false,`
`active: false,`
`autoHeight: false,`
`animated: false,`
`header: ".menuLink"`

Script 16.3 *continued*

```
●○○                    script
            <li><a href="pg6.html">
            → Hamlet</a></li>
            <li><a href="pg7.html">Romeo
            → &amp; Juliet</a></li>
        </ul>
    </li>
    <li><a href="menu3.html"
    → class="menuLink">Histories</a>
        <ul>
            <li><a href="pg8.html">Henry IV,
            → Part 1</a></li>
            <li><a href="pg9.html">Henry IV,
            → Part 2</a></li>
        </ul>
    </li>
</ul>
</body>
</html>
```

Script 16.4 While we've done similar menus previously, using jQuery means a lot less CSS.

```
●○○                    script
#theMenu { width: 230px; }

ul li ul {
    margin-left: 10px;
    padding-right: 10px;
    background-color: #A0DF82;
    list-style-type: none;
}
```

Script 16.5 And with jQuery, it needs even less JavaScript.

```
●○○                    script
$(document).ready(function() {
    $("#theMenu").accordion({
        alwaysOpen: false,
        active: false,
        autoHeight: false,
        animated: false,
        header: ".menuLink"
    });
});
```

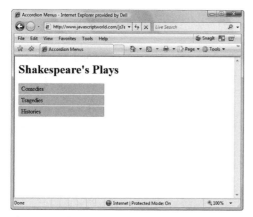

Figure 16.4 The accordion menu first loads, just the way we want it to: with all options closed.

Figure 16.5 Clicking on a menu header opens the new sub-menu (and closes any other that might already be open).

We need to set a few options, and that's done right inside accordion(). They are:

▲ alwaysOpen: should the accordion always have an option open? If not, our initial state looks like **Figure 16.4**.

▲ active: if the accordion should always have an option open, set this to the class of the option that should be open when the page loads.

▲ autoHeight: forces the accordion area to always have a fixed height (based on the largest area needed).

▲ animated: if you want menu items to display with an animated effect, set this to the name of the desired effect (e.g., "slide", "easeslide").

▲ header: how jQuery can identify the headers for each menu. Here, they all have the class "menuLink", and clicking on one of the headers gives a page that looks like **Figure 16.5**.

✔ Tips

■ There are additional options for accordion() besides the ones above—those are only where we wanted to override the default. If we'd wanted the accordion to open when the user hovered the mouse over a menu label (versus only when the user clicks a menu label), all we'd do is add this to the last step:

event: "mouseover"

■ Don't like the *Flora* theme, and don't want to design your own? Check out the ThemeRoller at http://ui.jquery.com/themeroller, where there are several others available for download. Still not quite satisfied? Select the theme that's closest to what you want, then click the "Roll Your Own" tab. From there, you can choose colors, fonts, textures, and more, and then download the resulting theme.

Creating Smarter Dialogs

Another common design element in modern
sites are dialogs that don't look like the usual
prompt(), alert(), or confirm() ones we
learned about back in Chapter 2. Instead,
they look more like the dialogs you see in
applications, such as modal dialogs, that is,
dialogs that force you to respond to them
before you can go back to the Web page.
Once again, jQuery makes it straightforward
to accomplish a task.

To create smarter dialogs:

1. `<link type="text/css"`
   `→ rel="stylesheet"`
   `→ href="jquery/theme/contrast.css" />`

   We've created our own custom theme
   here using ThemeRoller (as mentioned
   in the previous task), and named it
   contrast.css. Here's where **Script 16.6**
   loads it into our page.

2. `<script type="text/javascript"`
   `→ src="jquery/ui.dialog.js">`
   `→ </script>`
   `<script type="text/javascript"`
   `→ src="jquery/ui.draggable.js">`
   `→ </script>`
   `<script type="text/javascript"`
   `→ src="script03.js"></script>`

   We want to have a draggable modal dialog
   on the page, and the jQuery routines
   ui.dialog.js and ui.draggable.js will
   handle the work. The little bit of custom
   code we need is shown in **Script 16.7**.

Script 16.6 Again, we only need a few `<script>` tags
added here to start off our jQuery changes.

```
<!DOCTYPE html PUBLIC "-//W3C//DTD XHTML 1.0
Transitional//EN"
        "http://www.w3.org/TR/xhtml1/DTD/
        → xhtml1-transitional.dtd">
<html xmlns="http://www.w3.org/1999/xhtml">
<head>
    <title>Modal Dialog</title>
    <link type="text/css" rel="stylesheet"
    → href="jquery/theme/contrast.css" />
    <script type="text/javascript"
    → src="jquery/jquery.js"></script>
    <script type="text/javascript"
    → src="jquery/ui.core.js"></script>
    <script type="text/javascript"
    → src="jquery/ui.dialog.js"></script>
    <script type="text/javascript"
    → src="jquery/ui.draggable.js"></script>
    <script type="text/javascript"
    → src="script03.js"></script>
</head>
<body>
    <div id="example" title="This is a modal
    → dialog">
        So long as you can see this dialog,
        → <br />
        you can't touch the page below
    </div>
    <h1>Welcome to my page</h1>
    <div id="bodyText">Lorem ipsum dolor sit
    → amet, consectetuer adipiscing elit.
    → Nulla viverra aliquet mi. Cras
    → urna. Curabitur diam. Curabitur eros
    → nibh, condimentum eu, tincidunt at,
    → commodo vitae, nisi. Duis nulla lectus,
    → feugiat et, tincidunt nec, iaculis
    → vehicula, tortor. Sed tortor felis,
    → viverra vitae, posuere et, ullamcorper
    → a, leo. Suspendisse euismod libero at
    → orci. Pellentesque odio massa,
    → condimentum at, pellentesque sed,
    → lacinia quis, mauris. Proin ultricies
    → risus cursus mi. Cras nibh quam,
    → adipiscing vel, tincidunt a, consequat
    → ut, mi. Aenean neque arcu, pretium
    → posuere, tincidunt non, consequat sit
    → amet, enim. Duis fermentum. Donec eu
    → augue. Mauris sit amet ligula.</div>
</body>
</html>
```

Script 16.7 This tiny bit of jQuery code handles the modal dialog.

```
$(document).ready(function() {
    $("#example").dialog({
        modal: true,
        resizable: false,
        overlay: {
            opacity: 0.4,
            background: "black"
        },
        buttons: {
            "OK": function() {
                $(this).dialog("close");
            }
        }
    });
});
```

Figure 16.6 This modal dialog box can be dragged around the browser window, but you can't get to what's below it until it's closed.

3. `$("#example").dialog({`
```
    modal: true,
    resizable: false,
    overlay: {
        opacity: 0.4,
        background: "black"
    },
```

This code runs when the page first loads. It finds the `example` element and uses it as the basis of a dialog. That dialog is modal (because of the line `modal: true`) and is not resizable (because of the line `resizable: false`).

We've also added an overlay; as you can see in **Figure 16.6**, the page behind the dialog is darkened to show that it's inaccessible. That's done with the `overlay` options, where both the opacity and the background overlay color are set.

4. `buttons: {`
```
    "OK": function() {
        $(this).dialog("close");
    }
}
```

This dialog has a single button that says, "OK," and when it's clicked, the dialog closes. If you wanted more buttons or more actions to take place when the dialog is clicked, those would go here.

✔ Tip

- By default, dialogs are both resizable and draggable. If you want yours to be resizable as well, just do two things: add a `<script>` tag to call `ui.resizable.js` in step 2, and remove the `resizable: false` line in step 3.

Striping Tables

If your site has a lot of tabular data, you should add stripes to your tables—without them, the information can be difficult to read and understand. Unfortunately, there's still no way to use CSS to stripe table rows that works in all commonly used browsers. It used to be the case that using JavaScript to stripe table rows was so difficult that most people didn't bother. With jQuery, it's nice and simple as seen in **Figure 16.7**.

To create zebra-striped tables:

1. ```
   $("tr").mouseover(function() {
       $(this).addClass("over");
   });
   ```

   Script 16.8 (our HTML file) and **Script 16.9** (our CSS file) don't have anything new or original. The only thing that might be a little curious is that the CSS file sets rules for table rows with the class set to "over" and "even", but nowhere in the HTML is either of those ever set up. That's because it's all done in the JavaScript file, **Script 16.10**.

   This section of code acts as a rollover: whenever the mouse is over a row, the mouseover for that tr is triggered. That tells jQuery to add a class of "over" to that row, and our CSS tells the browser that it should now display that row in a different color (as shown in **Figure 16.8**).

continues on page 436

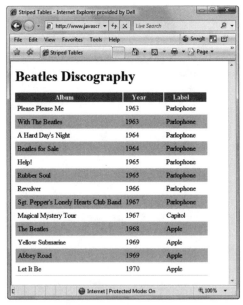

Figure 16.7 This list of albums, with its alternating stripes, is easy to read.

Script 16.8 The HTML for a very standard table, without any inline style or inline script.

```
script
<!DOCTYPE html PUBLIC "-//W3C//DTD XHTML 1.0
→ Transitional//EN"
        "http://www.w3.org/TR/xhtml1/DTD/
        → xhtml1-transitional.dtd">
<html xmlns="http://www.w3.org/1999/xhtml">
<head>
    <title>Striped Tables</title>
    <link type="text/css" rel="stylesheet"
    → href="script04.css" />
    <script type="text/javascript"
    → src="jquery/jquery.js"></script>
    <script type="text/javascript"
    → src="script04.js"></script>
</head>
<body>
```

script continues on next page
```

Script 16.8 *continued*

```
+------------------------------------+
| ⊖ ⊖ ⊖          script              |
+------------------------------------+
<h1>Beatles Discography</h1>
<table>
    <thead>
        <tr>
            <th>Album</th>
            <th>Year</th>
            <th>Label</th>
        </tr>
    </thead>
    <tr>
        <td>Please Please Me</td>
        <td>1963</td>
        <td>Parlophone</td>
    </tr>
    <tr>
        <td>With The Beatles</td>
        <td>1963</td>
        <td>Parlophone</td>
    </tr>
    <tr>
        <td>A Hard Day's Night</td>
        <td>1964</td>
        <td>Parlophone</td>
    </tr>
    <tr>
        <td>Beatles for Sale</td>
        <td>1964</td>
        <td>Parlophone</td>
    </tr>
    <tr>
        <td>Help!</td>
        <td>1965</td>
        <td>Parlophone</td>
    </tr>
    <tr>
        <td>Rubber Soul</td>
        <td>1965</td>
        <td>Parlophone</td>
    </tr>
    <tr>
```

script continues in next column

Script 16.8 *continued*

```
+------------------------------------+
| ⊖ ⊖ ⊖          script              |
+------------------------------------+
        <td>Revolver</td>
        <td>1966</td>
        <td>Parlophone</td>
    </tr>
    <tr>
        <td>Sgt. Pepper's Lonely Hearts
➝ Club Band</td>
        <td>1967</td>
        <td>Parlophone</td>
    </tr>
    <tr>
        <td>Magical Mystery Tour</td>
        <td>1967</td>
        <td>Capitol</td>
    </tr>
    <tr>
        <td>The Beatles</td>
        <td>1968</td>
        <td>Apple</td>
    </tr>
    <tr>
        <td>Yellow Submarine</td>
        <td>1969</td>
        <td>Apple</td>
    </tr>
    <tr>
        <td>Abbey Road</td>
        <td>1969</td>
        <td>Apple</td>
    </tr>
    <tr>
        <td>Let It Be</td>
        <td>1970</td>
        <td>Apple</td>
    </tr>
</table>
</body>
</html>
```

2. `$("tr").mouseout(function() {`
    `$(this).removeClass("over");`
`});`

Here's where that's turned off again: when the mouse moves off the row, its `mouseout` is triggered, and the class attribute of `"over"` is removed.

3. `$("tr:even").addClass("even");`

Yes, this is really all there is to adding zebra-striping. Because jQuery understands the concept of odd and even rows, we can tell it to just set all even rows to have a class attribute of `"even"`. And because our CSS has a rule that applies to `tr.even`, every other row is automatically colored, without us ever having to touch a bit of HTML.

✔ Tip

■ It's worth pointing out that no special jQuery routines were needed to create this functionality. The only script that was brought in was the always-required `jquery.js`.

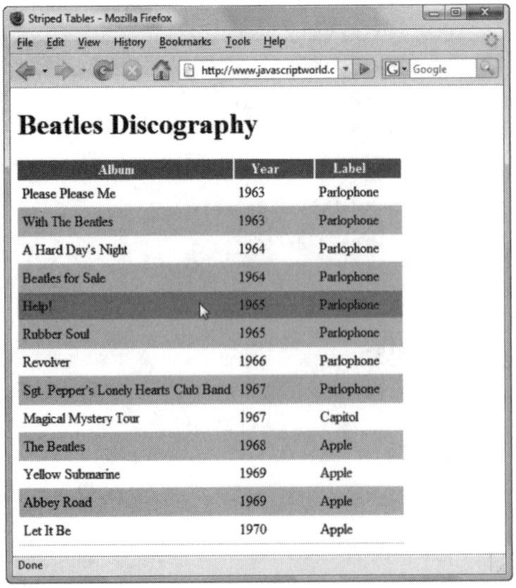

Script 16.9 A small bit of CSS, which will be enabled via jQuery.

```
table { border-collapse: collapse; }

tr.even { background-color: #C2C8D4; }

tr.over { background-color: #8797B7; }

td {
    border-bottom: 1px solid #C2C8D4;
    padding:5px;
}

th {
    border-right: 2px solid #FFF;
    color: #FFF;
    padding-right: 40px;
    padding-left: 20px;
    background-color: #626975;
}
```

Script 16.10 Here's all the code necessary to add striping to your tables.

```
$(document).ready(function() {
    $("tr").mouseover(function() {
        $(this).addClass("over");
    });
    $("tr").mouseout(function() {
        $(this).removeClass("over");
    });
    $("tr:even").addClass("even");
});
```

Figure 16.8 Hovering over any row highlights that row.

STRIPING TABLES

Script 16.11 You need to add very little to your HTML to add sorting to your tables.

```
<!DOCTYPE html PUBLIC "-//W3C//DTD XHTML 1.0
→ Transitional//EN"
        "http://www.w3.org/TR/xhtml1/DTD/
        → xhtml1-transitional.dtd">
<html xmlns="http://www.w3.org/1999/xhtml">
<head>
    <title>Sorted Tables</title>
    <link type="text/css" rel="stylesheet"
    → href="script05.css" />
    <script type="text/javascript"
    → src="jquery/jquery.js"></script>
    <script type="text/javascript"
    → src="jquery/jquery.tablesorter.js">
    → </script>
    <script type="text/javascript"
    → src="script05.js"></script>
</head>
<body>
    <h1>Beatles Discography</h1>
    <table id="theTable">
        <thead>
            <tr>
                <th>Album</th>
                <th>Year</th>
                <th>Label</th>
            </tr>
        </thead>
        <tr>
            <td>Please Please Me</td>
            <td>1963</td>
            <td>Parlophone</td>
        </tr>
        <tr>
            <td>With The Beatles</td>
            <td>1963</td>
            <td>Parlophone</td>
        </tr>
```

script continues on next page

Sorting Tables

While it's nice enough to have a table that's striped, sometimes you want a site that allows user interaction. Maybe the user wants to be able to sort the columns in a different order—instead of having the years increase, they want them to instead decrease. Or maybe they want to sort by name. Or maybe by name in reverse order. Or... you get the idea.

Here's the one example where jQuery doesn't contain this functionality out of the box—so instead, we'll have to use a plug-in. This one's called, meaningfully enough, `tablesorter`.

To create sortable tables:

1. `<script type="text/javascript"`
   `→ src="jquery/jquery.tablesorter.`
   `→ js"></script>`

   Script 16.11, our HTML file, is virtually identical to Script 16.8. There are only two changes: we added this line to bring in the new `jquery.tablesorter.js` routine, and we've added an id of `theTable` to the table itself.

continues on page 439

```
                 script
    <tr>
        <td>A Hard Day's Night</td>
        <td>1964</td>
        <td>Parlophone</td>
    </tr>
    <tr>
        <td>Beatles for Sale</td>
        <td>1964</td>
        <td>Parlophone</td>
    </tr>
    <tr>
        <td>Help!</td>
        <td>1965</td>
        <td>Parlophone</td>
    </tr>
    <tr>
        <td>Rubber Soul</td>
        <td>1965</td>
        <td>Parlophone</td>
    </tr>
    <tr>
        <td>Revolver</td>
        <td>1966</td>
        <td>Parlophone</td>
    </tr>
    <tr>
        <td>Sgt. Pepper's Lonely Hearts
     →  Club Band</td>
        <td>1967</td>
        <td>Parlophone</td>
    </tr>
    <tr>
        <td>Magical Mystery Tour</td>
        <td>1967</td>
        <td>Capitol</td>
    </tr>
    <tr>
        <td>The Beatles</td>
        <td>1968</td>
        <td>Apple</td>
    </tr>
```

script continues in next column

```
                 script
    <tr>
        <td>Yellow Submarine</td>
        <td>1969</td>
        <td>Apple</td>
    </tr>
    <tr>
        <td>Abbey Road</td>
        <td>1969</td>
        <td>Apple</td>
    </tr>
    <tr>
        <td>Let It Be</td>
        <td>1970</td>
        <td>Apple</td>
    </tr>
    </table>
</body>
</html>
```

Script 16.12 And the sort doesn't require much extra CSS either.

```
table { border-collapse: collapse; }

tr.even { background-color: #C2C8D4; }

tr.over { background-color: #8797B7; }

td {
    border-bottom: 1px solid #C2C8D4;
    padding:5px;
}

th {
    border-right: 2px solid #FFF;
    color: #FFF;
    padding-right: 40px;
    padding-left: 20px;
    background-color: #626975;
}

th.sortUp {
    background: #626975 url(jquery/images/
    → asc.gif) no-repeat right center;
}

th.sortDown {
    background: #626975 url(jquery/images/
    → desc.gif) no-repeat right center;
}
```

2. ```
th.sortUp {
    background: #626975 url
    → (jquery/images/asc.gif)
    → no-repeat right center;
}

th.sortDown {
    background: #626975 url
    → (jquery/images/desc.gif)
    → no-repeat right center;
}
```

These two rules are all that had to be added to **Script 16.12**, our CSS file. Whether the user wants to sort up or down, we want the table header to display an appropriately pointed arrow.

*continues on next page*
```

3. `$("#theTable").tablesorter({`

Here's our big change to the JavaScript code in **Script 16.13**: telling jQuery that we want users to be able to sort the contents of the table. That's done by this step and the next. We select the element with the id of `theTable` (as mentioned in step 1) and run the `tablesorter()` method on it.

4. `sortList:[[1,0]],`
   `cssAsc: "sortUp",`
   `cssDesc: "sortDown",`
   `widgets: ["zebra"]`

This is jQuery, so there must be several possible options in how we want our table to display. The ones we're using here are:

▲ `sortList:[[1,0]]`: we want the table to be sorted in a particular way when the page first loads (as in **Figure 16.9**), and here's where that's defined. Count your columns starting with zero; the column you want is the first parameter. Here we want our table to be sorted by the second column, so we pass a 1 (remember, JavaScript is zero-relative!). The second parameter is which way we want to sort: 0 is up, 1 is down.

Script 16.13 And finally, just a few lines of code, and our jQuery-enabled table is sortable and striped.

```
$(document).ready(function() {
    $("tr").mouseover(function() {
        $(this).addClass("over");
    });
    $("tr").mouseout(function() {
        $(this).removeClass("over");
    });
    $("#theTable").tablesorter({
        sortList:[[1,0]],
        cssAsc: "sortUp",
        cssDesc: "sortDown",
        widgets: ["zebra"]
    });
});
```

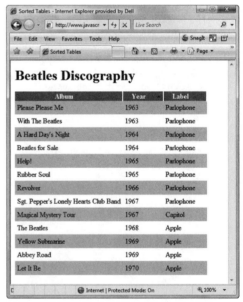

Figure 16.9 When the sortable table initially loads, it's sorted by year, increasing—and you know that because of the upward arrow to the right of the Year label.

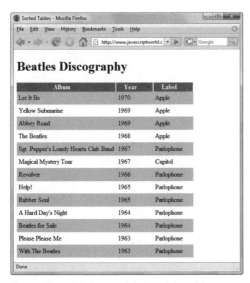

Figure 16.10 Click the Year label, and the table re-sorts itself in decreasing order and changes the arrow to point down.

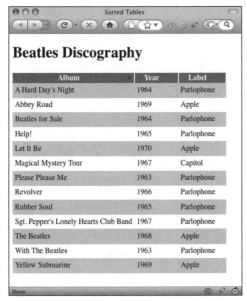

Figure 16.11 Click on any other label (such as Album, shown here) and then that column becomes the sort field.

▲ `cssAsc: "sortUp"`: when the user chooses to sort up, we want a new CSS rule to apply to this `th` cell. This will automatically assign a class of `"sortUp"` when that's what the user wants, which will then show an upwards-pointing arrow to the right of the label.

▲ `cssDesc: "sortDown"`: we want the user to know when they're sorting downwards instead, and clicking on the `th` cell again changes the class to `"sortDown"`, which displays a downwards-pointing arrow to the right of the label (**Figure 16.10**). Because you might want to sort on any column, not just the one the web developer decided to make the default, all a user has to do is click on a different `th` cell, and the results immediately change (**Figure 16.11**) without you having to add any more code.

▲ `widgets: ["zebra"]`: with `tablesorter()`, zebra-striping is a thrown-in freebie widget. Just say that you want to add the zebra widget, and you've got stripes.

SORTING TABLES

17

BOOKMARKLETS

You know that JavaScript can be used to control Web browsers from inside your Web pages. However, you can also use JavaScript to control your browser without using Web pages, by using what are called *bookmarklets*. Bookmarklets are bookmarks (or favorites, if you prefer Internet Explorer's terminology; sometimes bookmarklets are called favelets) that contain a call to the browser's JavaScript interpreter, instead of an external URL. The JavaScript in your bookmarklets can do anything from getting details about images, to giving you the definition of a word, to resizing your browser window. And because you know JavaScript, this functionality is easy to add to make your browser a smarter, better tool.

Bookmarklets differ from other JavaScript code that you'll write because they have a significant and interesting formatting limitation: they must be written all in one line. You'll use semicolons to string commands together.

In this chapter, you'll be introduced to a variety of useful bookmarklets, and with a bit of effort, you'll be able to go forth and write your own.

Your First Bookmarklet

Okay, **Script 17.1** isn't the most thrilling script you'll ever see. It's a variation on our old friend, the "Hello World" script. But what's important is that you're getting something to happen in a Web browser without ever loading a Web page. This example also demonstrates how to create and use a bookmarklet in the various browsers.

To create a bookmarklet (Firefox 2):

1. From the Bookmarks menu, choose Manage Bookmarks. The Bookmarks Manager opens.

2. From the File menu, choose New Bookmark. The Bookmark Properties dialog opens (**Figure 17.1**).

3. In the Name field, type the name you want to appear on the toolbar. In this case, type Hello.

4. In the Location field, type javascript: → alert('Hello World'); and then click OK.

   We'll return to the Bookmarks Manager dialog.

5. Choose the Bookmarks Toolbar Folder to ensure that the new bookmark appears in the Bookmarks Toolbar.

6. Click OK, and close the Bookmarks Manager. Our new button should appear on the Bookmarks Toolbar. Clicking the button activates the command and makes the alert box appear with the text "Hello World."

Script 17.1 Yikes! It's the return of "Hello World."

```
javascript:alert('Hello World');
```

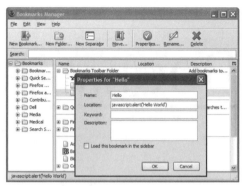

Figure 17.1 Firefox 2 (for Windows, in this case, but the Mac version is similar) allows you to enter bookmarklets in the Bookmarks Manager.

YOUR FIRST BOOKMARKLET

Figure 17.2 Firefox 3 for Mac has the New Bookmark menu item in the Action menu.

Figure 17.3 While Firefox 3 for Windows has the New Bookmark menu item in the Organize menu.

To create a bookmarklet (Firefox 3):

1. From the Bookmarks menu, choose Organize Bookmarks. The Library window opens.

2. In the left column, choose Bookmarks Toolbar. From the toolbar above, choose the Action menu (Mac, **Figure 17.2**) or the Organize menu (Windows, **Figure 17.3**) and select New Bookmark.

3. In the Name field, type the name you want to appear on the toolbar. In this case, type `Hello`.

4. In the Location field, type `javascript:` → `alert('Hello World');` and then click Add.

   We'll return to the Library window.

5. Close the Library window. Our new button should appear on the Bookmarks Toolbar. Clicking the button activates the command and makes the alert box appear with the text "Hello World."

✔ Tip

- If you can't see the Bookmarks Toolbar in Firefox, choose View > Toolbars > Bookmarks Toolbar to display it.

The Origin of Bookmarklets

The original idea came from the Netscape JavaScript Guide, which told how to add JavaScripts to the Personal Toolbar. Steve Kangas, who now runs the site Bookmarklets.com, coined the term "bookmarklets." His Web site at `http://www.bookmarklets.com` contains hundreds of useful bookmarklets; this chapter just touches on the possibilities. Some of the examples in this chapter are loosely based on scripts on his site and are used by permission.

YOUR FIRST BOOKMARKLET

To create a bookmarklet (Safari):

1. Make sure the Bookmarks Bar is visible by making sure that an item in the View menu displays "Hide Bookmarks Bar" and not "Show Bookmarks Bar."

2. In the Address Bar, type `javascript:`
   `→ alert('Hello World');`

3. Drag the globe icon (to the left of the text you typed) from the Address Bar to the Bookmarks Bar, and release the mouse button.

   A dialog appears, asking you to name the new bookmark (**Figure 17.4**).

4. Enter the bookmarklet's name, and then click OK.

   The new bookmarklet appears in the Bookmarks Bar as a button. Click the button to activate the command.

✔ Tips

- You can use Bookmarks > Show All Bookmarks to reposition the bookmarklet from the Bookmarks Bar to the Bookmarks menu, if you prefer.

- To remove a bookmarklet from the Safari Bookmarks Bar, drag it off the bar and into the browser window. It disappears in a puff of animated smoke. If you accidentally delete the wrong bookmark, undo the mistake by pressing Cmd-Z.

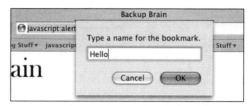

Figure 17.4 After entering the bookmarklet code in the Address Bar and dragging it to the Bookmarks Bar, Safari prompts you to enter a name for the bookmarklet.

Figure 17.5 Internet Explorer 6 requires you to edit a bookmarklet's properties to add the code.

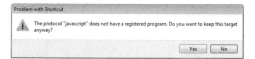

Figure 17.6 Internet Explorer adds an extra security dialog.

Figure 17.7 Internet Explorer 7 changes the Favorites dialog a bit.

To create a bookmarklet (Internet Explorer 6):

1. From the Favorites menu, choose Add to Favorites. The Add Favorite dialog appears.

2. In the Name field, type `Hello`.

3. In the Create in section of the dialog, choose the Links Folder to ensure that the new bookmark appears in the Links Toolbar, and click OK.

4. Right-click the new "Hello" book-marklet in the Links Toolbar, and choose Properties. The Properties dialog appears. In the URL field, type `javascript:alert('Hello World');` as shown in **Figure 17.5**, and click OK.

5. The Problem with Shortcut dialog should appear, if IE's security settings are appropriately set, as shown in **Figure 17.6**. This is to help prevent malicious scripts from being added to your browser. We're not malicious (at least towards our own computer!), so everything is OK. Click Yes.

6. Click the "Hello" button in the Links Toolbar to activate the command.

To create a bookmarklet (Internet Explorer 7):

1. From the Favorites menu, choose Add to Favorites. The Favorites Center dialog appears (**Figure 17.7**).

2. In the Name field, type `Hello`.

3. In the Create in section of the dialog, choose the Links Folder to ensure that the new bookmark appears in the Links Toolbar, and click Add.

continues on next page

4. Right-click the new "Hello" bookmarklet in the Links Toolbar, and choose Properties. The Properties dialog appears. In the URL field, we type `javascript:alert('Hello World');` (**Figure 17.8**) and, if you're fine with the icon IE assigns to the button (it's usually the icon of the current Web page you're on), click OK.

5. (Optional) If you want to change the icon, click Change Icon in the Properties dialog. The Change Icon dialog appears (**Figure 17.9**); choose the icon you want, click OK, and then click OK again to dismiss the Properties dialog.

6. The Problem with Shortcut dialog should appear, if IE's security settings are appropriately set. Click Yes.

7. Click the "Hello" button in the Links Toolbar to activate the command.

To create a bookmarklet (Internet Explorer 8):

1. From the Favorites menu, choose Add to Favorites Bar. The Add a Favorite dialog appears (**Figure 17.10**).

2. In the Name field, type `Hello`.

3. In the Create in section of the dialog, choose the Favorites Bar Folder to ensure that the new bookmark appears in the Favorites Toolbar, and click Add.

Figure 17.8 Add the code in IE 7's Properties dialog.

Figure 17.9 If you want a different icon than the one IE assigns to the bookmarklet, use the Change Icon dialog.

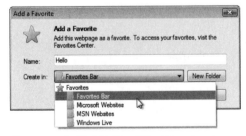

Figure 17.10 And in IE 8, it's a little different again; here's the Add a Favorite dialog.

Figure 17.11 Again, modify the properties to add the JavaScript code to your bookmarklet.

4. Right-click the new "Hello" bookmarklet in the Links Toolbar, and choose Properties. The Properties dialog appears. In the URL field, type `javascript:alert('Hello World');` (**Figure 17.11**) and, if you're fine with the icon IE assigns to the button (it's usually the icon of the current Web page you're on), click OK.

5. (Optional) If you want to change the icon, click Change Icon in the Properties dialog. The Change Icon dialog appears; choose the icon you want, click OK, and then click OK again to dismiss the Properties dialog.

6. The Problem with Shortcut dialog should appear, if IE's security settings are appropriately set. Click Yes.

7. Click the "Hello" button in the Links Toolbar to activate the command.

Bookmarklets vs. IE Security

It's no secret that Microsoft Internet Explorer has had many security problems, which Microsoft has addressed in various ways. Windows XP Service Pack 2 was heavily devoted to beefing up security, including changes to IE6. IE7, incorporating more security features, was initially scheduled to ship with Vista but shipped earlier after Vista was repeatedly delayed. More security was added with Vista, and then even more with IE8.

As of this writing, we're working with a public beta of IE8, and the behavior of bookmarklets between versions is, in our tests, inconsistent. We've discovered that some bookmarklets can only be run on some pages, and some bookmarklets can't be run at all, depending on a complex combination of which security settings you have enabled in IE. These settings include whether or not you have the pop-up blocker turned on and the many settings in the Security tab of Tools > Internet Options. In short, by adding successive layers of security to IE, Microsoft has made it harder for bookmarklets to work in Internet Explorer. It's possible to get more bookmarklets to work in IE by changing security settings, but because IE has such a history of security problems, we don't recommend that course of action.

Here's our advice: if you have to make a choice between lowering your security levels in IE or not running bookmarklets, we recommend using Firefox or Safari instead. This pretty much solves your browser security problems, and you'll get consistent bookmarklet functionality.

YOUR FIRST BOOKMARKLET

Resetting a Web Page's Background

Script 17.2 is simple but powerful. Have you ever visited a site that you knew had lots of useful information, but the background color was so close to the text color that the information was unreadable? Or worse, the page's author used violently clashing colors that made your eyes water? This little bookmarklet solves those problems. Note that at this point, using the bookmarklet changes the way that you're viewing someone else's page—that's part of the power of bookmarklets. Of course, it doesn't change the actual page, just the way that your browser displays it.

To reset the background of a page:

◆ `javascript:void(document.body.style.`
   `→ background='#FFF');`

   This script uses the `document. body.`
   `→ style.background` object and resets it to white. Now, we can see what's actually written, as shown in **Figures 17.12** and **17.13**.

✔ Tips

■ Note that the bookmarklet uses the form `javascript:void(command);`. This is because a bookmarklet must return some value, which would normally be used to overwrite the contents of the current page. By using the `void()` method, nothing is returned, and nothing is overwritten.

■ Bookmarklets use single quotes, not double quotes. This is because, behind the scenes, each bookmarklet is inside an `<a href="">` tag. Using double quotes would end the bookmarklet prematurely.

Script 17.2 This script, which changes the background color to white, improves many a design-impaired page.

```
javascript:void(document.body.style.
→ background='#FFF');
```

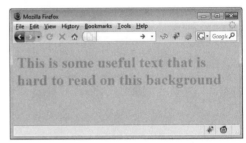

Figure 17.12 It's difficult to read the text on the page's original background color.

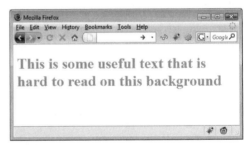

Figure 17.13 Against white, the text is much more legible.

Script 17.3 Don't be thrown off by the gray arrows; they're only there because of the limited size of this book's pages. Remember that the actual bookmarklet is all on one line. This script changes the styles on a page to make it more readable.

```
javascript:(function(){var nuStyle=document.
→ createElement('link');nuStyle.rel=
→ 'stylesheet';nuStyle.href='data:text/css,*
→ {background:#FFF !important;color:#000
→ !important;} :link, :link * {color:#00F
→ !important;} :visited, :visited *
→ {color:#93C !important;}';document.
→ documentElement.childNodes[0].appendChild
→ (nuStyle);})();
```

Changing a Page's Styles

The previous example works fine if the background color of an offensive page is set in the page's HTML. But it's ineffective if the page uses style sheets to change the background color, or to apply a background image to a page element. This next bookmarklet (**Script 17.3**) replaces the CSS styles for a page's background color, text color, and link colors. The background color changes to white and the text color to black; links will be blue; and visited links will be purple. You can see these sorts of changes in the example shown in **Figures 17.14** and **17.15**.

continues on next page

Figure 17.14 The original page can be a bit difficult to read, so we want to swap out the CSS styles to make it more readable.

Figure 17.15 By changing the background and link colors, the page is easier to read.

If you have trouble reading Web pages that use white text on a black background, or you get annoyed at sites that use too-similar colors for links and body text, this is the perfect bookmarklet for you. We use this one more than any other bookmarklet in our day-to-day Web browsing. Once again, we remind you that the bookmarklet just changes the look of the page in your browser, not the page itself. In fact, if you reload the page, it reappears in its original, hard-to-read glory. But with this bookmarklet, visual relief is just a button click away.

To change a page's styles:

1. `javascript:(function(){`

   We're changing things up here again a little bit: now, instead of using `void()` to return a null value to the browser, we're instead putting the entire bookmarklet itself into an anonymous function.

2. `var nuStyle=document.createElement`
   `→ ('link');`

   This line creates a new `link` element on the page and then stores that element in the new variable `nuStyle`.

3. `nuStyle.rel='stylesheet';`

   This line creates a new `rel` attribute for the newly created link and then sets its value to `'stylesheet'`. Here, the `rel` attribute tells the browser that we're linking to a style sheet.

4. `nuStyle.href='data:text/css,`
   `→ * {background:#FFF !important;`
   `→ color:#000 !important;} :link,`
   `→ :link * {color:#00F !important;}`
   `→ :visited, :visited * {color:#93C`
   `→ !important;}';`

This line adds a new href attribute to the newly created link element and sets the styles that we want to add to the page: the background will be white, the text color black, the links blue, and visited links purple. The !important forces these styles to override all other styles, and the * says that these new styles apply to all elements on the page.

5. `document.documentElement.`
   `→ childNodes[0].appendChild`
   `→ (nuStyle);`

   This line inserts the new link element into the Web page, causing the new styles to take effect and make the page readable.

6. `})();`

   Here we end the anonymous function we started up above (the `}`) and then end the function wrapper (the `)`). The `()` next just says, "You know that function you just created? Run it now."—which the browser then does.

✔ Tips

■ Does that seem like a lot of trouble to go to just to avoid the void()? Here's why it's particularly useful: JavaScript sees bookmarklets as running inside the current page you're on, and with the old way, there's no way to be sure that the variables you're using in the bookmarklet aren't already in use by the page itself. When you wrap the entire bookmarklet inside a function, the variables stay within the *scope* (covered back in Chapter 2) of the function, and you're guaranteed to be safe.

■ As mentioned in this chapter's introduction, a bookmarklet must be a single line of code. Putting the semicolons between statements allows you to put all the commands on a single line.

Word Lookups

If you use your Web browser for writing (email in particular), you'll find that you wish you had the dictionary and thesaurus tools that are available in most word processors. With **Scripts 17.4**, **17.5**, and **17.6**, you'll be able to have this functionality in all your writing. You do it using a bookmarklet to query an online dictionary or thesaurus. Because the scripts are so similar, we've presented them all in one task. Script 17.4 shows how to do a dictionary lookup in Safari and Firefox, Script 17.5 does a dictionary lookup in IE, and Script 17.6 shows how to do a thesaurus lookup in Safari and Firefox. Because the code is virtually identical to Script 17.5, we've omitted a script to do a thesaurus lookup in IE, trusting you'll be able to figure it out.

To look up a word:

1. `var inText=window.getSelection()+'';`

   or

   `inText=document.selection.`
   `→ createRange().text;`

   Our code will then use one of the above two lines. The latter works in IE, the former in Safari and Firefox. This line creates a new variable, inText, which is set to the value of the selected text in the browser.

   Note that in the first line, that very last bit is two single quotes, not one double-quote. That's done because both Safari and Firefox may return something that isn't a string, and this forces the result to be a string.

Script 17.4 This bookmarklet performs a dictionary lookup in Safari and Firefox.

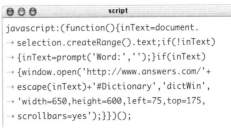

```
javascript:(function(){var inText=window.
→ getSelection()+'';if(!inText){inText=prompt
→ ('Word:','');}if(inText){window.open
→ ('http://www.answers.com/'+escape(inText)+
→ '#Dictionary','dictWin','width=650,
→ height=600,left=75,top=175,
→ scrollbars=yes');}})();
```

Script 17.5 This script does a dictionary lookup in Internet Explorer.

```
javascript:(function(){inText=document.
→ selection.createRange().text;if(!inText)
→ {inText=prompt('Word:','');}if(inText)
→ {window.open('http://www.answers.com/'+
→ escape(inText)+'#Dictionary','dictWin',
→ 'width=650,height=600,left=75,top=175,
→ scrollbars=yes');}})();
```

Script 17.6 This bookmarklet performs a thesaurus lookup in Safari and Firefox.

```
javascript:(function(){var inText=window.
→ getSelection()+'';if(!inText){inText=prompt
→ ('Word:','');}if(inText){window.open
→ ('http://www.answers.com/'+escape(inText)+
→ '#Thesaurus','thesWin','width=650,
→ height=600,left=75,top=175,
→ scrollbars=yes');}})();
```

Figure 17.16. Triggering the dictionary bookmarklet returns this window with the lookup's results.

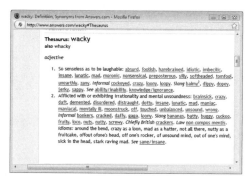

Figure 17.17. The thesaurus lookup results.

2. `if(!inText){inText=prompt`
`→ ('Word:','');}`

If we didn't select any text, then we ask for a word to be entered.

3. `if(inText){`

The user has had two chances, so they should have entered something to look up by now. Even so, we check before doing the look up.

4. `window.open('http://www.answers.`
`→ com/'+escape(inText)+`
`→ '#Dictionary','dictWin',`
`→ 'width=650,height=600,left=75,`
`→ top=175,scrollbars=yes');}`

or

`window.open('http://www.answers.`
`→ com/'+escape(inText)+'#Thesaurus,`
`→ 'thesWin','width=650,height=600,`
`→ left=75,top=175,scrollbars=yes');}`

We pick one of these two, depending on whether we want to do a dictionary or thesaurus lookup, as shown in **Figures 17.16** and **17.17**. Either opens a new window, with the information that we requested. You can change the window dimensions to fit the size of your screen by changing the `height` and `width` attributes of the `window.open()` call.

WORD LOOKUPS

✔ Tip

■ This has nothing to do with JavaScript, but it's cool and worth mentioning: if you're on a Mac running Mac OS X 10.4 or later, in Safari or many other programs, you can just place the cursor over a word and press Cmd-Ctrl-D, and the OS pops up a dictionary/thesaurus window, based on the Dictionary application (**Figure 17.18**). This works in any Cocoa-based program (great), so if you use Firefox on the Mac, it doesn't work (bummer). If you don't know what a "Cocoa-based program" is, don't worry about it; just give it a try and see if it works for the program you're in.

Figure 17.18 Under Mac OS X Tiger and later, a dictionary and thesaurus are built-in.

Why the Different Code?

The reason for the variations of the code for different browsers is, as usual, Microsoft's insistence on doing things its way, instead of following agreed-upon Web standards. Differences between browser's DOMs (Document Object Models) dictate that commands with the same results be written differently. That's more—and needless—work for coders everywhere. Arrrgh.

Script 17.7 You can view a table of page images with this script.

```
javascript:(function(){var iWin,i,
→ t='',di=document.images;for(i=0;i<di.
→ length;i++){if(t.indexOf(di[i].src)<0)
→ {t+='<tr><td><img src='+di[i].src+'
→ />/</td><td>'+di[i].height+'</td><td>'+
→ di[i].width+'</td><td>'+di[i].src+
→ '</td></tr>';}}if(t==''){alert('No
→ images!');}else{iWin=window.open('','IW',
→ 'width=800,height=600,scrollbars=yes');
→ iWin.document.body.innerHTML='<table
→ border=1 cellpadding=10 cellspacing=
→ 0><tr><th>Image</th><th>Height</th>
→ <th>Width</th><th>URL</th></tr>'+t+
→ '</table>';}})();
```

Viewing Images

A useful tool for designers is the ability to view all the images on a page, apart from the layout of the page. **Script 17.7** allows you to peek behind the scenes of someone else's page and see a list of the page's individual images, the height and width of the images (in modern browsers), and their URLs.

To view images:

1. `var iWin,i,t='',di=document.images;`

   The bookmarklet starts and initializes four variables: iWin; i; t, which will later contain all the output; and di, which contains the document.images object.

2. `for (i=0;i<di.length;i++){`

   We now loop through each image in the document.

3. `if(t.indexOf(di[i].src)<0){`

   In this step, we check to see if we've already put the image on the page. This line of code keeps that from happening more than once.

4. `t+='<tr><td><img src='+`
   `→ di[i].src+' /></td><td>'+`
   `→ di[i].height+'</td><td>'+`
   `→ di[i].width+'</td><td>'+`
   `→ di[i].src+'</td></tr>';}}`

   All the information we want is written out here, in a nice table format. The first cell contains the image; the second contains the height; the third, the width; and the last contains the URL of the image.

5. `if(t==''){alert('No images!');}`

   When the loop completes, check to see if we've found any images. If not, an alert window that says "No images!" is displayed.

continues on next page

6. `else{iWin=window.open('','IW',`
`→ 'width=800,height=600,`
`→ scrollbars=yes');`

If we found images, open up a new window for the image information.

7. `iWin.document.body.innerHTML=`
`→ '<table border=1 cellpadding=10`
`→ cellspacing=0><tr><th>Image</th>`
`→ <th>Height</th><th>Width</th>`
`→ <th>URL</th></tr>'+t+'</table>';}`

Here is where the new window is created and displayed. The image information, with heading information for each column, is written out, as shown in **Figure 17.19**.

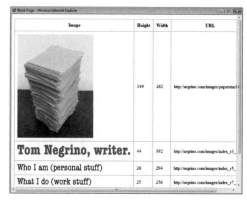

Figure 17.19 This script formats the images and information into an attractive table.

Script 17.8 Rather than look up an accented character in a book, let JavaScript generate a list whenever you need one.

```
javascript:(function(){var eWin,n,i,j,w,t=
→ '<table border=1 cellpadding=20 cellspacing=
→ 0>',l=document.createElement('p'),
→ v='aAeEiIoOuUyY',s=new Array('acute',
→ 'circ','elig','Elig','grave','ring',
→ 'slash','tilde','uml');for(i=0;i<v.length;
→ i++){for(j=0;j<s.length;j++){w=v.charAt(i)+
→ s[j]+';';l.innerHTML='&'+w;n=l.innerHTML;
→ if(n.length==1){t+='<tr><td>&'+w+
→ '</td><td>&amp;'+w+'</td><td>&amp;#'+n.
→ charCodeAt(0)+';</td></tr>';}}}eWin=window.
→ open('','EW','scrollbars=yes,width=300,
→ height='+screen.height);eWin.document.body.
→ innerHTML=t+'</table>';})();
```

Displaying ISO Latin Characters

If you're authoring Web pages by hand, it can be a hassle to remember codes for different characters like á and à. **Script 17.8** shows you a list of common variations of the vowels.

To display ISO Latin characters:

1. `var eWin,n,i,j,w,t='<table`
   `→ border=1 cellpadding=20`
   `→ cellspacing=0>',`
   `→ l=document.createElement('p'),`

   Start off the bookmarklet by initializing several variables.

2. `v='aAeEiIoOuUyY',`

   Initialize a string, v, which contains all the vowels.

3. `s=new Array('acute','circ','elig',`
   `→ 'Elig','grave','ring','slash',`
   `→ 'tilde','uml');`

   Here's an array, s, which contains all the diacritical character codes.

4. `for(i=0;i<v.length;i++){`

   This line sets up i to loop through the characters in the v string.

5. `for(j=0;j<s.length;j++){`

   And this line sets up j to loop through the s array.

6. `w=v.charAt(i)+s[j]+';'`

   In this line, we set up the variable w to be the vowel concatenated with the code, followed by a semi-colon.

   continues on next page

7. `l.innerHTML='&'+w;n=l.innerHTML;`

For an upcoming step, we'll need not the string representation of the entity, but the entity itself—that is, we want ã, not `&atilde;`. We can get that by taking our string w (set in the previous step) and put it (with a leading ampersand) into the innerHTML of an already created element, l. That converts it from the string value to its displayed value. In order to use that value, we set the variable n to the contents of that same `innerHTML`.

8. `if(n.length==1)`

In order to get every possible entity, our lists of vowels and diacritical characters have a few that don't combine to make up a valid result. We know when that's the case because the previous conversion step won't actually convert our string. That is, while `&aelig;` converts to æ and `&Aacute;` to Á, `&Aelig;` (while it looks like it should be Æ) isn't—and so, the previous step leaves it as a seven-character string. Valid entities, though, will end up as one-character strings, and will do the next bit of code.

9. `{t+='<tr><td>&'+w+'</td><td>&amp;`
`→ '+w+'</td><td>&amp;#'+n.`
`→ charCodeAt(0)+';</td></tr>';}`

We've got a valid entity here, and so we want to put it into our table. In the first column we want the entity itself, the second its string representation, and in the third, its numeric representation. We get that last value by using the `charCodeAt()` method on our entity.

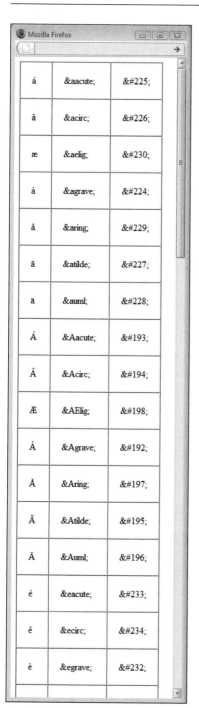

á	&aacute;	&#225;
â	&acirc;	&#226;
æ	&aelig;	&#230;
à	&agrave;	&#224;
å	&aring;	&#229;
ã	&atilde;	&#227;
ä	&auml;	&#228;
Á	&Aacute;	&#193;
Â	&Acirc;	&#194;
Æ	&AElig;	&#198;
À	&Agrave;	&#192;
Å	&Aring;	&#197;
Ã	&Atilde;	&#195;
Ä	&Auml;	&#196;
é	&eacute;	&#233;
ê	&ecirc;	&#234;
è	&egrave;	&#232;

Figure 17.20 The result of this script is a new window with all the possible variants of the vowels as HTML entities.

10. eWin=window.open('','EW',
→ 'scrollbars=yes,width=300,
→ height='+screen.height);eWin.
→ document.body.innerHTML=t+
→ '</table>';

When we're done, we open a new window and then write our table into it, as shown in **Figure 17.20**.

✔ Tips

■ Our table can be lengthy, so we've been a little tricky with the height of the window we're opening. Instead of giving it a fixed height, it's instead set based on the height of the user's display. If that's not what you want, you can set it to a fixed size instead.

■ If you're now wondering how to get an Æ in HTML, it's **Æ**—that is, it needs an upper-case E, not a lower-case e. Now you can see why we find bookmarklets like this so handy!

DISPLAYING ISO LATIN CHARACTERS

461

Converting RGB Values to Hex

Another useful little widget Web developers frequently wish they had on hand is an RGB-to-hexadecimal converter. This is useful whenever you need to translate a color value from a graphics program like Adobe Photoshop or Fireworks into a browser color, for page backgrounds or text colors. **Script 17.9** shows the conversion calculator done in JavaScript and turned into a bookmarklet.

To convert RGB values to hexadecimal:

1. `var s,i,n,h='#',`

   Start off the bookmarklet by initializing four variables.

2. `x='0123456789ABCDEF',`

   The variable x is set to the valid hexadecimal digits.

3. `c=prompt('R,G,B:','');`

   This line prompts the user for the requested RGB values, separated by commas, as shown in **Figure 17.21**.

Script 17.9 This script takes RGB color values and turns them into their hexadecimal equivalents.

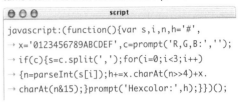

```
javascript:(function(){var s,i,n,h='#',
→ x='0123456789ABCDEF',c=prompt('R,G,B:','');
→ if(c){s=c.split(',');for(i=0;i<3;i++)
→ {n=parseInt(s[i]);h+=x.charAt(n>>4)+x.
→ charAt(n&15);}prompt('Hexcolor:',h);}})();
```

Figure 17.21 The first part of the script prompts the user for the RGB values.

Figure 17.22 Another prompt box provides the calculated hex value.

4. `if(c){`

   If the user entered anything, continue with the code. Otherwise, the value of c will be null, and the bookmarklet skips all the following steps.

5. `s=c.split(',');`

   Split the entry in c, separated by commas, and put the result into the s array.

6. `for(i=0;i<3;i++){`

   Loop around the following lines once for each of the three red, green, and blue color values.

7. `n=parseInt(s[i]);`

   Turn the current element of s into a number, and save it as n.

8. `h+=x.charAt(n>>4)+x.charAt(n&15);`

   This line converts n into 2 hexadecimal digits and adds the result to h.

9. `prompt('Hexcolor:',h);`

   The result (ready to be copied into an HTML page) is displayed via a prompt command, as shown in **Figure 17.22**. It's done this way instead of with an alert, so that we can copy the code and paste it later.

Converting Values

The possibilities are endless for the types of values that can be converted from one form to another. **Script 17.10** shows just one example: how to convert kilometers to miles.

To convert kilometers to miles:

1. `var t,expr=prompt('Length in`
   `→ kilometers:','');`

   The bookmarklet starts by prompting the user for a length in kilometers (**Figure 17.23**).

2. `if(isNaN(parseFloat(expr)))`

   Check to see if the user entered a numeric value.

3. `{t=expr+' is not a number';}`

   If not, set t to be an error message.

4. `else{t='Length in miles is`
   `→ '+Math.round(expr*6214)/10000;}`

   Otherwise, convert the value to miles and store it in t.

5. `alert(t);`

   Whether the input value is good or bad, we've stored the result in t. Here we display that result, as shown in **Figure 17.24**.

✔ Tips

■ It's a straightforward process to adapt this script into any kind of conversion you need. Just change the label in step 1, and replace the math expression in step 4 to the correct expression for the particular conversion you're looking for.

■ You can make up a bunch of bookmarklets with different conversions and then organize them all into folders in your Bookmarks or Favorites menu. Conversions can be just a mouse click away.

Script 17.10 You can create bookmarklets for almost any kind of unit conversion. This script converts kilometers to miles.

```
javascript:(function(){var t,expr=prompt
→ ('Length in kilometers:','');if(isNaN
→ (parseFloat(expr))){t=expr+' is not a
→ number';}else{t='Length in miles is '+Math.
→ round(expr*6214)/10000;}alert(t);})();
```

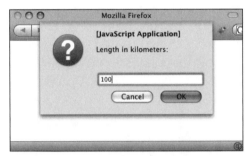

Figure 17.23 First, ask for the number to be converted.

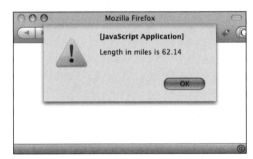

Figure 17.24 JavaScript returns the result of the conversion.

Script 17.11 Surprisingly complex equations can be evaluated with this bookmarklet.

```
                          script
javascript:(function(){var evl,expr=prompt
→ ('Formula...(eg: 2*3 + 7/8)','');with(Math)
→ try{evl=parseFloat(eval(expr));if(isNaN
→ (evl)){throw Error('Not a number!');}
→ prompt('Result of '+expr+':',evl);}
→ catch(evl){alert(evl);}})();
```

Table 17.1

JavaScript's Math Functionality	
FUNCTION	**DESCRIPTION**
abs	Absolute value
sin, cos, tan	Standard trigonometric functions; arguments in radians
acos, asin, atan	Inverse trigonometric functions; return values in radians
exp, log	Exponential and natural logarithm, base e
ceil	Returns least integer greater than or equal to argument
floor	Returns greatest integer less than or equal to argument
min	Returns lesser of two arguments
max	Returns greater of two arguments
pow	Exponential; first argument is base, second is exponent
round	Rounds argument to nearest integer
sqrt	Square root

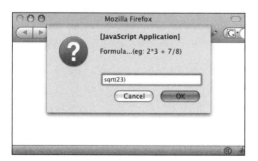

Figure 17.25 The user must be prompted for a formula.

A Bookmarklet Calculator

If you think about it, it's really a bit too difficult to do a full-fledged calculator with buttons and a running value on just one long line of code. However, you can use a bookmarklet like **Script 17.11** to do fairly complex calculations, using JavaScript's built-in Math functions, as described in **Table 17.1**.

To use a JavaScript calculator:

1. `var evl,expr=prompt('Formula...`
   `→ (eg: 2*3 + 7/8)','');`

   This line sets up a variable evl, and then prompts the user for an expression or formula, as shown in **Figure 17.25**, which is stored in expr.

2. `with(Math)try{`

   The next few lines need to be evaluated using JavaScript's built-in Math routines. The with(Math) part tells the interpreter that when any of these functions are seen, to evaluate them as Math commands.

   The try{} warns JavaScript that what we're doing may well fail, and if so, don't panic. In fact, don't even put up an error message if there's a problem, as we'll be handling the errors ourselves.

3. `evl=parseFloat(eval(expr));`

   Evaluate the expression, and turn it into a floating-point number, which is then stored in evl.

4. `if(isNaN(evl))`

   If the resulting value in evl is not a number (NaN), do the following line.

continues on next page

5. `{throw Error('Not a number!');}`

If we're here, for some reason what the user entered didn't work out to a number. When that happens we want to force an error message of "Not a number!" to display. Here's where the message is set; it will be displayed in step 7.

6. `prompt('Result of '+expr+':',evl);`

Otherwise, the expression was valid, so display the result, as shown in **Figure 17.26**.

7. `}catch(evl){alert(evl);}`

Here's the end of that `try{}` block that started in step 2. To get here, one of two things happened: either we ran into the error in step 5, or some other error entirely occurred. Either way, we "catch" the error that was "thrown" and put it up on the screen in an alert.

✔ Tip

■ Trying to remember where you've seen that `try/throw/catch` syntax before? It was originally covered back in the "Handling Errors" section of Chapter 2.

Figure 17.26 JavaScript returns the result of the calculation.

Script 17.12 Shorten those URLs with a single click of a mouse (and this script).

```
script
javascript:(function(){window.open('http://
→ tinyurl.com/create.php?url='+location.
→ href,'','width=750,height=500,scrollbars=
→ yes');})();
```

Figure 17.27 There are a number of uses for shorter versions of URLs, and this bookmarklet makes it simple to get that short URL.

Shortening URLs

There are a number of reasons why you might want a shorter version of a URL than the one of the page that you're currently on- maybe you're using a Twitter-like service with a short number of characters allowed, or maybe you're going to paste the result into an email and you don't want it to wrap. Either way, **Script 17.12** makes it simple.

To shorten URLs:

◆ `window.open('http://tinyurl.com/`
   `→ create.php?url='+location.href,`
   `→ '','width=750,height=500,`
   `→ scrollbars=yes');`

Here we're opening a new window, and using the TinyURL.com service to set our short URL. We pass it our current page location (found in `location.href`) and that's all the information it needs. Because TinyURL.com immediately puts the new shortened URL onto your clipboard for you, all you have to do (once you're on the right Web page) is click the bookmarklet, glance at the page that opens to make sure everything worked as it should (**Figure 17.27**), close it, and paste your new location wherever you want.

✔ Tips

■ There are a number of different URL-shortening services online. If you don't like TinyURL.com, check out `snurl.com`, `twurl.nl`, or `is.gd`.

■ If you're on Twitter, feel free to say "Hi!" to us at `@negrino` and `@dori`.

Validating Pages

When creating your pages, it's a great idea to make sure that you're making sites that adhere to Web standards; such pages load quicker in modern browsers and are easier to maintain. The easiest way to check a page that you're working on for valid code is by running it against the page validator maintained by the World Wide Web Consortium (W3C), at http://validator.w3.org. This bookmarklet, **Script 17.13**, checks the page currently shown in your browser for validity. It does this by taking the URL of the current page, passing it to the validator, and then opening a new window with the validator's results, as shown in **Figure 17.28**.

To validate your pages:

◆ window.open('http://validator.w3.
→ org/check?uri='+window.location.
→ href,'','width=800,height=900,
→ resizable=yes,scrollbars=yes');

This one, useful as it is, isn't exactly rocket science. First, we open a window and pass that window the URL to the validator. You'll note the validator has a parameter, uri, which accepts the URL of the current page, which we pass as location.href. The plus sign between the two concatenates the location object to the validator's URL. The rest of the line is just parameters for the window's size and other attributes.

Script 17.13 Use this script to make sure your pages contain Web-standard, valid markup.

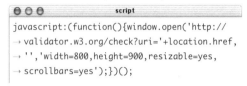

```
javascript:(function(){window.open('http://
→ validator.w3.org/check?uri='+location.href,
→ '','width=800,height=900,resizable=yes,
→ scrollbars=yes');})();
```

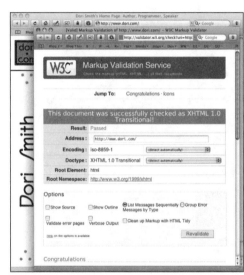

Figure 17.28 Running your page against the W3C validator returns this happy result, if you've written your page correctly.

Script 17.14 If you want to mail all or part of a Web page to someone, you can't make it much simpler than using this bookmarklet.

```
script
javascript:(function(){location.href='mailto:
→ ?SUBJECT='+document.title+'&BODY=
→ '+escape(location.href)+' \r'+window.
→ getSelection();})();
```

Figure 17.29 One click opens a new window, with the start of your mail already begun.

Mailing Pages

Sometimes you'll be surfing along, and you'll find a page that's so useful you need to share it with your co-workers, or maybe it's so funny you need to share it with your best friend. This bookmarklet, **Script 17.14**, takes the page you're on, plus any highlighted text, and uses it to create a new outgoing email

To mail a Web page:

◆ `location.href='mailto:?SUBJECT=`
  → `'+document.title+'&BODY=`
  → `'+escape(location.href)+'`
  → `\r'+window.getSelection();`

If you've ever put a `mailto` link on a Web page, you should recognize this syntax. All this does is act just as if you've clicked on a `<a href='mailto:'></a>` link. The subject of the email is set to the title of the current document, and the body of the email is set to the URL of the page plus any text you have currently selected, as seen in **Figure 17.29**.

✔ Tips

■ Because we're using `window.getSelection()` here, this bookmarklet won't work "as is" in IE. You'll need to modify it similar to the changes in "Word Lookups," above.

■ No, you don't have to be using Gmail, or even Web mail for this to work. Whatever mail client you've set up as the default on your computer is what will open and create the mail.

Resizing Pages

When you're working on a site, it's useful to be able to see how a page looks with a smaller display than the one you're using. This bookmarklet, **Script 17.15**, resets your browser window to 640x480.

To resize your page:

◆ `resizeTo(640,480);moveTo(0,0);`

The first command, `resizeTo()`, changes the dimensions of your browser window. The next, `moveTo()`, tells the browser where to put the top-left corner (**Figure 17.30**).

✔ Tips

■ By itself, this bookmarklet is only moderately useful. Where it shines is when you create a folder full of almost identical versions of this, with all the various sizes that you could want. As you can see, it's straightforward to duplicate this for any size window.

■ It's also useful (if your display is large enough) to be able to open windows side by side with identical dimensions. For instance, you can have one bookmarklet that resizes your window to be 700px wide by the max height of your display:

`resizeTo(700,screen.availHeight);`
`→ moveTo(0,0);`

And also this one:

`resizeTo(700,screen.availHeight);`
`→ moveTo(screen.availWidth-700,0);`

The latter resizes a page to the same 700px wide by the max height of your display, but positions the window such that it's against the right edge of your screen versus the left. If your display is 1400 pixels or more, you should see them perfectly aligned without overlapping, each flush against one side.

Script 17.15 If you want to see how your page looks at a different size, bookmarklets like this one come in handy.

```
javascript:(function(){resizeTo(640,480);
→ moveTo(0,0);})();
```

Figure 17.30 We can see at a glance that the small screen version of this site doesn't show much of the content.

JAVASCRIPT GENEALOGY AND REFERENCE

JavaScript has been transformed over the past decade or so, since its introduction as part of Netscape Navigator 2.0. This appendix briefly discusses the different versions of JavaScript and which browsers include which version of JavaScript.

You'll also find a JavaScript object flowchart as well as a table listing most of the JavaScript software objects up to and including JavaScript version 1.5, along with their properties, methods, and event handlers.

JavaScript Versions

The scripting language that you think of as JavaScript has several different names (depending on whose product you have) and almost a dozen different versions. Besides JavaScript, there are also JScript and ECMAScript. Here's a guide to which version does what.

Netscape's JavaScript

The first version of JavaScript, originally called LiveScript, was first released in Netscape Navigator 2.0. Netscape intended LiveScript to be a way to extend the capabilities of browsers, and to allow Web designers to add some interactivity to their sites. The JavaScript version in Navigator 2.0 is JavaScript 1.0.

Along with Navigator 3.0 came JavaScript 1.1, which added support for images, arrays, Java applets, and plug-ins, among many other changes.

With the release of Navigator 4.0 (also known as Netscape Communicator), JavaScript 1.2 was born, with more enhancements and refinements. Netscape 4.5 later shipped with JavaScript 1.3. JavaScript 1.4 was server-side only, and Netscape 6 introduced JavaScript 1.5.

Current versions of JavaScript are being developed by the open-source Mozilla project, mainly for the benefit of its Firefox browser. Firefox (and its spinoffs, such as Camino for Mac OS X) uses ECMAScript-262 Edition 3 (see below).

At press time for this book, the current version of JavaScript was 1.8, which is shipping with Firefox 3 (as seen in **Table A.1**).

Table A.1

Netscape/Mozilla JavaScript Versions	
BROWSER	JAVASCRIPT VERSION
2.0	1.0
3.0	1.1
4.0–4.05	1.2
4.06–4.7	1.3
6.0, 7.0, Mozilla, Firefox 1.0–1.41	1.5
Firefox 1.5	1.6
Firefox 2.0	1.7
Firefox 3.0	1.8

Table A.2

JScript Versions		
JSCRIPT VERSION	IE VERSION	WINDOWS VERSION
3.0	4.0	
5.0	5.0	
5.1		2000
5.5	5.5	
5.5		ME
5.6	6.0	
5.6		XP
5.7	7.0	
5.7		Vista
5.8	8.0	

Microsoft's JScript

As is so often the case, Microsoft implemented JavaScript in its own fashion, which is not always compatible with the Netscape version. Called JScript version 1, the Microsoft version of JavaScript was more-or-less compatible with JavaScript 1.0; there were some differences. Naturally, JScript appears only in Windows and versions of Microsoft Internet Explorer (MSIE).

On Windows, there was also a JScript version 2 (somewhat comparable to JavaScript 1.1) for Windows 95/NT that came with upgraded versions of MSIE 3.02 and later. Not all versions of MSIE 3.02 had JScript 2.0. If you happen to have one of these oldies, you can tell what version of JScript you have installed by searching your disk for "jscript.dll". Get the file's properties, and click the Version tab. If the file version does not begin with at least 2, you've still got the original.

On the Macintosh, MSIE 3.0 had no JScript, but version 3.01 did. That included JScript 1.0, but not the identical version as on Windows; there were differences between the Mac and Windows versions of JScript (for example, the Mac version supported the Image object for mouse rollovers, while the Windows JScript 1.0 did not). In 2003, Microsoft discontinued MSIE for Mac, ending official support in 2005.

Confused yet? You're in good company. But wait, there's more: JScript 3.0 was roughly equivalent to JavaScript 1.2, and JScript 5.x is roughly equivalent to JavaScript 1.5. Some versions of Windows are also associated with particular JScript versions, as JScript is one of the scripting languages that can be used to script Windows itself. **Table A.2** helps you identify which version of JScript you have, depending on which version of IE and Windows you're running.

AOL

Which versions of JavaScript do AOL browsers support? Given that AOL owns Netscape, you might guess that it ships with that browser, but you'd be wrong, unless you're talking about AOL for Mac OS X. For contractual reasons, AOL uses Microsoft's Internet Explorer. **Table A.3** shows which browsers shipped with which versions of AOL.

According to AOL, the Mac (for Mac OS 9 and earlier) and 16-bit PC versions come with MSIE embedded into the client, but 32-bit PC versions since AOL version 3 can use whatever version of MSIE is on the user's system. Consequently, these folks may have anything from MSIE 3 to MSIE 6 or later installed. AOL for Mac OS X uses Netscape technology to provide an embedded browser, which from the JavaScript standpoint is functionally equivalent to Netscape 7.

Table A.3

AOL/MS IE Browser Chart			
AOL VERSION	**16-BIT PC**	**32-BIT PC**	**MAC**
3.0	3.0	3.0	2.1
		3.01	
		3.02	
		4.01	
4.0	3.0	n/a	3.01
5.0		n/a	4.01

JAVASCRIPT VERSIONS

ECMAScript

In 1996, Web developers began to complain that Netscape was going in one direction with JavaScript, and Microsoft in a somewhat-compatible but different direction with JScript. Nobody likes to have to code pages to handle different dialects of JavaScript, or have their code work in one browser but not another. Developers wanted a standard. So Netscape went to an international standards body called ECMA and submitted the JavaScript language specification to it, and Microsoft threw in its own comments and suggestions. ECMA did whatever it is that standards bodies do and in June of 1997 produced a standard called ECMA-262 (also known as ECMAScript, a term that just dances off the tongue). This standard closely resembled JavaScript 1.1, but (sigh) was not exactly the same; subsequent versions rectified this problem. If you're interested in reading the official ECMAScript specification, you can download it from `http://www.ecma-international.org/`. Look for the Standards link and then follow it to the ECMA-262 specification.

ECMAScript also has several flavors, the most current of which is the third edition. At press time, work on the fourth edition was in progress but not yet finalized. It's important to note that ECMAScript is now driving the JavaScript standards process; all current browser makers have made their implementation of JavaScript ECMAScript compliant.

ECMASCRIPT

Microsoft claims that Internet Explorer versions 4.0 and up are ECMAScript-compliant, along with some extra, proprietary features that are specific to MSIE. So as long as you write ECMAScript-compatible code, it should run just fine under MSIE 4.0+ and Netscape Navigator 6.0+ (and its successors, the Firefox and Mozilla browser families). But you should always test your code with different browsers, platforms, and versions just to be sure.

Apple's Safari has always supported ECMAScript. The current Safari 3.0, which shipped with Mac OS X 10.5 ("Leopard"), supports ECMAScript-262 Edition 3.

ECMASCRIPT

Object Flowchart

Throughout this book, we've primarily used DOM scripting, relying on looking for particular ids versus particular objects. It's simply easier to use getElementByID() and access the element you want directly, rather than descending the object tree, as with document.form.button.radio. We recommend that you use DOM scripting in your code, as well.

If you want information about what objects are available to you, check out the Firefox DOM Inspector, shown in **Figure A.1**. While not everything is cross-browser, it will give you a number of places to start.

For older browsers, however, those options aren't available, and you need to know what properties exist and how they all fit together, and that's where this section fits in, as a reference to the older method of doing things.

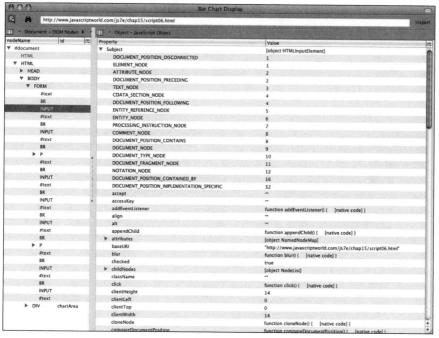

Figure A.1 With the Firefox DOM Inspector, you can see precisely how the browser sees your code.

JavaScript objects are connected together in a particular order, which you can think of in terms of an organization chart. The primary object in JavaScript is the current window, and all other software objects flow from that window, as seen in **Figure A.2**. This order of objects is often called the JavaScript object hierarchy, but that name is just a tad too self-important for this book.

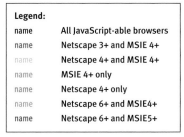

Legend:

name	All JavaScript-able browsers
name	Netscape 3+ and MSIE 4+
name	Netscape 4+ and MSIE 4+
name	MSIE 4+ only
name	Netscape 4+ only
name	Netscape 6+ and MSIE4+
name	Netscape 6+ and MSIE5+

Figure A.2

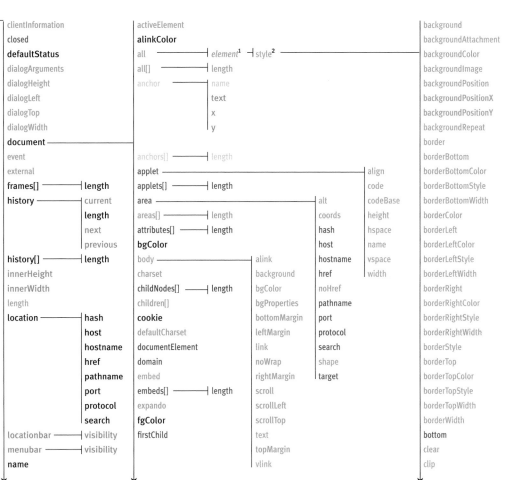

window (frame, self, top, parent)

1 The *element* object is just a placeholder for MS IE. In coding, it should be replaced with the actual name of the object.

2 Style and its properties are available in Netscape 6+, but only through document.getElementById, as described in Chapter 2.

OBJECT FLOWCHART

OBJECT FLOWCHART

navigator	form —	action		checked	color
offscreenBuffering		button —	form	defaultChecked	cssText
opener			name	form	cursor
outerHeight			type	name	direction
outerWidth			value	type	display
pageXOffset		checkbox		value	font
pageYOffset		elements[] —	length	form	fontFamily
parent		encoding		name	fontSize
personalbar —	visibility	enctype		type	fontStyle
screen		fileUpload		value	fontVariant
screenLeft[3]		hidden		form	fontWeight
screenTop[3]		length		maxLength	height
screenX		method		name	left
screenY		name		readOnly	lineHeight
scrollbars —	visibility			size	listStyle
self				type	listStyleImage
status				value	listStylePosition
statusbar —	visibility	password		defaultvalue	listStyleType
toolbar —	visibility	radio —	checked	form	margin
top			defaultChecked	maxLength	marginBottom
			form	name	marginLeft
			name	readOnly	marginRight
window (frame, self, top, parent) (cont.)			type	size	marginTop
			value	type	overflow
document (cont.)		radio[] —	length	value	padding
		reset —	form		paddingBottom
			name		paddingLeft
			type		paddingRight
			value		paddingTop
		select —	form		pageBreakAfter
			length		pageBreakBefore
			multiple		pixelHeight
			name		pixelLeft
			option —	defaultSelected	pixelTop
				form	pixelWidth
				index	posHeight
				selected	position
				text	posLeft
				value	posTop
			options[] —	length	posWidth
			selectedindex		right
			size		styleFloat
			type		tableLayout
			value		textAlign
					textDecoration
					textDecorationBlink
					textDecorationLineThrough

style[2] (cont.)

3. Exists as of MS IE 5+.

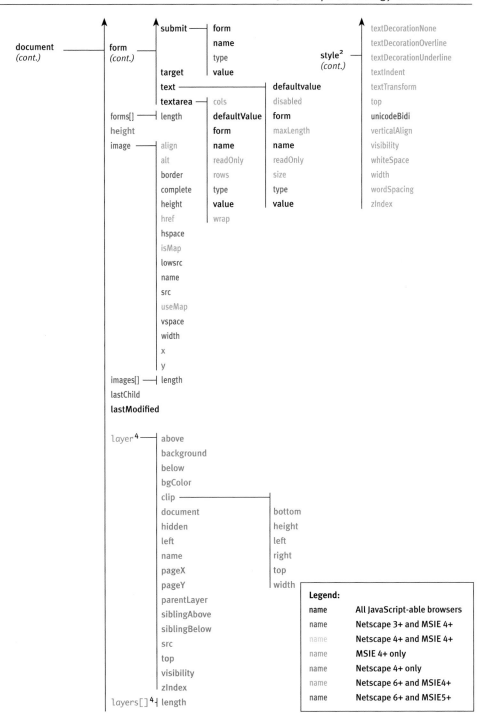

document
(cont.)

form
(cont.)

submit — form
name
type

target
text ——— defaultvalue

textarea — cols
forms[] — length
height
image — align

defaultValue
form
name

disabled
form
maxLength
name

style[2]
(cont.)

textDecorationNone
textDecorationOverline
textDecorationUnderline
textIndent
textTransform
top
unicodeBidi
verticalAlign
visibility
whiteSpace
width
wordSpacing
zIndex

alt
border
complete
height
href
hspace
isMap
lowsrc
name
src
useMap
vspace
width
x
y

readOnly
rows
type
value
wrap

readOnly
size
type
value

images[] — length
lastChild
lastModified

layer[4] — above
background
below
bgColor
clip
document
hidden
left
name
pageX
pageY
parentLayer
siblingAbove
siblingBelow
src
top
visibility
zIndex
layers[] [4] — length

bottom
height
left
right
top
width

Legend:	
name	All JavaScript-able browsers
name	Netscape 3+ and MSIE 4+
name	Netscape 4+ and MSIE 4+
name	MSIE 4+ only
name	Netscape 4+ only
name	Netscape 6+ and MSIE4+
name	Netscape 6+ and MSIE5+

4 The layer (and layers[]) object and its properties only existed in Netscape 4.x and were not included in later versions.

OBJECT FLOWCHART

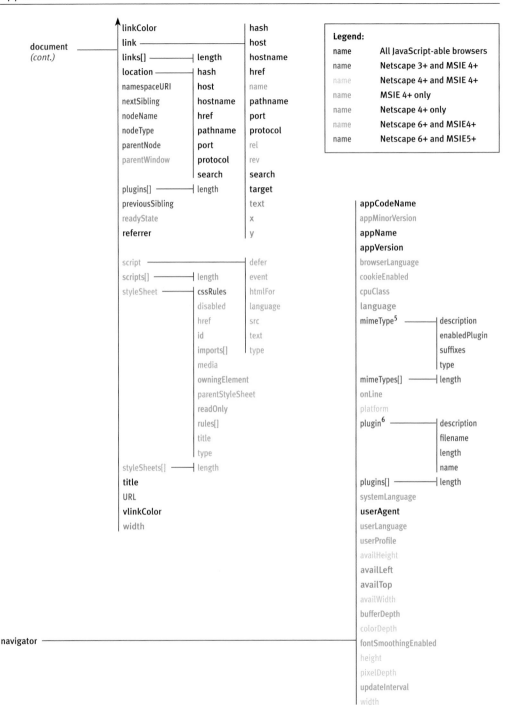

document
(cont.)

linkColor
link
links[] — length
location — hash
namespaceURI   host
nextSibling   hostname
nodeName   href
nodeType   pathname
parentNode   port
parentWindow   protocol
                  search
plugins[] — length
previousSibling
readyState
referrer

hash
host
hostname
href
name
pathname
port
protocol
rel
rev
search
target
text
x
y

Legend:

name	All JavaScript-able browsers
name	Netscape 3+ and MSIE 4+
name	Netscape 4+ and MSIE 4+
name	MSIE 4+ only
name	Netscape 4+ only
name	Netscape 6+ and MSIE4+
name	Netscape 6+ and MSIE5+

script — defer
scripts[] — length   event
styleSheet — cssRules   htmlFor
             disabled   language
             href   src
             id   text
             imports[] type
             media
             owningElement
             parentStyleSheet
             readOnly
             rules[]
             title
             type
styleSheets[] — length
title
URL
vlinkColor
width

appCodeName
appMinorVersion
appName
appVersion
browserLanguage
cookieEnabled
cpuClass
language
mimeType[5] — description
              enabledPlugin
              suffixes
              type
mimeTypes[] — length
onLine
platform
plugin[6] — description
            filename
            length
            name
plugins[] — length
systemLanguage
userAgent
userLanguage
userProfile
availHeight
availLeft
availTop
availWidth
bufferDepth
colorDepth
fontSmoothingEnabled
height
pixelDepth
updateInterval
width

navigator

5 This object (and its properties) exist in Netscape 3+ and MSIE 4+ (Mac).
6 This object (and its properties) exist in Netscape 3+ and MSIE 5+ (Mac).

The Big Object Table

No JavaScript book is complete without the whopping big table of JavaScript objects, along with their associated properties, methods, and event handlers (check Chapter 1 for definitions of these terms). **Table A.4** covers most of the JavaScript objects in the language up through and including JavaScript 1.5. We've omitted a few very obscure objects, as well as some older objects from earlier versions that have been superseded by new or extended objects in version 1.5.

Table A.4 JavaScript Object Table

Object	Properties	Methods	Event Handlers
Anchor	name text x y	none	none
anchors array	length	none	none
Applet	align code codeBase height hspace name vspace width	applet's methods blur focus	onblur onclick ondblclick onfocus onhelp onkeydown onkeypress onkeyup onload onmousedown onmousemove onmouseout onmouseover onmouseup onresize onscroll
applets array	length	none	none
Area	alt cords hash host hostname href noHref pathname port protocol search shape target	none	onblur onclick ondblclick onfocus onhelp onkeydown onkeypress onkeyup onload onmousedown onmousemove onmouseout onmouseover onmouseup onresize
Array	length	concat join pop push reverse shift slice sort splice toLocaleString toString unshift	none

Table A.4 **JavaScript Object Table** *(continued)*

OBJECT	PROPERTIES	METHODS	EVENT HANDLERS
Body	alink background bgColor bgProperties bottomMargin leftMargin link noWrap rightMargin scroll scrollLeft scrollTop text topMargin vlink	createTextRange	onblur onclick ondblclick onfocus onhelp onkeydown onkeypress onkeyup onmousedown onmousemove onmouseout onmouseover onmouseup onresize onscroll
Button	form name type value	blur click focus handleEvent	onblur onchange onclick ondblclick onfocus onhelp onkeydown onkeypress onkeyup onmousedown onmousemove onmouseout onmouseover onmouseup onselect
Checkbox	checked defaultChecked form name type value	blur click focus handleEvent	onblur onchange onclick ondblclick onfocus onhelp onkeydown onkeypress onkeyup onmousedown onmousemove onmouseout onmouseover onmouseup onselect
Date	none	getDate getDay getFullYear getHours getMilliseconds getMinutes getMonth getSeconds getTime getTimezoneOffset getUTCDate getUTCDay getUTCFullYear getUTCHours getUTCMilliseconds getUTCMinutes getUTCMonth	none

Table A.4 JavaScript Object Table *(continued)*

OBJECT	PROPERTIES	METHODS	EVENT HANDLERS
Date *(cont.)*		getUTCSeconds	
		getYear	
		parse	
		setDate	
		setFullYear	
		setHours	
		setMilliseconds	
		setMinutes	
		setMonth	
		setSeconds	
		setTime	
		setUTCDate	
		setUTCFullYear	
		setUTCHours	
		setUTCMilliseconds	
		setUTCMinutes	
		setUTCMonth	
		setUTCSeconds	
		setYear	
		toGMTString	
		toLocaleDateString	
		toLocaleString	
		toLocaleTimeString	
		toString	
		toUTCString	
		UTC	
		valueOf	
document	activeElement	clear	onblur
	alinkColor	close	onclick
	all	createElement	oncut
	Anchor	createStylesheet	ondblclick
	anchors	createTextNode	onfocus
	Applet	elementFromPoint	onhelp
	applets	focus	onkeydown
	Area	getElementById	onkeypress
	areas	getElementsByName	onkeyup
	attributes	getElementsByTagName	onmousedown
	bgColor	getSelection	onmousemove
	Body	handleEvent	onmouseout
	charset	open	onmouseover
	childNodes	write	onmouseup
	children	writeln	onpaste
	cookie		onresize
	defaultCharset		
	documentElement		
	domain		
	embed		
	embeds		
	expando		
	fgColor		
	firstChild		
	Form		
	forms		
	height		
	Image		
	images		
	lastChild		
	lastModified		
	Layer		
	layers		
	linkColor		
	Link		

Table A.4 JavaScript Object Table *(continued)*

Object	Properties	Methods	Event Handlers
document *(cont.)*	links location namespaceURI nextSibling nodeName nodeType parentNode parentWindow plugins previousSibling readyState referrer Script scripts StyleSheet styleSheets title URL vlinkColor width		
FileUpload	form name type value	blur focus handleEvent select	onblur onchange onclick ondblclick onfocus onhelp onkeydown onkeypress onkeyup onmousedown onmousemove onmouseout onmouseover onmouseup onselect
Form	action Button Checkbox elements encoding encType FileUpload Hidden length method name Password Radio Reset Select Submit target Text Textarea	handleEvent reset submit	onclick ondblclick onhelp onkeydown onkeypress onkeyup onmousedown onmousemove onmouseout onmouseover onmouseup onreset onsubmit
forms array	length	none	none
frames array	length	none	none

Table A.4 JavaScript Object Table *(continued)*

OBJECT	PROPERTIES	METHODS	EVENT HANDLERS
Hidden	form maxLength name readOnly size type value	none	none
History	current **length** next previous	back forward go	none
history array	**length**	none	none
Image	align alt border complete height href hspace isMap lowsrc name src useMap vspace width x y	none	onabort onblur onchange onclick ondblclick **onerror** onfocus onhelp onkeydown onkeypress onkeyup **onload** onmousedown onmousemove onmouseout onmouseover onmouseup **onreset** onresize onscroll **onsubmit**
images array	length	none	none
Layer	above background below bgColor clip document hidden left name pageX pageY parentLayer siblingAbove siblingBelow src top visibility zIndex	load moveAbove moveBelow moveBy moveTo moveToAbsolute resizeBy resizeTo	onblur onfocus onload onmouseout onmouseover onmouseup
layers array	length	none	none
Link	**hash** **host** **hostname** **href** name **pathname** **port** **protocol**	none	onblur **onclick** ondblclick onfocus onhelp onkeydown onkeypress onkeyup

Table A.4 **JavaScript Object Table** *(continued)*

OBJECT	PROPERTIES	METHODS	EVENT HANDLERS
Link *(cont.)*	rel rev search target text x y		onmousedown onmousemove onmouseout onmouseover onmouseup
links array	length	none	none
location	hash host hostname href pathname port protocol search	assign reload replace	none
Math	E LN2 LN10 LOG2E LOG10E PI SQRT1_2 SQRT2	abs acos asin atan atan2 ceil cos exp floor log max min pow random round sin sqrt tan	none
MimeType	description enabledPlugin suffixes type	none	none
mimeTypes array	length	none	none
navigator	appCodeName appMinorVersion appName appVersion browserLanguage cookieEnabled cpuClass language MimeType mimeTypes onLine platform Plugin plugins systemLanguage userAgent userLanguage userProfile	javaEnabled preference taintEnabled	none
Number	MAX_VALUE MIN_VALUE NaN NEGATIVE_INFINITY	toExponential toFixed toLocaleString toPrecision	none

Table A.4 JavaScript Object Table *(continued)*

Object	Properties	Methods	Event Handlers
Number *(cont.)*	POSITIVE_INFINITY	toString valueOf	
Object	attributes childNodes children className clientHeight clientLeft clientTop clientWidth dir firstChild id innerHTML lang language lastChild length localName namespaceURI nextSibling nodeName nodeType nodeValue offsetHeight offsetLeft offsetParent offsetTop offsetWidth ownerDocument parentNode prefix previousSibling readyState scrollHeight scrollLeft scrollTop scrollWidth sourceIndex style tabIndex tagName title	appendChild blur click cloneNode focus getAttribute getAttributeNode getElementsByTagName getExpression hasChildNodes insertBefore item releaseCapture removeAttribute removeAttributeNode removeChild replaceChild scrollIntoView setAttribute	onblur onchange onclick oncontextmenu ondblclick onfocus onkeydown onkeypress onkeyup onmousedown onmousemove onmouseout onmouseover onmouseup onreadystatechange onresize onscroll
Option	defaultSelected form index selected text value	remove	none
options array	length	none	none
Password	defaultValue form maxLength name readOnly size type value	blur focus handleEvent select	onblur onchange onclick ondblclick onfocus onhelp onkeydown onkeypress onkeyup onmousedown onmousemove onmouseout

THE BIG OBJECT TABLE

Table A.4 **JavaScript Object Table** *(continued)*

Object	Properties	Methods	Event Handlers
Password *(cont.)*			onmouseover onmouseup **onselect**
Plugin	description filename length name	refresh	**none**
plugins array	length	**none**	**none**
Radio	**checked** **defaultChecked** **form** **name** **type** **value**	**blur** **click** **focus** handleEvent	onblur onchange **onclick** ondblclick onfocus onhelp onkeydown onkeypress onkeyup onmousedown onmousemove onmouseout onmouseover onmouseup onselect
radio array	**length**	none	none
RegExp	input lastMatch lastParen leftContext multiline rightContext $1 $2 $3 $4 $5 $6 $7 $8 $9	none	none
regular expression	global ignoreCase lastIndex source	compile exec test	**none**
Reset	**form** **name** **type** **value**	**blur** **click** **focus** handleEvent	onblur **onclick** ondblclick onfocus onhelp onkeydown onkeypress onkeyup onmousedown onmousemove onmouseout onmouseover onmouseup onselect
screen	availHeight **availLeft** **availTop** availWidth	**none**	**none**

Table A.4 JavaScript Object Table *(continued)*

Object	Properties	Methods	Event Handlers
screen *(cont.)*	bufferDepth colorDepth fontSmoothingEnabled height pixelDepth updateInterval width		
Script	defer event htmlFor language src text type	none	onerror onload
Select	form length multiple name Option options selectedIndex size type value	blur focus handleEvent	onblur onchange onclick ondblclick onfocus onhelp onkeydown onkeypress onkeyup onmousedown onmousemove onmouseout onmouseover onmouseup onresize
String	length	anchor big blink bold charAt charCodeAt concat fixed fontcolor fontsize fromCharCode indexOf italics lastIndexOf link localeCompare match replace search slice small split strike sub substr substring sup toLocaleLowerCase toLocaleUpperCase toLowerCase toString toUpperCase valueOf	none

THE BIG OBJECT TABLE

Table A.4 **JavaScript Object Table** *(continued)*

Object	Properties	Methods	Event Handlers
Style	background	none	none
	backgroundAttachment		
	backgroundColor		
	backgroundImage		
	backgroundPosition		
	backgroundPositionX		
	backgroundPositionY		
	backgroundRepeat		
	border		
	borderBottom		
	borderBottomColor		
	borderBottomStyle		
	borderBottomWidth		
	borderColor		
	borderLeft		
	borderLeftColor		
	borderLeftStyle		
	borderLeftWidth		
	borderRight		
	borderRightColor		
	borderRightStyle		
	borderRightWidth		
	borderStyle		
	borderTop		
	borderTopColor		
	borderTopStyle		
	borderTopWidth		
	borderWidth		
	bottom		
	clear		
	clip		
	color		
	cssText		
	cursor		
	direction		
	display		
	font		
	fontFamily		
	fontSize		
	fontStyle		
	fontVariant		
	fontWeight		
	height		
	left		
	lineHeight		
	listStyle		
	listStyleImage		
	listStylePosition		
	listStyleType		
	margin		
	marginBottom		
	marginLeft		
	marginRight		
	marginTop		
	overflow		
	padding		
	paddingBottom		
	paddingLeft		
	paddingRight		
	paddingTop		
	pageBreakAfter		
	pageBreakBefore		
	pixelHeight		

THE BIG OBJECT TABLE

Table A.4 JavaScript Object Table *(continued)*

OBJECT	PROPERTIES	METHODS	EVENT HANDLERS
Style *(cont.)*	pixelLeft		
	pixelTop		
	pixelWidth		
	posHeight		
	position		
	posLeft		
	posTop		
	posWidth		
	right		
	styleFloat		
	tableLayout		
	textAlign		
	textDecoration		
	textDecorationBlink		
	textDecorationLineThrough		
	textDecorationNone		
	textDecorationOverline		
	textDecorationUnderline		
	textIndent		
	textTransform		
	top		
	unicodeBidi		
	verticalAlign		
	visibility		
	whiteSpace		
	width		
	wordSpacing		
	zIndex		
StyleSheet	**cssRules**	addImport	none
	disabled	addRule	
	href	removeRule	
	id		
	imports		
	media		
	owningElement		
	parentStyleSheet		
	readOnly		
	rules		
	title		
	type		
Submit	**form**	blur	onblur
	name	click	**onclick**
	type	focus	ondblclick
	value	handleEvent	onfocus
			onhelp
			onkeydown
			onkeypress
			onkeyup
			onmousedown
			onmousemove
			onmouseout
			onmouseover
			onmouseup
			onselect
Text	**defaultValue**	blur	**onblur**
	disabled	click	**onchange**
	form	focus	onclick
	maxLength	handleEvent	ondblclick
	name	select	**onfocus**
	readOnly		onkeydown
	size		onkeypress
	type		onkeyup

THE BIG OBJECT TABLE

Table A.4 JavaScript Object Table *(continued)*

OBJECT	PROPERTIES	METHODS	EVENT HANDLERS
Text *(cont.)*	value		onmousedown
			onmousemove
			onmouseout
			onmouseover
			onmouseup
			onselect
Textarea	cols	blur	onblur
	defaultValue	click	onchange
	form	createTextRange	onclick
	name	focus	ondblclick
	readOnly	handleEvent	onfocus
	rows	select	onhelp
	type		onkeydown
	value		onkeypress
	wrap		onkeyup
			onmousedown
			onmousemove
			onmouseout
			onmouseover
			onmouseup
			onscroll
			onselect
window	clientInformation	alert	onblur
	closed	back	onerror
	defaultStatus	blur	onfocus
	dialogArguments	clearInterval	onhelp
	dialogHeight	clearTimeout	onload
	dialogLeft	close	onmove
	dialogTop	confirm	onresize
	dialogWidth	focus	onscroll
	document	forward	onunload
	event	handleEvent	
	external	home	
	frames	moveBy	
	history	moveTo	
	innerHeight	navigate	
	innerWidth	open	
	length	print	
	location	prompt	
	locationbar	resizeBy	
	menubar	resizeTo	
	name	scroll	
	navigator	scrollBy	
	offscreenBuffering	scrollTo	
	opener	setInterval	
	outerHeight	setTimeout	
	outerWidth	stop	
	pageXOffset		
	pageYOffset		
	parent		
	personalbar		
	screen		
	screenLeft		
	screenTop		
	screenX		
	screenY		
	scrollbars		
	self		
	status		
	statusbar		
	toolbar		
	top		

JavaScript Reserved Words

Reserved words are words that have special meaning to JavaScript. Therefore, they cannot be used as variable or function names.

You'll recognize many of the reserved words from previous chapters, but others will be unfamiliar. Some of the latter group are future reserved words; i.e., it's expected that they might be used in future versions of JavaScript. They're being set aside now so that you won't have to revise your code when new revisions are released.

JavaScript reserved words

These words are part of the JavaScript language as of ECMAScript version 3.

break	for	throw
case	function	try
catch	if	typeof
continue	in	var
default	instanceof	void
delete	new	while
do	return	with
else	switch	
finally	this	

Additional words reserved for future use by ECMAScript 3

abstract	final	protected
boolean	float	public
byte	goto	short
char	implements	static
class	import	super
const	int	synchronized
debugger	interface	throws
double	long	transient
enum	native	volatile
export	package	
extends	private	

ECMAScript 4 Reserved Words

As of this writing, ES4's list of reserved words is in a state of flux. This is the currently proposed list, but it's likely to change before this book even sees print.

__proto__	if	switch
class	in	this
const	instanceof	throw
continue	interface	true
debugger	is	try
default	let	type
delete	like	typeof
do	namespace	use
dynamic	native	var
else	new	void
false	null	while
final	override	with
finally	return	yield
for	static	
function	super	

ES4 Contextually Reserved Words

ECMAScript 4 introduces a new type of reserved words: ones that are only *contextually* reserved. That is, they're only reserved at certain times and in certain places. For best results, though, we recommend that you not use the following words as variables names.

each	get	standard
extends	implements	strict
generator	set	undefined

The good news, though, so far as ECMAScript 4 is concerned: they've gotten rid of the concept of future reserved words. Barring any changes (unlikely though that is), there shouldn't be any more additions to this list in the future.

Other identifiers to avoid

The object names used in Appendix A aren't officially reserved (outside of the keywords above), but as they are part of the JavaScript language, you shouldn't use them as function or variable names. If you do, abandon all hope; the results will be unpredictable.

In addition, most browsers are case-sensitive, which means that they differentiate between Document and document. Internet Explorer is only sometimes case-sensitive, which means that, for example, it may not understand any difference between Document and document. Consequently, be aware that just because it works in one browser doesn't mean that it'll always work in others. Test, test, test.

CASCADING STYLE SHEETS REFERENCE

This appendix lists the CSS2.1 properties as defined by the W3C at http://www.w3.org/TR/CSS21.

The CSS 2.0 specification was standardized all the way back in May 1998, but as of this writing, some properties aren't implemented in any browser. The next version, CSS 2.1, was at the Candidate Recommendation stage at the time this was written. The goal of the CSS 2.1 specification is to clarify CSS2 so that it is closer to what browser makers have actually implemented. This list is complete except for the aural properties (those used for speech synthesis for the visually disabled), which are not (at this time) modifiable by JavaScript.

Because this is a book about JavaScript, we've only touched on a few of the cool things you can do with CSS. If you want to learn more, we recommend *Cascading Style Sheets: The Definitive Guide, Third Edition*, by Eric A. Meyer. The book lives up to its name, with exhaustive descriptions of CSS1, CSS2, and the in-progress CSS 2.1.

Table C.1

Basic Concepts	
PROPERTY NAME	VALUE
In HTML	link
	<style>...</style>
	<x style="declaration;">
Grouping	x, y, z {declaration;}
Contextual selectors	x y z {declaration;}
Class selector	.class
ID selector	#id
At-rules	@import
	@media
	@page
Important	!important

Table C.2

Pseudo-Elements and Pseudo-Classes	
PROPERTY NAME	VALUE
after	:after
anchor	a:active
	a:focus
	a:hover
	a:link
	a:visited
before	:before
first	:first
first-child	:first-child
left	:left
paragraph	p:first-letter
	p:first-line
right	:right

Table C.3

Color and Background Properties

PROPERTY NAME	VALUE
background	<background-color>
	<background-image>
	<background-repeat>
	<background-attachment>
	<background-position>
background-attachment	scroll
	fixed
background-color	<color>
	transparent
background-image	<url>
	none
background-position	<percentage>
	<length>
	top
	center
	bottom
	left
	right
background-repeat	repeat
	repeat-x
	repeat-y
	no-repeat
color	<color>

Table C.4

Font Properties

PROPERTY NAME	VALUE
font	<font-style>
	<font-variant>
	<font-weight>
	<font-size> / <line-height>
	<font-family>
	caption
	icon
	menu
	message-box
	small-caption
	status-bar
font-family	<family-name>
	cursive
	fantasy
	monospace
	sans-serif
	serif
font-size	<absolute-size> (xx-small– xx-large)
	<relative-size> (smaller– larger)
	<length>
	<percentage>
font-style	normal
	italic
	oblique
font-variant	normal
	small-caps
font-weight	normal
	bold
	bolder
	lighter
	100 – 900

CASCADING STYLE SHEETS REFERENCE

Table C.5

Generated Content Properties	
PROPERTY NAME	VALUE
content	<string>
	<url>
	<identifier>
	<counter>
	open-quote
	close-quote
	no-open-quote
	no-close-quote
	none
	normal
counter-increment	<identifier>
	<integer>
	none
counter-reset	<identifier>
	<integer>
	none
quotes	<string>
	none

Table C.6

Text Properties	
PROPERTY NAME	VALUE
letter-spacing	normal
	<length>
text-align	left
	right
	center
	justify
text-decoration	none
	underline
	overline
	line-through
	blink
text-indent	<length>
	<percentage>
text-transform	capitalize
	uppercase
	lowercase
	none
white-space	normal
	pre
	nowrap
	pre-wrap
	pre-line
word-spacing	normal
	<length>

Table C.7

Box Properties

PROPERTY NAME	VALUE
border	<border-width>
	<border-style>
	<border-color>
border-bottom	<border-width>
	<border-style>
	<border-color>
border-bottom-color	<border-color>
border-bottom-style	<border-style>
border-bottom-width	<border-width>
border-collapse	collapse
	separate
border-color	<color>
	transparent
border-left	<border-top-width>
	<border-style>
	<border-color>
border-left-color	<border-color>
border-left-style	<border-style>
border-left-width	<border-width>
border-right	<border-top-width>
	<border-style>
	<border-color>
border-right-color	<border-color>
border-right-style	<border-style>
border-right-width	<border-width>
border-spacing	<length>
border-style	none
	hidden
	dotted
	dashed
	solid
	double
	groove
	ridge
	inset
	outset

Table C.7

Box Properties *(continued)*

PROPERTY NAME	VALUE
border-top	<border-top-width>
	<border-style>
	<border-color>
border-top-color	<border-color>
border-top-style	<border-style>
border-top-width	<border-width>
border-width	thin
	medium
	thick
	<length>
margin	<margin-width>
margin-bottom	<margin-width>
margin-left	<margin-width>
margin-right	<margin-width>
margin-top	<margin-width>
padding	<padding-width>
padding-bottom	<padding-width>
padding-left	<padding-width>
padding-right	<padding-width>
padding-top	<padding-width>

Table C.8

Visual Formatting Properties

PROPERTY NAME	VALUE
display	block
	inline
	inline-block
	list-item
	run-in
	table
	inline-table
	table-row-group
	table-header-group
	table-footer-group
	table-row
	table-column-group
	table-column
	table-cell
	table-caption
	none
left	auto
	<length>
	<percentage>
right	auto
	<length>
	<percentage>
top	auto
	<length>
	<percentage>
bottom	auto
	<length>
	<percentage>
float	left
	right
	none
clear	none
	left
	right
	both
direction	ltr
	rtl
unicode-bidi	normal
	embed
	bidi-override

Table C.8

Visual Formatting Properties *(continued)*

PROPERTY NAME	VALUE
width	<length>
	<percentage>
	auto
min-width	<length>
	<percentage>
max-width	<length>
	<percentage>
	none
height	<length>
	<percentage>
	auto
min-height	<length>
	<percentage>
max-height	<length>
	<percentage>
	none
line-height	normal
	<number>
	<length>
	<percentage>
vertical-align	baseline
	sub
	super
	top
	text-top
	middle
	bottom
	text-bottom
	<percentage>
	<length>
position	static
	absolute
	relative
	fixed
z-index	auto
	<integer>

Table C.9

Visual Effects Properties

PROPERTY NAME	VALUE
overflow	visible
	hidden
	scroll
	auto
clip	auto
	<shape>
visibility	collapse
	visible
	hidden

Table C.10

List Properties

PROPERTY NAME	VALUE
list-style	<list-style-type>
	<list-style-position>
	<list-style-image>
list-style-image	<url>
	none
list-style-position	inside
	outside
list-style-type	disc
	circle
	square
	decimal
	decimal-leading-zero
	lower-roman
	upper-roman
	lower-greek
	lower-alpha
	lower-latin
	upper-alpha
	upper-latin
	armenian
	georgian
	none

Table C.11

Table Properties

PROPERTY NAME	VALUE
caption-side	top
	bottom
table-layout	auto
	fixed
border-collapse	collapse
	separate
border-spacing	<length>
empty-cells	show
	hide
border-style	none
	hidden
	dotted
	dashed
	solid
	double
	groove
	ridge
	inset
	outset

Table C.12

Page Properties	
PROPERTY NAME	**VALUE**
orphans	<integer>
page-break-after	auto
	always
	avoid
	left
	right
page-break-before	auto
	always
	avoid
	left
	right
page-break-inside	avoid
	auto
widows	<integer>

Table C.14

Units	
PROPERTY NAME	**VALUE**
Length Units	em
	ex
	px
	in
	cm
	mm
	pt
	pc
Color Units	#000
	#000000
	(RRR,GGG,BBB)
	(R%,G%,B%)
	<keyword>
URLs	<url>

Table C.13

User Interface Properties	
PROPERTY NAME	**VALUE**
cursor	<url>
	auto
	crosshair
	default
	pointer
	move
	e-resize
	ne-resize
	nw-resize
	n-resize
	se-resize
	sw-resize
	s-resize
	w-resize
	text
	wait
	help
	progress
outline	<outline-color>
	<outline-style>
	<outline-width>
outline-color	<color>
	invert
outline-style	<border-style>
outline-width	<border-width>

WHERE TO LEARN MORE

Once you've worked through this book, you should be well on your way to spicing up your Web sites with JavaScript. But there's a lot more to learn about the JavaScript language, and you'll probably have questions as you write your own code.

The best place to get those questions answered is online, as you might expect. There are many resources on the Web and elsewhere on the Internet that can help you out and deepen your understanding of JavaScript.

In this appendix, we'll point you to several of the most helpful JavaScript-oriented Web sites and some online forums where you can interact with other scripters, and we'll even mention a few other books that the authors found helpful.

But first, a gentle reminder: the Net is not a static, unchanging place. Web sites can and often do change the addresses of their pages, so it's possible that the URLs we list will become out of date by the time you use them. We're just reporting the URLs; we have no control over them. Sometimes, entire Web sites disappear. If you find a link that's become stale, check our companion Web site at `http://www.javascriptworld.com` to see if we have posted a new location for the page you were looking for.

Finding Help Online

The original JavaScript documentation is found at Netscape's Web site, but there's a lot of good information at sites from Microsoft and at independent JavaScript pages as well. Here are some of the best:

Mozilla sites

Since Netscape developed JavaScript, it's no surprise that the Mozilla project, the open-source creators of Mozilla and Firefox (the successors to Netscape's browser), has lots of great information about the language and further development.

JavaScript Center

```
http://developer.mozilla.org/en/
→ JavaScript
```

This site (**Figure D.1**) is designed for all levels of JavaScript users and includes links to tools, documentation, and online communities. The documentation includes the Core JavaScript Reference (covering JavaScript 1.5), which gives you a rundown on the basics of the language, and definitions and explanations of the concepts used in JavaScript. It suffers from a moderately geeky difficulty level and sketchy examples, but you should be able to puzzle it out once you've digested this book. Also found here is the Core JavaScript Guide, and explanations of what was added in JavaScript from versions 1.6 on.

Figure D.1 Mozilla's JavaScript section of their Developer Center is a good place for you to start furthering your knowledge of JavaScript.

Figure D.2 Firebug, an add-on to Firefox, gives you an extraordinary amount of control and ways to examine your code.

Figure D.3 If you aren't running Firefox, you can still run Firebug Lite—shown here inside Safari on the same page as Figure D.2.

Venkman Debugger

`http://developer.mozilla.org/en/Venkman`

When you need to debug your JavaScript, it certainly would be nice to have a good tool to use to help you. Wish no longer; Venkman, the JavaScript debugger from the Mozilla project, is a pretty good tool that works with Firefox, Thunderbird, and Mozilla, and allows you to step through your code, setting breakpoints, inspecting objects and variables as the script executes, and working with JavaScript source code.

Firebug Debugger

`http://getfirebug.com`

If you liked Venkman, you'll love Firebug (**Figure D.2**). You can use it with Firefox to debug not just your scripts, but your HTML and CSS as well. It's free, with good documentation, handy logging, and all the breakpoint and DOM support you could want.

If the only thing missing to make your (scripting) life complete is similar functionality for IE, Safari, and Opera, then you need to check out Firebug Lite at `http://getfirebug.com/lite.html` (**Figure D.3**). It doesn't have all the functionality of its big brother, but it's very handy to have a single common interface when trying to track down a random bug.

Other useful sites

When you get away from the Mozilla sites, you'll still find plenty of places where you can pick up script examples, find tutorials, and ask questions of JavaScript experts. Here are some of our favorite sites.

Microsoft's JScript Language

`http://msdn.microsoft.com/hbxc2t98.aspx`

Microsoft's own version of JavaScript—called JScript—has its own pages on the Microsoft Developer Network site (**Figure D.4**), where you can learn the similarities to (and differences from) Mozilla's JavaScript. You'll find a detailed JScript Language Reference and the JScript Users Guide.

Yahoo! User Interface Library

`http://developer.yahoo.com/yui/`

Yahoo! JavaScript Developer Center

`http://developer.yahoo.com/javascript/`

Yahoo! Design Pattern Library

`http://developer.yahoo.com/ypatterns/`

These three sites are excellent resources for new JavaScript and Ajax developers. The Yahoo! User Interface Library is a set of utilities and controls, written in JavaScript, for building richly interactive Web applications using techniques such as DOM scripting and Ajax. All of the examples are open source and can be used freely in your pages. The JavaScript Developer Center provides documentation for using Yahoo!'s services and APIs, and many code samples you can use to learn about JavaScript and Ajax. The Design Pattern Library (**Figure D.5**) provides many usable examples of JavaScript interface solutions that can be downloaded and dropped into your sites.

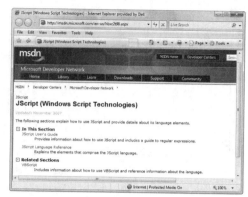

Figure D.4 Microsoft's Windows Script Technologies page gives you the lowdown on JScript, Microsoft's variant of JavaScript.

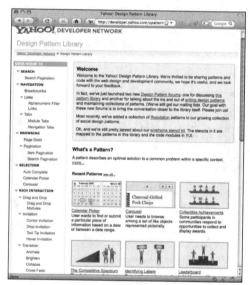

Figure D.5 You'll find many great JavaScript and Ajax examples at Yahoo!'s JavaScript developer pages. The Design Pattern Library gives you access to premade user interface solutions that you can integrate into your own sites.

Figure D.6 The Ajaxian blog is a good destination for JavaScript and Ajax news and information.

Figure D.7 Peter-Paul Koch's QuirksMode site often has JavaScript information well ahead of any others.

Weblogs

There are many weblogs devoted to JavaScript, Ajax, and DOM Scripting. Here are a few of our favorites, but these by no means form an exhaustive list.

Ajaxian

`http://ajaxian.com`

This is a good blog with news, lists of JavaScript and Ajax resources, podcasts with JavaScript and Ajax luminaries, and much more (**Figure D.6**). It can sometimes get a bit breathless over the fabulousness of Ajax, making you think that it's the cure for cancer and a terrific dessert topping all rolled into one, but we're sure that the blog's perspective will mellow over time. It used to have a bad habit of being a little confused about what Ajax actually *is* (no, Flash is *not* any part of Ajax); but over time they've learned a little more about that as well. And it's a great site to find out who's doing cool user interface tricks.

QuirksMode

`http://www.quirksmode.org/blog/`

Peter-Paul Koch is a JavaScript developer in the Netherlands. The best thing about his site (**Figure D.7**) is that he keeps it amazingly up-to-date with the latest news about browsers and their JavaScript capabilities. It's not a tutorial site, but along with the weblog there is a great deal of basic information that will be helpful to the beginning scripter.

Continuing Intermittent Incoherency

`http://alex.dojotoolkit.org`

Alex Russell is President of the Dojo Foundation, the organization behind the Dojo Toolkit (another major JavaScript framework). He's got plenty of opinions about JavaScript, and he's not afraid to share them.

Microsoft's JScript Blog

http://blogs.msdn.com/jscript/

This blog isn't just about JScript; the people who write JScript themselves write it. While it's not a place for questions about particular IE issues, it's a great resource to see what the team is working on and learn about their priorities and recommendations.

Yahoo! User Interface Blog

http://yuiblog.com/blog/

This is the companion blog for the Yahoo! sites listed above. It has discussions about the Design Pattern and User Interface Libraries, which help you to efficiently get the most out of today's browsers. The Yahoo! developers are regularly posting, answering questions, and discussing better ways to use their libraries.

Surfin' Safari

http://webkit.org/blog/

This weblog (**Figure D.8**) isn't just about JavaScript, but it *is* all about Apple's Safari browser—which isn't just for the Mac anymore. Here's where you can get information straight from Apple employees about what the next versions of Safari will and won't do, including downloadable nightly builds of WebKit (the open source engine underneath Safari), giving you features long before Apple ships them to the public.

Elsewhere

JavaScript Mailing List

http://lists.evolt.org/mailman/
→ listinfo/javascript

This list has been around for many years in one form or another. Once run by Louisiana Tech University (latech.edu), it's now hosted by evolt.org. The archives (at http://lists.evolt.org/pipermail/javascript/) contain

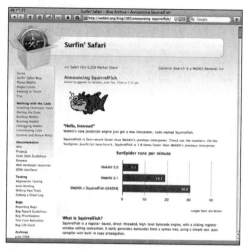

Figure D.8 To learn the latest about Safari (on Mac or Windows), you want to go Surfin' Safari.

FINDING HELP ONLINE

years of useful information. It's not as active as it once was, but it still gets at least a few questions per month.

SitePoint JavaScript Forum

```
http://www.sitepoint.com/forums/
↪ forumdisplay.php?f=15
```

WebDeveloper.com JavaScript Forum

```
http://www.webdeveloper.com/forum/
↪ forumdisplay.php?f=3
```

These two forums (**Figure D.9**) are fairly alike: they both use the popular vBulletin forum software, they both require you to register to post or answer a question, they both have years of searchable archives, and they both have an active community answering questions. We're not going to recommend one over the other; they're both worth your time if you need help.

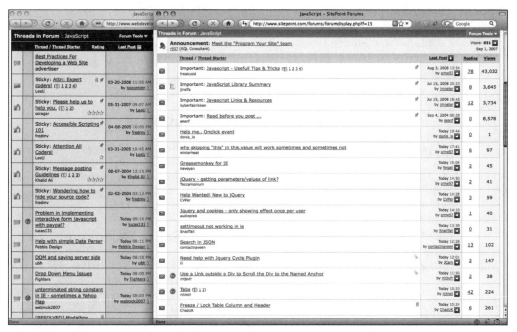

Figure D.9 The WebDeveloper.com and SitePoint JavaScript Forums are similar to each other in many ways, including their usefulness.

JavaScript Newsgroup

You can think of Usenet as a worldwide bulletin board system, where people from everywhere can post messages and join discussions about subjects that interest them. At last count, there were more than 100,000 newsgroups, covering virtually every subject you can imagine.

Naturally, we're interested here in the newsgroup that's devoted to JavaScript: `comp.lang.javascript` (also found on the Web at `http://groups.google.com/group/comp.lang.javascript/`), where there are many discussions about scripting, people asking questions about problems that have them stymied, and general talk among JavaScript developers. It's a good place to get answers and pick up tips. You'll often find that threads begun by other people will apply to your own question.

✔ Tip

■ Usenet can be a wild place, and `c.l.j` old-timers can be merciless to "newbies" who ask what (to the old-timers) seem to be foolish questions. It's best to hang around and just read other people's messages before you post your first message in a newsgroup. You may save yourself a lot of grief and avoid many nasty flaming responses. Never forget that your messages can be read potentially by millions of people worldwide. And always remember to read the FAQ before posting—chances are, you'll find that some of your questions will be answered in there, plus there's always other interesting information. You can find the latest `c.l.j` FAQ at `http://jibbering.com/faq/`.

Books

Though the authors would naturally like to think that the book you've got in your hands is all you'll ever need to become a JavaScript expert, they recognize that you might just want a bit more information after you've eagerly devoured this book. There are approximately a zillion JavaScript books on the market; here (in no particular order) are some of the books that we think are the best.

JavaScript, The Definitive Guide

Written by David Flanagan and published by O'Reilly Media, this is an exhaustive reference to the JavaScript language. Not for the faint of heart, this is where the experts turn to look up those weird operators and nail down that odd syntax. The 5th Edition of this book (the latest available as we write) is more than two years old and covers JavaScript 1.5, but it's still a valuable reference.

ppk on JavaScript

Peter-Paul Koch is one of the acknowledged masters of JavaScript. In this book from New Riders, he uses real-world script examples he created for paying clients to take you through a journey that is both theoretical and practical.

Bulletproof Ajax

In this New Riders book, Jeremy Keith (who also wrote *DOM Scripting*) covers how to build accessible, degradable, and robust Ajax-enabled sites. Yes, it really can be done, and this book is a good primer on how to do it.

Pro JavaScript Techniques

John Resig (of jQuery fame) wrote this book to help intermediate-level JavaScripters become advanced scripters. Not for the novice, it's a good book to take you onwards from where this book ends.

INDEX